OUT OF THE SHADOWS OF ANGKOR

MANOA 33:2
MANOA 34:1
DOUBLE ISSUE

UNIVERSITY OF HAWAI'I PRESS

HONOLULU

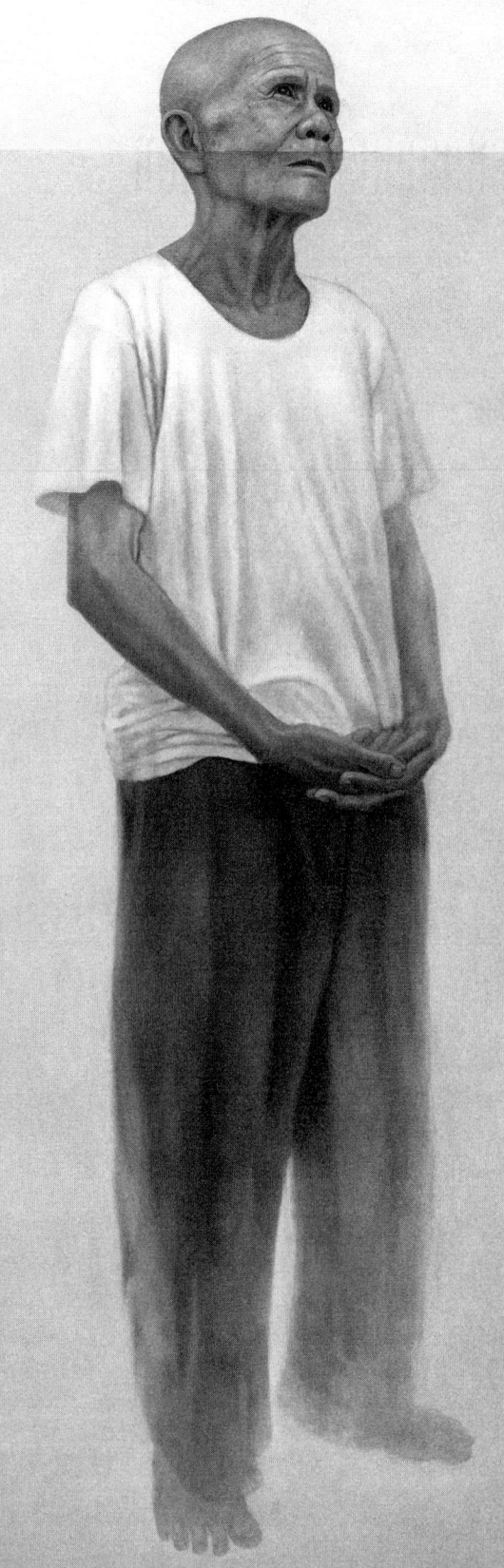

OUT OF THE SHADOWS OF ANGKOR

CAMBODIAN POETRY, PROSE, AND PERFORMANCE THROUGH THE AGES

Frank Stewart
SERIES EDITOR

Sharon May
Christophe Macquet
Trent Walker
Phina So
Rinith Taing
GUEST EDITORS

Achar, *2019*
Oil on canvas
from the series Surviving
by Cambodian artist
Theanly Chov.

Mānoa: A Pacific Journal of International Writing

Editor   Frank Stewart

Managing Editor   Pat Matsueda

Associate Editor   Noah Perales-Estoesta

Designer and Art Editor   Barbara Pope

Abernethy Fellow   Li Shan Chan

Consulting Editors
Anna Badkhen, Robert Bringhurst, Carol Moldaw, Michael Nye,
Naomi Shihab Nye, Gary Snyder, Julia Steele, Arthur Sze, Michelle Yeh

Corresponding Editors for Asia and the Pacific
CAMBODIA   Sharon May, Christophe Macquet, Trent Walker
CHINA   Chen Zeping, Karen Gernant, Ming Di
HONG KONG   Shirley Geok-lin Lim
INDONESIA   John H. McGlynn
JAPAN   Leza Lowitz
KOREA   Bruce Fulton
NEW ZEALAND AND SOUTH PACIFIC   Vilsoni Hereniko, Alexander Mawyer
PACIFIC LATIN AMERICA   Noah Perales-Estoesta
PHILIPPINES   Alfred A. Yuson
SOUTH ASIA   Alok Bhalla, Sukrita Paul Kumar
WESTERN CANADA   Trevor Carolan

Advisors   Laura E. Lyons, Robert Shapard

Founded in 1988 by Robert Shapard and Frank Stewart

Mānoa is published twice a year and is available in print and online for both individuals and institutions. Subscribe at https://www.uhpress.hawaii.edu/title/manoa/. Please visit http://muse.jhu.edu/journals/manoa to browse issues and tables of contents online.

Claims for non-receipt of issues will be honored if claim is made within 180 days of the month of publication. Thereafter, the regular back-issue rate will be charged for replacement. Inquiries are received at uhpjourn@hawaii.edu or by phone at 1-888-UHPRESS or 808-956-8833.

Mānoa gratefully acknowledges the University of Hawai'i and the University of Hawai'i College of Languages, Linguistics, and Literature; with additional support from the National Endowment for the Arts; Amazon Literary Partnership Literary Magazine Fund and Community of Literary Magazines & Presses; Cambodian Living Arts; and Mānoa Foundation.

outoftheshadowsofangkor.com (queries: shadowsofangkor@gmail.com)
manoa.hawaii.edu/manoajournal
uhpress.hawaii.edu/title/manoa/
muse.jhu.edu
jstor.org

CONTENTS

Vaddey Ratner   xi
   Foreword

Sokunthary Svay   xiii
   On Cambodian American Writers

Sharon May   xvi
   Out of the Shadows of Angkor

Trent Walker   xxv
   Cambodian Literature: An Introduction

CLASSICAL

600–1400

Inscription   3
   Warning to Thieves

Queen Indradevi   4
   In Praise of Sister Queens

Inscription   6
   Hymn to the Tree of Awakening

Khun Thepkrawi   8
   Hymn for the Elephants' Feast

1400–1700

Epic   11
   Reamker

Brah Sugandh   15
   Code of Old Sayings

Brah Rajasambhar   18
   My Soul of Gold

Chant   24
    Victory in the Eight Directions

Traditional Oath   26
    Goddesses of the Land

1700–1930

Folk Songs   30
    Ancestral Offerings
    In Bloom
    Windswept Pond
    Rowing the Boat

Folk Song   33
    The Point of the Cape

Buddhist Song Tradition   34
    The Thirty-Three Consonants
    This Life Is Short
    Hymn to the Buddha's Feet

Anonymous   42
    Thunder and the Crabs

Mai   46
    Code for Girls

King Ang Duong   53
    Kaki

Krom Ngoy   62
    A Garland of New Advice

Folklore   65
    A Cycle of Alev Stories

Ukna Suttantaprija Ind   69
    Journey to Angkor Wat

Brah Padumatther Som   78
    Tum Teav

POETRY

1930–2020

Prince Areno Yukanthor   83
   On the Threshold of the Khmer Narthex

Suy Hieng   85
   The Orphans

Khun Srun   86
   A Small Request

Khau Ny Kim   88
   A Hundred Scents, A Hundred Seasons

Chey Chap   90
   Don't Fight the Wind
   A Bunch of Coconuts

Prince Amrindo Sisowath   93
   A Cry

Pen Samitthy   95
   Bound to His Father

Huot Iv   96
   What Would You Like to Eat?

Kong Bunchhoeun   98
   The Race of the Quick

Yin Luoth   101
   The Fate of Bloodsuckers

Pich Tum Kravel   102
   The Ox with the Broken Hoof
   Man and Krasang
   The Sun Turns Leprous

Chath pierSath   105
   Exiting Interview
   My Brother Thay

Bunkong Tuon   107
   Moon in Khmer
   An Elegy for a Fellow Cambodian
   Living in the Hyphen
   Fishing for Trey Platoo

Princess Moon — 111
blessing dance
dance, dance, dance

Kosal Khiev — 115
Dream
Rewind
Peace in Pieces

Sokunthary Svay — 118
Reincarnation

Mylo Lam — 120
Ma's Canh Chua Recipe

Greg Santos — 122
Our Name
Dear Ghosts
Shall We Dance?

FICTION

1940–2020

Nou Hach — 129
Wilted Flower

Suon Sorin — 136
A New Sun Rises Over the Old Land

Christophe Macquet — 149
An Introduction to The Accused

Khun Srun — 155
The Accused

Soth Polin — 161
Command Me to Exist
The Anarchist
The Aroma of Desire in Fresno

Ty Chi Huot — 184
Sky of the Lost Moon

Sok Chanphal — 191
The Kerosene Lamp Ghost Stories
Buried Treasure

NONFICTION

1970–2022

Bunchan Mol   205
   Political Prison

Boreth Ly   212
   Of Performance and the Persistent Temporality of Trauma

Alice Pung   225
   Her Father's Daughter

Putsata Reang   231
   At Sea, and Seeking a Safe Harbor

Elizabeth Chey   235
   Painting History

Sokunthary Svay   243
   Cambodian Requiem

Rinith Taing   249
   *The Bookrenter of Battambang and
   the Master of Uselessness*

Phina So   265
   *Contemporary Writing and Publishing in Cambodia
   Freshwater Crayfish and the Trouble with Names*

Maria Hach   271
   An Archive of Haunting

PERFORMANCE

1960–2020

Ma Laupi   277
   *A Pair of Turtledoves
   The Fishing Eagle of Boeng Kansaeng*

Sinn Sisamouth   279
   Champa of Battambang

Kong Bunchhoeun   280
   The Shade of the Tenth Coconut Tree

Sim Chanya   282
   Farewell, Wild Guava Flower

Bassac Folk Opera 284
    When Ream Faked His Death to Win Back Seda

Ayai Folk Theater 292
    A Flirtatious Battle of Words and Wits

Songsaeng Rungrueangchai 298
    The Big Tusker

Kong Nay 301
    Lullaby: An Elephant Rocks Its Trunk

Sharon May 303
    A Musician's Life: An Interview with Kong Nay

Prumsodun Ok 314
    Moni Mekhala and Ream Eyso
    Here and Now, into the Future

Kalean Ung 322
    Letters from Home

GRAPHIC NOVEL

Tian Veasna 255
    Year of the Rabbit

About the Contributors   328
Acknowledgements   339
Sources   342
Permissions   350

VADDEY RATNER

Foreword

Food is not enough, my mother said. Without pralung, *they will always be hungry.*

Many months had passed since our arrival at Khao-I-Dang, a camp on the Thai-Cambodian border that burgeoned with refugees, like us, fleeing in the wake of the Khmer Rouge regime. My mother had recently been promoted to director at an orphanage within the camp. While most of the children there had indeed lost their parents, there were those too whose parents had purposefully left them, hoping they would at least have the security of shelter and food. They now had both, but my mother realized that they needed something more.

She made an appeal to the larger camp community for anyone with a shred of skill in the arts, music, dance, or poetry to join together in mounting a modest production to lift the spirits of the children. There were no experts, but what little knowledge people had protected and hidden by necessity to stay alive under Khmer Rouge rule, they now offered up. The adults quickly assessed and assigned children to the various roles of singers, dancers, narrators, and musicians. Some fashioned musical instruments from bamboo and coconut shells and nylon cord. Others pooled together to recollect fragments of song. Watching the buzz of activity around me, I realized it wasn't just the children who were hungry.

The Khmer concept of *pralung*—most often rendered as spirit, soul, or life-force—describes a quality that is at once individual and collective. All of us who survived were reduced by the violence and loss from which we emerged, starved in a multiplicity of ways. We longed for the nourishment of the arts that had been denied us, arts so centrally and viscerally connected to our identity as Cambodians. It wasn't only at Khao-I-Dang, of course. Despite the massive and disproportionate loss of life among artists of all types, I would later learn, countless Cambodians in the country and in the diaspora had begun committing themselves to quiet and often unheralded acts of cultural and artistic revival.

One of these quiet heroes was Pich Tum Kravel, who compiled stage versions of *lakhaon,* the classic theatrical dramas that he had performed in his youth, working from surviving scripts and from memory. Published in the early 1980s, only a few short years after the fall of the Khmer Rouge, when so much still lay in ruins, these texts—and eventually a full shelf of books he authored and edited on various traditional art forms—helped ensure that these masterworks would endure.

As a student later at Cornell University, I found in these texts a vital connection to my own cultural heritage. I pored over *Tum Teav,* learning how a young girl not only disobeyed her mother but also challenged a whole tradition in the name of love. I lost myself in *Mak Thoeung,* in awe of the courage of a humble perfume seller who stood up to a prince and then the King himself. While I had a childhood familiarity with bits and pieces of these tales, studying the written *lakhaon* I felt the weight of Khmer literature in a way I had never felt before. The beauty and subtlety of the language, the complexity of the moral dilemmas and questions that resonate across time... Here, I realized, we have not only records of our history but also touchstones to guide us in navigating the troubled present and uncertain future.

I may be a long way now from Khao-I-Dang, but I have never forgotten the wisdom in my mother's simple words. Art nourishes. And who among us, in a world marked by such division and displacement, would not stand to benefit from such nourishment and connection?

This anthology is so vital because it provides a glimpse into that rich tradition of Cambodian literature and writing that, particularly for English-language readers, too often remains obscured from view, unrecognized alongside the more visible marvels of architecture and sculpture of Angkor, or the splendors of classical dance. Here you will find not only fragments of *lakhaon* but also the thirteenth-century Sanskrit poems of Queen Indradevi and passages from the *Reamker,* the ancient tale adapted from the Hindu *Ramayana*. There are works from the pre-war period known as the Cambodian Renaissance, including Khun Srun's writing on political repression, and groundbreaking fiction by Nou Hach and Soth Polin. And there are samplings from a generation of emerging writers, poets, musicians, and performers, pushing boundaries with increasingly diverse reflections on contemporary Cambodia and the diaspora.

In these writings I hope that you find, as I have done, echoes of that *pralung* that animates and sustains us. And because it is only a taste, may it leave you—just so slightly—hungry for more.

SOKUNTHARY SVAY

On Cambodian American Writers

As a member of the 1.5 generation of Cambodian immigrants in the U.S., I could sense the fear of language loss within our community. When my generation was growing up, we were admonished at get-togethers for not being able to reply to our elders when they spoke Khmer to us. After so much had already been lost, the deep anxiety of losing this linguistic link was palpable. If we as the children of the first generation couldn't speak, read, or write Khmer, we couldn't communicate directly with the older generation or read the literature of our ancestors. And even those of us who could speak the language with fluency or at a practical level often missed out, during those early years of survival, on the exchange between parent and child in which we could learn about our history. My parents were typical; they didn't have time to sit and tell us myths, folktales, or family stories. Working several jobs at a time, they were frequently exhausted from cleaning other people's dirt. They were glad just to sit down at the end of the day with familiar food, knowing their children were safe.

Aware of what was missing to make us whole, I searched for language programs, but at that time, twenty years ago, there were only a handful, many of them expensive and out-of-state. The few that were accessible were taught by monks at temples and were likely to be unwaveringly strict and to rely on traditional rote instruction.

It's under these conditions that books became vital to my survival. They kept me company when my parents, believing the neighborhood to be unsafe, had me stay indoors most of the time. Books entertained me and took me to far-off, imaginary places. At other times, books taught me about the world and how things worked. But most exciting of all, I learned that words could be written down to teach: they could reveal to me things that my parents could not show me. I was able to soak up the information on my own. I could overcome the silence in my own family.

But, dear reader, at a certain moment, we—I mean you and me—realize that in all these books, we don't see anything about our community, what our families went through and that they are not written by anyone who looks like us. That's when the search for a Khmer diasporic identity began. Like scavengers, we searched libraries, the Internet, and college courses. In the late 1990s and early 2000s, there was not much. We ended up becoming unintended experts in Cambodian American literature. In certain works, we found writers with whom we had something in common. More important, we began to discover what we were looking for and what we needed, as well as the larger subject of legacy in a people's literature.

In the absence of stories passed down through your family, you understand that you need to become your own family historian, ethnographer, biographer, and narrator. In the absence of heirlooms, family photos, recordings, literature, and an archive to draw from, you are left with a profound emptiness. You need to (re)create a narrative of what happened to your elders during the Khmer Rouge, their losses and journey to the U.S. And you need to understand what the world was like for them before the Khmer Rouge regime.

Escaping from the trauma of Cambodia's crisis, our community arrived in the U.S. less than fifty years ago. We came without knowing the whereabouts of our relatives. In my parents' refugee application, both sides of my family were listed as either missing or dead. With finality, in capital letters, was the phrase NO OTHERS. This is how we and many other Cambodians entered the country: with no documents or belongings, no remnants or evidence of our lives before being pulled from the refugee camps. Our former history no longer applied here.

Those of you readers who are members of the Cambodian diaspora: I invite you to bring to your reading of *Out of the Shadows of Angkor* your discontents, hunger, and curiosity about what you've been missing all these years. This collection gives you a view, with a wide angle, of the majesty of homeland literature, as well as of the diaspora. There is a range of genres here that stretches from newly translated classical works to performance artists and spoken-word poets. For educators who might consider teaching from this collection, it is likely you have students who are from Cambodia or Southeast Asia and/or its diasporas, or students who are looking for more variety in a global literature course. These students are why you have good reasons to be holding this anthology.

The works in *Out of the Shadows of Angkor* stand alone, but would go well alongside the literature of other Southeast Asian countries, such as Vietnam and Laos, and the many ethnic communities that reside in the region. I would also urge educators to include in their curricula—in tandem with this literature—the diasporic works of immigrant groups in the U.S. and to juxtapose them with African American literature. As members of a relatively new diaspora who came to the U.S. as a result of war, we would do well to discuss those connections and to learn how others have coped, survived, and thrived. We are not the first to go through these trials.

It's exciting to see in one volume works from several centuries ago and more, from anonymous scribes and ancient royalty, from wedding songs to the songs of Lok Ta Sin Sisamouth and Lok Ta Kong Nay (masters in their genres of pop and folk). And to see spoken-word poetry, a play, and a graphic novel. Here are words from the homeland, classic and contemporary, revealing the earliest thoughts and concerns of Cambodians. I would suggest that, whenever possible, the works be read aloud in a variety of venues, the songs be sung, and the play staged. I hope that they will be discussed and recorded. Keeping them alive—on and off the page—will ensure their longevity, along with that of the Cambodian community.

When I saw the first *Mānoa* anthology on Cambodian writing—*In the Shadow of Angkor*, published in 2004—I was surprised there was enough material to fill a book. Almost twenty years later, I see that an attempt to contain what makes "us" in one volume will always be an incomplete effort. There are many writers who might have been added here if we had had more space to include them and enough time to translate further from Khmer, French, and other languages. So we gather what we can for now and look to the future for the next generation of voices and beyond.

SHARON MAY

Out of the Shadows of Angkor:
A Personal and Literary Journey
through Cambodian Literature

It has been twenty years since I was asked to guest edit *In the Shadow of Angkor*, a special issue of *Mānoa* focusing on Cambodian literature. The moment I arrived in Phnom Penh, an American journalist wished me luck, telling me that Cambodians can't write and there wouldn't be enough material to fill a book. As it turned out, the volume demonstrated just how wrong he was. Nevertheless, many Western readers are likely to hold the same mistaken belief; compared to the literature of other Asian countries, Cambodian writing remains largely unknown to the English-speaking world. We hope that this companion volume, *Out of the Shadows of Angkor,* will help to change that.

The search for the literature presented in this book began in the 1990s. At the time, guest editor Christophe Macquet was teaching translation at the Royal University of Phnom Penh and hunting for Khmer books out of a love of literature and the Khmer language. On his way to and from teaching, he would often stop his motorbike by the open-air street stalls on Pasteur Street (Street 51), near the Independence Monument. In plastic envelopes hanging from portable wooden stalls were books from the 1960s and 1970s—books that had miraculously survived the destructive wrath of the Khmer Rouge regime. Christophe bought many of them, including works of poetry and fiction. Among them he discovered a remarkable volume he had never heard of by Khun Srun, a brilliant writer in the 1970s. Srun was murdered in 1978 by the Khmer Rouge at age thirty-three, along with most of his family. Eventually, Christophe was able to reach Khun Srun's only surviving child, his daughter, Khun Khem, in a remote border village. He translated five Khmer writers, including Khun Srun, for the French journal *Europe*, which inspired *Un tombeau pour Khun Srun* (A Tomb for Khun Srun), a documentary film directed by Eric Galmard. In 2018, with Khun Khem's permission, he translated the entire book into French, which was published in Paris as *L'Accusé* (The Accused).

The street stalls in Phnom Penh have since disappeared along with the books. Like *The Accused,* many have never been republished in the Khmer language. Some, however, reemerged in badly retyped and cheaply printed versions in the early 2000s—with numerous mistakes, omissions, and missing pages. In order to reconstruct the original texts and translate the works, Christophe turned for help from Cornell University, which in 1989 had started a modest program to preserve Cambodian materials onto microfilm, saving many Khmer books and papers from oblivion. The microfilm was later given to the Center for Khmer Studies Library at Wat Damnak, in Siem Reap.

Despite these efforts and others, many texts could not be rescued. For example, one of Soth Polin's best novellas, *We Die Only Once* (1967), is lost forever. An enormously gifted writer, Soth Polin began publishing in the 1960s. After a friend's assassination in 1974, he escaped from Cambodia to France and later moved to the U.S.; he is one of the few to write and publish in all three countries.

Many people over the past thirty years have helped create *Out of the Shadows of Angkor*. They have sought out old booksellers; visited dusty and somewhat derelict libraries; tracked down authors or their relatives, in the city, countryside, and overseas; and contacted anyone who might have a photocopy, or microfilm, or posted work on the Internet. The permissions alone were a monumental task. Finding and translating the ancient texts preserved in stone or in fragile manuscripts and in ancient languages such as Sanskrit and Old Khmer also posed challenges. For example, much of the poetry of Brah Rajasambhar (a seventeenth-century contemporary of John Donne) has been lost to time. The only complete copy of some of his poetry is a black-paper manuscript hidden in the vaults of the British Library. Fortunately, guest editor Trent Walker identified this Cambodian treasure on a research trip and translated it for the first time for this book. The story of finding this text is no less dramatic than its content. It's a love poem by a king who abdicated his throne for his lover, written while they were separated; the two ran away together but were eventually tracked down and killed. Finally, there are challenges documenting the songs of bards such as Prach Chhuon and Kong Nay, and the dramatic works of troupes that perform *lakhaon bassac, yike,* and *ayai*—whose ephemeral art is often improvised and rarely recorded, much less translated.

Many Cambodian writers were killed during the Khmer Rouge regime from 1975 to 1979. Others became refugees or went into hiding; to survive, they took on menial jobs, such as driving taxis, selling toothpaste, or even transporting chickens, as Soth Polin describes in his novella *The Aroma of Desire in Fresno*. When I first contacted him twenty years ago, he was reluctant to talk to me, thinking I was a political agent sent to track him down—a reminder of the many difficulties in building trust in a community that has suffered one of the greatest collective traumas of the twentieth century. Cambodia's great lyricist Ma Laupi ran a donut shop and convenience store in Northern California; not knowing who he was, I once worked several nights for him, redoing his floors.

For me, the creation of this book has had many unexpected echoes of the last volume. Once again, Christophe and I met at cafés in Phnom Penh, most notably the Bright Lotus, near the Mekong River. We spent so many hours there working on this book—drinking coffee and tamarind juice, ordering the occasional bowl of Vietnamese sour soup (despite its name, a Cambodian dish), and taking up valuable space from better-paying customers—that eventually we were both banned from the Bright Lotus.

Temporarily at a loss, we found the café of Cambodia's National Museum, in the vicinity of some of the greatest works of Cambodian sculpture, and right next to the museum's stage. Each day we worked to the sounds of a traditional Khmer orchestra and the keening of singers accompanying dance practice. It reminded me of my days working in Site II, a camp for displaced persons on the Thai–Cambodian border. The instructor of the dancers on that National Museum stage turned out to be none other than *neak kru* Voan Savay—former principal dancer of the Cambodian Royal Ballet, and the same teacher of the child dancers who, thirty years before, I had photographed and watched perform the *Reamker,* the Cambodian *Ramayana.* She and her husband, Meas Vonroeun, a folk-dance specialist and musician, had turned down an offer to leave for France and instead chose to stay in Site II, where they created a performance center, school, and refuge for dancers and musicians, recreating a lost classical and folk repertoire from memory.

Each day after working with Christophe at the National Museum, I watched the end of dance practice and met with Savay and Roeun Sarum—one of the young dancers in Site II, now also a teacher—to identify the dancers and musicians in the photographs I had taken in the camps for a book and museum exhibit. We talked about who had lived, who died, who left Cambodia, who stayed, who became a dance teacher or a soldier, who became the leader of the Royal Phnom Penh Orchestra. The book recounts stories of those young performers and old masters who worked together to revive and preserve their art in war's shadow.

One late morning, I arrived at the museum in a daze. "You look terrible," Christophe said. That morning, in the span of a few minutes, I had learned that my home and the entire town of Paradise, California, where I live, had been destroyed by a wildfire—and that my father was dying. Christophe was the first person I told. We had planned to work on "Bound to His Father," a poem by Pen Samitthy about a calf tethered in a field. An old frog emerges from her burrow to tell him that he's an orphan and that the shinbone used to stake him to the ground is all that is left of his father. It is a poem I love. But I couldn't concentrate. I was thinking of my own father, who was not yet gone, but would be soon.

As usual, I met later with Savay. She was the second person to whom I told my sad news. The third would be Trent Walker, who was also in Phnom Penh. That evening, Savay responded with the compassion of one who has suffered such losses and many more. She told me about the day she returned to Site II (after going to a hospital outside the camp) to find that in her absence, fire had destroyed all of their homes. Her own hut and everything in it had burned, leaving nothing but a charred patch of red earth. Lost were all the photographs, notes on music and dance before the Khmer Rouge regime, dancers' costumes, and musical instruments—along with her just-completed book on Khmer dance, which she had illustrated by hand after ten years of work. As it turned out, my photographs (whose negatives were also now burned) were the only record she and the dancers had of their years in the camp.

The irony of having my own home and work destroyed while I worked to resurrect the careers of Cambodian authors—some of whom perished in war, and others who lost nearly everything to it—has been etched into my mind. The night before I left, Savay took my hands in hers and said fervently, "If your house is burned, rebuild it. This is how it is. If our house is burned, we remake it." That is exactly what Cambodian artists, dancers and musicians, poets, playwrights, bards, and writers have been doing for generations.

And so this book seeks to bring Cambodian literature out of the shadows of the great temples of Angkor and out of the ashes of a war that killed most of the country's authors and destroyed countless irreplaceable books, whether by fire, neglect, or being turned into cigarette wrappers or toilet paper. The works collected here illuminate fourteen hundred years of a tradition in which the oldest surviving poetry is inscribed in stone—a classical literature of complex, clever, and nuanced beauty, written in ancient, rarely translated languages. At the same time, it presents contemporary Cambodian writers who have risen to the challenges faced by refugees of war, rebuilding a literary community out of devastation. And it presents the children of the diaspora living in countries from Australia to the U.S., Canada, and Europe.

The earliest recorded writings in Cambodia are carved in stone in Sanskrit and Old Khmer. The great temples of Angkor have many beautiful poetic inscriptions, invisible and unknown to the tourists who pass by. These include Queen Indradevi's moving elegy to her sister, composed around 1200 AD at the height of the Angkor era, and "Hymn to the Tree of Awakening," both inscribed into the temple of Phimeanakas and included here.

Around the fifteenth century, the Khmer language was transformed into what is now called Middle Khmer. By the eighteenth century, it lost most of its original voiced consonants and doubled its number of vowels (making it one of the most vowel-rich languages in the world). The multisyllabic vocabulary from Pali and Sanskrit, combined with the largely monosyllabic, highly alliterative and onomatopoeic native vocabulary, created a diverse orchestra of sounds and a wonderful rhythmic and melodic palette embraced by poets. Among these early compositions are long, varied lists and beautiful descriptions of species of birds, fish, animals, plants, and even place names invoking the spirits of the land in every corner of Cambodia. The beauty of language and sound—in Khmer, *piruoh* (melodious, melliflluous)—is greatly valued. There is a Khmer expression, *chhnganh trachiek*—which literally means delicious (like food) for the ears. Wit, word play, poetic speech, musicality, and the ability to tell a good story are all highly appreciated in Cambodia, whether one is literate or not—and this has been reflected in its literature over the centuries.

Classical Khmer poetry has over sixty forms, using complex meters and intricate rhyme schemes. The epics, or verse novels, were composed in thousands of stanzas and could take days to chant. Perhaps the most famous epic poem in Cambodia is the *Reamker*, which has been recited, sung, and danced in various forms for centuries. These verse novels continue to influence writers today. Kong Nay learned to improvise by memorizing verse novels; Ma Laupi studied all the classical poetic epics.

The majority of the translated material here appears for the first time in English, including the large section of classical texts from the AD 600s to the AD 1900s, thanks to guest editor Trent Walker. Among these translations into English is Mai's *Code for Girls*, now controversial for its rules of proper conduct for women, but a text that can also be read as a subtle critique of men behaving poorly. *Thunder and the Crabs*, a classic teaching text, consists of a humorous and lively dialog between Thunder and the vulnerable crabs he is about to leave to the various dangers posed by men.

Many of the surviving versions of wedding songs, Buddhist chants, and folktales presented here were recorded only in the late nineteenth and twentieth centuries—after being been passed down orally for untold generations. Modern Cambodian literature began to emerge in the early twentieth century. Khmer poet and scholar Ukna Suttantaprija Ind (1859–1924) was a pivotal figure in its creation. His poem *Journey to Angkor Wat* describes his travels to attend King Sisowath's visit to the Angkor temples in 1909. The manuscript, discovered among his possessions after his death, represents a transition between classical tradition and modernity. In the excerpts translated here, the poet recounts his river journey as a meditation on life, desire, and impermanence, and also describes his first seeing the great stone lions of Angkor—one of the most famous passages in Cambodian literature.

In the early 1900s, the Buddhist Institute, which initially printed *Journey to Angkor Wat* and other literature, became the nation's first major publisher. Khmer-language newspapers and journals appeared in the 1920s, although the first Khmer-owned and operated newspaper, *Nagaravatta* (Angkor Wat), did not appear until 1937. The first Khmer modern novels appeared soon afterward. A new Khmer term was invented for the novel, *pralaom lok*—which means a story written to seduce the hearts of human beings—a term coined by Soth Polin's maternal great-grandfather, the poet Nou Kan. Many of these early works featured ill-fated lovers and contained moral and social critiques. As with some of the nineteenth-century work of Dickens and Tolstoy in Europe, many Cambodian novels of the 1900s were serialized in newspapers or journals, first in Buddhist publications and later in secular periodicals. Among these was the literary supplement of *Reatrey Thngai Sau* (Saturday Night), which inspired a whole generation of writers, including Soth Polin, who secretly read its pages while hiding in his mother's closet.

In 1915, the Buddhist monk Brah Padumatther Som composed his version of the famous *Tum Teav*, based on an earlier tragic love story, considered Cambodia's *Romeo and Juliet*. The classic story of separated lovers would become the subject of many modern novels—from Nou Hach's *Wilted Flower*, in 1947, to Ty Chi Huot's *Sky of the Lost Moon*, in 1985—often interwoven with issues of social or class divisions. All three of these classics are excerpted in *Out of the Shadows of Angkor*. Som's *Tum Teav* is translated by Trent Walker, whose love of Cambodia's classic literature began when he learned to sing its Buddhist poetry. *Wilted Flower* is beautifully translated by Vaddey Ratner, and *Sky of the Lost Moon* is translated by guest editor Rinith Taing, who first discovered the novel when he was a teenager searching for literary gems in a dusty library. Rinith's essay, "The Bookrenter of Battambang and the Master of Uselessness," is an homage to his passion for books.

The love of books, the arts, and the country—often in the face of great loss and adversity—is among the prominent themes of this volume. It is present in the foreword by Vaddey Ratner and the preface by Sokunthary Svay, both living in the U.S., and in the work of guest editors Phina So and Rinith Taing, both living in Cambodia. Indeed, during Cambodia's struggle for independence, literature became inextricably linked with national identity. Cambodians in France began writing decades before independence, among them Makhali Phal, daughter of a Cambodian woman of royal lineage and a minor French official, and Prince Areno Yukanthor, son of the rebel Prince Yukanthor. Both wrestled in different ways with aspects of colonialism and the divide between East and West.

Following Cambodia's independence from France in 1953, literacy, education, and publication expanded. In 1961, Suon Sorin published *A New Sun Rises Over the Old Land*, an ideological novel that describes the hardships of a *cyclo* driver's life and remains popular today. This was the heyday of Cambodian rock 'n' roll, the "golden" voice of Sinn Sisamouth, and a vibrant sophisticated community of writers and intellectuals, among them Khun Srun and Soth Polin. Fluent in both Khmer and French, they were creating new Cambodian literature, despite being threatened by censorship, disappearance, assassination, the closing down of presses, and the war spilling over from neighboring Vietnam.

After the 1970 coup that deposed Prince Sihanouk, a war ensued between the Khmer Republic and the Khmer Rouge, but this turbulent period of political upheaval and unrest nevertheless saw a flourishing of music, poetry, fiction, and memoir, largely unknown to English-speaking readers today. Among the works represented here are Bunchan Mol's memoir of his imprisonment in the 1940s in the French colonial prison on Poulo Condor (Koh Tralach, in Khmer), a penal island off what is now the coast of southern Vietnam. Khun Srun's *The Accused*, published in 1973, is about his first imprisonment by the

Lon Nol regime; after his second imprisonment, he joined the Khmer Rouge but was executed by them in Tuol Sleng prison just days before the fall of the regime—murdered in the very same high school where he had taught as a young man. In his introduction, Christophe Macquet writes, "*The Accused* is moving, finally, because of its resistance to life's oblivions. To be able to read *The Accused* by Khun Srun seems miraculous. The original Khmer-language book is nearly impossible to find in Cambodia today." In "A Small Request," Khun Srun asks to be buried under a small mango tree. This haunting poem was written when he was just twenty-four years old in 1969, before the Khmer Republic and the Khmer Rouge regime.

On April 17, 1975, less than four decades after the publication of Cambodia's first novel, the flowering of Cambodian literature and scholarship abruptly ended with the Khmer Rouge takeover. Reading and writing were virtually abolished, as was music, except for purposes of propaganda. Kong Nay describes being forced to sing Khmer Rouge propaganda until that too was silenced. Revealing one's education, wearing glasses, or being an artist could get one killed—as many people were. Buddhist monasteries, the traditional repositories of literature, were ransacked and used as prisons. The National Library of Cambodia was used to raise pigs; in fact, it has never fully recovered and only twenty percent of its pre-war collection was preserved. Of more than six hundred librarians, only three survived.

On January 7, 1979, Vietnamese-backed troops ousted the Khmer Rouge. Artists, writers, and citizens found themselves in a shattered country. The nation's infrastructure had been destroyed and the land seeded with mines and unexploded ordnance. Poverty and illiteracy were widespread. Considering the devastation in the country, it is surprising that anyone wrote at all. But they did. Almost as soon as the Khmer Rouge regime ended, a new literature appeared: novels were handwritten, often in pencil, on the cheap graph-lined paper of student notebooks, then photocopied or recopied by hand and rented out by the day at market stalls. Guest editor Phina So in her essay, "Contemporary Writing and Publishing in Cambodia," recalls her mother renting out these hand-copied novels, including those by Tonsai (Rabbit), the pen name of Mao Somnang, and describes what it's like to be a writer, editor, and publisher in Cambodia today.

With the advent of video culture and capitalism, many of the older texts— even those written as recently as the 1980s and 1990s—ceased to be printed or copied and became difficult to find. Even *Sky of the Lost Moon,* the most popular novel of its generation, fell into obscurity. However, new writers have emerged in Cambodia, such as fiction writer and lyricist Sok Chanphal, two of whose stories are included here, one of them a ghost story in the tradition of Chuth Khay. Kong Bunchhoeun, born in Battambang province, resumed his writing career, which had begun in the 1950s. He escaped execution during the Khmer Rouge era thanks to a cadre who had read his novels and testified to his "profound sense of social justice."

Modern poetry—which began in Cambodia with the publication of Keng Vannsak's *Virgin Heart* in 1954, and continued with such volumes as Koy Sarun's *Black Flowers* in 1970—resumed in the 1980s with work by poet and scholar Chey Chap, poet and journalist Pen Samitthy, poet and actor Pich Tum Kravel, and Yin Luoth, now a Khmer-language lecturer in the U.S.

Meanwhile, another era of Cambodian writing began overseas: a literature of exile, to be transformed into other forms by younger artists, who often live and work between different countries. In France in the 1980s and 1990s, Cambodians were writing poems in Khmer, such as Khau Ny Kim's "A Hundred Scents, A Hundred Seasons," first published by Pech Sangwawann's Association of Khmer Writers Abroad. Others writing in French include Prince Amrindo Sisowath, whose poem "A Cry" was written and published while he was in the Sainte-Anne mental asylum. Soth Polin wrote *The Anarchist* in French, an excerpt of which was translated by Penny Edwards for this volume. In addition, literary scholars such as Khing Hok Dy were gathering, preserving, and translating Khmer literature into French. Rithy Panh, whose work is presented in our previous volume, began his groundbreaking film career. Tian Veasna's three-volume graphic novel about the Khmer Rouge period was first published in France, then in Cambodia, and finally in English as *Year of the Rabbit*.

Fiction, essays, and memoirs have begun to be published in recent decades by talented Cambodian writers in the U.S. Recent fiction ranges from the novels of Vaddey Ratner to the short stories of Anthony Veasna So. Other modern prose writers include Danny Thanh Nguyen (of Khmer Krom heritage) and several essayists included in this book writing about the arts: Sokunthary Svay on music; Elizabeth Chey on painter Vann Nath; Prumsodun Ok on sacred dance; and Boreth Ly on photography. International journalist Putsata Reang has contributed "At Sea, and Seeking a Safe Harbor," which is a prelude to her memoir, *Ma and Me*. Living in Australia, Alice Pung is represented here by an excerpt from her second memoir, *Her Father's Daughter*, about her return to Cambodia.

Poet U Sam Oeur, who survived the Khmer Rouge years by feigning illiteracy, received an MFA from the Iowa Writers' Workshop in 1968. His bilingual book of poems, *Sacred Vows*, was translated and published in the U.S. in 1998; his work appears in our previous volume. Other Cambodian poets who are publishing in English in the U.S. include Chath pierSath, Bunkong Tuon, Sokunthary Svay, Mylo Lam, and Monica Sok. Poet Greg Santos, a transracial adoptee of Cambodian descent, publishes in Canada.

Cambodia's rich oral tradition of poetry and storytelling is carried on today by traditional artists such as the bluesy, improvisational *chapei* master Kong Nay, who recently collaborated with rap artist Vann Da. Younger generations of spoken-word poets in the U.S. and Cambodia include praCh, Kosal Khiev, and Princess Moon.

While writing is the most solitary of pursuits, the creation of literature and the communities from which it comes are often made from literary friendships, wherever in the world they reside. In the "golden age" of Cambodian literature in the 1960s and 1970s, a community of writers thrived through such friendships and literary partnerships. Khun Srun helped publish his mentor Koy Sarun; Soth Polin started his own newspaper and published many of the most brilliant voices of his day, including those on the opposite end of the political spectrum.

This book has likewise grown out of literary friendships and mentorships over the years. It would not have been possible without our dedicated team of guest editors and the expertise of Frank Stewart and the editors of *Mānoa: A Pacific Journal of International Writing,* who published *In the Shadow of Angkor* in 2004 (and years earlier, my first short story). I met Christophe Macquet, my literary cohort, in Phnom Penh twenty years ago through my friendship with Soth Polin; we communicated in our common language, Khmer, to the amusement of the café workers at the places we met; Christophe has spent a large part of his life translating and documenting Cambodian literature, as well as translating foreign literature into Khmer. I first encountered Trent Walker fifteen years ago on a sunny afternoon at Stanford University, when he was an undergraduate and had just spent a year learning *smot* singing in Cambodia; he has since become a brilliant translator of ancient Cambodian languages and an endlessly patient and generous literary colleague through the years of working on this book. I met Phina So in Cambodia years ago when the only literary festivals were not in Khmer; she has worked tirelessly to remedy that by becoming a writer, editor, publisher, and passionate community advocate for Cambodian literature and arts. The Khmer Literature Festival she founded in 2017 is now an annual event. I remember standing on the steps of the CKS library at that first inaugural festival, in October 2017, at Wat Damnak, in Siem Reap, in the same spot where, fifteen years earlier, a young poet had told me, "I am a Khmer writer. I don't have much experience. But in my heart, I feel addicted to writing." Rinith Taing has been writing perceptively about Cambodian authors and artists for many years as a journalist based in Phnom Penh; he worked intensely on translations for this volume. Others who contributed to this book are too numerous to mention in this overview, but have our heartfelt and enduring thanks. Their names can be found in the Acknowledgments.

The work included in *Out of the Shadows of Angkor* is just a part of the vast, diverse repertoire of Cambodian literature created by those born in Cambodia, in the camps, and in new lands. Soth Polin once told me, "What we have lost is indescribable... What we have lost is not reconstructable. An epoch is finished. So when we have literature again, it will be a new literature." We hope this book brings out of the shadows some of the lost, hidden, and emerging gems of Cambodian literature—past, present, and moving into the future.

TRENT WALKER

Cambodian Literature: An Introduction

When Cambodians speak of literature, they speak of *aksar-sel* (Sanskrit *aksharashilpa*), "the art of letters" and *aksar-sah* (*aksharashastra*), "the science of letters." Khmer writers who succeed are celebrated not only for the creative genius of their art but also for their technical mastery over the bewildering variety of forms and genres Cambodian authors have developed. In Khmer, authors are known as *neak nipun*, literally "those who bind together," from Sanskrit *nibandha*, "tying down." The work of composition demands virtuosity in fastening words to one another. In many Cambodian genres, this work of binding involves controlling impressive arrays of linking rhymes and layers of hidden meanings. Even prose authors are tasked with holding together long strings of serial verbs and adjectives, evoking the sonic qualities of assonance and balance so valued in Cambodian poetry.

I entered Cambodian literature through the door of sound. My first intensive encounters with its literary forms were as a student of Buddhist chant and poetry recitation in rural Kampong Speu province, Cambodia, for thirteen months from 2005 to 2006. My teachers, *lok kru* Prum Ut and *neak kru* Koet Ran, had exacting standards for diction, melody, and moral conduct, and knew that their role as masters of an exceptionally musical form of chant called *smot* meant instilling such standards in their students. I was only eighteen at the time, fresh out of high school in San Francisco, and was at first a failure in their eyes. I mispronounced the words, put trills and glissandi in the wrong places, and once ran away to a nearby mountain temple when I couldn't stand the pressure of complete immersion in Khmer village life. Despite my transgressions, they took me under their care. Under their tutelage, I repeated short phrases until I got it right or until my throat, irritated by the silty tea we drank out of dimpled beer mugs, simply gave out.

In studying with Prum Ut and Koet Ran, I had unwittingly been steeped in the way Cambodian literature had been transmitted for the past fifteen hundred years. Koet Ran, who became blind after the Khmer Rouge period, stressed the oral method alone: she would sing, I would repeat, then she would critique me and sing again. She had memorized well over a hundred chants and had high hopes I would have such a fine memory. But here again I failed, fumbling for the words whenever I set down my notebook. Prum Ut offered a dual method, both oral and written. At night, he would sit me down on the creaky floors of his one-room home, light a slender candle, and take a thick *krang* off the altar. This paper manuscript, folded in the leporello or accordion style, guided my studies of *smot* and sparked a lifelong passion for traditional Southeast Asian books and manuscripts. Prum Ut chanted Khmer and Pali texts from the *krang* in ornate, flowing melodies as I did my best to keep up. By day, I returned to the manuscript, transcribing and translating the texts we had studied the night before.

My failures notwithstanding, these are the core methods that Cambodians have used in teaching literature and the performance of literature to new generations since at least the seventh century of the Common Era. For many Cambodian authors throughout history, their rigorous approach to language built the foundation for the expressive art of literature. Since this issue of *Mānoa* looks at literature as art rather than science, I offer my essay here as a kind of counterweight, carving out a peephole into the precise, intricate workings that make traditional Cambodian literature tick.

The borders of the modern nation-state of Cambodia are home to a plethora of languages. In addition to the ninety percent who primarily speak the national language of Khmer, there are also large communities of Vietnamese, Chinese, and Cham speakers, the latter being an Austronesian language closely related to Malay (and very distantly to Hawaiian). On Cambodia's hilly borders with Vietnam, Thailand, and Laos, there is also an extremely diverse range of indigenous communities living in the forest, beyond the margins of wet-rice cultivation. Most of these groups speak related languages from the Austroasiatic family and have lived in Cambodia for several thousand years or more. This volume—like so many representations of Cambodia—focuses on voices from the numerically and politically dominant community of Khmer speakers. But language and ethnicity are never airtight categories. Many of the writers featured in this collection are of mixed heritage, including several with both Khmer and Chinese traditions in their families and one who was born in Vietnam. Sinn Sisamouth, far and away the most celebrated Khmer singer and songwriter of the twentieth century—a performer included here—had both Lao and Chinese grandparents.

To complicate the picture further, Khmer speakers are not limited to Cambodia. They have lived in the southern provinces of modern-day Vietnam since at least the middle of the first millennium, if not considerably longer. Vietnamese toponyms such as Saigon have older Khmer names; *sài gòn* is probably derived from Khmer *prey kor* "Kapok Forest" or *prey nokor*, "City in the Forest." The whole Mekong Delta region is sometimes known as Kampuchea Krom, or Lower Cambodia, and the Khmer dialect spoken there is mutually intelligible with that in Cambodia proper. The political reach of past Khmer kingdoms once extended far into what is now Laos and Thailand, particularly before Lao and Thai speakers arrived in mainland Southeast Asia in the early centuries of the second millennium. Even today, in the southern provinces of northeastern Thailand, especially Surin, Buriram, and Sisaket, there is a robust community speaking a dialect known as Northern Khmer, which in recent centuries has diverged significantly from Modern Khmer as spoken in Cambodia. One song in Northern Khmer appears in this volume, Songsaeng Rungrueangchai's "The Big Tusker."

The Cambodian diaspora has brought Khmer speakers to many corners of the globe. Large refugee communities formed in France, the U.S., Australia, Canada, and elsewhere after the collapse of the Khmer Rouge regime in 1979. Many Cambodian authors abroad continue to read and write in Khmer, while others have made their literary mark in English, French, and other languages. Khmer literacy is still taught in diaspora communities, particularly in Buddhist temples. It is also fostered at university academic programs. Maintaining the Khmer language in aggressively monolingual environments such as the U.S., with its long history of anti-Asian racism and xenophobia, is an enduring challenge for members of the Cambodian diaspora. Limited resources are available for language programs, especially in comparison to programs in other Asian diaspora communities. My personal hope is that this volume may remind the Anglophone world of the depth, range, and beauty of Cambodian literature, and so foster support for more language programs, especially those serving diaspora communities.

Where does the national language of Cambodia come from? Khmer, along with Mon and Vietnamese, is one of the most prominent representatives of the Austroasiatic language family, as basic to human history as Indo-European, Sino-Tibetan, or Dravidian. Austroasiatic languages are the primary indigenous languages of mainland Southeast Asia, and their distinct grammar, phonology, and vocabulary have shaped all subsequent languages that have entered the region. It is hard to pinpoint exactly when the Khmer language arose; it probably diverged from its closest Austroasiatic cousins between two and three thousand years ago. Like other languages in the same family, Khmer has several fascinating properties that have guided its development as a literary vehicle.

First, Khmer is distinguished by its mix of monosyllables and sesquisyllables. The latter refers to words composed of a weak syllable followed by a strong syllable. The rhythmic structure of Khmer verse thus tends to be iambic, with an alternating stress pattern. Second, these sesquisyllables are generally derived through prefixes and infixes that can easily change verbs into nouns, actions into agents, and ordinary verbs into causatives. In simple terms, this means that every verbal root in Khmer can be grammatically transformed by adding a weak syllable to either its front or middle. An old verbal root, *ser/sir*, meaning "to make a line" (now obsolete in Khmer), can be transformed into *sar-ser* ("to write"), *smer* ("a scribe, a writer"), and *samner* ("a piece of writing"). Third, these verbs and their derived forms may be combined with other verbs to form complex strings of serial verbs. In poetry, key nouns such as the subject and object may be dropped or only implied, leaving behind a sequence of verbs for the reader or listener to weave together into a grammatical sentence. These features give Khmer authors great flexibility but pose particular challenges when translating into a radically different language such as English.

In addition to its distinctly Austroasiatic features, Khmer literature has been shaped by words borrowed from other languages. The vocabulary of Khmer received a massive influx of words from Pali and Sanskrit, a transformation already visible in the earliest dated Khmer-language inscription from 612 CE. Later cultural contacts brought a smaller number of words from Thai, Chinese, Vietnamese, and French. By the mid-twentieth century, Khmer writers, concerned about the increasing share of foreign borrowings, either coined new words from Indic roots or adopted Khmer-derived terms for describing the new protocols and technologies of the modern world. The result of these centuries of borrowings and new coinages is an Austroasiatic language with a rich set of Indic-derived words, similar to the preponderance of Romance-language vocabulary in English.

Cambodia is home to one of the longest continuous literary traditions in Southeast Asia. The oldest writings in Sanskrit by Cambodian authors date to the fifth century, and hundreds of Khmer-language inscriptions survive from as early as the seventh and eighth centuries. To speak of the Sanskrit inscriptions first, these are almost entirely in verse and reflect the linguistic genius of their Cambodian authors. The dominant form of Sanskrit verse in Cambodia is known as *prashasti* ("praise"), the genre of ornate, eulogistic inscriptions that spread throughout South and Southeast Asia during the first millennium and early into the second. Surviving examples of this genre by Khmer authors number in the hundreds. A short except from one of them appears in this volume, under the title "In Praise of Sister Queens." This celebrated inscription, among the oldest known works by a female author in Southeast Asia, was etched in stone at the temple of Phimeanakas in the heart of the ancient royal palace.

Sanskrit *prashasti* by Khmer authors are just as magnificent as those produced in India. Indeed, the Sanskrit inscriptions of Cambodia are only matched by the magnificence of the stone monuments on which they are carved. Dense with royal and religious imagery, many such inscriptions overflow with an ingenious literary technique called *shlesha* ("embrace"), in which whole stanzas are intended to be read in two completely divergent ways based on small ambiguities in the Sanskrit. By breaking up Sanskrit words in different ways, Khmer poets embraced two possible meanings for their verses, with the hidden reading often revealing a sophisticated interpretation of Hindu or Buddhist philosophy. In many ways, Cambodia's Sanskrit literature is better known outside Cambodia than its Khmer literature, having been assiduously studied and translated by generations of Cambodian, Thai, Indian, and European scholars from the late nineteenth century onward.

Very little classical literature written in Khmer has been available to Anglophone readers. Khmer falls into three linguistic stages: Old (seventh to fourteenth centuries), Middle (fourteenth to mid-eighteenth centuries), and Modern (mid-eighteenth century to the present). The distinctive metrical structures of Cambodian poetry have their roots in Old Khmer, but many of the key forms and meters were only developed during the Middle and early Modern phases of the language. Khmer poets refer to this versified poetry as *kaby* (pronounced "kap"), derived from Sanskrit *kavya*, meaning the style of complex literary verse used in *prashasti*. Though Khmer poets borrowed aesthetic concepts from Sanskrit genres, the meters they created are completely Southeast Asian in character, and best suited to the linguistic structures of Austroasiatic languages. Khmer meters are distinguished by the following features: fixed patterns of syllable counts per line, usually between four and nine; stanzas of three to seven lines each, with four being the most common; complex rhyme patterns that link together lines both within and between stanzas; and an emphasis on alliteration and other forms of assonance. These features, coupled with diverse traditions of melodic recitation, have favored the aural dimensions of Khmer poetry throughout its history.

Meters (known as *pad*, pronounced "bot") featured in this collection include the Narration (*bamnol*, "pumnol"), Brahma's Song (*brahmagiti*, "prumakit"), Crow's Gait (*kakagati*, "kakkate"), Serpent's Lilt (*bhujang lila*, "phuchung lilea"), Four-Syllable (*baky puon*, "peak buon"), Seven-Syllable (*baky prambir*, "peak prampir"), and Eight-Syllable (*baky prampi*, "peak prambei") varieties. Each meter is associated with up to a dozen or more styles of a cappella recitation. Cambodian folk and popular songs are based on the same set of meters, particularly the Four- and Seven-Syllable meters, allowing for an ever-expanding horizon of melodies to be applied to Khmer poetry.

The metrical forms and musical dimensions of Khmer poetry pose a range of conundrums to the translator. How can we hope to capture in English the beauty generated through subtle arrangements of Khmer sounds and musical tones? Several approaches for literary translation are possible, each with their own merits and limitations. One, we can focus on the meaning alone and ignore the rhyme patterns and syllable counts of the Khmer. If the goal is a fluid, readable text in English, this is the most direct method, and most of the translations in this book adopt such an approach. In all but a few cases, the original stanza divisions have been respected, and in my own translations I try to maintain a regular line length and syllable count to more faithfully convey the rhythmic qualities of the original.

Another approach is to ignore rhyme but still preserve the exact syllabic structure of the Khmer poem. For poems in the Crow's Gait meter, for instance, this entails creating an unrhymed English translation of four syllables per line and seven lines per stanza. I frequently follow this method in my translations, as it makes the structural qualities of the Khmer visible to the reader without compromising too much on meaning. A third approach, represented only by

"This Life Is Short" in this collection, is to reproduce both the syllable counts and rhyme scheme in the English. The risks of this mode of translation usually outweigh the gains. But such examples do allow readers unfamiliar with Khmer to appreciate the kinds of intricate rhyme patterns that structure most of the poems composed in Cambodia up to the present.

In addition to their metrical form and musical performance, the materiality of Khmer poems has also shaped their transmission and reception, particularly in the Middle and early Modern phases of the language. As I learned from Prum Ut, the key material object for the transmission of Cambodian literature has long been the manuscript, including handwritten documents in a variety of formats. We know that manuscripts were used extensively between the seventh and fifteenth centuries, but none of that age have survived Cambodia's hot and humid climate. From the sixteenth through nineteenth centuries, however, we have direct knowledge of Middle and early Modern Khmer literature from manuscript copies made in the nineteenth and early twentieth centuries. Most of the translations of pre-twentieth-century literature in this book were made either directly from manuscripts or from academic editions based on such manuscripts.

Carved on the long, pliant leaves of the talipot palm or inked on the folded pages of bark-paper manuscripts, these texts hail from a period when handwriting was king and print not yet born. Buddhist monasteries were traditionally the primary places for the creation, curation, reading, and safeguarding of both secular and religious manuscripts. These documents are thus imbued with a sacred aura. In the weeks leading up to my temporary ordination as a novice monk, Prum Ut guided me through the specific bows and gestures involved. Careless and clumsy in my practice robes, after completing one bow I lost balance and fell back on his leporello manuscript. He rebuked me, stating it was a grave misdeed to disrespect a book in this way. This reverence for manuscripts was a key factor in the preservation of old literary works well into the twentieth century.

Print technology arrived late in Cambodia. The first European-style printed books appeared at the end of the nineteenth century, but print technology only fully supplanted the use of traditional manuscripts in the 1960s. Verse novels from the early twentieth century were still composed and transmitted on palm leaves or recited by itinerant bards from memory. When the modern prose novel emerged in the 1940s, it coincided with a wider availability of printed material and a burgeoning book culture in Cambodia. The Buddhist Institute in Phnom Penh played a key role in this process, publishing early-twentieth-century works by Suttantaprija Ind *(Journey to Angkor Wat),* Padumatther Som *(Tum Teav),* and Krom Ngoy ("A Garland of New Advice"). These authors, all featured in this volume, had previously only been accessible in handwritten or oral form.

In contemporary Cambodia, though traditional manuscript materials have fallen out of use except in rare circumstances, the practice of hand-copying continues. Koet Ran's sighted husband copies down all the texts she has memorized in paper notebooks. On the rare occasions when her memory falters, he is there by her side to cue the next verse. In the 1980s, a vibrant literary world emerged from the circulation of novellas hand-copied on notebook paper, which were rented out to an eager circle of readers. As Rinith Taing's essay in this volume describes, the practice of renting printed books continues to the present. The material basis may have shifted, but little has changed about Cambodians' reverence and passion for literature.

As documented in Phina So's essay in this collection, spaces for the literary arts continue to flourish in Cambodia, despite the plethora of challenges. That such a thriving culture of writing exists today can hardly be taken for granted. It took a tremendous amount of effort on the part of Cambodian writers in their homeland and beyond. The tumult and tragedy of the twentieth century visited unimaginable horrors on Cambodians everywhere. Throughout these trials, writers have been punished, banished, and executed. But they have persisted in bringing pen to page and letters into song.

Each year, more and more Cambodians study Old Khmer inscriptions at the Royal University of Fine Arts and other institutions. Classes and research on Khmer literature from the Middle and Modern periods are burgeoning at the Royal University of Phnom Penh, and manuscript digitization initiatives are promising unprecedented access for Cambodians hoping to read traditional forms of Khmer literature. Senior bards such as Kong Nay, master of the *chapei dang veng*, represented in this volume, are celebrated anew as younger songwriters find ways to incorporate traditional forms. Contemporary poets continue to push the boundaries of their craft, even as they compose in meters now hundreds of years old. Collaborations between writers in Cambodia and those in diaspora are beginning to emerge, paving new paths. Cambodian literature rests on a much deeper history than the Khmer Rouge dared to imagine, and the future looks bright. This collection is an invitation to explore, celebrate, and be moved by what Khmer writers have offered the world through the ages.

NOTE ON SOURCES, TRANSLITERATION, AND NAMES

We have presented the essays, contributions, and notes in the main portion of this collection entirely in Roman script and without diacritics. For students and researchers looking for more precise information, we have included two additional resources in the back matter. For complete citations of all of the pieces gathered in this volume, with Khmer and Roman script as appropriate, including diacritics, please consult the Sources in the back. For more on the authors and translators, including Khmer-script names of the relevant authors, consult About the Contributors.

In presenting Khmer words in Roman script, we have followed three basic conventions: (1) respecting precedent and the choices of individual authors, (2) transcribing terms in contemporary contexts phonetically, and (3) transliterating older terms based on the graphic system favored by scholars. Our goal is not consistency but rather making the process as straightforward as possible for both general readers and those who would like to learn more about Cambodian literature.

In detail, these three conventions are as follows. First, for proper names for which a commonly accepted Roman-script version exists, such as *smot*, Angkor Wat, the *Reamker*, Krom Ngoy, or Sinn Sisamouth, we have followed conventional practice. Many contemporary Cambodian authors who write and publish primarily in Khmer have their own preferred romanization of their names, which we have followed.

Second, for names and terms discussed in relation to the past one hundred years, we have used a simplified, diacritic-free version of Frank Huffman's Franco-Khmer phonetic transcription system, itself based on common Cambodian practice during the mid-twentieth century. Most writing on contemporary Cambodian history and literature uses a variation of this system.

Third, for names and terms relevant to contexts from more than one hundred years ago, we have used a diacritic-free version of the graphic transliteration system widely used by scholars of Ancient, Middle, and early Modern Cambodia. This system is not phonetic, but we use it for older words, works, and authors to make it easier for readers to follow up on such items in existing publications. When appropriate, we have also added phonetic transcriptions in quotation marks, based on the Franco-Khmer system.

For terms in other languages, we have followed simplified, diacritic-free versions of a widely accepted standard, such as RTGS for Thai and IATS for Pali and Sanskrit.

In Cambodia, names are usually presented with the family name followed by the given name, as in "Kong Bunchhoeun." Cambodians who publish in other languages or who live abroad in Anglophone or Francophone contexts often present their name in the Western sequence of the given name followed by the family name, as in "Kalean Ung." We have endeavored to respect contributors' preferences for the sequence of their names. The About the Contributors section is alphabetized by family name, marked in bold; therefore, **KONG BUNCHHOEUN** appears before **KALEAN UNG**. To facilitate ease of reference, we have also used family names—or single personal names, in the case of many pre-twentieth-century writers—in the abbreviated footers that appear in the book. However, when discussing individual authors who write primarily in Khmer, we defer to Cambodian practice and use either full names or given names only, as in Kong Bunchhoeun or simply Bunchhoeun.

THEANLY CHOV

Oil paintings from the series Surviving, *by Cambodian artist Theanly Chov.*

ACHAR, 2019
ii

KIMRY, 2019
2

HOUNG, 2017
82

HEOUB, 2016
Lysath Loeuk Collection
128

CAKE SELLER, 2019
148

KRAMA, 2019
203

AYUTTHYEA, 2019
204

SOVIET, 2019
224

TOUCH, 2018
Julien Seroussi Collection
276

INSCRIPTION

Warning to Thieves

This short inscription from Choeung Ek Monastery in Kandal province, slightly more than a mile north of the contemporary Choeung Ek "Killing Fields" memorial, records the seventh- or eighth-century founding of a Shaivite temple along with a stern warning to any vandals who might steal or disturb what has been donated to it. TW

The decree of My High Lord:

That of My High Lord Siddhayatana in Cun Muh was pooled together with the property of My High Lord Sri Acalesvara, including slaves, cattle, buffalo, rice fields, harvested rice, gardens, lowlands, and crop fields. The people gave all these to the Lord.

Anyone who steals them from here, anyone who seizes people from here, anyone who infringes upon here, anyone who misuses what is listed here, anyone who petitions here, anyone who collects taxes here, anyone who takes cattle, carts, or boats from here, anyone who transgresses this decree—they shall be punished.

Translated from Old Khmer by Trent Walker

QUEEN INDRADEVI

In Praise of Sister Queens

Queen Indradevi is the earliest known female poet in Cambodia. "In Praise of Sister Queens," inscribed in the late twelfth or early thirteenth century, reveals a nearly flawless command of the Sanskrit language and its complex poetic forms; the passage here includes verses in the indravajra, vamsastha, vasantatilaka, *and* sloka *meters. This excerpt from the great stele of Phimeanakas includes just the final twelve stanzas of a 102-stanza poem, which was discovered in the rubble of the ancient royal palace near Angkor Thom in 1916. In 1297, the Chinese emissary Zhou Daguan described a gold tower within the royal palace, presumably a reference to Phimeanakas. The inscription eulogizes Indradevi and her younger sister Jayarajadevi, both queens to Jayavarman VII, the most powerful monarch in Cambodian history and a patron of Mahayana Buddhism.* TW

What the last Lord of the Land built in stone—
this temple, called Ornament of the Earth—
Queen Jayarajadevi piously swathed in gold,
making it ornament of both earth and sky.

On a mountain known as Shiva's City,
she reverently raised golden icons
of her three venerable masters,
bedecked with gems, blazing like suns.

Ever wise, she built statues across the land,
images of her parents, siblings, and friends,
along with her relatives and more distant kin,
both those she knew and those she knew of.

Even on her deathbed, bound for perfect peace,
she remained devoted to her husband, the king,
waiting until he'd finished his midday rites
before slipping away into supreme repose.

Jayarajadevi brought more joy to her people
than even their own mothers, and once she passed,
her elder sister Indradevi was crowned as queen,
guiding the people from burning grief to peace.

In every city, Indradevi erected numerous icons
of her sister, herself, and her king, Jayavarman.
Yet within her own palace, she cherished only
the splendor of the Victorious Buddhas.

Her Grace surpassed the grace of mere beauties,
her Learning bested the eloquence of sophists,
her Fortune's splendor outshone all adversaries,
steadily making true her own name.

At the Buddhist abodes of Mountain-Chief Summit
and Highest Ornament, peaks of erudition on Earth,
she was named preeminent professor by the king
and ceaselessly taught an array of royal women.

In her lovely residence at Hermitage of the Kings,
she reigned in brilliance, beloved by the Earth-Holder
for her supreme learning. Adored by her students,
she aided them like Saraswati made flesh.

First in the city called Elephants' Rest,
then in the city named Saraswati,
and at last in the capital, Yashodharapura,
this half-Brahmin, half-royal girl rose to chief consort.

Indradevi, who raised the king's soles to her bowed head in respect,
surpassed Ganga, who poured her river's feet on Shiva's crown in wrath.
The queen scattered her lord's favors, the pleasures of knowledge,
among the lovely ladies of the court, who longed for learning.

Wise by nature, a true savant, perfectly pure,
she was true to the king, glorious Jayavarman.
Having composed this perfect poem of praise,
eclipsing the skills of all others, she gleamed.

Translated from Sanskrit by Trent Walker

INSCRIPTION

Hymn to the Tree of Awakening

"Hymn to the Tree of Awakening" praises the bodhi tree, the sacred fig under which the Buddha awakened, and is a rare example of a Sanskrit inscription followed by a precise translation into Old Khmer. It is located in Phimeanakas, the same temple that bears the long Sanskrit poem of Queen Indradevi. TW

SANSKRIT

Your base is Brahma, your body is Shiva,
your branches are Vishnu, everlasting tree!
King of the forest, endowed with blessings,
you give refuge to all, O giver of fruits!

Neither lightning bolts nor axe blades,
neither gusts of wind nor pious flames,
neither rogue kings nor angry elephants:
may none drag you down to destruction.

Blinking eyes, twitching brows,
nightmares, unsettling thoughts:
O sacred fig, appease them all,
be they human or divine.

KHMER

O sacred tree of awakening, O you whose trunk is Lord Brahma, O you whose body is Lord Shiva, O you whose branches are Lord Vishnu, O you who will last forever, O you who are king of all trees, O you whose fortune is massive, O you who are the refuge of all worlds, O you who bear fruit in all seasons!

May lightning never strike you, my Lord, may axes never fell you, may winds never snap you, may fires never burn you, may Lords of the Lower Realm never destroy you, may angry elephants never trample you.

As for the ominous twitching of eyes, the ominous twitching of brows, ominous dreams, ominous thoughts—anything ominous at all, be they of heaven or humans—may you make them disappear.

Translated from Sanskrit and Old Khmer by Trent Walker

KHUN THEPKRAWI

Hymn for the Elephants' Feast

"Hymn for the Elephants' Feast" may be the oldest surviving rhymed poem in Khmer. The archaic language, transitional between Old and Middle Khmer, suggests it was based on now-lost ritual texts of the Angkorian kings. Across the region, "Hymn for the Elephants' Feast" and similar poems would have once been recited in conjunction with royal rituals to capture wild elephants from the forest. Such elephants were essential to Southeast Asian monarchs, not only for labor and for battle but also as palladia that symbolized the potency of a king's reign. The process of rounding up elephants in the jungle was orchestrated as an elaborate Brahmanical rite, accompanied by chants and offerings to various Hindu deities.

This chant was intended to be recited at the beginning of such rituals. The first deity invoked, Ganesha, is celebrated as a remover of obstacles, and so is afforded the first spot. Son of Shiva and Parvati, Ganesha is distinguished by his human body and elephant head. According to one Indian narrative, referenced obliquely in the Khmer poem, Ganesha's ordinary human head was destroyed by Saturn, a planet and deity known for his destructive gaze. Most of the stanzas of "Hymn for the Elephants' Feast" are devoted to Vanaspati, literally "Lord of Trees," or brah brai *in Khmer. Vanaspati is the Hindu god of the whole plant kingdom, a personification of Nature Himself. The text briefly invokes another deity, Devakarman, a powerful elephant god who serves as the symbolic leader of the flesh-and-blood elephants rounded up during the ritual. The feast of offerings to Devakarman and his pachyderm troops is regarded as a gift to Vanaspati, the ultimate ruler of the jungles where the elephants live.

Very little is known about Khun Thepkrawi (a court title meaning "divine poet"), the author or editor to whom most manuscripts ascribe this text. He was said to come from the northern Siamese city of Sukhothai, which flourished as an independent kingdom in the thirteenth to fifteenth centuries before its absorption into Ayutthaya. The structure of Khun Thepkravi's version of "Hymn for the Elephants' Feast" alternates between portions in Brahma's Song meter and others in the Narration meter. The English translation uses these changes in meter as a basis for dividing the poem into discrete sections.

Given the difficulties and uncertainties in the text and its transmission, the translation is necessarily speculative in some passages. The deep Brahmanical erudition and keen poetic sense of the author are readily apparent, however. TW

Homage to you, Ganesha, made of space and heaven,
victor over Lalita and her lunar goddesses.
Please, O Lord, destroy all obstacles and binds;
cut our karmic knots to keep us well and free.
May you, Ganesha, mighty Lord of Elements,
practice your harsh penance to conquer all the spheres.
Long ago, Lord Shiva transformed you, his dear son,
from a magic boy into the Lord of All His Hosts.
O Saturn, fiercest planet, don't come out at dusk.
Take your path across the sky, but don't intersect too much;
your deadly stare might fell Ganesha's head once again.

Wet with creeks and rivers, streaming, splashing, and surging
beneath the wide-mouthed heavens and the dazzling solar orb,
soaring high in lofty beauty, alive since ancient time—
Nature Himself, Vanaspati, shines with striking splendor.
The charm of the Lord of Trees, Vanaspati, exceeds all other gods.
I praise him with these words and foods both fine and coarse.
Vanaspati sprouts high and low, in ponds, in lakes, and rushing
    streams,
their sparkling flows now hushed, for soon a king shall come.

Devakarman, King of the Elephants, lead your troops
across the woods, where sounds echo all around!
We offer this fish, this flesh, this rice and wine
for you to consume, in worship of Vanaspati.
Candles, incense, puffed rice, and flowers
are gifts for Nature Himself, above all lesser gods.

In glades and mountain crags, swift winds burst forth;
trees sough in lovely tunes. High on the towering peaks,
you shine, Vanaspati, your figure white as snow.
Hear the hymns of birds, who praise you day by day.
Fierce rains pour down; gales blow in concert with reed flutes.
Barbet calls and cicada cries pierce through the wild din.
Rain roars ten thousand sounds, more sonorous than horns;
oboes play old plaintive tunes to please Vanaspati.
An orchestra of gongs resounds with martial beats,
with bugles and pounding drums to rouse the Lord from sleep.

Quiet grow the trees, some great, some small, in clusters and long
    rows.
The thick air swells with birds in songful choirs, as roosters crow,
    forlorn.

Owls hoot and eagles screech as they swoop down to take their verdant perches.
The woods erupt in cries, the trees alive with sound; cacophony breaks out.
At midday, peacocks scream and small beasts flee, leaping from cliff and cleft.
By evening, partridges warble and wail—how shrill and sorrowful!
Your grace and glory, Vanaspati, outshines all other gods.
We praise you with this hymn—please take our gifts, O Lord of Trees!
Protect His Majesty, our earthly king; may he reign for years to come.
Help him secure success on the throne and thrive throughout a long life.

Translated from Old Khmer by Trent Walker

EPIC

from *Reamker*

The *Reamker* (*Ramakerti*, "The Glory of Rama") is the title given to the Khmer versions of the Ramayana. The most famous version, Reamker I: Early Episodes, is also the oldest extant recension, having been composed in Middle Khmer during the sixteenth or seventeenth centuries. Of its twenty-one episodes, the first two are translated here. Much of the remaining narrative is found only in the eighteenth-century text Reamker II: Later Episodes. Both were likely composed for shadow-puppet theater. A number of other versions of the *Reamker* have survived in oral traditions, typically in prose. Whether performed on the stage or recited in village festivals, the *Reamker* remains one of the most beloved pieces of classical literature in contemporary Cambodia.

The first episode introduces us to the might of Prince Rama (pronounced "Ream" in modern Khmer), known to Cambodians as both an avatar of the Hindu god Vishnu and a previous incarnation of the Buddha. The episode narrates Rama's slaying of a demon who disrupts a ritual at his teacher Vishvamitra's forest hermitage. The second episode begins with the birth of Sita, discovered in a furrow in a plowed field by her father, King Janaka of Mithila. Janaka holds a contest, offering Sita in marriage to anyone who can lift a magic bow. After all the other gods fail, Vishvamitra calls for Rama to try his hand; he wins easily.

The poetic sensibility of the *Reamker*, particularly Reamker I, is among the finest in all of Khmer literature. The diction is by turns graceful and arresting. The emotions of humans and gods are more restrained than in Reamker II, but compelling nonetheless. **TW**

EPISODE I: RAMA SLAYS THE DEMON KAKANA

I tell of when the prince of seers, Vishvamitra,
was most pleased. Great as the greatest kings,
he sat sealed within the walls and carved columns
of his high-vaulted hall, a place of pure penance.

Beyond these sacrificial grounds, where blazing pennants waved,
fire-red leaves filled the woods, spreading refreshing shade.
Fresh streams cascaded down to cleanse the poisoned stones

with sparkling-clear waters that splashed over tiny falls.
Amidst the hermits' cells grew areca and coconut,
their trunks arrayed in rows, their yields fit to be plucked.

All kind of trees—*kruc*, *kray*, *pangau*, *phniev*, plus *sragam*, *guy*, and *krasamn*—
grew thick and lush, laden with fruits that grant undying life.
Atop their limbs, timid squirrels hid from civets and apes,
as throngs of gibbons swung in joy from branch to branch.

Now at that time there was a demon named Kakana.
When conches blew for Vishvamitra to start his rite,
she used her powers to change into a crafty crow.
Swooping in to peck at the burnt oblations,
she made much noise, her piercing squawks filling the air.
Flowers, palm fronds, and flags fell down as she scampered away.

Rama's holy teacher, Vishvamitra, mighty hermit,
ablaze with powers, virtues, and sacred writ,
had made offerings to seal his potent vows.
He saw the vile demon disturb his ritual and said,
"I'll call for my godsons, the two princes,
Lord Rama and his brother Lakshmana.
This snag shall be resolved once I speak with
the sons of the great king Dasharatha.
I'll then perfect my powers on the Lord Buddha's path,
with incantations drawn from deep within the old scriptures,
to make Rama and Lakshmana endowed with strength,
filled with ascetic fire such that victory burns bright."

"O Rama!" he cried out, "O Lakshmana!
Come quick, for the auspicious hour now draws near!"
The royal seer led Prince Rama and his brother
to the ashram's platform for sacred rites
to craft a mighty bow infused with spells.
"Rama and Lakshmana, you whose power beats all!
Shoot off this arrow toward that demon Kakana.
Make known the massive might of Dasharatha's sons!"

Lord Rama nocked a lone arrow
and loosed it toward the demoness.
Kakana fell at once, collapsing lifelessly.
Yet Rama's magic bolt kept on, as she
fell down and down
      to the nagas' nether abyss, as she
fell down and down, through every realm,
      till the arrow pursued her to the death.

EPISODE II: RAMA WINS SITA'S HAND IN MARRIAGE

I tell of an auspicious day in May
when Janaka, dutiful king of Mithila,
summoned his men to turn the earth
to please the people with a rite of old.

He grasped the golden plow, his oxen proud as lions.
When he reached the Yamuna, a golden girl emerged
upon a jeweled lotus, her purity beyond compare.
The king was filled with joy for his divine issue.
The overlord of Mithila corralled his troops
to make a swift return to the palace.
He brought along the gorgeous nymph,
as if she had emerged from his own core.

Arriving home to keep his people's peace,
the king announced a rite to name this child.
She was to be Sita—"furrow" or "white"—
since her body shone brighter than the moon.
The king gazed out on his daughter's fine form,
her elegance unmatched in the heavens.
With his wisdom, the king intoned a spell,
enchanting a bow with this solemn vow:
"I shall give my precious Sita
    to the most mighty god."
With that, the ten directions shook.
    The heavens quaked,
        waking the hosts of gods.

All of the deities who lived in realms above
then hurried to descend from their abodes:
Indra, shining with brilliant rays,
    atop the elephant king;
Lord Fire, blazing with fervent force,
    atop his fierce rhinoceros;
Lord Wind, the sky filled with his gusts,
    atop his rake of colts;
Lord Rain, titan of all the sparkling seas,
    atop his serpent ride;
Candrakumara, awash with gold,
    atop his fine peacock;
Brahma, bound by his vows,
    atop the king of swans;
Nerirati, powered by pure penance,
    atop a fierce ogre;

Vaishravana, most mighty lord,
    atop his palace in the sky;
Shiva, beyond all the three realms,
    his body packed with violent force,
    atop his fearsome bull.

These gods and kings soon saw the magic bow
and one by one measured their proper strength.
But none could lift the bow, and so sat down in sad defeat.
The sage Vishvamitra thought of Vishnu, Rama himself—
by his colossal strength might that bow be lifted yet.
As Shiva and the other gods prepared to return home,
Vishvamitra brought Rama and Lakshmana to Mithila.
Rama went at once to tell the king he wished to try the bow.
Janaka replied, "Please demonstrate the mark of your prowess."

Lord Rama beamed, seeing that gods and kings had failed.
He, too, would test his might, with sages as witness.
Immensely strong, he showed his power, second to none—
    he lifted the great bow!
All gods and men within the spheres rejoiced,
offering unending praise of Rama's might.
He nocked a bolt out of sheer strength,
and drew the bow till it curved round,
    fringed by his shapely hands.
King Janaka, having witnessed Rama's rare feat,
was overjoyed and blessed the great victor.
He gave precious Sita, the perfect girl,
    in homage to the Lord.

Translated from Middle Khmer by Trent Walker

BRAH SUGANDH

Code of Old Sayings

Didactic poetry is the foundation of Middle Khmer literature. Prior to the twentieth century, the first texts young students learned to read were cpap *(pronounced today as "chbap"): short, aphoristic poems aimed at moral edification. This influential example of the genre, attributed to a sixteenth- or seventeenth-century monk styled Brah Sugandh, strings concrete images and pithy instructions into a garland of memorable verse.* TW

Here go the old sayings: you're blind to your own faults
yet make mountains out of the minor flaws of others.

In the forest of wild beasts, you call friends to join the hunt,
but once the honey's found, you sneak back home and eat it all alone.

You get some yet want more. You search but don't reflect.
You look at others, yet see only your own face.

You're served the finest food, but fail to chew it well.
You mistake all you see: Cham for Pnong, Chong for Kuoy,

grandpa for grandma, your son for your nephew,
two things when one will do, and sorrow for pure bliss.

Unshaven with a monk's robe, eyes closed before a mirror,
a horse becomes an ass, an elephant a mouse.

These are the words of old. Reflect on them to see clearly.
Don't mix up ponds and roads; you'll get mired in the mud.

The wise uphold these ageless words: follow precedent.
Don't choose a violent path—the ancients warn against it.

These words come from the past; you ought to ponder them.
Don't go around showing off, thinking you're all that.

Sleep at night, don't sleep in, lest scandal come your way.
Don't stuff yourself with food; save enough for others.

❧

Only lift what you can carry, or you'll throw out your back.
Employ others with kindness; avoid endless complaints.

Take your time, don't rush; think things through before you act.
That's the best way to avoid infamy and disgrace.

Don't mistake raw for cooked; civilization has its rules.
Don't think you're so smart you can disregard the past.

Prepare your words with care; don't take the easy path.
Be still, scan wide, peer deep; look out for blind spots.

❧

The ancient ones advised: don't try to raise tigers.
They spoke in metaphor: if you act, do it right—

grasp a snake's neck tight, lest it whip back to bite.
Drag your boat, but not the mud; leave waters unclouded.

Leaves don't move on their own; they're shaken by the wind.
Clear waters, if made cloudy, must have been churned by waves.

❧

Don't subjugate the weak; bring them into the fold.
If rich, don't trample the poor; learn to step carefully.

For the rich protect the poor, like cloth covers skin;
the wise shield the unschooled, like a junk a little sampan.

The high protect the low, per ancient law.
The full feed the hungry, the strong defend the meek.

Take care of one another, without any sense of obligation,
for all ages to come, since even hedges need their thorns.

❦

Don't seek your fill alone, forgetting that so many
mouths wail in hunger; feed them till they're full.

Don't be so vain as to cross a stream on a crocodile's back.
Don't chop down your own fence just to cook a pot of rice.

To set sail, you'll need lines, push poles, anchors, paddles,
thole pins, and mooring bollards—you'll need every last part.

To guard against a storm and fend off mighty waves,
take note of every detail—this is called true care.

❦

You ought to bear in mind these old words of advice;
what the sages said is worth some deep thought.

These are your instructions to keep as your sure code.
Hold to them fast and firm, secure them without fail.

Here ends my recital of these timeless words.
Keep them in mind, take them to heart, memorize them well.

Keep these sayings on your lips, oh good people, don't forget!
May their meanings long endure; this poem is now complete.

Translated from Middle Khmer by Trent Walker

BRAH RAJASAMBHAR

My Soul of Gold

According to Cambodian chronicles, the Khmer king Brah Rajasambhar (pronounced today as "Preah Reachsamphear," also known as Dhammaraja II) died in 1631. "My Soul of Gold," like most of his surviving poems, was written for Princess Pupphavati, his great love. When he abdicated the throne, his uncle took her as a consort. The lovers were long separated, and when they secretly reunited, the new king sent soldiers after them; they were shot dead in remote Kratie province.

Most of Brah Rajasambhar's works were thought to be lost. In 2016, while recataloging Khmer manuscripts in the British Library, I came across a magnificent set of bark-paper manuscripts; all were dated to the 1830s. Purchased in Southeast Asia by a British official, they sat in the British Museum for decades before being transferred to the British Library. One of these manuscripts contains a robust collection of Brah Rajasambhar's romantic poetry, including "My Soul of Gold." What follows here is not only the first translation of the poem, but also the first complete publication of this text. The four-syllable, seven-line Crow's Gait meter of the Khmer is largely retained, though without the original rhymes. TW

My soul of gold!
Midday has passed,
the sun descends
across the sky,
swept clear of clouds
by a fresh breeze,
calm ripples of wind.

My soul of gold!
When drafts would blow,
I'd hold you close,
my dear princess,
on your soft bed,
your face a mirror,
as bright as faith.

My soul of gold!
Afternoon fades.
Birds fly in flocks,
circling in rings.
Calls fill the air,
echos resound
across the sky.

My soul of gold!
I hear the birds,
their coos and caws
just like the sweet
and honeyed tones
of your words, love,
when we're alone.

My soul of gold!
Evening arrives.
The trees grow lush
in verdant rows,
their branches wide.
Their fine bouquets
pervade the air.

My soul of gold!
A soft breeze blows,
infused with flowers,
just like your scent:
exquisitely yours,
expanding outward,
extending over all.

My soul of gold!
The sun is setting
behind the woods.
How sad and strange:
birds circle above,
then drop to the trees
to preen and cry.

My soul of gold!
I listen as birds
erupt in song.
Some swoop and dive,
some weep and wail,

some pause and perch
near their partners.

My soul of gold!
The sun has set
and slipped away.
I wait for you,
for your beauty
brings to blossom
flowers in your hair.

My soul of gold!
I've searched across
the worldly plane,
yet none can match
your radiance,
a light that blazes
brighter than fire.

My soul of gold!
Now twilight falls,
the sun is gone,
but feelings remain.
Wind sweeps the skies
and all shines clear.
White clouds retreat.

My soul of gold!
Twilight has come,
the sun's rays hide.
How bright the moon:
its disc soars high.
Soft light scatters
and darkness glows.

My soul of gold!
The moon glimmers,
chief of the stars.
When all is hushed,
birdsong carries.
A rustling wind
douses the dusk.

My soul of gold!
Evening arrives.

The moon orbits
around the pole
of Mount Meru,
its slopes gleaming
with lunar light.

My soul of gold!
Moonbeams shimmer.
I see your face,
perfect and round,
bejeweled by gems
of twinkling stars
far from the earth.

My soul of gold!
Nighttime has come.
The moon grows full,
its orb enwrapped
by constellations,
as the lone lord
of starry skies.

My soul of gold!
Here in this world,
there's only you,
my golden friend.
Your skin exudes
the finest bliss
in realms of lust.

My soul of gold!
Midnight is near.
A tender breeze
caresses me,
a rush of cool
as floral scents
perfume the air.

My soul of gold!
At such moments
my love would swell.
We'd sing as one,
in search of bliss,
our bodies joined
to the same tune.

My soul of gold!
Peals of thunder
rock me in waves,
as if you were here,
our limbs entwined,
murmuring nothings
to draw out the time.

My soul of gold!
I long to share
your silk pillow.
Why have you gone
so far away?
Doesn't your love
move you like mine?

My soul of gold!
Midnight is here.
I hear the birds
call out and cry.
Their sounds echo
throughout the cold
and sunless dark.

My soul of gold!
At times like these
birds find their mates.
Why must I stay,
loveless, alone,
broken from you,
shattered inside?

My soul of gold!
Your body fills
my memories,
my mind scattered
by winds and wings,
their fresh refrains
a shower of tones.

My soul of gold!
Midnight gives way
to the wee hours.
Your face haunts me.
I long, my pith,

for inner bliss
in your embrace.

My soul of gold!
In the small hours,
I yearn for you.
Absent your care,
my heart stops dead.
Why break the ring
that rounds our love?

My soul of gold!
The late hours fade
and first light looms.
The birds fall quiet.
How many more turns
of night and day
must I still wait?

Translated from Middle Khmer by Trent Walker

CHANT

Victory in the Eight Directions

This is one of the oldest vernacular chants still performed in Cambodia. Part of a group of Pali and vernacular blessing texts that surfaced in the sixteenth or seventeenth century across mainland Southeast Asia, the chant is frequently sung today at weddings and other auspicious occasions. The martial tone suggests that its original purpose was different: to bless Cambodian troops preparing for battle.

Today it is recited by monks in a spare, haunting melody that gradually increases in intensity. The composition itself uses an extended form of the Narration meter, in which the usual six-four-six syllable arrangement is jettisoned in favor of longer lines. To capture the martial rhythm of the original, this English translation is rendered into blank verse. Although the first line of the text is in Pali and explicitly Buddhist, the otherwise Khmer text of "Victory in the Eight Directions" presents a rare reflection of Cambodia's diverse religious heritage, with Hindu deities such as Shiva and Vishnu receiving special emphasis. **TW**

Our Lord Buddha is the Fount of All Boons.
We bow down low to the holy Three Jewels.
We seek to win, we long for magic might,
we pray, O Shiva, to trounce, to best, to beat.

Bless us, O gods, O gods of the East!
Fly here in flocks, our heads beneath your feet.
Bless us, O gods, O gods of the Southeast!
Summon your troops, soldiers by the thousands.

Bless us, O gods, O gods of the South!
Gather here as one and guard our good fortune.
Bless us, O gods, O gods of the Southwest!
Grant us the force of your trials and your tests.

Bless us, O gods, O gods of the West!
Guard us and keep us and seal our success.
Bless us, O gods, O gods of the Northwest!
Rally, rank and file; cheer us with joy and mirth.

Bless us, O gods, O gods of the North!
Come, join as one; increase our wealth and ease.
Bless us, O gods, O gods of the Northeast!
Descend from on high to hand us happiness.

Bless us, O Vishnu, refuge of mankind!
Bless us, O Shiva, lord of all creatures!
Bless us, O Indra, from your high heaven!
Bless us, O Brahma, from formless realms!

Bless us, O gods, who gather all around:
gods of the earth, who raise our very feet,
gods of the sea, and gods of Himavant,
the jungle maze of fruit, brute, and beast.

Bless us, O gods, from every source and point:
you who dwell in soils, in homes, and in haunts,
perched high on tree crowns, crags, and crests.

Lead us, O gods, lead us onward to victory!
Give us the power to crush their whole army.
Vanquish our foes! Make them shrink in fright.
Ward off bane and bale; keep death out of sight.

Translated from Pali and Middle Khmer by Trent Walker

TRADITIONAL OATH

Goddesses of the Land

This legal document, simply titled pranidhan *(truthful vow), has been dated to 1693 CE. It is one of a few oath texts that survive from this period. Such oaths were recited in legal proceedings to invoke the gods, including Buddhist, Hindu, and local deities, to help determine the identities of guilty parties. The main portion of the text, composed as a poem in the Crow's Gait meter, offers an impressive litany of powerful local spirits who have been at the core of indigenous Cambodian religion for the past fifteen hundred years. Each goddess (literally, white lady, or* me sa*) is associated with a specific place in Cambodia. The poem uses* me sa *for all of the local deities mentioned, including famous male tutelary deities (anak ta) such as Klang Moeung, today known as Khleang Moeung. Together they construct a complete geography of the kingdom.* **TW**

May there be prosperity, good fortune, vast splendor, and extraordinary success in this year of 1614 of the Saka era, Year of the Rooster, third waning day of the twelfth month, a Monday, an auspicious hour! It was at this moment that His Majesty the King, his heart filled to the brim with mercy and grace, spoke to the assembly of judges in the royal courthouse, informing them of all they needed to know with regard to making oaths, including the texts for chanting solemn oaths, should the occasion arise.

Should a party to a dispute make an oath to prove their innocence, whether by drawing lots, swearing via a proxy, or forcing a confession, the judge should examine both parties carefully. Having created a secure record of their testimony, the judge should never fail to make them swear upon this very testimony, as follows:

Hear, O Deities! O Shiva, O Vishnu! O Brahma, Creator!
To bind this oath, we call you down to join us here.
Make haste, my lords, come quickly! Join as our witnesses.
We bow in joy to the dust that clings to your feet.

We bow to Maitreya, glorious Buddha of the future,
to the Dharma and the Sangha, and to the Five Lords.
We bow to Indra and to Yama, to all the Brahma host,
to the Sun, the Moon, the stars, and Lord Vishvakarman.

We bow to Vaishravana, replete with power and glory,
to the Earth herself, and to gods both great and small.
O Rain, O Wind, O Sacred Flame, all gods above,
be our witness, both day and night, at dusk and dawn.

O gods of trees, of caves, of Himalayan peaks,
of streams, clefts, craters, thickets, and vast fields!
Hear us, O Lord of Death; hear us, O God of Time!
Come here at once; bear witness to their claims in full.

Rishis of pure virtue, *gandharvas* of finest scent,
vidyadharas of magic might, and *kinnaras*
who frolic with the *kinnaris,* travel with speed
from all quarters—help be our court's sincere witness.

Hear us, O gods! Come here, O guardian deities,
native spirits both great and small, known and unknown.
Goddess of Klang Moeung, Center of the Realm, highest of all!
Come here now with your retinue; serve as our chief.

Goddess of Banteay Pech, bright your beauty, lofty your rank!
Come and listen to this solemn oath; be our witness.
Goddesses of Phnom Bat, Preah Theat, and Phnom Preah
    Reachatroap!
Goddess of the Tavatimsa Stupa at victorious Udong!

Goddesses of Sla Khav, Koh Chen, Krang Ponlei, Srah Kaev,
    Phsar Daek!
Fearsome Goddess of Ponhea Leu, mighty Goddess of Peak Proat!
Goddesses of Kampong Khong, Lvaek, Anlung Koh Ream, Thnal
    Cham,
Ach K'aek, Kampong Ko Chraek, and lovely Prambei Chhaom!
Goddesses of Chveang Peang Sangkae, Chik Preah Srae, Prei Chrap,
Chhuk Chral, Sandan Thma Sa, and Bapreng—come one and all!
Spirits of Phoey Pao Tralak! Come here with your whole group.
Most excellent spirit of Phnom Baset! Bring your entourage here.

Goddess of Kampong Roteh, bearer of much merit and power!
Goddesses of Praek, Kong Meas, and Kampong Kdar, joy of the gods!
Among the goddesses of all districts, Goddess of Santuk, you stand tall!
Goddess of Kampong Svay and Goddess of Peam Traen—we invite you here.

O guardians who abide everywhere, in Sdi Bet Meas, hidden in sand and rice,
in *teal* groves, in the ponds and plains of Saen Snay, and in distant temples!
Goddess of Phnom Banan, Goddesses of Pursat and Battambang,
Goddess of Babor, Goddess of Khlung, Goddesses of Krang and Kragar!

Goddesses of Peal Nhaek and Peam Lok in Traok, mighty Goddess of Banhas!
Goddess of Trates, curt Goddess of Phnom Mlu—come here to listen.
Goddess of Indapattha, Queen of Angkor Wat! Goddess of the Bakan!
Brave Queen of Wat Athvear! Goddess of Bathleip, Goddess of Bakheng!

Goddess of Treang, proud Goddess of Bapeal, prominent Goddess of Barach,
Fearsome Goddess of Choeung Tan Thom! Come here; show off your might.
Goddesses of Kampot and Kampong Som, whose names prove your power!
Goddess of Koh Ream, goddesses of deltas and currents, come here quickly!

Goddesses of Banteay Meas, Prei Krabas, Nokorathibadei,
Kampong Putrea, Prei Puoch, Bati, and Samrong Tong!
Goddess of Phnom Choap, Goddess of Rolea P'ier, join as one!
Mighty goddesses and guardians great and small, come join us!

We invite you and your retinues, Goddesses of Rumduol and Svay Toap.
Come from the north, O bold Goddess Daeng, come all forest spirits!
Please come, O Goddess of Ba Phnom and other great guardians.
Come, O Goddesses of Tuol Chneang, Prei Khduoch, and Prei Khla!

Goddess of Prei Veng and Goddess of Srei Santhor, endowed with might!
Goddess of Tboung Khmum, from north of Khal and down to Slaeng!
From the Goddess of Peam Reang all the way to the Goddesses of Prang
and Moat Khnung, travel here on roads both smooth and clear.

Goddess of Kok Seh! We invite you here, along with you of Choeung Prei,
Ba Chey, Steung Traeng, Preah Beung, Sambok, and Sambour.
Goddesses of rivers and reservoirs, of vast lakes, ponds, and streams,
like those of Sopoar Kalei—come and hear this testimony.

Once the two parties have argued frankly against one another,
their testimonies must each be examined for boasts and truths.
Hence we now invite you to preside over this unfinished case—
serve as our witnesses. May the Earth herself be our alibi.

Should either party lie, intentionally breaking the oath,
may the deities of all places destroy them—bring them to ruin!
Part them from their children, wives, parents, and relatives.
Scatter their wealth. Smite them, O Lords, crush them.
In their next life, let them burn away their sins in the hells,
for such faults lead to birth in Avici, the lowest realm.

O deities! As for those who are honest and kind,
may all you gods and goddesses postpone their deaths.
Supply them with abundant wealth, with goods and gems.
Lengthen their lives and swiftly grant them utmost bliss.

O deities! We, the assembly of judges in this court,
beseech you now—kindly serve as our chief witnesses.
Hear us, O gods! May these prayers be swiftly answered.
O guardians! May this, our solemn oath, be soon resolved.

Translated from Middle Khmer by Trent Walker

FOLK SONGS

A Selection of Wedding Songs

Cambodian weddings have long been multi-day affairs, replete with dozens of major and minor rituals. Each of these rituals typically features a singer accompanied by a handful of traditional instruments, including woodwinds, strings, and percussion. The contemporary wedding music repertoire includes hundreds of songs. Their lyrics no doubt have changed across the generations, but some pieces are at least several hundred years old. In selecting these, I have favored the oldest versions available, which often differ from contemporary versions of the same title.

Not all of these songs were composed for weddings, however; some are folk songs in a broader sense, while others may still be heard in spirit possession rituals and other non-nuptial rites. The selection featured here represents the variety of themes and images in Khmer wedding music. "Ancestral Offerings" and "Rowing the Boat" reflect how Cambodian weddings are bookended by inviting ancestral spirits to partake of offerings and bless the new couple. The remaining songs capture the symbolic play and restrained eroticism of much of the genre. **TW**

ANCESTRAL OFFERINGS

Knees bent, hands in prayer,
I sing a melody
of offerings—
listen, O ancestors!

I call you from the mountains,
foothills, lowlands, and plains—
come now and partake
of these gifts:

cooked rice, both white and brown,
arrayed in porcelain bowls,
rice wine, hot tea, betel,
areca, cigarettes,

well-fermented fish paste,
dishes grilled and stewed,
all arranged on fine trays
for your pleasure.

Once you've had your fill,
please return at your leisure
and grant us blessings
for our health and happiness.

IN BLOOM

Fair bride, body in bloom! Why are you tiptoeing
out from your bed chamber? In your left hand: cigarettes;
in your right: betel nut. Where do you tiptoe,
        bearing such gifts for me?

I ask for some betel, you claim to have none.
I take your hand, see what you're hiding.
"Betel and areca— these I can give you.
As for my own body, that I must withhold."

Blooming mangrove blossom! I hold you in my arms,
in our bronze palace, with walls of lime and sand,
stones packed edge to edge. Here in this gleaming tower,
        I shall take you as mine.

WINDSWEPT POND

Man:
Down by the windswept pond,
immersed in waters clear,
I bathe, I bathe with you,
scrubbing your fair skin clean.

Woman:
Darling, you've scrubbed my front,
but you've ignored my back.
Please rub, please scrub my skin,
cleansing your bride's body.

Together:
Down by the windswept pond,
bathing with a blessed bowl,

may we, may we win joy,
freed from all obstacles.

Down by the windswept pond,
bathing with a gold bowl,
may peace, may peace and bliss
come to us, bride and groom.

ROWING THE BOAT

Oh the winds to ferry,	my darling,
I pine for the winds to ferry!	
Oh the winds to ferry,	my precious,
I pine for the winds to ferry!	
I chop bamboo for a raft,	my darling,
to ferry you back home,	oh dear, my dear, my darling,
to ferry you back home.	
I gaze out at the mast,	my darling,
and lo, the billowing sails!	
I gaze out at the mast,	my precious,
and lo, the billowing sails!	
They ferry you back home,	my precious,
for health, for joy, for ease,	oh dear, my dear, my precious,
for health, for joy, for ease.	
Oh how the rolling waves,	my darling,
how they slosh and spray.	
Oh how the rolling waves,	my precious,
how they slosh and spray.	
They carry all the offerings,	my precious,
with every kind of fruit,	oh dear, my dear, my darling,
with every kind of fruit.	
Pig heads, chickens, ducks,	my darling,
and trays of rice and soup.	
Pig heads, chickens, ducks,	my precious,
and trays of rice and soup,	
all for your journey home,	my darling,
to bring us happiness,	oh dear, my dear, my darling,
to bring us happiness.	

Translated from Khmer by Trent Walker

FOLK SONG

The Point of the Cape

This bawdy wedding song was transcribed by Albert Tricon (music) and Charles Bellan (words) for their 1921 collection of traditional Khmer music. Forgotten for nearly ninety years, it was revived in 2009 through a collaborative effort led by Cambodian musicians and musicologists. **TW**

> I pass the point of the cape
> and I have no regrets, *oeng oey*, no regrets.
> But if I miss the points of your breasts,
> the loss will strangle me, *oeng oey*, strangle me.
>
> Astounding how the frangipani
> and rose-apple announce themselves!
> Rough cocklebur grows all around.
> Hacking through this tangled jungle,
> I see a tiny island, rising low, *oeng oey*,
> rising low, *oeng oey*, out of the water.
>
> The naga grows angry, rising up strong.
> Leaving his eggs behind, he storms
> the little island with its deep cavern.
> He struggles to squeeze inside,
> until his body is swallowed, *oeng oey*,
> swallowed, *oeng oey*, and disappears.
>
> He explores the cave a good long while,
> emerging from the isle from time to time.
> The naga can't linger, or he'll be destroyed.
> So he pulls himself out and returns to brood,
> *oeng oey*, to brood, *oeng oey*, his eggs.

Translated from Khmer by Trent Walker

BUDDHIST SONG TRADITION

from *Until Nirvana's Time*

Cambodian Buddhist poems are little known outside of Khmer-speaking communities in Southeast Asia and in the global diaspora. However, for the past seven hundred years, most Cambodians have practiced Theravada Buddhism, and their Khmer-language poetry reflects a deep intimacy with the Dharma. The three poems selected here from Until Nirvana's Time: Buddhist Songs from Cambodia *(Shambhala Publications, 2022) were composed by anonymous authors in the eighteenth and nineteenth centuries.*

At one time, the majesty of the Khmer Empire held sway over much of what is now Laos, Thailand, and southern Vietnam. The terror unleashed by the Khmer Rouge was in some ways the culmination of the many traumas the Khmer people have faced in recent times: brutal warfare; colonial subjugation; migration and resettlement; poverty, violence, and erasure. Lost in this erasure have been the nation's many contributions to Buddhism, literature, and the arts. Khmer-language poems on Buddhist themes are among Cambodia's most precious gifts to the world.

The poems translated here are "Dharma songs" (dharm pad, pronounced "thoa bot"), verse texts meant to be recited with complex melodies known as smot *in dusk-to-dawn rituals of mourning, consecration, and remembrance. Khmer poetry is traditionally chanted aloud in dozens of different melodies, each of which has spawned several variations. Some melodies are fast paced and use only a few musical pitches. Others are slow, highly ornamented, and require a wide vocal range to reach their many notes. A single stanza can take up to three minutes to recite, a whole poem several hours. Each word of the Khmer is designed to linger in the air, carried by breath and music. As readers and listeners, we must be patient, letting the meaning gradually reveal itself to us.* **TW**

THE THIRTY-THREE CONSONANTS

The virtues in the consonants are thirty-three in all—
I've learned them as the letters that gave birth to my being.
The Pali phrase *in the body* means "within our very selves."
And hence inside my body, I find these thirty-three:

KA gives birth to the hairs on the head;
KHA to those covering the body.
Our heads sport some nine million,
the rest of the body ten times more.

GA is the nails, twenty in all;
GHA gives rise to the teeth.
Our Teacher, Lord Buddha,
had forty teeth in total.

People these days aren't so complete,
with thirty-two or maybe thirty-three.
Some poor folks have only twenty teeth,
and hence there's no fixed number.

ṄA is the skin, wrapped around
our bodies like a jujube fruit.
Conjure this image, clear as day,
and hold it within your mind.

CA is the flesh, thirty muscle groups;
CHA the sinews, pulled to and fro.
JA is the bones, three hundred in all;
JHA the marrow; ÑA the kidneys; ṬA the heart.

ṬHA gives birth to the liver.
In the bodies of the ignorant,
those whose wisdom is blocked,
this organ is bulbous as a pika fruit.

But the livers of the wise,
those endowed with courage,
are sharp as lemongrass,
barbed like spiked betel.

ḌA is the diaphragm,
holding in digested food.
ḌHA, the stomach's bag, is foul;
contemplate its transience.

ṆA is the lungs, pressed to the chest;
TA the intestines; THA the mesentery—
study them, remember them well
to perfect your magical power.

Buddhist . Until

DA is undigested food,
the daily source of life.
DHA is digested mush:
odious, rank, and vile.

NA becomes the gallbladder.
PA gives rise to phlegm;
PHA to pus; BA to blood;
BHA to sweat, flooding our pores.

MA is fat, whorled in endless little rings;
YA our tears, seeping from our eyes.
RA is grease, our flesh soaked through;
LA becomes saliva, knower of tastes.

VA is mucus, oozing daily,
and constantly changing;
SA is the fluid of passion,
obscuring right and wrong.

HA is urine, a stinky dribble,
staining the earth below;
ḶA is known as the skull
and A the brain within.

"A" marks a glottal stop consonant in Khmer.

Thus the letters are expounded; study and see them in your mind.
Divide them as appropriate; memorize them beyond doubt.
Twenty-one consonants are gifts of my father:
KA to DHA is his share, along with lonely ḶA.

My mother gave me twelve, from NA to HA, plus A.
Wise monks know these thirty-three and honor their true legacies.
What great rewards redound to the pious men and women
who learn and prize these words! For ancient scriptures say:

One who daily chants these letters
shall be reborn for hundreds of lives
as a blissful, righteous monarch,
blessed with beauty and speech divine.

THIS LIFE IS SHORT

This life is short: you are born
with bodily form that can't last.
You'll never be free or get past
the shadow cast by distress.

Nothing is yours: all is void,
all is devoid of essence.
No fame, no rank, no parents,
no one precious, nobody,

not even those born before,
not even your family.
Your own body is empty.
Listen to me: make this known.

Discarded deep in the forest,
with none to trust as your own,
save wild beasts who grunt and groan,
you'll be alone, through and through.

Your wealth, the worst poverty:
you can't take anything with you.
You'll lie there, nothing to do,
your body truly worthless.

All merit gone in your wake,
your kin will take your carcass
to woodlands cloaked in darkness.
They'll leave, tearless; there you'll stay.

The dead must be abandoned,
their bones and flesh thrown away.
Your body's bound to decay;
your name, they say, soon unsaid.

Reflect on this and be stirred.
Don't be deterred but instead
take refuge in what's well said.
Hear this and tread the right course.

Give gifts, keep rules, train your heart:
three ways to start from the source.
To wipe your brow of remorse,
don't do what's coarse. Thus I preach:

Buddhist . Until

Build your merit. Guard your mind.
Always be kind. Strive to reach
all those in need. Make your speech
match those who teach the true path.

HYMN TO THE BUDDHA'S FEET

To his two feet I bow in praise. I humbly bend
down to the earth beneath his feet, shining as bright
    as radiant jewels.

Here's my own head, instead of flowers, here's ten fingers
for gold candles, here's my two eyes to take the place
    of glowing lamps.

My words express and pay homage to the Marked Lord
in place of whiffs of fine incense, my mind in place
    of fragrant tastes,

my whole body presented as a golden jar,
bedecked with gems: all these offerings I humbly give
    to his two feet.

The Marked Lord's soles have wheels adorned with a thousand spokes
and wrought axles; auspicious symbols; fine parasols
    from all quarters;

golden bullhooks; towered temples, spires soaring high,
replete with jewels; gem-studded thrones; white umbrellas
    and royal swords;

fans of palm leaf and peacock feathers; whisks made of gold;
diamond-tipped pikes; girls clutching candleholders;
    exquisite crowns;

ribbons fringed with mottled gemstones; wish-granting stones;
bowls of radiant gold and silver; bowls forged from jewels;
    lotus flowers;

water lilies; gorgeous gold trays; silver pitchers;
jugs made of jewels; the lush woods of the Himavant;
    the world's sheer edge;

Mount Sumeru and its foothills, the Seven Bands;
the Seven Seas, the Sidantara, successive rings
     of oceans deep;

the Sun; the Moon, rising lustrous, sky-chief among
the host of stars, of radiant rays; four continents;
     two thousand isles;

conch shells; the king who conquers all, his ministers
in tow with flags and parasols; Indra; Brahma;
     Shiva; Vishnu;

the mountains and Seven Rivers; delightful ponds
in seven rows; the salty sea, its limits vast
     and most profound;

fish of silver and fish of gold; golden turtles,
sharks, and serpents in deep waters; junks and frigates,
     gold and silver;

nagas, garudas, lions, tigers; Uposatha,
the elephant king; Balahaka, king of horses;
     the snowy peak

called Mount Kailash; gold swans and geese; the elephant king
Eravana; lovely starlings; kinnara, parrots,
     and Mekhala;

karavika birds; peahens; peacocks with tails displayed;
the violent king of the vultures; waterfowl with
     blazing red hues;

lions who stand and those who walk; white bulls and cows,
with suckling calves; all the pleasant heavens above,
     six layers tall;

pure Brahma realms, sixteen in all, with gold mansions—
all these appear on the Lord's feet, his marks totaling
     one hundred and eight.

The Three-World's Lord strode on his feet to cross the earth,
saving beings in all kingdoms, with lotuses
     sprouting up

from the earth to meet the Sage's soles at every step,
with no footprints left in his wake; only when he was seated
    did the blooms cease.

From time to time, flowers might fail to greet his feet,
as when he walked on paths where winds cleared away
    all motes of dust

beneath his heels, carrying them up and far away
then blowing them back to earth as crystalline sands
    that soon dissolved.

No matter where the Lord would walk no prints remained,
lest anyone should tread upon his holy feet
    and incur sin.

❧

Our mighty Lord, nirvana bound, had goodwill for
all deities, gandharvas, gods, titans, nagas,
    humans, and beasts.

And so to save them he made five shrines for his footprints:
one pair on the summit of Mount Suvannamali,
    a pure abode;

one pair on the summit of Mount Suvannapabbata;
one pair on the isle of Lanka, on the fine Mount
    Sumanakuta;

one pair on the mountain known as Saccabandha,
where people may gather all kinds of offerings
    to worship them;

one pair on the Nammada's banks, where the Lord stepped
into the mud so that the fish might bow down low
    in reverence.

Before he went to nirvana, the Ten-Powered Lord
saved beings through these five footprints, made to last for
    five thousand years.

Alas, we are born too late to meet the Lord;
only his true Teachings remain. We can't even
    go near those shrines.

We thus bow down from far away, chanting in praise
to all five pairs. May there be joy, fortune, power,
    and victory.

May greed be beat, so too hatred, folly, danger,
suffering, sorrow, illness, and fear. May there be joy
    till nirvana!

❧

Whoever aims to know the marks on the Lord's feet,
who learns them well, free from all flaws, who always strives
    to chant them aloud,

they're like someone who's born in time for the Buddha,
leaving behind the four base realms, those filled with woe
    and vile karma;

for one hundred thousand eons, they'll know no pain,
never falling into the hells, tasting the joy
    of their merit;

their whole body will be complete, without a fault,
besting all men, flawless and fit, most lovely and
    most loved by all;

they'll know merit, sin, and virtue; work and duty;
the meaning of texts; reputation, determination,
    and firm ethics,

they'll be born in a lofty line of warrior caste;
rulers with full sovereignty, lords of all lands,
    mighty and strong;

their enemies from all quarters shall crouch down low
out of sheer fright, cowering in humble submission
    to such majesty;

and they'll be wise, skilled in all arts, their doubts removed
till nirvana—such boons arise from chanting the praise
    of the Lord's feet.

Translated from Khmer by Trent Walker

ANONYMOUS

Thunder and the Crabs

This is one of the most common didactic tales recorded in Cambodian manuscripts. Frequently paired with other moralistic poems, this amusing story sets up an extended metaphor between a teacher, Thunder, and his students, the crabs. As the rainy season comes to an end in late October, Thunder too retreats, and rural Cambodians may more easily gather the small freshwater crabs who live in the flooded rice paddies. As he departs, Thunder warns the crabs to watch out for the dangers posed by hungry humans. One particularly clever crab offers a response to the teacher's warnings. The main dialogue is composed in the Crow's Gait meter. The final portion of the poem offers a Buddhist reflection written in the Brahma's Song meter. **TW**

Thunder rolled at dawn out of pity for the crabs,
his offspring on earth, born of the same clouds.
Now, at monsoon's end, he must soon retreat
and leave them behind. Moved by love,
Thunder admonished his crustacean kin:

"Hey there, my little crabs! Listen up, you simple beasts.
Don't forget: it's time to burrow. Dig your holes deep.
Since my time has come, I've called you here today
to warn you of the dangers bound to come your way.

Think hard, dear crabs! Find spots to dig your secret dens.
Search for nooks and crannies down by the water's edge.
Use your claws; don't delay! If you wait until I'm gone,
the mud will dry, too hard for you to pierce.

For I have heard that men have set their sights on you.
They'll catch you for your meat, for your shells are filled
with creamy fat and flesh, perfect when roasted just right.
I've heard them say you're best when ground with tamarind,
pea shoots, and sprigs of *ma'om*, plucked straight from the field.
Once all is mashed together, I've seen them start to drool!

Connoisseurs know that crabs are best right after the rain.
They rise before dawn to hunt you down and dig you up.
With baskets full of crabs, they avenge all the stalks of rice
you snipped and stole away. Watch out, dear crabs, take heed!
Warn your kin. Don't be too bold; look out for your own lives.

How brazen can you be? Boring through berms
and draining paddies so that their rice can't grow?
They'll dig you out to make themselves a greasy snack.
They'll throw you on the grill; your fat will melt away
over the blazing coals. Once you're nice and cooked,
they'll grab and gulp you down with day-old rice:
crunch-crunch, *kriep-kruop!* They'll gorge on your flesh,
joking, 'Mmm, so good, better than a bonk on the head!'
If they gobble you up before the rice runs out,
they'll soon catch some more of your friends to toss on the fire.

Dear crabs, my little ones! Go find a solid, rock-lined pond.
Slip down into the cracks and take refuge there, hidden away,
wedged in so well and deep you're impossible to snatch.
Watch out for those humans! They'll stoop low to hunt for you.
Quick! Hole up underground, beyond the reach of hands.
Burrow into the earth, where they can't steal you away.
Call me kind, call me mild, but I'm here to set you straight:
Men are perverse. They'll hunt you down for a tasty meal."

Thus Thunder admonished his young kin, the crabs.
Hearing Thunder's words, a clever crab replied,
"Have mercy on us, great Thunder, our true father.
You gave us life and made the places where we dwell.
You have counseled us so well, profound in all senses.
Our debt to you is vast; how can we repay it?
We're bound to heed your words for years to come.
But please, O Master, let me first tell you a tale.

One bright morning, not long ago, I left my hole
in hopes of finally finding the biggest puddle of all.
But then I saw some men coming out of the brush.
They spotted me too and tried to stomp me flat,
but thanks to these swift legs, I slipped their grasp.
I hid beneath a stump, beyond their prying eyes.
Hungry but thwarted, the group cursed me out:
'Damn you, big fat crab, up yours! So much for lunch!
You botched our big chance. Go to hell, decapod!'

Though I escaped, they kept looking elsewhere,
stuffing all the crabs they could fit into their baskets.
Inside I saw bowed heads of crabs, frogs, and toads,
encaged by well-laced reeds. Would I be next?
The Buddhist truth is clear: nothing lasts for long!
I'm rocked by fear, for humans are so strong.
I'm fed up with their pokes and prodding hands.
I'm scared to death they'll smash my shell to pieces
and beat me to a pulp; why must I end up as a snack?
Even if I stay right here and carve myself a cave,
safe from human hands, the problem is the frogs,
our noisy next-of-kin. Even the kindest of their kind
still have those big mouths! At the first drop of rain,
they croak in chorus, leaping in joy, helter-skelter.
They fear nothing—what's their secret power?

But frogs never learn. They're dried and grilled,
served as snacks, or brought to market,
where skilled human butchers lop off head and limb
to make dead amphibians ready for one last steam.
With ginger, pepper, garlic, fish paste, lemongrass,
and a bed of cabbage, frogs become a tasty treat.
One bite and grown men cry, 'Mmm hmm, so good!'
They feast on fatty frogs, chatting and cracking jokes.
This tiny snack can't fill them up, so soon they start
to scheme in search of something more.

O Thunder, my Master, my claws are large and fierce.
Men can't stop me! I'll pinch their digits with such force
their bloody gaping wounds will take them out for good.
My mind is racked by fantasies of avenging wicked men.
How hot the hate that boils within, how cruel my rage!
I see them tiptoe in the fields, always on the prowl.
They call out for their friends: 'Hey man, get over here!
Bring some baskets too. Let's catch some crunchy crabs!'
Hearing their voices, I shudder and shake with fright.
I scurry down my hole so that they can't snatch me away.
For if they could, they'd smash my shell and roast my flesh.
How lucky I am to slip their grasp and live another day!"

Most folks these days don't care for virtue or charity.
In worlds to come they'll soon be reduced to nothing.
With virtue and charity, we plant wholesome seeds
that can transform into sweet fruits in future lives.
I set this tale in verse based on what old sages said;
don't let my heirs assume that I penned it all myself!

Translated from Khmer by Trent Walker

MAI

Code for Girls

There are several texts in the Khmer corpus known as "Code for Girls." This version, probably written in the late eighteenth century, remains the most famous. Mai was a male aristocrat, a former monk with the feudal title "min," who also composed "Code for Boys," which focuses on the virtues of domestic and agricultural labor and the dangers of gambling, wine, and womanizing. "Code for Girls," by contrast, focuses almost exclusively on obedience to one's husband and avoiding marital conflict at all costs. Many Cambodians have sharply criticized its misogynistic tone in recent decades. The poem's portrayal of cruel, incompetent husbands can also be read as a veiled attack on men.

The literary merit of this text is without question. It is one of few surviving extended poems in the Serpent's Lilt (bhujang lila) *meter: three lines of six, four, and four syllables, respectively. The English translation is rendered primarily in fourteen-syllable lines, mirroring the metrical structure and iambic patterns, though not the interlocking rhyme scheme, of the original. A few parts of the text suggest a faulty transmission; my translation smooths over these difficulties.*

Like other moral codes (cpap), *"Code for Girls" was written for memorization by young students learning to read and write. The narrative, concerning the naga Vimala's advice for her daughter Irandati before marrying the wicked ogre Pannaka, is drawn from the canonical* Vidhurapandita-jataka, *one of the most celebrated past-life narratives of the Buddha in Southeast Asia. Parts of the text, including the description of the types of wives, are likewise drawn from Buddhist scriptures. The bulk of Vimala's instructions, however, appear to be Mai's invention and reflect elite male ideals of marriage and gender relations in eighteenth-century Cambodia.* TW

Here goes the Code for Girls, arrayed in lines of Serpent's Lilt:
I tell the long-gone tale of the naga Princess Irandati.
On the evening before she was to marry Pannaka,
a powerful ogre who sought to slay the Buddha-to-be,
Queen Vimala, the bride's own mother, advised her thus:

Soon you must follow your groom, leaving our home, the naga realm,
for that of men and ogres. Listen and learn to serve your husband.
Do your duties daily—don't give him cause for anger.
He's now the lord of your home, lord of your life; don't dare mock him.

O my darling daughter! It's hard to follow the Code for Girls.
It's hard for the shy to use sweet words to please their kin.
It's hard for the simple to invite their in-laws to chew betel.
Whether you're rich or poor, use kind words to win their love.
Don't be rude or stingy; devote yourself to your new family,
for their own wealth, health, fame, and joy all depend on you.

When you're about to talk, guard your good name; don't speak in vain.
Don't babble like a child. If you see a boy, don't skirt too close.
Don't laugh without thinking, or crazy men will get all stirred up.
Such behavior debases you: ill-bred, uncouth, and bad-mannered.
Fickle and immodest, your words lack strength; you know no shame.
If you eye every guy you see, teasing, taunting, and laughing at them,
your good name will be in ruin, and you'll fear no fault of your own.
At work, don't sit in ways that hardly suit a proper woman.
Don't fail to guard your man's heart or let others make fun of him.
Girls like this are unbecoming, lacking both manners and etiquette.

When weaving, sewing, or pressing clothes, finish what you start.
Don't save tasks for later—only fools say, "I'll get back to it."
When weaving flowered silk, set up the loom before you begin.
Keep at it; guard your name. Don't wander off to chat with friends.
Take care, my dear, my soul. You should work hard while you're still young.
Once wed, what can you do? Your kids will cry; you'll have no time.
You'll be trapped by one child after another whining for food.
You'll fuss and fret to find sweets and snacks to shut them up.
When weaving patterned skirts, raise the warp high, beyond their reach,
so that they won't tangle the strands or jumble your work.

O my darling daughter, pay attention and be mindful.
Master the Code for Girls, respect your man, lord of the home.
Do your duties with care in order to guard the Three Hearths.
Light these fires, stoke them daily, and constantly blow their flames to life.
But don't let them spread or get too hot, for you'll get burned.
Keep outside fires without, and inside hearths always glowing.
Take care so that inner fires don't spark a blaze beyond the home,
inciting flames so fierce they sear your kids—what sin, what shame!

Be vigilant, my girl. Keep the Three Hearths always burning.
These three will guard your name and lift your life to lofty ranks.
They'll bring you great renown, abundant wealth, and all things fine.
The first two Hearths are your mother and your father.
Follow the proper path of deference to your guardians.
Strive hard to care for them; give them the food you cherish most,
rather than hoarding it all for yourself—serve them daily.
Endure all their advice, run their errands, or they'll feel hurt.

The third Hearth is your husband, lord of the home, to love for good.
Respect him without fail—don't even think of offending him.
Revere him, for you're just a girl; don't claim you're his equal.
Should your tiffs and tussles end in harsh words, step back and think.
If he should speak cruelly to you, don't dare tell his mother.
Anger will grow and spread if they start whispering about you.
No peace: things fall apart as arguments rage back and forth.
No calm: coarse words ignite, fierce conflicts burn, no end in sight.
Arguments explode, silence is gone, and words don't cease.
Such fights split friends apart, and joyful times won't last for long.

These are the Three Hearths—I call on you to guard them well.
No matter what cruel or merciless crimes your man commits,
bury them in your heart; don't dare mock him behind his back.
Don't swear or spar; if he's poor, weak, or dull, don't disdain him.
If he's stupid or slow, give him guidance mixed with sweet words.
Even if he spews a stream of vile curses in his anger,
his rage inflamed, unquenched, unrelenting, his heart still piqued,
if he keeps muttering insults and jibes, his heart still pained—
try hard to bear it, dear, until it ends and wrath subsides.

Don't be too proud or firm, and don't talk back to your husband.
Don't speak out of anger; as a woman, don't be coarse.
Don't protest with cruel threats or sarcasm to set off rage.
Don't be too stubborn, dear; don't stare at him or incite anger.
Don't mock him with snide words that lead you both to scrap and snap.
Don't call him a dog or cat, and never hint in ways that hurt.
Don't toss or throw your things or smash your stuff against the floor.
Don't be hard to shut up, or ever scheme to defeat him
to make yourself feel good—such sly women sully their names.
O my daughter dearest! Their faults are grave; don't be like them.

Should your husband curse you, go back to your own room and think;
when you come out again, show him kindness; pardon his crime.
Should he admonish you, embrace his speech with your whole heart.
Never dismiss his words lest you do wrong, as you've been warned.
For if you don't listen to your man's words, conflict ensues,
joy ceases, your name rots, and your quarrels will never end.
This is not becoming, to be so rude, a tramp, a whore,
who seeks to best her spouse and boasts to others.
Such a girl, unless told, won't even get out of his way.
If he gives an order, don't be lazy and just sit there.
No matter how near or far, get up and go; don't make him swear.
Don't dawdle while you're out; busy or not, hurry back home.

O my daughter, my soul! To be a girl is very hard.
Your body may look great, but who cares, if you shirk your chores?
You'll earn no one's respect; instead you'll face the Nine Misfortunes.
A real beauty knows her wifely duties and so is praised.
One can be fine and fair, incomparable, but forget the rules.
What use is witless beauty? Those who are dark may do good work;
these well-mannered women know the proper way to act.
They are the ones the ancients call real beauties, full of virtue.

O my darling dearest, now I shall name the Nine Misfortunes.
One: a wife plucking lice from her man's head, without bowing first,
is like a crane alighting on a roof, portending ill.
Two: stepping over his legs in haste to leave is lewd and vile,
like a corpse-dove diving straight down at you, spawning sickness.
Three: coming or going through a door without closing it,
thoughtless or by mistake, such that others may see inside,
is like lighting a lantern to guide thieves in to steal your wealth.
Four: laughing so loud people three houses away can hear,
like a kingfisher cackling in the village—how ominous!
Five: lying down to sleep with your back turned to your husband,
like a vicious snake inside the house—how odious!
Such evil portends the swift coming of all things foul.
Six: letting down your locks of long hair while dawdling idly
by village gates or wells, like a wild cat showing its claws—
how infelicitous, to loiter there with unbound hair!
Seven: treading heavily on your skirt hem like an earthquake,
ripping and tearing the cloth; stomping as loud as thunder booms,
rushing about in haste, making floorboards roar like crashing waves,
rocking homes three doors down—worse than crooks hauling your
   goods away.

Eight: seeing riches along your path, but passing them by.
Your wealth won't last for long if you don't keep your house in order;
money will drain away—discord and strife, certain ruin!
Nine: slyly snatching food and then secretly scarfing it down.

My dear child, such are the Nine Misfortunes. Bear these in mind
so that you might steer clear of them and learn of the Seven Wives
that our Teacher, the Buddha, described in sermons of Pali verse.
I'll start with the Four Good Wives, each free from fault and blame:
the Mother-Wife, the Sibling-Wife, the Friend-Wife, and the Servant-Wife.

As for the Mother-Wife, she's as good as his own mother.
She acts in these three ways. One: she aims for her man's best,
lifting up his good name, never letting him lose prestige.
Two: should he need new clothes, she gives him hers and wears the old.
She's skilled in preparing and serving him the finest food.
Three: should her man fall ill, she frets, she cares, she brings a cure,
finding doctors, healers, and astrologers to tend to him.

As for the Sibling-Wife, she's just as good as one's brother.
Close as a sibling in heart and flesh, she acts in these two ways.
First: she guards everything well; all his earnings are carefully kept.
Second: should anyone smear her man's good name or spread slander,
she refutes the rumors and guards his fame so all ends well.
Should he suffer, she puts his welfare first by taking his place.

As for the Friend-Wife, her acts are good in these three ways.
First: like one's own best friend, she does her best to keep him well.
Second: like meeting a friend after a long time apart,
her heart is bound to his; their reunion brings only joy.
Third: with faultless conduct, she never falls for other men.

As for the Servant-Wife, she's like her husband's handmaid.
Her qualities are four. First: fearing his slaps and curses,
she works hard to avoid embarrassment and stern rebuke.
Second: should his anger flare, she doesn't dare argue with him.
Third: should he grow violent and strike, shouting, "You little whore!"
she never dares fight back or make a fuss, lest rumors spread.
Fourth: she's skilled in cooking, but doesn't dare eat while he's away,
fasting till her husband returns so they can partake as one.
Such is the Servant-Wife, as preached by the Lord Buddha.
Any girl who listens well and takes this code to heart each day,
will at the end of her life be reborn way up in Tusita,
a heaven filled with bliss, forever free from pain and fear.

Now for the Three Bad Wives. The Slayer-Wife has four grave faults;
don't dare embody them. Cast them out before sin strikes.
One: her only thought is to trample on and crush her man.
She's too stubborn to say she's wrong, since she thinks she's so fine.
Arguing back and forth, she seeks to best and defeat him.
Two: too lazy to work, she bullies him to boost her pride.
Haughty, she runs him down; he just listens, though she's the fool.
Three: she's quick to lust, filled with desire—a treasonous tramp!
Four: she's so vicious and mean, she'd murder him for someone new.
She'd chop, slay, and stash the body away to get rid of him.

As for the Enemy-Wife, her wicked ways number seven.
One: she disrespects him; when he gives commands, she talks back.
Two: she's hard and silent; he asks but she doesn't reply.
Three: he explains good ways, manners, and codes, but she doesn't care.
Four: she doesn't help him achieve success or rise in rank.
Five: she's haughty in speech, bold in her views, and sticks to her guns.
Six: when he buys a slave, a girl who'll serve him faultlessly,
she burns with anger, hate, and jealousy, cursing the girl.
Seven: when he takes a lover, she rips his name to shreds.

As for the Thief-Wife, her evil ways have three aspects.
One: she spends her man's money till it's gone, not saving any.
Two: while her husband tries his very best to build their wealth,
she steals it for her parents. When he inquires, she lies to him.
Three: she neglects her work, then claims she's at it constantly.
When she gets caught lounging as she pleases, she swears she's ill
and groans under the sheets. All out of tricks, she pretends she's dead.

Such are improper wives. Women who hold fast to these ways
will descend to the Four Realms of Woe once their time is up,
condemned to misery. They'll be born as third-sex people
due to their evil acts, stuck on the shore of transgressions
and foolish conduct, having ignored this Code for Girls.

Pali scriptures describe eight forms of contempt women have for men.
The first contempt: your man is broken and impotent,
so you loathe and spurn him, instead of seeking cures from healers;
filled with impatience, you fervently pray for his death.
Two: your husband is poor, with a bequest far less than yours.
You blame him nonetheless, "Too lazy to work, you pissed it all away!"
Three: your man's a nobody, while you descend from a known line.
You make him serve you, and when you argue, you mock his kin.
Four: your husband is dull, sluggish—in short, a stupid dunce.
Rude and pitiless, bold as can be, you call him a dope.

Five: your man is ugly, his fierce flesh dark, his face pockmarked,
his figure fat and formless, his hair white, his paunch a cask.
Yet your own beauty shines, your skin most fair, so you mock him.
Six: your man is indolent; he loafs around and ditches work.
You hurl harsh words at him; you curse and swear, way out of line.
Seven: your man drinks wine; he spurns his job and staggers drunk,
shouting nonsense so loud the dogs join in, waking the kids.
Hearing him, you become enraged and fiercely cuss him out.
The eighth and last contempt: your ardent man playfully pokes,
pinches, and fondles you without respect, so you curse him.
Seeing his love for you, you utter the most brutal words.
You rage, then turn blasé; mad, then detached. So coy, so sly,
neither of you finds peace—such is the eighth form of contempt.

Thus goes the Code for Girls, for you, my dear, to learn and guard.
Hold it fast in your mind so that you'll win the joy you seek,
both in this world and for lives to come in other realms.
Should you vow to become the mother of a future Buddha
your prayers will be fulfilled. You'll gain a trove of vast riches
and the highest renown for many lives, just as you wish.
This code is most precious; those who study it are fortunate.
Rare is the chance to hear it. Having listened, learn it by heart
to reach the paths that lead to nirvana—don't forget it.

These meanings are expressed in truthful verse and perfect rhyme.
The sage who rendered them—rank *min*, name Mai—conceived this poem
in perfect faith, his mind serene and pure, suffused with joy.
Vowing to reach nirvana, he composed stanzas made to last.
Should there be any faults, rectify them; please don't blame me.
May my labors extend the dispensation of the Buddha
by laying down this code, a code that has reached its true end.

Translated from Khmer by Trent Walker

KING ANG DUONG

from *Kaki*

Like many Khmer, Lao, and Thai verse novels of the period, Kaki (pronounced "Kakey") is framed as a past life of the Buddha; however, the story is racier than typical Buddhist fare and is not found in the scriptures. It tells of a complex entanglement of lovers centered around the beautiful Kaki, Brahmadatta's queen. The Buddha-to-be, a half-eagle/half-man or garuda, *is endowed with special powers and can transform himself into a handsome youth. King Ang Duong has long been celebrated for his efforts to revive Khmer arts and literature. In the prologue, omitted here, he notes that he translated this novel into Khmer in 1815, while exiled to Bangkok as a young prince. The portion printed here is about a fifth of the whole text and includes the scene in which Kaki and the* garuda *fall in love. A* gandharva *is a type of demigod, sometimes depicted as a celestial musician. A* babil *(pronounced "popil") is a Cambodian ritual object that is used as a candleholder and is the size and shape of a hand mirror. Airavan, the mount of Indra, king of the gods, is usually depicted as a three-headed elephant.* **TW**

> I tell a tale of the Buddha,
> our great Lord, most merciful,
> back when he was still perfecting
> the path to highest awakening.
>
> Once in his long journey,
> he took birth as a winged beast,
> a lord among the garudas,
> eagles with the limbs of men.
>
> He lived in a wooded retreat,
> deep in the Simbali forest,
> near the axis of the world,
> the summit known as Sumeru.

⁂

At that time there was a king,
Brahmadatta his true name,
who reigned in the supreme city,
the Ganges-edged Varanasi.

There he built a vast fortress,
soaring high like a tall peak,
its stone walls sealed secure,
ringed by rivers dark and deep.

Gates and towers bound all sides,
each climbing high above the last,
with stone pavilions lined above,
guarded by fearsome gargoyles.

Walls crisscrossed on every flank,
their crenellations well incised,
each facet sculpted artfully,
faces carved with finest skill.

Hand-hung red roofs were raised in rows
on top of miniature mansions,
laid out on intersecting streets
between bustling market stalls.

⁂

Above it all rose palaces
in five-towered, quincuncial arrays,
topped by Shiva's sharp tridents,
gleaming against the dazzling sky.

There were buffalo chins, Brahma faces,
quartets of spires and sky blossoms,
with fierce garudas and nagas
locked in perpetual battles:

all was bedecked in gold and gems,
all was coated in silver gloss,
finer than the heavens themselves,
as if fashioned by holy hands.

The royal beds, built of gold,
inlaid with thousands of shining jewels,
shone and shimmered, like perfect prisms,
breathtaking beauty brought to life.

❧

The king's three-storied royal palace
was filled with dazzling ornaments,
shaped like lotus leaves and buds,
all interlaced in twisted braids.

On top were angels bent in prayer;
beneath them, nagas fought their foes.
Down on the bottom, fierce ogres
supported all the weight with clubs.

Canopies and parasols, leafed in gold,
sparkling with their blazing fringes,
studded with rows of precious jewels,
glittered under the solar light.

His audience hall was ornamented
with floral prints from floor to ceiling;
his harem with its feminine forms
had walls inlaid with glowing gems.

Icons and scriptures were preserved
inside a most elegant library.
The many-tiered seraglio
glimmered daily with fresh allure.

The royal stables were crowded full
with kingly carts and elephants;
the sovereign storehouse with weapons
and vast treasures, piled in heaps.

Gathering halls, glowing white,
sprouted in verdant delight,
among green gardens lush with trees,
complete with cooling ponds and pools.

❧

The royal court was always packed
with ministers, tasked with governing;
with poets, charged with the pen;
with priests, entrusted to chant;

with wise sages and astrologers;
with craftsmen skilled in every trade;
with top singers of every tongue;
with dancers of dazzling beauty.

The king had an army and a navy,
with burly men, brave to the bone,
superbly skilled in arts of war,
possessed of brutal, fearsome strength.

His millions of hardened, loyal troops
amassed in rows and neat arrays.
Veterans of the fiercest fights,
they never shrank from duty.

The king had a mighty guardian,
a gandharva named Natakuven.
whose skill and genius in magical arts
were long celebrated in all known realms.

Natakuven's gifts on the harp
matched the glories of the gods.
He sang in perfect rhyme as he strummed,
composing brilliant stanzas of verse.

King Brahmadatta reigned in peace,
savoring the bliss of supreme rule.
Lords of one hundred and one lands
paid him tribute in silver and gold.

Brahmans, elders, fortunetellers,
high ministers, and all the rest—
the king's people lived in true ease,
thanks to the grace of His Majesty.

His dear consort was named Kaki,
fairer than any in the land.
No girl could match her fine beauty;
she was the queen of womankind.

Her birth was a pure miracle:
as if burst forth from a lotus.
Her face gleamed brighter than the moon;
her hair darker than a bee's black stripe.

Her forehead glowed like a *babil*,
clear in complexion, full of charm.
Her smile bloomed in effortless bliss;
her lips were full, her words winsome.

Her cheeks were bright as marian plums,
plump little orbs of orange-rose light.
Her pleasing nose was so delicate,
as if an artist had painted its lines.

Her ebony teeth, stained darker than ink,
flared from within, like black sapphire.
Her shapely ears, with lovely lobes,
opened like fresh lotus petals.

Her dark eyebrows, glistening black,
were curved like graceful hunting bows.
Her glass-clear eyes, bright as lust,
shone clearer than a polished mirror.

Her rounded neck was perfectly plump,
folded thrice in the right places,
her shoulders broad and beautiful,
her arms as lithe as Airavan's trunk.

Her silk-soft hands tapered to her
slender fingers, as thin as vines.
Her sparkling nails, supremely fine,
gleamed brighter than well-cut gems.

Her stunning breasts swelled with charm,
as round and full as lotus buds.
Her winning waist was slim and slight,
suiting the curves of her figure.

Her thighs, white as banana blossoms,
were smooth and supple, free from flaws.
No girl's body could match Kaki;
she was beautiful in every way.

Her every limb and every fold
bested the women of the world.
Her yellow glow, like purest gold,
delighted the eyes of all around.

Her musky scent, strong and soulful,
could not be topped by any flower.
Her flesh exuded rich flavors;
her fragrance feminine to the core.

If any man became her lover,
and shared the pleasures of her touch,
the scent would linger on his skin
for as long as seven nights.

❦

Every time King Brahmadatta
slept with his queen, his heart found bliss.
His love grew full and round for her,
as cherished as his own two eyes.

They joined in union on the bed,
nestled so close, so intimate,
by day, by night, without tiring,
that the king made her his chief consort.

She was surrounded by a host
of the king's gorgeous concubines,
who served their lord on bended knee,
their talents proven in song and dance.

❦

Now at that time a garuda
was dwelling atop the Simbali woods,
ruling from his floating palace,
fashioned like those in realms divine.

Blessed with fearless, daring strength,
he flew across the vaulted sky,
blazing and bounding through the blue,
soaring a league in a single dive.

His might took him across the oceans,
flying over the Seven Ringed Seas.
Endowed with magical mantras,
he could metamorphose as he pleased.

The garuda loved the thrill of chance,
and often came down to bet on dice
with mighty King Brahmadatta;
their long-running game was nearly tied.

Every seven days, the garuda
would feel the pull of the game,
and longed to leave Simbali
to throw dice with the king.

He flew and blazed across the sky,
crossing seven sets of mountains
and seas to reach Varanasi,
alighting in a banyan tree.

The garuda then transformed
from a beast into a man,
graced with a handsome form,
his face beaming with charm.

Descending from the limbs of the tree,
he walked straight towards
the marvelous palace
of King Brahmadatta.

If any woman, hot with passion,
should have laid her lustful eyes
on his strapping form, she'd thirst
to clasp him close as her lover.

The transformed youth headed toward
the king's court to present himself.
Upon glimpsing the monarch's visage,
he bowed low in a show of fealty.

His Majesty, the illustrious king,
saw the winsome youth had arrived.
In honeyed tones, the monarch said,
"Come here, my lad, come here, my friend."

The king scooped up the dice with glee
and shared the pleasures of the game
with the Lord of the Garudas,
the pair entranced in their delight.

❦

At that moment, Queen Kaki,
the foremost lady of the court,
as the afternoon gave way to dusk,
was looking for her happy king.

For he had not yet returned
to take his place on their shared bed,
the most auspicious spot of all,
so she called out and asked:

"Ladies of the harem, where is my lord?
Where has His Majesty gone?"
They bowed in reply, "Great Queen,
our Master now sits in repose,

in his court for games of chance,
playing with a handsome youth.
The young lad's body is perfect;
no man could ever compete with him.

His dashing looks are free from fault;
completely suited to the game at hand."
The lovely Queen Kaki, having heard
her ladies' words, was filled with joy.

Knowing the looks of this dashing youth
exceeded all other men of the world,
the gorgeous queen wished to see
him for herself and crept up to the door.

She stopped and stood to catch a glimpse
of the garuda's body and fell in love,
her heart filled with such excitement
to take that bird-man as her mate.

The garuda, still playing with the king,
happened to glance toward Kaki
and felt the thrill of love arise,
delighting in desire's rush.

Silently he thought, "How stunning
is that lady! This is what is called beauty.
I'm overwhelmed by my good fortune;
no other girl can compare with her.

This is charm; this is elegance.
A match to her could never be found.
I've seen many beings in this world,
but never a lady as lovely as her.

Even the angels in the heavens
couldn't match the girl before me.
Not one blemish can be found
upon her resplendent body.

She seems to be the king's consort,
or else she would not dare
to stand and stare so fearlessly."
Gazing at her, he too fell in love.

⁂

As for Kaki, she caught the garuda
staring at her body. She smiled coyly and
looked at him from the corners of her eyes,
fanning the flames of his love.

Whenever the garuda locked eyes with her,
she giggled and smiled, then shrugged it off.
In furtive joy, she shot him glances
and flashed him a secret smile.

Seeing all this, his skin tingled
and his belly leaped into his chest.
Lost in love, dice gave him no relief;
he thought only of carnal bliss.

He turned away to focus on the game,
then turned back, stealing a gander.
He peeked for a sideways glance
his eyes never tiring of her sight.

She feigned a fall, letting her sash slip down
from her shoulder, revealing a pert breast.
His heart quavered, stirred by the thrill.
Aroused, he longed to ravish her,

and almost rushed to embrace her
and whisk her away at once,
but realizing his repute would suffer,
wrested himself back to the game.

Translated from Khmer by Trent Walker

KROM NGOY

from A Garland of New Advice

Anak Brah Bhiramy Bhasa U, born Uk U and popularly known as Krom Ngoy, was one of Cambodia's most influential bards of the late nineteenth and early twentieth centuries. Celebrated as a poet of the people, he went from festival to festival in the Cambodian countryside, singing his poems while plucking his collapsible one-string khsae diev *for accompaniment. His moralistic verse—full of humor, wit, and vivacity—has struck a chord with Cambodian audiences for generations. These two excerpts from Ngoy's best-known composition, A Garland of New Advice, offer a modern take on the centuries-old tradition of didactic verse, or* cpap. *The opening excerpt (stanzas 1 to 10) introduces the violence and immorality of the colonial era. The second (stanzas 31 to 38), perhaps the most famous passage in all of Ngoy's poems, urges Cambodians to uphold Khmer traditions in the face of French domination. Ngoy's compositions were recorded in 1930, near the end of his life, thanks to Suzanne Karpelès, who invited him to the Buddhist Institute and asked Khmer scholars to transcribe his compositions. His work continues to influence Cambodian poets and* chapei *singers today.* TW

[EXCERPT 1]

My name is U, my royal title "Blissful Eloquence."
I bow to the Buddha, the Dharma, and the Sangha,
to whom I owe a massive debt, and to my parents.

I bow to the monk who ordained me in my youth,
who held my palms and taught me my first chant:
hair, teeth, nails, skin ... and to my other preceptors.

I recall my debts to the consonants of Khmer,
each a part of my body, twelve from my mother,
twenty-one from my father, thirty-three in all.

I penned this poem in April nineteen twenty-two,
as a new moral code for boys and girls today.
Dear friends, young and old, please listen close.

These days we take wrong for right, mad for sane.
If at fault, we play dumb; offered peace, we fight.
We count on gold, count on silver, count on cunning.

We're crooked, we're cruel, we count on chops,
on stabs, on feet, on fists. We count on cuffs,
on kicks, on chains, the gallows and the guillotine.

Hear me out, children—don't count on these.
Remember the truth: our country is poor,
and poor it will be for years to come.

Our faith wanes as joy ebbs and pain crests.
Born in this immoral age, we're left to care
for our ancestors' words, so keep them close.

Believe old sayings. Hold them in your heart.
The brave come home with their skin flayed;
only cowards return with theirs intact.

Don't hang out with thieves or gamblers;
take all good people as your true kin.
Make friends with strangers if they're kind.

Don't warp the standard or stray from the path.
Don't defy your mother or veer from your father.
If you see white hair, quickly lower your head.

[EXCERPT 2]

Don't fan conflict. If other men lack brains,
don't crave their wealth or shame their wives.
Follow the new rules, but don't drop old codes.

Don't belittle peasants, don't forget you're Khmer.
Don't be a fraud who bows only when convenient.
Don't pretend you're rich, never mock the poor.

Remember your debts to your first teachers,
who taught you math, who taught you to read.
Don't shake their hands; bend your neck instead.

Don't talk back to them; they're not your peers.
If people seek refuge in you, talk to them kindly.
Harsh words spark anger, searing your own name.

Get over your station. Speak with courtesy,
for gentle words only raise your reputation.
Don't start quarrels or provoke the strong.

Don't detest the weak, for they might be misguided.
Bring them under your wing, before things go wild.
But if you think you can squeeze smoke into a ball,

your pride will blow up in your face.
Study Chinese and Vietnamese ways,
but don't lose yourself in the process.

Don't let success swell your big head.
Don't wear leather shoes in the temple.
Doff your hat, fold up your umbrella,

and bow down low, your forehead to the floor.
Don't just eat as you please, don't get too cocky.
In keeping French laws, don't lose your religion.

Translated from Khmer by Trent Walker

FOLKLORE

A Cycle of Alev Stories

Tales about the unscrupulous trickster Alev are part of the oral folklore of Cambodia and may have originated in the eighteenth and nineteenth centuries. From 2005 to 2006, some of these tales were collected in the four volumes of the New Cambodian Folktales Project of the Buddhist Institute, a collaborative initiative organized by Penny Edwards, directed by Sor Sokny, and executed by a team of Cambodian graduate students and myself. The following Alev stories were recorded as told by Mr. Su Lang of Angkuonh Dei village, Kampong Siem district, Kampong Cham, in 2005. EWD

INTRODUCTION

"Grandfather, have you heard the story of Alev?"

"That story's been around and told forever!"

"Do tell this story to me, please! Please, Grandfather, let the younger generation hear and read this story. I want to know it. How does it go?"

"All right, all right! This is the story of Alev, a boy who was sometimes lazy and sometimes not; sometimes too bold, and sometimes too tricky."

DOGSHIT CAKES

Once upon a time, a family had a little boy named Alev. When he got to be seven or eight years old, his parents took him to the temple to serve a monk so that he could learn and study a bit.

Whenever the monk went on his alms rounds, he ordered the young students to guard the temple grounds and keep the dogs from shitting all over the place.

When it was Alev's turn to stand guard, the monk told him, "Look: guard the temple well and don't let the dogs shit in here at all! If you fail, I'm going to make you eat every last bit of shit." Saying that, the monk left, expecting Alev to do as instructed.

Alev went home to his mother and had her make sesame cakes, which he told her he would take to the temple to eat. Once there, Alev mashed the cakes into small lumps shaped like a thumb, and scattered them in groups of two and three all around the central sanctuary of the temple.

When the monk came back from his alms rounds, he saw dog shit all over the temple grounds. Infuriated, he beat Alev and forced him to eat the dog shit. Alev, of course, wasn't afraid to eat the turds, since they were actually sesame cakes. Every time he ate one, he'd say, "Delicious!" The monk would give him a blow for each turd he ate until there was only one left.

The monk exclaimed, "Amazing! Are they really delicious, Alev?" And Alev gave a piece to the monk. Placing it in his mouth, the monk exclaimed a second time, "Wow! This is some sweet dog shit! No wonder you're eating it!"

The monk asked Alev, "So … which dog's shit is this? Go get some more."

"It's the black bitch's shit."

The monk commanded Alev, "Give that bitch lots of food to eat so that she'll make lots of shit for us." Then he tied a bowl under the dog's butt to collect shit.

A few days later, the monk had some visitors. Having nothing to offer them, he told Alev to fetch the dogshit cakes from the overflowing bowl he'd tied behind the dog.

After the monks had talked for a while and drunk some tea, one of the monks ate a piece of the dog shit. He immediately vomited violently because, of course, dog shit is disgusting.

Furious with Alev, the monk kicked him out of the temple, beating him as he ran, and told him to never come back.

ALEV KILLS HIS PARENTS FOR SOUP

So, Alev went back to live with his parents. One day, he craved some spicy Chinese soup, but didn't know how to get any. At that time, his father had gone to build a guard hut near the rice fields, and his mother was at home. Taking advantage of the situation, Alev told his mother, "Mom! Mom! Dad is dead! You should make soup to offer his spirit; make it spicy Chinese soup, if you can." His mother, who seldom asked questions, did as he requested.

When Alev had eaten his fill of bread and soup, he walked to his father's new hut near the fields and told him, "Mom's dead! Daddy, go offer some soup to her spirit!" In this way, Alev managed to get even more soup to fill his belly.

Next, Alev figured out how to convince his father to take another wife to replace his mother, who wasn't actually dead.

His father said, "And where will I find this wife? I'm already old!"

Alev replied, "Leave it up to me, Dad!"

Then he went to his mother to get her to replace his father, who also wasn't actually dead. "Mom!" he said, "you should take another husband; life for a woman alone is too difficult."

His mother replied, "Son, I have always acted according to your plans. Do as you see fit; I leave it up to you."

With this, Alev went to his father, saying, "Dad! Daddy! I've found a wife for you, but she says the wedding has to be tonight!" Agreeing, the father prepared rice and water for the wedding offering, and at nightfall went with Alev.

When Mother and Father saw each other at a distance, Alev's father thought, "Wow, she looks just like Alev's mom!" And Alev's mother thought, "Wow! He looks just like Alev's dad!"

Curious, they lit a lamp and saw that, indeed, they were Alev's parents, though each had thought the other dead. Both of them hollered, "Damn! Alev's tricked us again!" And they chased him away from their home, beating him as he ran.

ALEV PIMPS FOR A MONK

So Alev ran back to the temple and asked the monk for permission to live there again. Because so much time had passed, the monk was no longer angry and so agreed.

One day, Alev asked the monk, "So, grandfather, do you desire a woman?"

The monk retorted, "Don't talk like that! I'm ordained, and must shun all women; don't say anything more."

But of course, in reality, the monk did desire a woman and was simply trying to hide the fact.

"And anyway," continued the monk, "even if you did bring me a woman, you'd only go and tell everyone all about it. If you did that, I'd stop feeding you at the temple entirely."

Alev said, "That's not true; I will help you hide her, grandfather, as long as you pay me."

To this the monk replied, "How much?"

"Just one baht," answered Alev.

But of course, Alev had no idea where to procure a woman. So he went looking for a Chinese man.

When he found one, he asked, "Do you desire a woman? If you do, I can get you one."

The Chinese man did desire a woman and said yes.

The Chinese man paid Alev, who returned to the monk, saying, "I've found a woman; she wants you to meet her in the temple."

At around seven or eight that night, Alev led the woman to the temple—of course, it was actually the Chinese man.

Since it was dark, the monk confused the Chinese man for a woman, and the Chinese man confused the monk for a woman. They jumped and tried to grab each other. Struggling, each tried to get the upper hand until, finally, the weaker monk fell down with the Chinese man on top of him. When the Chinese man lifted up the monk's robes, he saw they had the same tools. Overcome with shame, each realizing that the other person was a man, they ran away in opposite directions.

Afterward, the Chinese man went to Alev to demand his money back, but Alev threatened to tell everyone what had happened. When the old monk realized he'd been tricked, he went to Alev to beat him and throw him out of the temple again. But Alev threatened, "If you dare to beat your humble servant, I'll tell everyone that you, grandpa, really do desire a woman."

Defeated, the monk went out to collect a begging bowl of money as payment for Alev's silence—not just one coin, but a bowl full of coins. When Alev got the money, he left the temple and returned to his home.

Translated from Khmer by Erik W. Davis

UKNA SUTTANTAPRIJA IND

from *Journey to Angkor Wat*

Composed in 550 stanzas, Journey to Angkor Wat *is Ukna Suttantaprija Ind's most celebrated poem. It recounts his first trip to Siem Reap, in 1909, when he was invited to accompany the Khmer provincial governor and his French counterpart to attend King Sisowath's official visit to the temples of Angkor. It was most likely written between 1909 and 1915, but was only published posthumously in 1934. The poem is in a Thai genre,* nirat *(pronounced in Khmer as "nireas"), that had recently been adopted into Cambodian literature. Nireas are poems of departure, with the poet reflecting as much on the journey taken as on the beloved left behind at home. Ind's text abounds with reflections on the shifting political landscape of Cambodia, the melancholy majesty of Angkor's ruins, and his own struggles with the ascetic strictures of Buddhist ethics. The excerpts selected here include stanzas 1 to 51 and 237 to 256. The latter is perhaps the poem's most famous passage, immortalized in countless Cambodian textbooks.* **TW**

[EXCERPT 1]

A journey to the gem of Angkor Wat
weighs down my mind as I leave you behind,
beloved partner of this life, my bliss, my love.

༄

Of royal line our noble king descends,
named Sisowath Preah Kaewfa Sulalai,
ruler of the Kingdom of Kampuchea,
who vows to tread the bodhisattva's way.

He's due to lead a rite at Angkor Wat
to mark the restoration of the old,
making lavish gifts of royal riches
to one day reach the state of a Buddha.

He's set to leave during the waxing moon,
the ninth day of the tenth lunar month,

Thursday, fifth of the week, a rooster year,
right when the sun's bright rays begin to fade.

❦

The governor of Battambang province,
who leads the work of the new French regime,
and the plenipotent *commissaire*
are both honest and deeply loyal men.

When all is set and all are in their suits,
they shall welcome the lofty king himself.
The governor kindly invited me along
that I may glimpse the ancient city too.

In the slightest dissent to his decree
I fear the harm that would befall my life,
so I resign to leave my beautiful,
my fated mate as fate forces farewell.

❦

Now's the time; the dignitaries must depart.
They board the carriage pulled by peerless steeds.
The skilled coachman takes hold of the reins
and steers down toward the quay on the Sangkae.

Khmer, Annamite, and French civil servants
have dressed their best for the dazzling departure.
The black-booted soldiers stationed by the boat
all stomp in step to stride and strut aboard.

The captain pulls the cord to sound three times
a loud whistle while deckhands weigh anchor.
The boiler fills and we head north along
the watercourse's way to which we hew.

The Annamite captain deftly steers straight,
guiding the boat between the river's banks.
The thundering wheel slaps hard against the waves
as townsfolk rush from all around to watch.

❦

I gaze out from my perch on the steamer
as we speed toward a distant customs house.
A lamppost stands in front of the cabin,
barely befitting the rank of customs chief.

House, roof, and deck, crippled, crumbled, and cracked,
its Khmerness lost, it's just a shack raised high.
This customs crew could really use some cash,
yet they hardly even check those who pass by.

No toll or tax to excise or extract,
the staff simply let us swiftly steam off.
This taxless customs house struggles to last,
living off naught but its own fields and farms.

The Siamese regime built this office,
but levies were not even properly charged.
Impressive that the customs chief remains
despite the new regime giving no aid.

The officers tend to their crops instead;
they don't traffic or trade like city folks.
Praise them who win their wealth without warped ways,
who brave the muck and mud without a word.

❧

How transient that lithe-limbed girl's life,
stooping to sow seedlings, scorched by the sun,
her face plastered with mud and dusty earth.
I mourn the strife and strain of those born poor.

If she had riches, rank, and great renown,
she'd dine and doze in lofty luxury;
adorned with fine perfume and fair powder,
hair trimmed and dyed, her complexion would shine.

she'd flaunt her charm to captivate rich men.
she'd be looked over, never overlooked.
But stained now by the sun and by the soil,
she can ensnare and earn their love no more.

I eye the tiny girl and pity her,
born to a wretched race with the wrong roots.
Subject to struggle, strain, and suffering,
she'll wait until she's far too old to wed.

Once aged she can't project her own beauty;
rare is the man who would bargain for her.
With her brideprice reduced, men feel deceived;
coupling and consummation cannot come.

Ind . Journey

Fortunes failed, wealth withered, she's bound to bear
the wear and tear of eking out a life.
Those with the means can brighten their bodies,
unlike this fair-skinned one besmirched with mud.

❧

I sit perplexed, my gaze still on the girl.
We reach Ansong Sok, "Molting Monitor."
The snaking stream divides into four channels
and floating slicks of sticks and scum abound.

The captain guides the wheel to the debris
to slice clear through, but the steamer sticks fast.
Deckhands use bamboo prods to pole the boat;
the wheel pushes the vessel back around.

The polemen poke away the sticks and scum.
The steamer seems to briefly break away
but stuck to sticks, the blades still strive to spin.
Pity the wheel now clogged and choked by scum!

I see how tight the scum girdles the boat,
as lust would mount flesh when morals fade.
Our bodies soon are trapped in that dark place;
the real is shrouded off, the light is screened.

Lust sears and singes creatures in the world
to rue and regret base earthliness.
The vessel's frame is like our human form;
those short of insight cannot see the real.

The blades are wisdom that slices and shears;
the floating scum is lust, now dropped away.
Escape from the shallows of sorrow and strife
depends on brave wisdom, the paddle wheel.

The boat's innards are our body's workings:
earth, water, fire, and wind, the four bases.
The helm's the post of wakeful remembrance,
the bamboo pole's the clear mind's reflection.

The sticks and scum are meditation's foes,
preventing us from seeing what is real.
The water whirls around like birth and death,
drowning creatures in this carnal abyss.

Alas, that this body does not spurn lust;
instead it's spun around, as in a gyre.
In woe we weep and wail, for we forget
to follow our Lord's flawless words of truth.

Reflecting on myself, shaken and stirred,
thwarted by thirst for all earthly delights,
I've seen the truth, but it's for girls I pine,
fodders for lust and fonts of mystery.

Lust yields not, for straining seals it tighter.
My poor heart and its love are wrenched apart.
Even if I take sacred writ as rule,
worldly lust stands unhampered, unhindered.

Ditching the Dharma can't help douse this fire;
desire's pitch-black, like night with shapes unseen.
Seldom sloughed off, lust fades but never's gone.
Can washing tar-stained silk remove the coal?

To scrub's no use, the color changes not;
tar stains are ever bound to their blackness,
as taints are tied to creatures thus enthralled.
Don't fancy you could somehow wipe them clean.

Straining to let go I'm locked in tighter.
Practice is stopped, not steady; stayed, not stilled.
I sit to rule myself with the Dharma,
like deckhands clearing all the scum at once.

Once we pass through, the sticks and scum float back,
again settling into the selfsame clumps.
The sticks and scum are like thirsting desire;
we chop and clear but choked remains the stream.

◈

Near an orchard the scum sticks to the shore,
strewn with the carcasses of cats and dogs.
They ooze, they fester, their entrails erupt;
vultures and crows compete for carrion.

Seeing the corpses consumed by the crows,
I'm shaken, thinking of my own body.
These crows swoop in whenever death arrives.
The dead, devoid of life, are jettisoned.

In life they're fierce, ferocious as can be;
no other beasts would dare to nip their flesh.
In death they're set adrift upon the stream,
where carrion birds now feast voraciously.

How transient the lives of all creatures!
Once bodies break apart and minds collapse,
no one will dare approach the vile stench.
Let us all dwell on life's impermanence.

I humbly strive to quake at corpses' sight,
yet lust still must be burning inside me.
For I think of my darling, my dear love;
"impermanence" is only on my lips.

Reflecting on the foul should purge desire,
crush lust, and take me to the edge of trance.
A true yogi would seize upon the object;
I've lost my calm and can't focus at all.

To see a dog's dead corpse as my body
cannot help disenchant me, my dear friends.
Oh what am I to do? Whoever's now
protecting me, oh please point out the path.

᎗

Now I also doubt "Molting Monitor."
A name that takes on such a sense is strange.
Since when was there a monitor that molted
so that it could give rise to such a name?

Monitor lizards never seem to molt at all,
so why would a village take on this title?
Perhaps some beast's shed skin was found near here
and was inscribed as this village's name.

I strive to understand, yet cannot see
how this strange name is anything but wrong.
Whoever named this "Molting Monitor"
his name remains up to this very day.

But maybe men of old deserve our praise
for they came up with all the names we know.
Though in the bush they lived, they still knew how
to designate a proper toponym.

I mull and muse upon a cool, fresh breeze.
The ship advances toward Krabau Canal,
where water slows and flows not one bit more,
deep black, yet shining pure and free from mud.

This water's clearly from the Tonle Sap.
The stream counters its flow right where they meet,
such that the current stops and flows no more.
Still, I ponder this strange Krabau Canal.

Just where did this canal branch off?
Here lies the end but where's its origin?
Maybe it lies too low and now is clogged?
Jungle channels must hide many secrets.

[EXCERPT 2]

I gaze upon the moat, a watery sea,
a vast expanse that circles Angkor Wat.
The kings of old had dug it for defense:
a ditch, a dam, a dyke to ward off foes.

The moat's waters expand, a wide, wet field,
all lined with stone, a dense array of rock,
its steep walls carved in shells, spirals of gems,
descending stairs sculpted in fragrant flowers.

In the center a bridge extends in stone,
its road both long and imposingly wide.
Yet its exact measure in length and width
conforms to the secret manuals of old.

A triple courtyard sits where the bridge starts,
guarded by standing lions at every edge.
Some of the sandstone beasts remain intact,
while other guardians lost their heads or limbs.

Pity these stone lions, the ancients' craft!
Their posture roars with life amidst decay.
But now they're chipped and cracked and smashed:
alas that these sculptures meet such an end!

Perhaps some savage folk, cut off from thought,
whetted their knives against the lions' backs,
ruining what still remains of their fine form,
without a shred of care for art of yore.

O lions! You stood rock-still, eyeing all those
who sharpened swords and daggers on your spine.
Why didn't you erupt in rage and crush
your enemies between your fearsome jaws?

Damn those who damaged these lion sculptures—
they don't know what's a puddle and what's the sea.
How shameful, then, what artists made with care
could be so heedlessly defaced by foes!

⁕

Down the causeway, I see the tight-packed rock:
a board of stones, their edges closely set.
Even an elephant can't make it sway.
The bridge still works, despite some sinking blocks.

The balustrades are carved in naga form;
each with ten heads, like a hand of bananas.
Their hoods are raised: bold snakes ready to strike,
a serpentine display, a knot of necks.

These naga kings, endowed with might and brawn,
sport long bodies; their faces guard the gates.
They slither along the bridge's balusters,
their tails entwined above rock-lined courtyards.

O naga lords, undaunted by the garudas,
your sworn rivals, you fight them with vigor.
Should they dislodge you from your wall,
just dive into the safe waters below.

O stone nagas, fashioned by the ancients!
In days long gone, your beauty surpassed all.
But now your bodies are broken and cracked;
you're only a ruin, your glamor all but gone.

Your backs are split, your heads torn from your necks.
Only the row of columns below remains.
Alas, the masterworks of old must fade,
unable to endure forevermore.

How transient the life of stone nagas!
Meant to last for ages beyond count,
they've gone to ruin, far before their time,
falling to pieces, scattered here and there.

Is this our fate as beings in the world?
No matter what, all that's born must soon die.
And the Buddha's teaching is clear as day:
all things, once aged, shall be scattered in death.

If even rock can meet its end in dust,
then what of us, with our fragile bodies?
Thus any pith of life to which we cling
will be destroyed, the plaything of disease.

Born in this form, we're bound to end in death,
our bones only a means to seed the soil.
Grow weary of the world; lessen your lust;
let Angkor's stone nagas weigh on your chest.

Though I still meditate upon these truths,
my mind doesn't settle on its object,
for thoughts of my beloved still arise.
When we're apart, how our two minds wander!

Alas, my mind is no more than a monkey,
never at peace, never silent or still.
Seeing this, I think of that; I can't stop.
These words? Useless. If I can't sit, no bliss.

Translated from Khmer by Trent Walker

BRAH PADUMATTHER SOM

from *Tum Teav*

Tum Teav (spelled Dum Dav in Khmer) is the tragic love story of a novice monk named Tum and a beautiful girl named Teav. When Tum and his friend Pech leave the monastery to sell trays and recite sermons in a distant village, Teav is enraptured by Tum's stunning voice, and Tum by Teav's beauty. The pair fall in love, but a nobleman named Archun and the king himself come to desire Teav as well. This story of jealousy, misunderstanding, and violent retribution ends with the death of the lovers. Based on legendary events from the seventeenth or eighteenth centuries, the story soared in popularity during the late nineteenth century. Brah Padumatther Som's 1915 version, the most popular retelling today, has been read by almost every Cambodian high-school student since the 1950s and inspired numerous stage, film, and musical adaptations. TW

Let me recount the tale of a boy named Tum,
raised in the paddy fields of Ba Phnom province.
Though born to two parents as is the rule,
little was known about his mother and father.

Once Tum had grown and reached a suitable age,
his mother knew that he was old enough
to lay aside his toys. She dressed him up
to begin his studies at Wat Vihear Thom.

The master there accepted him with joy,
training Tum to be skilled in magic spells
and steeped in deep wisdom with each new day,
until the boy sought to become a monk.

In his preceptor's long-lived lineage,
there was another novice monk named Pech,
a fellow acolyte of equal skill.
The two young monks made offering trays to sell.

Tum was keener in eloquence and wit,
paired with a lovely voice and youthful face.
With his good looks and winsome smile,
he thought of Pech as his younger brother.

Yet Pech made warm tones on the oboe,
and was adept at every melody.
So the two boys competed head to head,
resentful that their skills were so well matched.

But they worked side by side to sell their trays
to a small base of nearby customers.
When the new season came and cool winds blew,
the two boys shivered in their misery.

Unwholesome thoughts weighed down on Tum's body.
He confessed to Pech, as if the two were one:
"Novice Pech *oey!* Come on, help me out here.
We're selling just a few trays at a time.

Profits are down; soon our business will fail.
Don't you wonder about that old saying?
In every place... that's close and near...
there's only rest... if my girl's here...

The ancients did not err in their true words,
for we too are young men here in this world.
We know nothing beyond begging for food.
Shouldn't we break the mold and travel far?"

They thought it through and made a certain plan,
but couldn't restrain themselves a moment more.
Candles and incense in hand, they hurried off
to make an offering to their teacher.

The abbot soon made his suspicions clear:
"Just where do you think you two are going?"
The novice monks replied reluctantly,
"Master, please don't worry. Be kind to us,

for we now bow down low in deep respect
to take our leave of you, O Venerable!
We are planning to set off on the road
to preach to people out in distant lands.

Here at the monastery, we're on edge,
our bodies all worked up without a break.

We're listless, Master; we're feeling dull,
filled with an urgent need to wander far.

Swift winds now blow. A cold season awaits.
This is the right moment to take our leave,
for if we take a load of trays with us,
prospects are good; here we barely scrape by."

The abbot offered his well-tempered words:
"Well, why not go if that's what you both want?
You've said you're off to sell your little trays;
why waste your words by asking me again?

Go, by all means, but stay out of trouble.
Don't act the fool if you see a girl.
You shouldn't clown about or play around,
lest your behavior spoil my good name.

The shame of worldly disgrace and scorn
defies the rules the Buddha set for monks.
So once you've sold your load, hurry back here.
Don't tarry there to tally losses and gains."

The two young monks then bowed in obeisance,
and took leave of their master to rush off.
Swiftly preparing everything to leave,
they neatly placed the trays all upside down

to pack them in their cart. They scrambled for food
to wrap up tight. Then in a panic they found a sack
to stuff with raw rice grain in case the road
was turned to mire by the season's rains.

Once the two monks had readied their supplies,
insurance for the long journey ahead,
they strained to lift their ox-pulled cart upright.
That done, they yoked their cattle and set off

around the eighth hour of the morning.
The sun's bright rays emerged from eastern skies
with brilliant reds that lit the horizon
and blazed across the paddy field expanse.

A stretch of grass and puddles soon appeared.
They rushed to stake the oxen. The monks ate rice

while their beasts chomped the green and slurped the sky.
Once the cattle were re-hitched, the monks pressed on.

They came to a village to sell their trays.
The local people bought a healthy share;
the rest they sold to folks along the road
as they kept going towards Tboung Khmum.

Near the provincial border with Toteung Thngai,
they stopped when people gathered around,
wanting to buy their wares. Some stared with spite
at Tum, resenting his handsome body.

Some fantasized of taking him back home:
"If only I could snatch and snuggle him close,
I'd have my way with him." As they got near,
they bristled with delight before his face.

Pressing their new heartthrob towards a well,
the frenzied crowd gathered at a shaded knoll,
the site of a lovely town named Po Choeng Khal.
Men and women alike amassed, aroused by Tum.

The boys set down their cart in the village.
The laypeople felt sorry for the monks
and quickly bought their trays, finding them fine.
They then cajoled the novices to stay awhile,

to rest a bit, perhaps for many days.
They loved the boys and wouldn't let them go
to head back home. The novices were told
that given the season they ought to stay.

Some of the villagers nurtured the thought
that the two novices could take a break
and recite sermons from palm-leaf scriptures,
seeing that the boys were smart and charming.

Tum's chanting voice was crisp and smoooth and sweet.
When he sang, all the people of Tboung Khmum
rushed over to listen: young lads, old men,
widows, and fresh maidens all gathered round.

Translated from Khmer by Trent Walker

PRINCE ARENO YUKANTHOR

from *On the Threshold of the Khmer Narthex: Nonsense about the Conflict between East and West*

Prince Areno Yukanthor was born in 1896 and moved to Paris in 1919. There, he painted in the style of Orphic Cubism and wrote Symbolist poetry, works that bordered on vengeful frenzy, semantic hallucination, and a search for artistic salvation through mysticism. My thanks to Gregory Mikaelian for rediscovering this forgotten Cambodian artist-prince. CM

THE WORLD OF SIGNS

Humanity lies between Heaven and Earth. It is through humanity that Heaven may unite with Earth. And it is through an audience that a work of art comes alive...

Art is a magical destination. We must return to it...

In the subconscious darkness, an unreal blue light swirls in purplish clouds, illuminates this strange scene: a tall, slender young girl, veiled and dressed in silver-gray muslin, with a complexion more precious than gold, makes a long, weary gesture of picking a double LILY IN SHADOW... that opens in full bloom! Oh! What horror! Is it a toad? A satyr? What repulsive voluptuousness expresses itself in this lipped face without a forehead, a cranium pointed and shining like an abscess! And these hands! These hands! Inert as those of a fetus, and flaccid! Thicker than those of an abattoir slaughterman! These infamous hands that embrace the precious, aristocratic girl and pull her against him and his ugly, satisfied face! As she reaches for the LILY, a radiant crimson flame burns the ground and the Monster! Oh, these hands that penetrate muslin!...

The embers of TANHA [desire] spark and rise in flame. The flame becomes woman. On a blue background, the woman is motionless, masked, twisting her hair (or the veil that masks her—maybe both, veil and hair)...

She is like a sun casting trembling and revolving multicolored shadows. This fantasy is none other than the DANCE OF DESIRE around the FEMALE FLAME. The Flame is reborn and dies and is reborn in the same instant, and thus creates the rhythm of the Word in the Abyss of Being...

More exoterically, the Dance of Desire is the reflection of the individualized

Universe. And what we call in Khmer MANAS [thought] is the immediate moment—the volitional moment—that follows the contact of our complex and ephemeral individuality with all that is contained in the Whole from which individuality arises. This contact is not only material. It is also, above all, spiritual. As we said in *Angkorean Cantata*,

> There is no Matter
> There is no pure Spirit
> Separate from each other:
> Life is a dazzled Dream that persists.

We insist on the word PERSIST…

Thus, the Universe is subtly One. Matter and spirit, substance and essence, space and time, merge. The Universe is only a fusion that "persists." Thought, hatched in the mind, wrings itself free of the metaphysical world, like the fabulous ENTRI [eagle] that soars from Hembova Jungle towards the sun's glare and hovers in the ether—drunk on both ether and glare, drunk on the terrestrial landscapes made wide by the horizon, reaching toward that geometric place where all points of origin and departure meet…

Every leaf that falls from the branches of the CHAMPA *[Magnolia champaca]* describes its own harmony in the overall harmony; every blade of grass, even the most humble, plays its part in the harmonious rhythm that dissolves into ONE.

Translated from French by Christophe Macquet

SUY HIENG

The Orphans

Suy Hieng is one of Cambodia's first female novelists. From her youth, war was present in her life and writing. In 1952, she published Veasna Nei Neang Nakry (Destiny of Miss Nakry), *which begins with the American bombing of Phnom Penh in 1945, during Japan's occupation of Cambodia. In 1964, she had stopped writing for ten years but resumed after the tragedy of Chantrea—in which a town in Svay Rieng was destroyed when American and South Vietnamese forces bombed it with tons of ordnance and napalm. After going to the scene of devastation, Suy Hieng wrote the novel* Chantrea: Khmer Territory, *which was a huge success and adapted for the cinema. Its epigraph, "The Orphans," was later set to music by Pov Sipho.* **CM/SM**

The river unrolls the ribbon of its beaches.
My heart is tight, the boat is about to depart.
We'll return in the planting season,
when rice seedlings are nurtured in the fields.
Phum had just earned enough money to buy a car.
Kolap will no longer have a constant fear of missing out;
she will no longer struggle to sell flowers.
Phum will no longer toil to sell bread.
We hear the waves slapping the shore.
Large clouds flee across the high, cold sky.
The horizon is immense, as vast as ignorance.
With a heavy heart, I leave behind the orphans.
The wind blows from the south,
charged with a sweet scent,
as hundreds walk away.
Some children, in the distance, fly kites.

Translated from Khmer by Christophe Macquet and Sharon May

KHUN SRUN

A Small Request

When I die, my dear, please
bury me at the base of a small mango tree
so that my flesh may turn into compost.
Don't let me suffocate in a thick wooden coffin.

My soul will be happy if this young tree
flowers and bears fruit, if there is some land
around it to grow rice, and enough wood
for a Khmer to build a home for his family.

Please don't weep for me—if in this life
I have harmed any other living beings,
by making this tree a refuge for birds
and fellow creatures, I will be blessed.

What good is a tomb anyway?
I will be dust, I will be nothing.
In any case, I won't be there for long.
In the end, there is nothing inside tombs.

My dear, don't hope for help from my soul either.
Death will have already sent me
spinning to my destiny—to a place
beyond suffering, or maybe to Hell.

And finally, I beg you, don't bring me
any offerings of food. It will only rot
and reek. The angels won't touch it.
And the demons don't deserve to feast.

Translated from Khmer by Christophe Macquet and Sharon May

KHAU NY KIM

A Hundred Scents, A Hundred Seasons

I want you to wake before dawn and come with me,
I want you to see the sky washed by the night's rains,
I want you to breathe in nature as yet unspoiled,
Open the door of our thoughts and the cherished scents of our memory:

The *rumduol* flower that intoxicated me near the temple of Preah Khan,
Candles and incense before the Buddha footprint at the top of Phnom Kulen,
The guano of bats huddling in a gallery of Angkor Wat,
Dead leaves mixed with earth on the path to Ta Prohm.

The muddy pond where children gather to catch fish,
Ripe mangoes in the baskets of vendors in the town market of Ta Khmao,
The *prahok* that a farm family carries in a cart on the way to Prek Pnov village,
Salted crab in open jars in the Kampot market.

Fresh sugar-palm fruit picked to make *akao* cakes,
Pickled cabbage marinated in jars at Chbar Ampov,
Duck *kakor* soup in the market by the river in Battambang,
The first toasted rice when the cold Kadek winds blow from the North.

The seaweed left at low tide on the beaches of Kep,
The roasted chicken that little girls offer to bus passengers in Tram Khnar market,
The grilled bananas sold by old women sitting near the high walls of Wat Langka,
The rows of jars filled with palm sugar in the market of Baek Chan.

And the smell of the earth welcoming the first rains,
The aroma of *ma'om* growing in paddy fields filled with young rice seedlings,
The scent of sap from the hevea trees growing in the rubber plantations of Memot,
The Khmer perfumes and powders sold in the narrow lanes of Si Nhek market.

And I remember with you,
The scent of flowers floating in the night along Norodom Boulevard,
The smoke of candles and incense on holy days before the altar of
    Preah Ang Dorng Keur,
The aroma of cakes and dishes during the Festival of the Dead in the
    temple of Stung Meanchey,
And this—the perfume of your hair that the wind once brushed against
    my face.

February 1980

Translated from Khmer by Christophe Macquet and Sharon May

CHEY CHAP

Two Poems

Chey Chap is one of the most respected living poets in Cambodia. A master of formal poetic forms, he taught Khmer rhetoric, writing, and poetry at the University of Phnom Penh for many years and held positions in the Ministry of Education. His verses are distinguished by their sonorous rhymes, alliteration, and clever word play, giving his work a formal beauty in Khmer that is impossible to capture in translation. He composed most of his poems in the 1980s and 1990s; the two poems translated here were composed in 1985 and 1986, respectively, and first published in his influential 1994 collection, O Khmer Land. *In "Don't Fight the Wind," the Khmer word* phlieng *(rain) echoes* phleng *(music).* CM/SM

DON'T FIGHT THE WIND

Rain falls endlessly,
in drops large and small,
and tones high and low,
the liquid music joining
thunder's percussive clamor
throughout the night.
The angry rain
drives its torrent
to inundate the earth.
Tender grasses
drown in the deluge,
disappearing in silence.

When the rain is done
the wind takes over.
Its first hoarse whisper
becomes a howling gust.
The pounding tempest
lifts trees, spins them
in the swirling gale,
uproots them whole.
They struggle
against the wind
but destruction
will prevail.

The night fills with
a cacophony of frogs
and burrowing toads,
the dry clacking and
clicking of *kdak* shells.
Earth's creatures call and answer,
exchanging tales of suffering.
An exhausted army of ants
will surely perish in the dark.
Thus all living forms meet their end:
life and death woven
in the leaving of this world.

A BUNCH OF COCONUTS

See the coconut tree,
its upraised fronds
buried in the sky,
shuddering in the wind.

The unripe fruit
huddles close
in sleep together.
At its base, a mother
trembles in sorrow
longing for news
of her missing
children.

She's heard nothing.
She burns in pain,
her chest aflame squeezing
the orb of her heart.

Where have they disappeared to?
They used to sleep
arrayed
large and small,
like coconuts in a cluster.
Her children scattered,
her children gone forever,
the mother inconsolable.

Translated from Khmer by Christophe Macquet and Sharon May

PRINCE AMRINDO SISOWATH

A Cry

Written and published in the mental asylum Sainte-Anne

A cry rings out to the far end of night
A cry that rises from heaven's throat
Oh, these uncertain abysses into which we fall
These hands that save us from slipping away altogether

A cry like a cloak of light
Covering the nakedness of the present moment
And then these dreams raised like scaffolds
To reach our inner joy
As if we had no other company than ourselves
A chapped cry from the winter of our lips
A cry that scratches itself along the nape of our bones
A cry silent as a bridal veil
A hesitant cry that staggers, swirls at the edges of our teeth
A cry that hurries as if late for a rendezvous
A cry of a dying beast
A cry that wants to reclaim an abolished past
A cry that's remained in a glove compartment
Like a bullet in a revolver
But this cry is not mine
It belongs to another who looks like me
This cry of a desperate woman
This cry that now dances around the heaps of your eyes
It asks for cues from no one
A cry that is sovereign unto itself
This cry is only a visitor in me
It puts on its white overcoat to walk in the rain
Now it crosses the Danube of your sex
And launches fireworks at your loins

This cry that needs no urging
Is now happy to scream
As if it were about to go on television
This cry that can't be held back by a sea of humanity
Is building barricades around the Ministry of Human Rights
And gathers now around a puddle of blood
This cry that had no birth
It remembers now
The original source

That first cry on the first morning of the world.

Translated from French by Christophe Macquet and Sharon May

PEN SAMITTHY

Bound to His Father

A calf reaches to see what's beyond the embankment
but the rope passed through his nose restrains him.
In pain from the recent piercing, he retreats,
lowers his head and sniffs the ground, stuck.

The nearby seedlings look so fresh and tender.
The wind flutters through them, he aches with hunger.
But the taut rope holds him back
and fetters his hopes—he's not going anywhere.

An old frog emerges from her burrow,
awakened by a drumroll of thunder. Its message:
rain is coming, prepare yourself
for the blessings of the gracious sky.

She sees the poor, tethered calf
whose nose has just been pierced.
Her heart swells with pity, she whispers:
Do you see the post to which your rope is attached?

That is the shin bone of your father.
It's your karma, little one, to be roped to his bones.
He died and all that's left of him is his tibia
which a peasant made into a stake to tie you down.

The calf stands, dumbstruck, shaken to the core.
The inheritance from his father, to whom
he owes so much respect, is a spike driven in the earth,
binding him in place, where he turns in endless circles.

Translated from Khmer by Christophe Macquet and Sharon May

HUOT IV

What Would You Like to Eat?

Huot Iv wrote this poem in 1993 while living in France. In 1996, he set some of his poems to music and recorded an album, with singing by Koy Vanna, which was popular in the Khmer diaspora in Paris. "What Would You Like to Eat?" is from that record and is sung to the tune of "Chanthou" (Tuberose Flower), a famous Sinn Sisamouth song. CM/SM

Tell me, beautiful, what would you like to eat?
An orange, elephant apple, June plum, lychee, or mangosteen?
What fruit makes your mouth water?
A green *lhuot* mango or a tart santol?
Pineapple, jackfruit, durian?
Star gooseberry, gold apple, or carabao teats so red and velvety?
How about a mango of the *pumsaen* variety?

The fruits of our Khmer country have such particular flavors:
Mango plum, sour or sweet; tangy cherry plum, ripe jungle fruit fresh off the
    kuy vine,
Milk fruit, egg fruit, banana, figs of such distinctive taste,
Sliced sugar cane, wild red korlan, Burmese grapes,
Or just coconut milk and honey?
How about a round, firm persimmon, or hard *kralanh*?
Or the pale jelly of the sugar palm used in tasty cakes?

Tell me, my sweet, what would you like to eat?
I'll cross mountains, forests, plains, all roads for you.
Tell me, my heart, what makes you dream?
A great elephant mango or fragrant muskmelon?
A *ktih* coconut with perfumed flesh, or sour tamarind picked along the road?
Jujube, Bengal quince, plumrose, or jambolan?
Or just a few lotus seeds, a few grains of boiled corn?

Dearest, which of our country's fruits delights you most?
Sapodilla, starfruit, papaya, *okrang* mango?
A watermelon too large to wrap your arms around?
Guava, custard apple, kusum clusters, braids of longans?
Or would you prefer those bananas growing by the fence?
Let me pick them for you and place them on your tongue,
then pluck the courage to take your hand and cross Love's Bridge.

Translated from Khmer by Christophe Macquet and Sharon May

KONG BUNCHHOEUN

The Race of the Quick

Editors' Note
A comprehensive Cambodian peace agreement was signed in Paris in 1991, promising Cambodians sovereignty and free elections. However, multiple parties vied for power, most significantly the Khmer Rouge; the Cambodian People's Party, headed by Hun Sen; and King Norodom Sihanouk's royalist FUNCINPEC party, headed by his son, Prince Ranariddh. A compromise led to a government with two rival prime ministers, appointed by Sihanouk, who had been reinstalled as head of state. By 1997, military clashes had broken out among multiple factions, cooperation was in tatters, and the country was in chaos. "The Race of the Quick" was written in 1994.

Those who've come to know
the Khmer might say the word
"Khmer" really means "quick":
Quick to meet, quick to love;
Quick to change and change back;
Quick to conceal, then reveal;
Quick to anger, quick to heal;

Quick to fear, but then fearless;
Quick their fill, quick their hunger;
Quick to give, then take back;
Quick to cry, quick to laugh;
Quick to lack, quick to exceed;
Quick to meet, then take leave;
Quick to grovel, quick to stand;

Quick to be rich, quick to be poor;
Quick to evil, quick to good;
Quick to value, quick to cheapen;
Quick to bend, quick to break off;

Ploys and wiles, cons and tricks;
Quick to bloom, quick to fade;
Quick to bow, quick to rise;

Quick to win, quick to lose;
Quick to vex, quick to enrage;
Quick to loathe, quick to kiss;
First loyal, but then a traitor;
First scared, then aroused;
Quick to awe, quick to fright;
Quickly tickled, quick to take flight;

First bland, then too salty;
Quick the night, quick the day;
Quick to run, quick to walk;
First weak, then too strong;
Quick to roast, quick to burn;
Quick to halt, but then not quite;
Quick to rise, quick to fall;

Quick to learn, quick to forget;
Quick to listen, but quickly deaf;
Quick to "No!" then quick to "Yes!";
Their unity so quickly breaks,
But just as quickly is restored;
Quick to hate, quick to love;
So skinny, then so fat;

Quick to heat, quick to cool;
Quick the depths, quick the shallows;
Quick to walk, quick to run;
Quick the bitter, quick the sweet;
Quick to take more, quick to do without;
Quick to join, quick to part;
Quick to stumble, quick to watch out.

Because of this "quick"
The Khmer slipped and fell
Into the muck and mire.
Now that we're free
The Khmer should try not
To slip and slide down
To such darkness again.

If we are still quick,
then things will be a mess.
They'll tear us in shreds.
We must think with care
Before changing our approach,
For if we bungle things again,
What methods will free us?

Don't be quick to panic.
When tongues only click,
you hiss and strike.
Worried the hare will fly,
You let the snakehead go.
Peace, that thin waif,
might it slip away again?

Translated from Khmer by Trent Walker

YIN LUOTH

The Fate of Bloodsuckers

Not all mosquitos that suck our blood
suffer the same fate.
Some do their work at night,
others go about it in broad daylight.

Some bite us right on the face,
and we put an end to them with a slap.
Others escape destruction
by staying just out of reach.

Some gorge themselves until
their bellies swell like balloons,
stuffed beyond reason
until they can no longer fly.

Some, bloated with blood, graze
the sheets. And when we see them there
we want to crush them without mercy,
wipe them off the face of the earth.

Translated from Khmer by Christophe Macquet and Sharon May

PICH TUM KRAVEL

from *Songs of the Fighting Crickets*

Actor, playwright, and poet Pich Tum Kravel was one of the most famous performing artists in the 1960s and 1970s. After the Khmer Rouge regime ended, he was instrumental in restoring Cambodian arts from the 1980s until his death in 2015. "The Ox with the Broken Hoof" is written in me buon *meter (four lines of four syllables), a very compressed form often used in folk songs. "Man and Krasang" is composed in Crow's Gait meter (seven-line stanzas of four syllables per line). "The Sun Turns Leprous" takes up a classical Khmer theme, since the fall of Angkor, of the "upside down world"—its surreal images of eclipses and comets draw on traditional Asian prophecies.* CM/SM

THE OX WITH THE BROKEN HOOF

Because an ox with a broken hoof
has limped all day,
its brutal master beats
the animal near to death.

Alas for the big boss
with the thick brain
who batters his ox's back,
it's not the beast who will perish.

Nearby a cobra full of venom
clowns around the man's feet.
At just the right moment,
it strikes him dead.

MAN AND KRASANG

In the dry season
a man stops to rest
and roll a cigarette
in the shade of a *krasang* tree.
He smokes under its branches,
next to an earthen ridge,
in front of a pumpkin field.

krasang (Feroniella lucida) is a fruit-bearing tree native to Southeast Asia

He grumbles to himself:
"If you think about it
deeply you'll see that
this world is flawed.
Nature got things wrong.
Why make a pumpkin
the size of a basket?

Why give such magnificence
to a lowly breed that creeps
as a vine along the ground,
while the tall *krasang* tree,
with its generous shade,
gets fruit smaller than your wrist?
It's just not right.

Now if the great *krasang* had fruit
the size of ripe pumpkins—
that would be fitting and make sense."
Just then a whirlwind rises,
roaring through the *krasang*
like an airplane, spinning
through the branches.

The wind charges the boughs,
nearly breaking them.
The violent shaking
knocks the fruit to the ground.
One lands *bang!*
on the head of our man,
who briefly sees stars.

Startled, he covers his head
with his hands and cries:
"*Yi!* Mother Nature was right!
As hard as iron, if the *krasang* fruit
was the size of a pumpkin,
it would have smashed my skull
and surely sent me six feet under!"

THE SUN TURNS LEPROUS

The sun turns leprous
under its mosquito net.
The moon catches scabies,
and a star grows a tail.

A mosquito carries an elephant
in its mouth to use as bait.
A smelly old tiger
swallows the mosquito's lure.

The tiger's caught on the hook,
but a mouse deer feels the pain.
And that is how the mosquito
sucks the blood of all creatures.

A chicken egg takes offense
and makes a terrible decision.
For the honor of his clan,
he challenges a stone.

The egg makes a flying start.
He's weighed the pros and cons
and knows he will be broken, but at least
he will have soiled the stone.

Translated from Khmer by Christophe Macquet and Sharon May

CHATH PIERSATH

Two Poems

EXITING INTERVIEW

Do you remember the month or the exact day of your birth?

Have you been anywhere outside your village?
Do you have properties in your name?
Do you want to go now or do you want to stay?
How many children are you leaving?
Do you have any other relatives who will care for them when you're
    gone?
How old are your children?
What inheritance are you leaving for them?
Is this your thatched-roof house?
How about these pots and pans?
Do you own land?
Are these your regrets?
How often have you known grief and sorrow?
Who mistreated you?
How did you arrive in poverty?
How did you come to loneliness?
Did you have a first love?
Was the marriage what you expected?
Was it an arranged marriage?
Who was your husband?
Do you know him?
Do you have AIDS?

MY BROTHER THAY

That night he slept under the guava trees
On a bamboo bed beneath a canopy of stars.
His older brother feared that he would infect his children
If he let him inside his thatched house.

He died with his eyes open.
The virus spread its attack and pushed him with cold stiff feet.
It was silly to be monogamous.
There was no point to quit either drinking or smoking
The night he slept under the guava trees.

BUNKONG TUON

Four Poems

MOON IN KHMER

You are light
when the sun is punched out
and darkness reigns.

You are the antidote
to what came before:

black blood, black heart,
hands tied, kneeling before
a ditch of human bones.

Your laughter pierces
the silence of night
that bore witness
to the once blood-soaked land.

Your existence is resistance
to the genocide that orphaned
your father and drove
his family out of the homeland.

You are love against
the hate of the Khmer Rouge.

This is the meaning
of your name, Chanda.

This is how to defeat Pol Pot.

AN ELEGY FOR A FELLOW CAMBODIAN

The reason Vannark got into that fight
    was because Rob had called him a dog-eater.

LIVING IN THE HYPHEN

Thanksgiving.
Driving home from school with a migraine
I pulled over and vomited on the side of Route 2.
I had been working on an article exploring
the implications of Bhabha's third space, searching
for a theory of an authentic hyphenated, diasporic, transnational,
(or was it post-national?) transglobal Asian-American identity.

When I arrived at my family's home,
my fifteen-year old cousin Thearith, the tallest
in our extended family, was having dinner.
Born in the States, he greeted me in his perfect
Bostonian accent. I watched him attack his steak.

On the table, with the dishes
of rice and steak, were two plates:
One contained a Khmer dipping sauce,
made of *prahok*, lime juice, lemongrass,
grilled peppers, garlic, and Thai chilies;
the other, **A.1.** Steak Sauce
from the local Stop & Shop.

"Thearith, why do you have two sauces for your steak?"

"Well, when I get bored with one sauce, I go for the other.
It's all good, bro."

FISHING FOR TREY PLATOO

You might have seen them
fishing on the shores of the Cape Cod Canal:

My uncle in his fisherman's hat
pulling in a one-foot scup, my aunt in her pajama-like

pants walking backward up the bike path,
snapping a line that's gotten stuck between the rocks,

my other aunt reeling in a sea bass,
her husband by her side directing.

Bikers, joggers, teenagers and their dates,
families with their children look curiously on.

Or maybe you have seen them
lining up all three sides of a pier in Salem,

their wrists jerking in a language
that bewitches the squids below.

They are not the only ones.
Other Cambodians and Vietnamese, once enemies,

fish side by side on the same American pier.
Other immigrants—Chinese, Spanish, Portuguese

speaking languages I can't understand—come together
on this spot: sacred rods in hands, beckoning the squid.

Or maybe you have seen them
under a bridge fishing the Providence River,

looking for *trey platoo,* a type of mackerel
they used to eat in the refugee camps in Thailand.

Sometimes, my aunts and uncles run into an old friend
from those long-ago days. They talk about the lack

of food, of sneaking out at night to fish, and of running,
always running, from the Thai police.

They exchange phone numbers, share fishing secrets,
and set up a time and place where they'll fish together again.

When they get home, my aunts gut the fish,
clean them, fry them, and put them in a boiling stew

of galangal, lemongrass, and kaffir leaves.
My uncles and aunts sit in a circle on the floor,

eat, and tell stories of how this fish got away
or how one of them got caught by the Thai police.

No matter how hard they try, they can never understand
why my cousin and I ever bother with fishing—

why we catch and release food, as if it's some sport.

PRINCESS MOON

Two Poems

BLESSING DANCE

bless the full moon,
our eldest ancestor.
your fingers gently combing through the Mekong River.
bless the apples harvested by my mother during the war.
bless her first bite during starvation.
bless this game of death.
how quickly I've learned that the bruised are discarded.

bless the fireworks,
the red wine,
the American dream.
bless my mother's triggers,
the loud celebrations that make her cringe.
bless the sun that turns her skin red.
how she stays inside to hide from it now.
bless the factory jobs,
especially the illegal ones,
the only ones in our new English-speaking cities.

bless my father.
bless his ghost.
bless our parents and their silence.
bless the invention of internalization.
the fears we were born with.
bless my mother for not knowing how to cope with
my traumas, my sister's traumas,
my brother's traumas.

bless us for not knowing how to help our mother heal.
bless the generational gap.
this undeserving culture shock.
bless my first language and my parents' second.

bless my second language and my parents' first.
bless the Khmer phrases my mother has taught me.
how they sound simple like *troam* but mean
to survive this heartbreakingly painful struggle in your life.
bless not knowing how to describe your tormenting pain.
bless our girls.
please.

bless our mothers.
bless the men who know how to make our mothers cry.
bless the first time I heard her cry in the shower.
bless the first time she cried in front of me.
how she was sharing her stories of the ghosts of the genocide.
how we both would be ghosts if she didn't escape.
bless our survivors
and bless our war babies.
bless the stomachs that birthed us of landmines and starvation.
bless the conditions that still leave us hungry,
crying,
begging for more.
bless the boys I still love that only tried to kill me.
bless the broken homes I've learned from.
bless the men my mother only loved to keep us alive.
bless this strategy.
bless my former stepfather.
the one that shattered the glass coffee table with his foot.
how I wish it were my mouth then.
bless my sister for finding me in the closet.
the first fear I've ever felt.
bless my second fear of being watched.
bless my babysitter,
and his newborn daughter.
bless her the most.
bless that he doesn't repeat history with his own kin.
bless the men that were supposed to be my heroes,
but bless them for the fucked-up things they have to live with.
bless my brother,
a true gentleman.
bless this dance we were born to perform.
how exhausting it is to do this to our bodies.
to dance around death,
but also,
to survive.

DANCE, DANCE, DANCE

my parents met in the dark while
    escaping the genocide.
they relied on the reflection of the pale moon
    against their skin for guidance.
dad said that mom was glowing like an angel.

in the Cambodian culture,
an apsara is a goddess of earth and water.
they are heavenly dancers.
I've learned about them to know what it means
    to be Cambodian.
I've read somewhere that
apsaras are often the wives of musicians.
I do not know if this is true,
but it makes a lot of sense to me.

back in the day,
dad used to be quite the charmer.
before the PTSD kicked in,
he was a ghostwriter for the Cambodian music label,
The Golden Butterfly.

if you listen closely to all the albums,
you'll know exactly which songs are about mom.
she learned how to dance in a refugee camp
    in Thailand.
she's never stopped practicing.

it's been twenty years now
that dad's been gone,

but you can still hear his voice ringing in the hallway.
a scratched vinyl on a broken record player,
all your favorite cassette tapes
                  s t r e t c h e d   a p a r t
and thrown into the wood stove.
I catch my mom dancing in the kitchen.
she says,

      the acoustics here are the best.

dad is a distant choke gargling in the sink.
I watch her move for him.
her wings
draped in gold
and heavy with
the curse.

we are both in constant battles with our bodies.
mom tells me to stop dancing
in fear that I will become
my mother's daughter:
a lover of men who leave after teaching us
               how to move for them.
she says,

marry someone with the music not stitched into their skin.
or you'll just end up like me.
a sad snake returning home
to its charmer.

KOSAL KHIEV

Three Poems

DREAM

I sometimes dream of a cell
with a cold stainless-steel sink,
polished with toothpaste.
Shiny glossed mirror reflects back my humble beginnings.
I sometimes hear the key chains dangling
Chiming echoes of yesterday's meal
being fed through a steel slot.
Hearing fishing lines swish like cars built too reckless,
too fast to notice the wreckage
they've left behind.
I sometimes feel their longing
To belong, and be a part of something much greater than themselves.
Feel their thundering rage in a cage too small to contain.
And when one falls
Like a tree cut down in a dense forest.
Only the surrounding foliage weep.
The world sleeps in silence.
And I, along with them, dream.

REWIND

Step back rewind relapse recap my mind see if you can feel that..
Young cat strap with dreams of big cash.
Snap-back
Hat flip back tryin to flip racks…
But the hood was full of snitch rats…
Turned through the *click clack*…
Back then when we was riff raffs…
Running cold, with that hood rag…
Trying to be good…
But misunderstood with a no-good dad…
But don't misunderstand I never had…
So, I ran with the hood, till I got wrapped by them new jacks…
Never knew the hood could do that…
Pulled fourteen plus an extra year for that hood laugh…
So, tell me now, if I should have pulled that…
But too late…
That hammer came with a good slap…
Shook my world, and I was gone for a good lap…
The first step was brutal…
The next thousand crucial…
Forked roads, that moved through the sutures…
With a future unknown, I was moving towards my future…
But by the next thousand, I was drowning…
Under ice…
Heart pounding, frozen in life…
I was in nomansland…
A man with no country, I was in Nomansland…
With a spirit so hungry, with a yearning to understand…
But a learning had to be done first hand…
Now it's back to the homeland…
Back to the first strand…
Seems like mother been calling all of her nomads…
Come back home but I'm still roaming like no dad…
It's so sad… so I flow rap…
Naw more like poetry, without a toe tag…
Cause this is life giving and I'm giving it back…

PEACE IN PIECES

My heart cries after mass, collided with mass.
The blast deafening.
What's left, is flesh turned to ash.
Our own reckoning.
When can we scream, "At last, at last"?
But the wars never cease to be ending.
In streets, and blocks,
in countries, in locks,
in mass, and mosques,
in masks,
beneath the cloth.
For causes forgotten, long before we ever remembered,
    if we ever had cause.
So, this is a cry to the forgotten, and lost.
For the ones rotten, and gone.
Buried beneath stone, and rubble.
Where gunpowder meets metal.
Where the power of the sun, is held, and wielded by men,
    who claim to be God's sons.
But none held truth.
Only lies, twisted through the tongues of snakes,
    forked to hiss out venom.

So you tell him.
Why his mother and father is gone?
Why his sisters and brothers isn't home?
Why he's alone?
In a world too cold to care if he's warm.

So, I'm storming these walls.
Refracting light in spite of being born in the dark.
"Hark" the raven's call.
Witness how angels fall.
See, how we strangle, and dangle, struggling to walk?
While some voices, struggle to talk.
You see, my heart cried after mass, collided with mass.
The blast deafening.
What's left, is flesh turned to ash.
Our own reckoning.
When can we scream at last, at last?!?!

Reincarnation

I came of age
in the arms of Lord Shiva.
He welcomes with stone,
sculpted arms.
I slurp curry, crimson
as a monk's robe
tinged with the sun
on his morning alms,
what locals call "pig's blood."

I think of you
as the wind in Battambang.
I hear Mother's murmur
as she searches for her past
on the stranger's land.
What remains of you is gone.
Sandals kick the dirt
into a hiss of spray.

The cold night you died
boughs of palm trees shuddered.

A smokescreen of incense covers our relatives.
Palms clutch apologies
chant in Pali before your name,
inscribed on offerings.

We are a family of alliterations,
shared consonants echo
generations in every utterance.

Sothear, Sothy, Srou, Sri, Srau, Sreng,
Sarah, Soriya, Han, Haun,
Phai, Phoun, Phoum, Pho, Pheng
Sokunthary, Sokuntharith.

MYLO LAM

Ma's Canh Chua Recipe: April–December 1975

This poem was years in the making, spanning decades of listening to and overhearing my mom share pieces of her eight-month journey from Phnom Penh to the border of Vietnam in 1975. It was impossible for me to learn all the details of her story in one sitting, especially one of bloodshed, which was told in a language other than English and occurred thirteen years before I was born in Saigon. I overheard the first fragment when I was eight and walked into a room where my mom was speaking softly to my crying older sister, telling her about seeing blood in a morning river, presumably from murdered Cambodian prisoners. One of the last pieces was told in a car on the way back from the hospital where my dad was dying; I asked my mom if she would have married him if they hadn't been forced to flee from the Khmer Rouge. Even now, I don't have the story right. The narrator in this poem is unreliable; the gaps are canyons filled with mist. But I work to see glimpses of something more on the other side.

Canh chua is the Vietnamese version of "sour soup." It has derivations in many Southeast Asian countries, including samla mchu *in Cambodia.*

INGREDIENTS

¾ cup of "I barely know this man"
½ teaspoon of "I barely know his father"
6 cups of "I guess we're all running away together now"
2 tamarind pods – picked from the tallest tree in the middle of a storm
1 pineapple – quartered and sliced (good luck)
2 tomatoes – quartered and sliced (good luck)
  bean sprouts – as many as you can get your hands on
1 catfish – avoid the blood swimming downstream, if possible
  Protein alternatives:
  • 1 handful of escargots (i.e., edible snails)
  • 1 non-venomous snake (go for the head with a blunt object)
8 cups water – again, avoid the blood
dash of whichever herbs and spices you can scrounge or barter for:
  • Thai basil
  • red chili pepper
  • garlic
sugar (get some from a fruit?)
1 deck of cards

INSTRUCTIONS

1. Two weeks before April 17, have a dream. All around you is fire except for a 40-foot statue of Quan Am off in the distance.
2. Flee Phnom Penh. When your boyfriend tells you to run away with his family, refuse. That relationship isn't going to last anyway.
3. Be on the run for two weeks. Then, while running through the fields, see your boyfriend and his father chasing after you. No one else in their family is with them.
4. For safety reasons, collect ingredients late at night/early in the morning and with a lookout.
    - For the tamarind, have someone at the base of the tree, ready to catch it.
5. Add water to a pot and bring to a boil.
    - While water boils, play cards to pass the time.
6. Add catfish/escargots/snake to pot.
7. Add sugar.
8. Mash tamarind to a fine pulp (feel free to use same blunt object used to kill snake).
    - As your boyfriend sits there, realize you'll probably have his children.
    - Look over to your boyfriend's dad, realize he'll be your father-in-law.
    - Say nothing.
9. Add tomatoes and cook for 2 minutes, then turn off heat.
10. Toss in bean sprouts, garlic, and Thai basil.
11. Quietly enjoy this meal.
12. Eight months later, get to the border of Vietnam.
    - Wait until the sun rises on January 1st.
    - Have your future father-in-law use what little Vietnamese he knows to get you in.
    - Hope you can get the ingredients needed to make proper canh chua.
13. Have a dream you're walking down a narrow concrete stairway, leading to the outside. At the base is a two-headed snake gazing at you.
    - Realize you're pregnant with your first daughter.

GREG SANTOS

from *Ghost Face*

I grew up in Montreal, Quebec, as a transracial adoptee of Cambodian descent who was raised by Canadian immigrant parents of Portuguese and Spanish heritage. My comfort foods included rotisserie chicken, fries, sugar pie, chorizo, paella, and pastéis de nata—*Portuguese egg-custard tarts. I have to admit that I didn't really know what Cambodian food was; nor did I know anything about Khmer heritage. Considering I was not immersed in its language or culture, how could I?*

In elementary school, I never understood why my teachers would confuse me with the two South Asian boys in my class. My name was Gregory. I am not from India. For much of my life, I did not identify as Asian, even if I looked the part. I was a Montrealer with Iberian heritage and spoke Spanish with my grandparents.

As the story goes, my adopted parents had always wanted children but were unable to have any of their own. A family acquaintance who worked with immigrants and refugees knew my birth mother, a teenager who was unable to raise me but was steadfast about finding a loving family for me. From the time I was an infant, I was part of a supportive environment and was always made to feel cherished. My adopted family raised me to be "color blind," and would tell me I would be loved and appreciated no matter my color.

It wasn't until I became a parent with two children of my own that I realized if I were to dig deeper into my own roots, it would help them reclaim and understand the diversity of their heritages. My collection Ghost Face, *from which the following poems are gathered, is the result of my working on this for over ten years. I view the book as a memoir in a poetic stream, touching on themes of absences, family mythologies, loss, parenthood, and ultimately hopefulness. These poems are a gift to my children and family. They are a record of my grappling with questions of identity, struggling with losses such as the devastating death of my adopted father when I was a teenager, and learning how to embrace the full spectrum of my Canadian, Khmer, Spanish, and Portuguese heritages.*

I carry on trying to fill in some of the gaps of my childhood by connecting with other adoptees and fellow Khmer diaspora writers and artists. I am so grateful to have been welcomed with such warm and generous spirits.

Thank you. A kun. Gracias. Obrigado.

OUR NAME

Can I ask you something?

Yes.

What was your name?

I don't know.

What do you mean you don't know?

I don't know if you don't know.

But we have a blood connection.

Yes.

Do you know if we had any siblings?

… A sister named Preah Neang.

Whoa.   Really? Do you know what that name means?

It means princess in Khmer.

That's amazing. How did you know that?

I Googled it. Or how about Pich? That means diamond.

Oh.

DEAR GHOSTS

On a cold rainy spring evening
as I was drifting off to sleep
M showed me a passage
from a new book.

> *Here, a part about the universe:*
> *Atoms.*

Atoms, such a beautiful word.
Like cellar door and hope.

> *Read this.*
> *You might want it for your book.*

In it, I read how when things die,
their atoms don't disappear or cease to exist
but are redistributed.

An ancient fern becomes coal.
This lump of coal becomes a diamond.
And on and on until
the atoms of the fern are nothing but

>   a speck

in the web of my open palm.

Your faces flash
in the attic of my memory.
You are welcome spirits.

I toss off the covers, rush to my office.
I am struggling to capture this moment,
how do I grasp these silvery apparitions?

> The moment is gone
>   and I'm left grasping
>   grasping for something to hold.

The distant sound of our dishwasher,
some light rain outside and it's

                        gone gone gone.

    Redistributed away.

Dear ghosts,
where do your atoms reside?

Father.

Tata. Nano. Vovo. Chico. My grandparents.

The birth family I never knew.

I like to think that you still inhabit our planet.

    We contain multitudes, right?

The galaxy in the speck of a birthmark—
the one that I call my chocolate spot
    My *chocolatito plus*
that cannot be smudged off.

A planet. A galaxy.
The cosmos. Heaven.

In the palm of my hand.
The size of a mustard seed.
Head of a needle.
Where angels reside.

SHALL WE DANCE?

The Mars InSight Lander
touched down on the red planet
on November 26, 2018.
I am 37 years old.
At the beginning of December,
some space wind blows past a seismometer
and is recorded by NASA to study Marsquakes.
How odd it feels to write down that word!
On this date, December 7, 2018,
as my children cut through water
during their swimming lessons,
twirling about as if in zero gravity,
I click on a link from my laptop.
Wind blasts across the Lander's solar panels
and I am an earthling on this tiny blue planet
listening to Martian wind for the first time.
Today I get a haircut,
shrug on a blazer for an evening party,
mingle amid the clinking of wine glasses.
We celebrate the holidays.
Listen.
Heard best with earphones,
can you hear that low pitch?
It is Mars's heartbeat.
There is so much darkness right now,
the building of walls,
our deep-rooted fear of aliens.
Yet we are alive.
We are alive to hear a Martian zephyr,
so privileged to hear the first sounds
ever recorded on another planet.
Today I woke up to my son snuggling me,
awakened by his words,
"You are the best daddy ever."
I feel so lucky.
To be the best daddy ever.
To be alive right now.

I admit I do not always feel this grateful.
Small irritant, micro-aggressions
have a tendency to ruin the day.
The gravity of our world
always pushing down on our fragile bodies.
We are not always thankful.
But today I am.
I hope you are, too.
For an instant in the grand scheme of things,
I am thankful.
To feel this alien wind blow across my heart
is but a reminder that I have lived
to hear my children's breath,
a zephyr,
a reminder that I am sharing this tender moment
between our planet and Mars.

Dear Earthlings and Martians,
may we continue sharing this
grateful space dance together for eons.

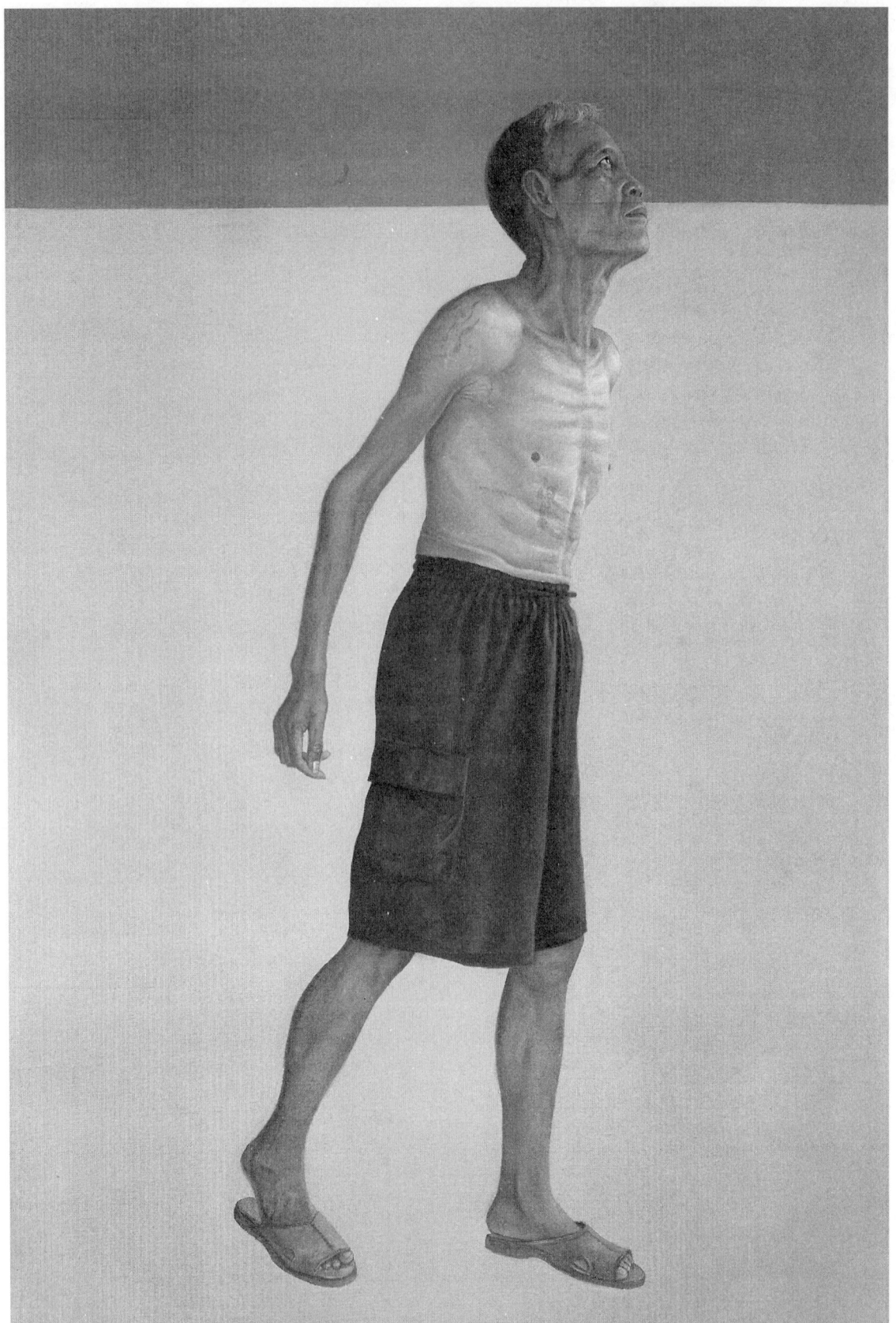

NOU HACH

from Wilted Flower

First published in 1947 in the weekly Kampuchea, Wilted Flower *(Phka Srapon) remains one of the most widely read and influential pieces of modern literature in Khmer. Appearing in book form in 1959, it was incorporated into the official high school curriculum in 1969 and is still taught today. Within a tradition of Khmer literature as social critique, Nou Hach became one of the early Khmer writers to experiment with the novel form. Set in Battambang province, the story follows the journey of two young people on the cusp of adulthood. What sets it apart from other love stories of the period is the attention Nou Hach gives to the female protagonist. While the author endows Vitheavy with the outward virtues of a traditional Khmer woman, his portrayal lays bare her inner turmoil. The first two chapters, translated here, showcase his elegant and engaging style.* **VR**

CHAPTER 1

The train barrels like a cyclone through hollong forests and bamboo groves. It hurtles past streams and cuts through mountains, emitting a thundering roar that resounds through the earth. Soon it leaves behind the mountain range and jungle. If one peers through any of the windows, one sees the dark-gray dikes of rice paddies forming a checkerboard darting in reverse. Rice fields! Rice fields!—vast and continuous, reaching all the way to the edges of the woods, a vista of endless emerald. Water brims the paddies, sparkling and clear, rippling with waves in the breeze, young shoots swaying in undulating green. Here and there flowers bloom—purple morning glory, crimson cosmos, and deep-yellow marigold—as if to further embellish a landscape already endowed with rolling sky and the warmth of a blazing sun. White and blue egrets, in flocks or pairs, search for food, feasting on snails clustering in the water. A little farther away, wild ducks chase one another among the water lilies. Farmers in muddied black clothes look up from their planting to stare at the speeding train, eyes blinking curiously.

A group of high school students is traveling together back home to Battambang for a two-month break. In celebration some play their bamboo flutes, others clap along and thump on the wooden floorboards, while still others bellow out movie tunes sung by the French actor Tino Rossi. A boy named Bunna, with a peculiar talent for impersonation, parodies the Kru Achar, their teacher, causing an explosion of laughter to reverberate in a deafening cacophony. Those of a gentler nature are content to stand at the windows and watch sparrows in flight, peasants at work, scene after moving scene, feeling a kind of camaraderie with the landscape.

A grand vacation! Understandably, happiness fills the students' hearts. Two months! The very notion opens wide the horizon, the possibilities ahead. They feel as exhilarated as birds released from a cage, their bodies so light it seems they could as well drift away with the clouds. Like drunks, they are intoxicated with their newfound liberty. Two whole months! They've never had a break this long, experienced the sustained joy of knowing they are free from daily lessons. Goodbye, heavy books with subjects that make the head throb! Goodbye, the voice of the Kru Achar that threatens and forces, chastises, and critiques! Goodbye, flea-ridden beds! Goodbye, cafeteria that assaults the nose with putrid smells! And alas, goodbye, friends and rivals... *Goodbye, goodbye!* They will see again their families and loved ones. They will sleep as long as they wish, eat until they're no longer hungry, and romp about as they please. *A break for two months!—hooray!*

It's hard to imagine how anyone could be sad amid the rowdy jubilation. But there's an eighteen-year-old who sits alone, looking forlorn. He appears to be of Chinese descent, an athletic-looking youth of average height, with an oval face and light skin and thick black hair that flutters wildly in the wind. His white clothes, cut in European fashion, are stained all over, intensifying the gravity of his expression.

Ou Sralau Station! The young man stands up and looks out the window to the east. Suddenly, memories come unbidden, soothing his spirit like a welcome breeze in the hot months. Oh, these fields of rice, this stretch of stream! Oh, the clangs of wooden bells on herds of cows and water buffaloes grazing the grassland! No matter how many times he encounters these sights and sounds, the young man never tires of them. If anything, he feels his attachment to the land deepen, as though it were a beloved friend. "Oh, birthplace of mine," he thinks to himself, "you're separated from me only by two more rivers."

The train rumbles onward. With only fifteen kilometers left until their destination, the students collect their belongings and close their suitcases. Those concerned with appearance rush to the restroom to wash their faces, comb their hair, straighten their hats and ties, put on their sunglasses. Bunthoeun, the youth with the grieving expression, pulls the train ticket from his pocket and heaves his suitcase, the leather worn from frequent traveling back and forth. He feels his heart beating faster as the train nears his beloved town. It trundles past the rest stop of Ou Dombong, crosses the steel bridge, pauses briefly at Wat Kundeng Temple, and then rounds the stretch of paddies to the left of the Sangkae River. Finally, the gray wall of the town jailhouse appears, followed by wooden homes and buildings. The train crawls slowly toward the station, where a crowd is waiting, and the passengers all rise from their seats. The horn blares, and the locomotive comes to a complete stop alongside the station. Amid shouts, laughter, and hubbub, the passengers push against one another to disembark.

Bunthoeun dons his white cap, grips his suitcase with one hand, bids farewell to a couple of friends, shaking their hands, before extricating himself from the crowd to move toward the ticket collector standing at the door. He gives the man his ticket to examine and punch. Then he climbs on an auto rickshaw and says, "Take me to Kampong Preah."

The road from the town of Battambang to Kampong Preah village is the first colonial road, now known as National Route No. 5, which goes all the way to Phnom Penh. It's been tarred over and smoothed. The rickshaw soon passes out of the township, leaving behind the clusters of houses and residential buildings. Surprisingly, the next stretch is not desolate as he expected. Along the way, Bunthoeun encounters oxcarts and foot travelers and other motorized vehicles like his. Amid the distant hoots of the train, the road fills him with a sense of nostalgia as he recalls the voices and laughter of childhood friends. The sorrow he'd suppressed during the train journey now suddenly rises to his throat. He slips open the letter his sister Sopheak had sent before he left Phnom Penh and rereads it:

> *Dear Brother,*
>
> *I'm afraid to hide from you the misfortune that has recently befallen us, lest you accuse me of negligence. As you already knew from my previous letters, our father had ten thousand bushels of rice loaded onto his business partner's merchant boat to be transported to Saigon via the Tonle Sap Lake. I've just received definitive news that the barge capsized in the middle of the Great Lake during a typhoon. There is no hope of retrieving the grain. It is an enormous loss to us.*

As the words resound in his mind, Bunthoeun is once again overcome by shock. His dream vanishes, melting like salt in water. *I suppose I'll have to abandon my schooling and return here to help my parents in the fields.* He knew his father had struggled to gather the capital to purchase the grain, using up their savings as well as borrowing funds from creditors. Even if his father sells their home and land, there will be barely enough for them to live on after he repays the debts and interest incurred. *Such foolish ambitions I had with school—to go abroad, to further my studies—not to mention the promise made to my love that I'd take care of her in our life together… Father, Mother—I'm in turmoil…* The rickshaw speeds past villages scattered along the road. Anlong Vil… Chronik… Svay Kang. Villages with rich, fragrant soils. Bunthoeun does not take a moment to admire any of it, his feelings entangled in worries for the hardship ahead.

CHAPTER 2

A quiet night. Electric streetlamps cast bolts of golden light into the dark water of the Sangkae River, which flows and whirls swiftly. It is already ten o'clock.

On the eastern shore, crickets chirp languidly, and every so often an auto rickshaw buzzes across the metal bridge, carrying passengers back home to their villages from the market square where they've enjoyed a late-night snack of seafood porridge. Along the harbor lined with large tamarind trees growing in luxuriant profusion, young men gather in kiosks here and there to bask in the breeze and talk at leisure. In Wat Po Knong village, directly in front of the dock pointing toward a school on the opposite shore, sits a small stand beneath a sweet tamarind tree. But because there are not as many young men here as in other villages, the stand remains empty without a crowd to animate it.

On this night of our story, if a traveler came to rest at the stand beneath the sweet tamarind tree, he would hear a female voice, warm and melodious, floating softly from a house surrounded by greenery—a voice adrift in the air scented with the aromas of roses and jasmines, a voice as pure as crystal that leaves the listener besotted with its owner. Hearing it, the traveler would find it difficult to walk away, for it's rare to chance upon such music. If he turned his gaze eastward, he'd catch the glimmer of a kerosene lantern through the foliage and see a brick path leading to the stairs of a house with a gable roof, a covered veranda, and unvarnished wood plank walls that have turned pale gray in the rain and sun. In a plot near the veranda stands a small abode with metal sheet roofing and a rail of wooden posts along the front. Inside gleams a dark platform made from the heartwood of a bur tree, on which the inhabitants often recline in the breeze before turning in for the night. In this haven, protected by a sturdy enclosure and steady calm, live three women.

In her fifties, Old Mrs. Noun has begun to show signs of gray here and there, her hair shorn close to her scalp in keeping with the Buddhist precepts she faithfully observes. Her bright, piercing eyes and strong jaw reveal she is a woman of resolute, forceful character. Once her mind is made up, no one can convince her otherwise. Since her husband died, leaving her on her own, she has abandoned all business endeavors, focusing her efforts instead on protecting her possessions and assets for her daughter, whom she loves above all else.

Vitheavy is seventeen years old, a lovely girl with gentle manners, an oval-shaped face, and shoulder-length black hair. Quiet and shy, she always obeys her mother. When she was a young child, she studied at Wat Po Veal School, where her teachers constantly praised her sharp intellect. Upon entering womanhood, she stopped studying at her mother's bidding and instead occupied herself with household chores. But, in her free time, she would study Thai language and embroidery from a woman who lived nearby. In the span of several months, she'd learned enough to be able to read stories in Thai and become so skillful in her needlework that she would embroider decorative patterns onto curtains and pillowcases.

Finally, there's Grandma Phai, an elderly servant who's worked for the family since before Vitheavy was born. Many years older than the widowed Mrs. Nuon, Grandma Phai is wrinkly and silver-haired, with hardly a black strand visible. Vitheavy has always regarded her as family. Likewise, Grandma Phai has loved and cared for Vitheavy since infancy. She's never once entertained the thought of leaving her to go live elsewhere. To this day, she still calls Vitheavy "Little One."

On this night, Old Mrs. Nuon is full of worries, and to distract from her anxiety, she's asked Vitheavy to read to her from the *Legend of Preah Leaksenavong*. A large kerosene lantern is perched above them, and every time Vitheavy turns the page, the single stone on her ring flickers in the light, playing against the textures of her black traditional sarong and satiny rose-colored top. She reads with a resonating, melodic voice, captivating beyond compare. It's the same voice that the traveler would hear floating gently toward the mouth of the dock.

Old Mrs. Nuon lies solemnly beside her daughter on the platform, her gaze searching the ceiling, her mind on a quandary as jumbled as a ragged old broom that has neither end nor tip. Leaning against a wall, arms hugging her knees, Grandma Phai listens raptly with her mouth slightly ajar. When the ancient tale reaches the part in which Prince Leaksenavong—misled by the lies and deceits of the seductress Yisun—orders the executioner to kill his dear Pream Kaesar, the elderly servant cannot stop crying, the tears rolling furiously down her face. At another moment in the story when Pream Kaesar descends into madness because of the prince's betrayal and runs shrieking shamelessly through the market square, Grandma Phai angrily jumps up and exclaims, "I told you!—I told you not to fall for him. Men these days are like that—out with the old, in with new, without a care whatsoever!"

At these words, Vitheavy stops reading and turns to see Grandma Phai gesturing wildly. Giggling, the girl asks, "Why, what's the matter, Grandma Phai?"

The old servant looks dazed, as if she'd just woken. She stands stock-still for a second, then finally says, "Forgive me, Little One. It's just that I'm so angry! Angry at those who give no thought to their actions!"

Jolted out of her reverie by the servant's words, Old Mrs. Nuon sits up straight and murmurs, "Vy, that's enough reading. It's late now. We must rise early tomorrow to tend to our tasks."

Vitheavy hurriedly straightens up, pins her hair back in place, closes the book, and with the lantern, goes inside. Grandma Phai collects the betel-nut box and drinking bowls scattered on the floor and carries them inside. Soon after, all the doors and locks clang shut. Vitheavy blows out the lantern and scoots into bed next to her mother.

"Vy, are you feeling sleepy yet?"

"Not yet, Mother. Is something the matter?"

"Oh, nothing ... I want to talk with you a bit, though. You know Bunthoeun, don't you?"

Hearing his name, Vitheavy feels a surge of joy, but then, as she thinks about him, her apprehension grows. She fears something awful might have happened to her beloved. Hiding her agitation, she says, "Of course, Mother. I ... remember him well. When we were children, we used to play together."

"Then you probably know the story ... You see, when your father was still alive, he'd maintained a strong connection to Bunthoeun's family. Your father and Bunthon—the boy's father—were close friends who'd had much success together in their business ventures. So…" Old Mrs. Nuon pauses, as if unable to find the right words. "So, before he passed, your father made me promise that I keep you for Bunthoeun once he finishes his studies. Your father dared to think ahead about your marriage because he knew that his friend Bunthon had enough wealth to bequeath his children a comfortable life. But now… I'm very concerned. You see, their circumstances have been greatly reduced. In short, the family is nearly impoverished."

"Oh, may the Lord Buddha have pity!—I feel for them."

Old Mrs. Nuon acts like she hasn't heard her daughter and continues, "Over the years Bunthon has suffered loss after loss with his grain business, forcing him to dip deeper and deeper into the family's coffer. This rainy season, he borrowed a huge amount from the bank—ten thousand riels for the purchase of rice to be shipped to Saigon by way of the Tonle Sap. But now, you see, a storm has sunk the boat…" She lets her voice trail off.

Vitheavy again feels a rush of sympathy for Bunthoeun. If she had her own resources, she would hasten to help his family in their time of need. She tries to gauge her mother's feelings, her sense of generosity, but knows she cannot count on it.

A moment passes, then Old Mrs. Nuon resumes throatily, "Their savings are gone, along with the gold and silver. Whatever property they still have—their land and rice paddies—they'll have to sell it eventually in order to repay the bank and the people they've borrowed from. Once it's all gone, the hardship is inevitable. I don't know what I should do. I think of you first and foremost, of course. I don't have much to begin with, just enough to pass along so that you don't have to struggle. But now that Bunthoeun is poor…"

"Mother… it's wrong for you to speak like this. Bunthoeun may lack wealth, but he possesses something far more valuable: education. Once he gets his diploma—"

Annoyed with her daughter, Old Mrs. Nuon impatiently retorts, "He's the kind who'll roam around aimlessly, drink until he's drunk, and abandon his wife and children to their miseries."

"Mother, I've known Bunthoeun since we were both little children. He'll never become such a person."

"Who knows—who can ever tell! I see through you, understand all your feelings and thoughts. You want to depend on that diploma salary of thirty-plus riels a month! No matter how you budgeted it, it wouldn't be enough to feed yourselves, even with no debt to contend with. If he took on more loans, you'd surely be penniless. If I gave you any inheritance, your husband would use it to pay off what they owed. Believe me, daughter, in this world if you have money, any difficulty or challenge can be overcome. The way I see it, Bunthoeun bears an unfortunate karma. He's not meant to be your partner. That's why the *tevo-das*—the angels who protect and guide you—have caused such misfortune to befall his family, to show you that you have no connection to each other, you're not bound together by fate."

The widow takes a long pause; Vitheavy remains mute in the dark, eyes wide in alarmed dismay. Then her mother continues, "Don't be cross with me. You must take care to keep your emotions in check. Forget Bunthoeun. One day when you know security and ease, you'll realize that your mother was right."

The clock tolls the midnight hour. Old Mrs. Nuon says no more. She turns her back to her daughter and promptly falls sound asleep.

Vitheavy, choked with grief, lets her tears flow. She knows her mother is wrong about so many things, but she's a girl who's been taught to always listen and obey. She has never defied her mother. Moreover, she's shy and timid by nature, and when it comes to talk of marriage, she never voices her preferences or desires one way or another.

Bunthoeun!

She imagines him standing right in front of her. She recalls their childhood when they would play house together. She remembers a day not long ago when he waved goodbye to her as he left for Phnom Penh to take his entrance exam. Every evening during their separation, she would burn incense and pray to the *tevodas* for his success. She recalls how happy he was when he returned home after accomplishing what he'd set out to do. She remembers the time he read to her from the novel *Paul et Virginie*. She'd teasingly called him "my darling Paul," and he, in reply, had called her "my little darling Virginie." On the day he was leaving to study in Phnom Penh, he whispered in her ear, "Darling, four more years and we'll be together forever, never to be separated again."

Vitheavy, now in the throes of agony, cannot sleep, tossing and turning as if the bed and mat had burned to embers. Next to her Old Mrs. Nuon snores raucously. Outside the wind moans, hurling palm fronds onto the rose-apple trees. A rooster crows faintly every now and then, while a barn owl hoots, sending a chill even through those submerged in sleep.

Translated from Khmer by Vaddey Ratner

SUON SORIN

from *A New Sun Rises Over the Old Land*

Editors' Note
First published in 1961, eight years after Cambodia gained independence from French colonial rule, A New Sun Rises Over the Old Land *by Suon Sorin is an iconic work of modern Khmer literature. The novel follows the life of Sam, a young man who leaves the countryside to find work in the city as a cyclo driver, navigating a three-wheeled bicycle-taxi through the streets of Phnom Penh before the nation's independence. Sam wants to earn an honest living, but is constantly beaten down by greedy and corrupt landlords, factory bosses, and politicians, until he eventually becomes a local community leader. The following comes from one of the first full-length English translations of a modern Khmer novel.*

CHAPTER 2
THE LIFE OF A WORKER IN THE CITY

In the middle of the monsoon season, the rain falls heavily, saturating the land almost every day. This makes it hard for *cyclo* drivers to earn any income, since there aren't many passengers. Sam had to use some of the money that he had saved to pay the rental fee for his *cyclo*—the *cyclo* that would soon wear him out completely.

The sky had been darkened with rain for three days already; it rained almost without stopping.

And this morning was soaked with rain again. Sam sat in their little hut, his arms wrapped around his knees. He was worried about his poor wife, Soy. There was nothing at all of any value in the hut, just a mat for the floor, a pillow, and an old mosquito net. The *cyclo* was parked in front. Sam's face was dark with worry. He hadn't been able to pay the rental fee yesterday. He wondered what they could do if the *cyclo* owner came to take away his vehicle... It would be very difficult to find someone else to rent a *cyclo* from, because he would need a guarantor, and money for a deposit, too.

"What else can we do, Soy?" Sam asked his wife sadly. "Perhaps you think I'm lazy, and stopped driving the *cyclo* just to enjoy myself. But I promise, I've been working so hard, hardly even stopping for a break, but there have been no passengers at all. And if the rain continues like this, there will *still* be no passengers, since people don't really go out in this weather."

Soy was a beautiful-looking woman. She was around seventeen years old, with a pretty, pale complexion and a good figure. She was well liked, a quiet woman who didn't talk much, but was always honest with her husband.

Sam's words made Soy very upset. "No, my dear!" she replied. "I never think that you're lazy. Driving a *cyclo* is a risky job, and it's just bad luck to have no passengers! Today, you need to earn at least sixty riels to be able to pay the rental fee. You should hurry! If the madam who owns the *cyclo* comes, I'll lie and tell her that you've been unwell since yesterday, and couldn't take the rental fee to her. Please, my dear, hurry off!"

"Let's see how it goes today," Sam answered with a long sigh. "If I can't earn sixty riels, the madam owner will take the *cyclo* back for sure. And perhaps you and I will die from hunger, who knows?"

Soy sighed and looked pityingly at her husband's face. "Give it a try, my dear. Maybe today you'll have better luck."

Sam smiled at his wife and answered, "Yes, I'll go now, darling. I've done nothing but sit here while the rain falls, and it's almost noon already. If I come back a bit late tonight, please don't worry about me, okay?" He stood and walked out of the hut.

Sam drove away on the *cyclo* as the rain fell. Whenever there was heavy rain, the road in front of the hut would turn to deep and sticky mud. One of the front wheels of Sam's *cyclo* got stuck in a pothole; he had to get down from the seat and pull it from the front to get it out of the mud. At that moment, suddenly a car appeared. The driver's head emerged and glared angrily at Sam, screaming, "Damn you! Why have you stopped your *cyclo* in such a stupid place? I almost crashed into it and killed you! Get out of here, quick! Sheesh, look at me—I mean it!"

Feeling belittled, Sam tried to smile. From the way that this driver was talking and acting, it was clear that he looked on Sam with utter contempt. Sam wanted to answer rudely, but he stopped himself in time. "Oh!" he thought. "This is a rich man. If anything happens, I'll lose to him for sure." Thinking like this, Sam tried to stay quiet and not say anything. He hurriedly pulled his *cyclo* out of the way to let the car pass. Then he jumped onto the seat and turned the vehicle away. And in that moment, Sam was suddenly stunned: he looked up and saw a woman standing with her hands on her hips in front of the coffee shop. It was Mrs. Kim Leang, the wife of Mr. Kim Chhun, a wealthy man who owned around thirty *cyclos* that he rented out, including the *cyclo* that Sam was driving.

Mrs. Kim Leang was short and fat. She didn't bother to dress herself up much, but she loved money more than anything. This woman had a filthy mouth and the meanest of all faces.

At that moment, Sam almost lost his senses; he was terrified that the woman would take the *cyclo* back and deprive him of his livelihood. Seeing Mrs. Kim in the middle of the road like this, Sam stopped his *cyclo* and jumped off to beg for mercy.

"What the hell are you doing, damn you? This isn't like you! Why didn't you bring me the money for the *cyclo* yesterday?" As the woman spoke, her face was filled with a mean arrogance.

"Sorry, madam!" Sam answered while lifting his hands in a *sampeah* gesture of respect. "Yesterday I earned only ten riels. I'll bring the money to you this evening."

Mrs. Kim Leang laughed cruelly and said, "Damn you, you're all like this! Ugh, I'm so sick of doing business with the likes of you."

Sam lifted his hands in a *sampeah* once more. Mrs. Kim Leang's manner of speaking was upsetting to his ears. *Damn, damn*: they were harsh words, rude and disrespectful. All the workers who rented this woman's *cyclo*s had to endure this kind of language from her.

"Go on then," the woman continued. "You've never done the wrong thing by me before. You told me that you couldn't earn the money, and I'll take a chance and believe you this time. But if you don't bring the money for me this evening, I'll send someone to take back my damned *cyclo!* There's nothing more to say. I won't waste my time to come and find you again. Damn it, I hate doing business with the likes of you!"

Although he was hurt by these words, Sam smiled. "Thank you so much, madam! This evening I will bring you the money."

"Ah, get out of here! I'm going." Mrs. Kim Leang left.

Sam was terribly worried. He jumped back onto the *cyclo* and drove off immediately.

From the morning till noon, the rain poured down without stopping. Sam drove all over the city trying to find a passenger. He could earn only twenty riels, but he needed to pay sixty riels this evening! Thinking of this, Sam refused to take a break at all. He kept on driving his *cyclo*, searching for a passenger to hail. He needed to earn at least sixty riels to pay the rental fee, but as for the cost of food for him and his wife, Sam wasn't so worried. In the house, they still had enough rice and *prahok* fish paste to eat for two or three more days ... He ate only so that he could live to drive his *cyclo*, not to enjoy the taste.

Sam drove down Ohyer Street. He was overjoyed when he saw a Chinese man raise his hand to hail the *cyclo*. Sam hurried over to the man.

But ... Sam had to slam on the brakes immediately because there was a policeman nearby who ordered him to stop.

"Why are you riding in the middle of the road like that?" the policeman asked.

Sam's heart fell. The joy of finding a passenger had made him forget to watch the road, and he'd crossed the line by more than two meters.

Sam quickly jumped off the *cyclo* and raised his hands in a *sampeah* to the policeman while apologizing. "Please accept my apologies, sir. I wasn't looking."

The policeman's face was mean. Shaking his head, he answered immediately,

"You damn people! You always have an excuse. The signal I made was loud and clear! How could you miss it?" The policeman spoke very strictly. "Look, bring me the *cyclo* license book."

Sam politely passed the book to the policeman with both hands. This policeman had never forgiven anyone in his life. He carefully inspected the license book, and then pulled out his own small notebook. When Sam saw this, he was terrified because he knew that he would have to pay a fine of at least twenty-five riels.

"Your excellency!" Sam spoke with a trembling voice, his eyes pleading with the policeman. "Please kindly forgive me this time, sir!"

The policeman shook his head. "I have never forgiven anyone who did the wrong thing. You damn well know the rules, and when you break the law, it is my duty to fine you!"

Sam was terribly distressed … Driving a *cyclo*, he drenched himself in sweat just to earn a living, and even then it was usually not enough! Not only that, but he also had to be careful not to break the law, because if he came across a policeman, he would have to pay a fine. Sam stopped pleading with the officer and simply stood still and pretended to ignore him. When the policeman had finished writing out the fine, he passed it to Sam.

"Get out of here!" The policeman said. "Tomorrow you must go to Police Station Number Two."

That evening, Sam returned home a little before seven o'clock. In his shirt pocket, there was only thirty riels. His clothes were soaked in sweat. He was utterly exhausted, having ridden the *cyclo* from morning till night without finding any customers and without earning enough money to pay the rental fee for the *cyclo*. And not only that, but the policeman had fined him, too! Soy sat waiting in the doorway of the hut, anxiously watching for her husband's return. When she saw the *cyclo* arrive, she rejoiced and quickly stood and rushed to meet her husband. Sam stopped the *cyclo* in front of the house, got off, and walked in despondently. From his facial expression, Soy knew immediately that he hadn't made enough money to pay the rental fee.

"Dear Soy!" Sam told his wife, "I made only thirty riels. What can we do? I feel terrible. And a policeman fined me as well. Tomorrow morning I have to go to the station and pay at least twenty-five riels."

Soy was overcome with disappointment. "How did that happen? What did you do to make the police fine you?"

"I drove the *cyclo* on the wrong side of the road."

Soy said nothing else. She brought her husband into the hut. Sam dropped to the floor, sat next to his wife, and hugged his knees to his chest, as was his habit.

"I think we're out of options! I don't know when we'll get to live easily like other people do." As he spoke, Sam looked at the food that his wife had served. There was nothing but one plate of rice and one dish of *prahok* fish paste. Their lot in life left no room to breathe. And their biggest problem was the money that they had to pay the next morning.

Sam sighed deeply. "The police fine is the most important thing because if I don't pay that, I'll have to go to prison."

Soy's eyes widened. "Go to prison?" she asked in wonder.

"Of course!" Sam answered. "They'll bring me to prison if I don't pay the fine. Tomorrow I will beg the *commissaire* and tell him honestly that I have only thirty riels. Perhaps he'll take pity and not fine me more than that. But as for this *cyclo*, even though it works perfectly well, I've lost hope that I'll ever be able to ride it again. I'll keep it here for Mrs. Kim Leang to take back. Even if I stay here to plead with her, she won't agree because she is never lenient with anyone!"

Tears flowed from Soy's eyes. "Our time is up, my dear. I can't just sit here and do nothing. I have to find a way to help you to earn an income. I'll do any kind of work to earn some money to survive! You never let me go and work, or even just sell a few things here and there. But this time, please don't disapprove of what I will do. We must help each other to find an income. I can go and earn a wage anywhere, because these days there's nothing to be done at home."

Sam stroked his wife's back gently and lovingly. Before he could answer her, he heard the sound of a woman shouting their names from in front of the hut. Sam felt a chill through his body because he knew immediately that it was the voice of Mrs. Kim Leang. He stood and walked out of the hut with a trembling heart. Mrs. Kim Leang was standing with her hands on her hips in an angry pose, next to a man.

"What the hell is this?" Mrs. Kim Leang asked. "You promised you'd bring the money for the *cyclo* rental this evening. I waited for you until dark! I don't need to hear your damned excuses. Come! Give me the money! You damned people are all the same. None of you are any good, not one. You all owe me money until I come to your house to take it. And then you claim that you're not feeling so well, or that your wife and child aren't well."

"I have no excuse, Mrs. Kim Leang, other than to plead with you. I truly cannot find any income. Truly! Please, madam, please forgive me!"

Mrs. Kim Leang raised her hand to silence Sam. "No! I can only take pity on those who pay the price of the *cyclo* rental. I bought these *cyclo*s for tens of thousands of riels so that you could ride them. So what can I do? I need the money! If you don't have it, then stop riding my *cyclo*. You can go find someone else's to rent, go on! You people are terrible; you make some money, then you just use it to gamble, or smoke marijuana, or drink alcohol. You never think about the owner of the *cyclo* at all!" When she'd finished speaking, Mrs. Kim Leang turned to the man who was standing next to her. "Go on, Kuch! Take the *cyclo* back to the house!"

Kuch, her servant, obeyed her orders immediately, and she followed after him. Sam stood and watched them go, tears flowing from his eyes. He gritted his teeth in silence for a moment, and then slowly began to speak. "Oh gods! Lord, you have no mercy on us poor people!"

Soy walked up close to her husband and spoke. "My dear, whatever happens, we aren't starving to death yet. Even though they've taken the *cyclo* away, there are still other jobs we can do."

"Darling!" Sam said despairingly. "I've always stuck to an honest way of life. I've accepted poverty and hardship, but never agreed to do anything deceitful or illegal. But these good principles that I've lived by for so long haven't brought me any happiness at all! My dear, I want to become a thief. Perhaps that will make life a bit easier."

"Sam!" Soy protested. "Don't think like that! You should stick to the good way of life. Surely one day the gods will help us—surely."

Sam laughed in anger at their life; it was so dark and hopeless. They had no one to support them—no friends or relatives that they could depend on—and worst of all, no money to spend. Must he suffer such hardships for his whole life?

"Go wash up and change your clothes," Soy said to Sam. "Then let's eat, and we can discuss how to make enough money to keep on living."

During such difficult times as these, Soy was the only one who could comfort Sam and give him any sense of hope. He turned to his wife and said, "Darling Soy! I pity you so much. You should never have come to join in this suffering with me. Ever since we married, we've encountered nothing but hardships. Sometimes we even go hungry."

"Sam! You should understand me better than that," she answered in a trembling voice. "My happiness doesn't come from money. It comes from loving and caring for you, and nothing else. I've told you many times: I could happily eat a block of salt as long as I have your love."

Sam caressed his wife's shoulder and smiled despairingly. "It's true, my dear. You are my heart and soul—there is nothing in this world that I love more than you, Soy. If I ever find a higher station in life than this, then I will gather all the happiness I can find and give it to you."

"My life and my body have been given to you," Soy replied. "I strive to be with you in suffering as in happiness, to be a good wife to you. My dear! Please don't think too much; it makes you sad and helpless. Please remember that the life of the poor people is always like this. We must grit our teeth and never tire of struggling until the day we die. Today, we have escaped death, because we have rice to eat. Even that alone is something to be glad about. We shouldn't think yet of what we will do tomorrow—poor people have no future. We can only live from day to day."

Sam nodded his head slowly, delighted by these rousing words from his poor wife. "My darling Soy, you're right. Life is struggle—so I must search hard for a new job."

CHAPTER 3
NO JOB AND NOTHING TO DO

His beloved *cyclo*, which had shared so much misfortune with him, had been taken away by its capitalist owner, because Sam had failed to pay the rental fee for just two days. And so Sam had become a worker without a job. The very last money he had was just thirty riels, and even this he had used to pay a fine, because he had ridden his *cyclo* on the wrong side of the road.

A week passed. Anything in the hut that they could pawn, Sam had resigned himself to losing, in order to turn their lives around, and escape from the daily threat of death. Sam tried desperately to find a job. He went everywhere: to the shops, to the ports, to the warehouses, everywhere. But no one would agree to take him on. In some places, they yelled at him: "Do you have money to pay a deposit? If you have 500 riels to deposit, then tomorrow you can come to work!"

Every day, Sam returned to the hut feeling hopeless. One evening, just as he arrived back home, Sam ran into their landlord, an old man named Grandfather San. He owned many rental houses, but was completely without any sympathy for even the poorest people. Sam and Soy's neighbors knew that the capitalist old man would never agree to let them delay their rental payment, not even by a day. In fact, the hut that Sam rented was one that Grandfather San had originally built as a temporary hut, when he first bought this plot of land. It was built as a guard hut, and when Sam went to rent it, Grandfather San profited in two ways: first, he had the rental income from the hut; and second, he didn't have to pay anyone to guard his land.

"What the hell, Sam?!" Grandfather San spoke like someone who knows he can depend on the power of his money. "You used to pay your rent very reliably, but this month you're overdue by seven or eight days. What the hell are you thinking?!"

Sam answered in gentle and respectful voice. "Please forgive me just this once, please!"

"Forgive? You mean you want me to give you some extra time to pay the rent, is that right?"

"Yes, sir."

"No! I cannot!" Grandfather San answered immediately. "I spent a lot of money to build this house, and I have to pay the taxes, too. You damn well need to understand: if you don't have the money to pay the rent, then you need to get the hell out of here!"

Sam lifted his eyes to look Grandfather San in the face, and smiled fearfully. "I have never done you wrong, sir. Please sir, please allow me just fifteen more days, sir."

"No! I cannot, damn you!" Grandfather San spoke very strongly. "I'll give you just one more day."

"Sir..." Sam spoke with a choking voice. Grandfather San had no desire to listen to Sam's pleading words. He hurried away from the hut. Sam watched the old capitalist walk away until he disappeared from view, then turned back to his wife, who was standing behind him.

"Darling!" Soy said to her husband. "If that's how it is, what are we to do?" Sam gritted his teeth, feeling defeated by all the misfortune in his life. The way forward for them both seemed very dark, almost too dark to see. "My dear Soy! I'm at the end of my wits. The rent is 100 riels. Where can we get that much money in time to pay him?"

Soy's eyes were despondent, as if she was about to cry. "So where can we go?" she asked.

"Wherever we are when night falls, we'll sleep there," Sam answered in frustration. "But I think we have no choice but to desperately struggle for our lives, until the day we die. Poor people like us have no hope of happiness, my dear."

"No matter how hard it is," Soy answered, "I know I will continue to bear it together with you."

Before he could say anything in reply, Sam heard the sound of a man calling his name. He turned and saw in front of him a handsome, well-dressed man with a thin moustache running along his upper lip. The man was wearing fashionable clothes, with his hair combed neatly to one side, and he stood in front of Sam and Soy's hut. This young man's name was Sav, and to make a living, he was an expert thief. Sav was staying in a house near Sam's hut with several young male friends. He had plenty of money to throw around, and wore only the most expensive clothes. Sav had chosen to rent a house in this neighborhood because it was quiet, and because most of the people here were workers who every evening would spend only what little money they'd earned that morning. There was no one around here who would care to notice what it was that Sav did for a living. Sam called out, and went to greet the young man. Sav smiled through his moustache and patted Sam lightly on the shoulder.

"How are you, Sam? What did you do to make Grandfather San carry on so loudly? You owe him the rent, do you?"

Sam nodded his head, and before he could say anything, Sav took him by the hand and led him over to sit down at his house. Sav encouraged Sam to chat about this and that, while several of his friends left to go to work in the market.

"Hey, Sam!" Sav said. "I really pity you, you know. Now you've stopped driving a *cyclo*, right?"

"Yeah, Sav," Sam replied. "I owed the *cyclo* rental fee, and the owner came and took it away."

"So what are you doing for work these days?"

Sam laughed ruefully. "I'm looking for a job. I'll do anything, as long it's honest work."

"Oh, Sam," Sav said with a smile. "You're so stupid! So stupid that there's nothing I can do to help you. I've invited you many times to come and make money like I do. It's so easy. Even on a bad day you can make 100 riels, and on a good day you can make thousands—just imagine! We're poor people; if we spend our time thinking about honor and goodness, then we'll starve to death. You think about it, Sam! Money is a god … It is the jeweled chalice. People always say that rich people are good, and poor people are bad. If you have money, then everyone respects you and honors you as a good person, but the way you are these days, no matter what kind of morality you have, you cannot avoid the wealthy people looking down on you. They always think that they're superior and that a poor person like you is just the slave beneath their feet. Oh, Sam! The capitalists and the excellencies, most of them build their happiness and their power on the backs of the poor. They rob the Khmer people and they rob the Khmer nation. The way I see it, we should go and steal all of that back. I really like your quiet character, Sam. And now you have no work, so I want to want to invite you to make some money with me."

Sam smiled fearfully at Sav. "Thank you very much, Sav, for wanting to help me like this. But I can't do what you do…"

"Because you have these stupid ideas about morality, right? It's for nothing, Sam. No one sees the morality of the poor. There is no job that can make money like thieving—these days, I live happily and I eat well, and I have nice clothes that I can wear to watch the movies in any cinema."

"Your happiness and mine are very different, Sav," Sam answered. "You are happy with a life of thieving, but I'm happy with having an honest job. No matter how much the work makes me sweat, I'm still happy to do it. Let me tell it to you straight: in my life, I will never do anything dishonest or illegal."

"Well, that's up to you, Sam," said Sav. "If you're happy to starve to death, then go ahead. But as for me, I can do anything if it makes money."

"But your work is very dangerous."

"That's true, Sam," Sav answered. "Do one thing wrong, and I'll go to jail immediately. But for people like me, jail is not such a big deal. I've been to jail before, and in a way, it's easy, too: when it comes time to eat, there's a meal prepared for you, and there are people to guard you, too." When he'd finished speaking, Sav put his hand in his pocket and pulled out 100 riels to show off to Sam. "Look at this, Sam! I left the house for just a moment and made almost 2,000 riels while a shopkeeper was distracted going to buy a movie ticket. Think about it! Two thousand riels in one day!"

"Sorry, Sav," Sam said. "I can't do what you do. I'm stupid, just like you said. I'm determined to starve to death instead of doing something dishonest. So that's it! Goodbye, Sav…"

Sav shook his head. "Go and sleep on it for a night, my friend! If you agree to work with me, I'll buy some nice new outfits for you to wear, and give you some money to spend so that you have nothing to be embarrassed about. Ever since I gave the landlord 100 riels a year ago, he still doesn't dare to open his mouth to me. Because he knows that even if the rent goes up to 1,000 riels, I'll still get it for him…"

Sam had nothing more to say, and he stood and walked out of Sav's house, not knowing what to think.

The next evening, Sam and Soy met the callous capitalist Grandfather San again. Sam wasn't feeling very well, since returning home from looking for work and finding nothing, just like on every other day. But he tried hard to smile for his landlord, and pleaded with him to give them an extension. Sam even pointed out how poor they were, so that the landlord would understand, but the only response from Grandfather San was a barrage of curses.

"Your poverty is not my concern!" Grandfather San said harshly. "I cannot help you. All I need is the money you owe me for rent, there's no need for you to explain anything more than that. If you don't have the money, then you have to get out of my house! In fact, I should take the rent that you owe me for these past seven or eight days, too. But I won't take it, just as long as you leave this evening."

Sam almost couldn't bear it. He tried to look at Grandfather San, and even though he was furious, tried to plead with him once again.

"Sir, you should take pity on poor people like me, sir. Ever since I arrived, I have never paid you the rent late even once, until this time. I beg of you, sir…"

Grandfather San laughed angrily. "If I spent my time pitying people like you, I might never make a living! If I'm not strict with people like you, then in the future no one will pay their rent to me. I have nothing more to say to you. Give me the money, or don't; it's up to you."

"Please give me another half a month, sir."

The old capitalist shook his head, and said forcefully, "I told you already, I cannot. So now will you give me the money or not?"

"Sir!" Sam said, his voice shaking. "I don't have it yet, sir."

"If that's the case, then you have to get out of my house! Get out tonight." It was too much, Sam couldn't bear it. He said nothing more to Grandfather San, and the old man walked away.

Sam thought that it was surely true that poor people like him had no chance to argue with rich people, because money was more powerful than anything, even honor. And whenever money was involved, it could be used unjustly, too.

Sam sighed deeply while he looked at his wife. Then he told her to pack up their things so that they could leave Grandfather San's hut.

Since they had no other option, that evening Sam took his wife to sleep out in the open, under the eaves of the Vietnamese monks' quarters in Wat Toul Prosrey temple. Sam had no belongings other than a mosquito net, a pillow, a mat to sleep on, and two changes of clothes for himself and his wife. What's more, Sam and Soy had with them just ten riels, which was the very last money they had to keep them alive. Now, they were trapped without a home, no different from beggars.

The atmosphere in Wat Toul Prosrey temple was quiet and deserted, and it felt very lonely. Sam and Soy sat hugging their knees to their chests, looking sorrowfully at one another. In front of the western corner of the temple, there were two or three dogs lying lazily at the end of a leash. Sometimes they snarled, sometimes they barked, and sometimes they attacked each other.

Five days passed! Five days that passed in sadness and sorrow for Sam and Soy.

One evening, Sam was fast asleep and snoring loudly on their torn mat. Near him was a small basket.

It was seven o'clock already. Soy was rushing through the gate toward the temple, carrying in her hands a packet of rice and food that she'd bought at the market. Her expression was more cheerful than usual.

As soon as she set foot in the temple grounds, Soy called out to her husband. Sam woke, then got up and looked curiously at his wife.

"Gosh! It's so late," Sam said sleepily. "When did you go to the market? I didn't realize. I was just lying there thinking, then suddenly I fell into a deep sleep."

Soy put the package of rice and food on the tiled floor, and sat down close to her husband, smiling at him. Then she told Sam that when she'd been at the market, she'd met an old lady. This old lady was looking for a woman to work for her boss, a man named Hok, to do the cleaning and take care of his house. Soy explained that she had already agreed to go and live with him, because he would pay a salary of 200 riels each month. Tomorrow, Soy would meet with the old lady, so that she could bring her to meet the boss, Hok.

Sam listened to his wife, and sighed. "Soy, my dear, I don't want you to be separated from me. But what can we do? We're drowning. We have no choice but to live separately for a while. If you can really earn an income by staying with them, then I think I'll travel to the countryside for five or ten days, too, since now it seems as though the Issarak rebels have quieted down a bit. I'll go and sell some things in the countryside, maybe make some money to bring back and go into business with someone."

Soy looked at her husband, and asked doubtfully, "But dear, where will you get the money for a train ticket?"

"Don't worry about that!" Sam replied. "We still have one mosquito net we can sell, and if I'm a bit short, I'll go and borrow a bit of extra money from a friend… Oh, and tomorrow, I'll take you to Hok's house. If he's generous, I can ask to sleep there, too, and I'll happily do any work he demands, if I can stay close to you."

Sam and Soy looked at each other and smiled. "Darling," Soy said. "Please don't worry. Even if you can't stay and work there together with me, no matter where you go, I'll ask the boss to let me go and see you at least once a week."

"Oh! When will we be able to enjoy life like other people do?" Sam cried out.

Soy undid the package of rice and food, and shared it between them. They ate in silence, filled with a feeling of sadness.

The next morning, the old woman that Soy had met at the market came to bring her to meet the boss, Hok. Sam took the opportunity to go along, too, so that he'd know where the house was, and so that he could ask for a job, too.

Hok was a middle-aged man, a trader with piles of money. He was a widower, and even though he was about forty years old, he still looked young and fit, because he was rich. Hok's house was big and spacious, with two or three cars, and more than ten servants, both men and women. To an outsider, Hok seemed like a good man. He was of Chinese background, but he didn't behave like a Chinese man. Hok was a person who everyone knew and liked, just because of the power of his money.

From the very first moment that he saw Soy's face, Hok was delighted by her appearance. But he didn't like Sam at all, once he knew that he was Soy's husband.

"I agree to take you on as my woman-servant immediately," Hok said. His conduct seemed to be nothing but kind and generous. "To begin with, I'll give you a salary of 200 riels a month, but as for your husband, I'm very sorry but I don't have anything suitable for him to do. But if he ends up visiting you often, then maybe I'll find something for him to do."

These very kindly words, although they came from a heart that was most cruel and slovenly, were enough to win Sam's total respect for this capitalist Hok. Sam held Hok in the highest esteem, even though he had the heart of a thief. His words were enough to make Sam have hope that in the future, his wife would find happiness under the roof of this capitalist's house…

"I'm delighted!" Sam said, in the most respectful terms, while lifting his hands in a *sampeah* gesture of respect to Hok. "I'll be glad to send my wife to you, your excellency."

"Don't worry! Don't worry! I always have nothing but kindness and compassion for all of my servants, as if they were my own children."

Before Sam and Soy parted, she walked with him to the outside gate. They looked at each other with passionate desire. "Soy, my dear! Please work hard to truly serve his lordship, you hear me?" Sam told his wife. "This man seems very kind, and not at all snobbish."

"So when are you going to the countryside? When you get back, please come to see me right away, yes?"

"I want to go tomorrow, and I'll go for just seven or eight days. I'll be back. Goodbye, my dear!"

Sam and Soy separated from each other, filled with desire. Sam walked away from her, but in his mind he still saw nothing but Soy…

Translated from Khmer by Roger Nelson

CHRISTOPHE MACQUET

An Introduction to The Accused

But how many [writers] have come back from it? A whole national literature is buried there, plunged into oblivion, not only without a tombstone, but without clothes, naked, with only a number tagged to its toe.... Where a peaceful forest could have grown, there remained, after all the felling, only two or three trees spared by chance.

Aleksandr Solzhenitsyn (reception speech
for 1970 Nobel Prize in Literature)

A WRITER IN THE CIVIL WAR

1863–1953   French colonization
1953–1970   Independence and autocratic rule of Norodom Sihanouk
1970–1975   US-backed coup d'état and Khmer Republic under General Lon Nol
1975–1979   Fall of Phnom Penh and Khmer Rouge regime

Khun Srun was part of a generation of writers who came to maturity in the late 1960s and early 1970s, during the brief "golden age" of twentieth-century Cambodian literature. To briefly cite the names of this era: Chou Thani, Chhut Khay, Hak Chhay Hok, Koy Sarun, Laing Peng Siek, Nuon Khoeun, Soth Polin,[1] Vong Phoeurn, Yim Guechsè. All were born during World War II. All symbolized the success of the education system established under Prince Norodom Sihanouk.[2] All were exiled or killed under the Khmer Rouge regime.

Khun Srun was born in 1945 in Takeo province, fifty kilometers south of the capital. His father died when he was eight, and his mother, Chi Eng, a small grocer and devout Buddhist, raised him and his six brothers and sisters.[3] An excellent student, Khun Srun left home to attend secondary school in Phnom Penh. While completing his teacher training in the Institut Supérieur de Pédagogie, he passed the mathematics baccalaureate while also studying literature and psychology. He read avidly, and began to write. Galvanized by a growing left-wing protest movement, he entered the political fray in 1967. Srun—an admirer of the ideals of the French Revolution, and a reader of Victor Hugo, Albert Camus, and Jean Paul Sartre—initially saw in General Lon Nol's 1970 coup against Sihanouk the possibility of a new 1789. But he was rapidly disenchanted.[4] For his opposition to the new regime, he was arrested in 1971 and again in 1973.

Despite imprisonment, he remained committed to his vocations. A professor of mathematics, he served on the commission to create Khmer-language textbooks for schools. He continued to work as a journalist, essayist (on psychology, literature, and philosophy),[5] novelist, and poet. Faithful to a vanishing socialist orientation that rejected both Lon Nol's right-wing republicanism and the violence of Maoist leftists, and sickened by the carnage of the civil war, he decided to leave Cambodia.

By December 1972, everything was ready for his departure. He had succeeded in obtaining the equivalent of a diploma in literary studies from the Université de Rennes in Haute-Bretagne and planned to settle in France. At the last minute, however, the Interior Ministry forbade him from leaving the country. In 1973, after great soul searching, he decided to join the revolutionary resistance, the Khmer Rouge.

Khun Srun's meteoric literary life was over, but he left behind an unconventional, intimate oeuvre of exceptional literary quality. In just four years, he invented new forms and styles that drew the contours of a brilliant, modern literature. His works include *Kumhoenh* (My Views I, II, III, 1969–1970), three mixed-genre books of poetry, récits, and philosophical fictions, reissued in 1971 as a single volume, *Samrah Chivit* (Life Is Beautiful); and two autobiographical books, *Lumnov Chong Kraoy* (Last Home, 1972) and *Chun Choap Chaot* (The Accused, 1973). He also wrote a final volume of poetry, *Chun Neari Mneak* (For a Woman, 1973).[6]

THE ACCUSED

The Accused is at once prison literature, confession (after Rousseau), a provocative mingling of speculation and contemplation (after Montaigne), and Buddhist meditations on death. The narrator—Khun Srun's literary avatar, Chea Em[7]—wants to leave, find meaning, make a grand leap, reach a land of asylum far from conflict, far from pervasive death. The book is a cry against the civil war raging around Phnom Penh; a cry against life itself and against the human condition. He retains a vision of fugitive happiness kept alive by fragile threads: peace, studious frugality, dreams, love (with the beautiful Sophary), and freedom.

The narrator wants to flee his country because he has been "accused." He is "under examination" in all senses of the term: (1) He must prove his innocence under interrogation in a place where the workings of justice are hidden—a situation that mirrors Srun's first arrest. Imprisoned for more than seven months in the headquarters of Lon Nol's secret police, Srun's progressive beliefs and refusal to collaborate had only hardened. (2) He examines himself and the world in which he is confined. (3) He must turn in his examination papers (everything occurs as if he has never left school).

The Accused—an ambiguous, composite book folding together autobiography and fiction—is composed of four distinct parts. The first, dated January 1973 and signed Khun Srun, takes the form of a preface. The second, dated 1971 to 1973, is unsigned. The third, undated, unsigned, appears orphaned. It eludes and alters reality: the narrator is the son of a rich father who is described in detail (Khun Srun came from a poor family and lost his father at a young age) —yet does not attain the autonomy, or security, of a piece independent from the other sections. The fourth, which lends its title to the whole, has a fictional surface—the narrator is named Chea Em—but resembles the preceding parts as if made from the same skin and bone. It describes detention, liberation, existential doubt, the agonizing presence of death, and the determination to flee. It is an unusual design, stunningly modern, in which Khun Srun, at the close of the book, signals that a fictional artifice could be "real."

A SUBJECTIVITY REDUCED TO DUST

The book is moving, firstly, because it is the last known work of Khun Srun. It is a testament. After its publication in 1973, he was again placed under preventive detention by the judiciary police. One week after his release, he joined the resistance of the Khmer Rouge. He was twenty-eight years old. His life as a writer was finished.

The book is powerful, too, because Khun Srun's life is emblematic of the Cambodian drama and of an immense catastrophe. How did a young, promising writer—a humanist and pacifist, a reader of Heinrich Böll[8] and Aleksandr Solzhenitsyn, a defender of liberty and human rights—become a fighter for a political ideology that brought to life a nightmarish universe of concentration camps? Under the Khmer Rouge, every space under the open sky, gripped by a reign of terror, was transformed into a prison.

How to associate Srun—a pacifist incapable since childhood of standing the sight of blood—with one of the most horrifying mass exterminations of the second half of the twentieth century? How did this teacher-at-heart, kindred of Chhuk Meng Mao (theorist of the "Khmer soul"),[9] who cherished knowledge and intelligence above all else; this critical spirit worthy of representing the young, turbulent modernists of his era; this defender of the individual in a feudal society where the "I" is "detestable" (autobiography, as a literary genre, was only beginning to be conceivable), where fiction is considered collective, where authorship and originality are without status (a writer is simply a vehicle for an eternal truth and beauty), where the only person who has the full right to say "I" is the sovereign, "master of lives and souls"—how could he find himself under the banner of an ideology as pitiless and "anti-subjective" as the Khmer Rouge?[10]

There were, of course, people of complex leanings at the heart of the Khmer Rouge—a name invented by Sihanouk for the Khmer left-wing—including reformers, moderates (the "roses"), and royalists (the "Khmer Rumdah").

All were methodically eliminated by a hardcore faction led by Pol Pot, Nuon Chea, and Ieng Sary. They actively sought out Cambodian graduates living abroad, enticed them to come home, then massacred them on their return to Phnom Penh.

Chhuk Meng Mao, one of Khun Srun's mentors, was among those executed. He wanted to put his expertise as an educator to use in his country, yet quickly found himself at S-21, the notorious prison also known as Tuol Sleng,[11] interrogated and ground to dust. Hundreds like him, the most celebrated of the country's educated class, met the same fate.

Like the intellectuals who joined the Khmer Rouge late in the civil war, Khun Srun was transferred to a camp for indoctrination in the Special Zone (administered by the office of propaganda) to prove his reliability. Afterwards, he was assigned the position of workshop foreman in the railway system.

Survivor of wave after wave of purges, Khun Srun was a victim of the last. He was arrested on December 20, 1978, two weeks before the fall of the Pol Pot regime. Incarcerated at Tuol Sleng, he was murdered along with his wife and his two youngest children.[12]

He was thirty-three years old.

In light of the events of his life, we read *The Accused* in a different way. Its echoes are terrifying. Its words are prescient. The story's ironies are cruel. Tuol Sleng was a school after all. A person has no choice but to hand in examination papers.[13]

AGAINST OBLIVION

The Accused is moving, finally, because of its resistance to life's oblivions. To be able to read *The Accused* by Khun Srun seems miraculous. The original Khmer-language book is nearly impossible to find in Cambodia today. It has never been republished. Throughout *The Accused*, Khun Srun touches on the disappearance of books, and the mystery of the survival of the written word. Khun Srun evokes the oblivion, the nothingness, which seems to await him.

When I first stumbled upon a copy of *The Accused* fifteen years ago, I decided to translate an excerpt for the French magazine *Europe*,[14] in 2003. After reading our translation, filmmaker Éric Galmard decided to make a documentary on the life of Khun Srun, *Un tombeau pour Khun Srun / A Tomb for Khun Srun* (Dora Films, 2015). Then, after seeing Éric Galmard's film, the publishing house Éditions du Sonneur, in Paris, committed to publishing a translation of the book in French, *L'Accusé* (2018).[15]

Things do not happen by chance.

We translated Khun Srun because we were moved by his singular voice. Tomoko Okada, a Japanese scholar of Khmer literature, without any communication between us, decided to translate *Lumnov Chong Kraoy* (Last Home) two years before the issue of *Europe* was published. The Canadian writer Madeleine Thien, moved by the destiny of this young Cambodian writer, wished also to translate fragments of *The Accused* into English.

We believe readers of Khun Srun do not forget his voice. *There is something here*, as they say. Something frank, sincere, almost ingenuous. And also tragic. As Khun Srun himself wrote in *The Accused*,

> I have a hope (I clasp my hands and secretly pray)...
> There is a place, far from the road of honors and riches. A place for something else. A place for learning. A place to meditate.
> There is a voice. In the concerted, deafening sound of power. A voice to which no one, or almost no one, listens. This is the voice of the poet (of the minuscule writer, negligible, despised, the flea)...
> I have a hope. That this voice, however weak, will not die.

We share this hope.

NOTES

Thank you, Im Lim, for friendship and for rereading, with me, the last draft of this translation; thank you, Khun Ngeth, Sim Chanya, Yim Guechsè, and Khing Hoc Dy for your invaluable insights into the life and work of Khun Srun.

1. See *L'Anarchiste*, La Table Ronde, 1980.

2. Most of these young people will turn against him.

3. According to Khun Ngeth, one of Khun Srun's brothers, their father was a Chinese national who had fled communism.

4. A known leftist, Khun Srun was considered amenable to the Republic, and was initially courted by the regime. According to Khun Ngeth, he repeatedly refused "gifts" from Lon Non, the brother of Lon Nol (gifts such as a villa, car, cash).

5. *What Is Knowledge? Book for the Use of Young People,* 1971; *What Is Love? Book for the Use of Young People,* coauthored with Peng Soeung, 1971 (2nd edition, 1973); *Questions of Khmer Poetics,* coauthored with Ing Yeng, 1972; *Jean Paul Sartre and Albert Camus,* 1972.

6. This book is an enigma. Announced as "forthcoming" at the start of 1973, in all likelihood it was never published.

7. Chea *(chie)* means "free" and Em *(aem)* "sweet" (*aem* perhaps also refers to *sraaem*, which means "dark and golden skin").

8. According to the poet Yim Guechsè, a friend and former classmate at the Faculty of Letters, Khun Srun greatly admired the German writer.

9. Chhuk Meng Mao was a seminal figure in the fields of education and pedagogy. He directed Prince Sihanouk's literacy program, which in 1969 won UNESCO's Mohammad Reza Pahlavi Prize. Khun Srun's book *Last Home* is partly dedicated to Chhuk Meng Mao's wife. The theory of the "Khmer soul" advocates a return to ancestral rural Cambodian values: gentleness, tolerance, goodness, self-reliance, courage, moderation, humility, patience. It is part of a Buddhist framework, the path of smiles, forgiveness, knowledge, and wisdom (Jean-Jacques Rousseau's

influence can be detected, as well as the non-violent eco-anarchism of Leo Tolstoy or Henry David Thoreau).

10. See Christophe Macquet, *Écrivains du Cambodge,* in *Europe* 889, mai 2003, pp. 197–201.

11. See the films by Rithy Panh, notably *S-21: The Khmer Rouge Killing Machine* (2003) and *Duch, Master of the Forges of Hell* (2012).

12. Only his eldest daughter, Khem, who was nine years old at the time, will survive.

13. The irony becomes even more terrible when we know that (1) S-21 was briefly situated, in 1975, within the premises of the judiciary police where Khun Srun was imprisoned; (2) S-21 was relocated to Tuol Svay Prey (Tuol Sleng), the former high school where Khun Srun, as a young man, began his teaching career; (3) Duch, the leader of the executioners of S-21, was almost the same age as Khun Srun. Both were Sino-Khmers born into impoverished families in the provinces, and both men were teachers of mathematics.

14. *Europe* 889, May 2003, pp. 244–255.

15. "Fragments from *The Accused,*" *Brick* 97, 2016.

Translated from French by Madeleine Thien

KHUN SRUN

from The Accused

Published in 1973, The Accused *is Khun Srun's last novel. The narrator is a writer imprisoned by Cambodia's military government. He asserts that he is not a person of politics or even a man of conviction, simply an observer and a writer. A lover of literature, he wants to flee the country and be part of the wider world; yet he wants, also, to have the courage to risk his life for his principles.*

Shortly after The Accused *was published, Khun Srun left Phnom Penh and joined the Khmer Rouge. He was eventually assigned work as a railway engineer. In December 1978, Srun, like so many who had committed their lives to the socialist ideals of the revolution, was arrested. He was held in the most notorious prison of the regime. Days after his arrest, Srun, his wife, and two of their children were executed. Only their nine-year-old daughter, Khun Khem, survived. Two weeks after Srun's execution, the Khmer Rouge fell from power.*

I first read an excerpt of Srun's work nearly a decade ago. I was struck by the deep turmoil beneath the disturbing calm of his prose. Lines he wrote at the height of Cambodia's civil war have a conscious dissonance with his collapsing society: the words are measured, reserved, quiet as the nation explodes in war.

I unexpectedly encountered Srun's work again when French filmmaker Eric Galmard screened his documentary, Un tombeau pour Khun Srun, *at the 2015 Cambodia International Film Festival in Phnom Penh. The film affected me deeply. Afterwards, I sought out Galmard, who had portrayed, so powerfully, the dissonances as well as the longing in Srun's work. "There is a repulsion to violence," Galmard told me, "but, at the same time, a critique of populist Buddhism, of fatalism and accepting things as they are." He said that Srun had a Socratic impulse, and in his brief life sought to live an examined existence, true to his principles. Galmard sent me the few translated fragments he had of* The Accused *and put me in contact with Khmer–French translator and writer Christophe Macquet, who kindly gave his permission for the following translation.* MT

My name is Khun Srun. I was born in 1945, in Roveang commune, Samrong district, Takeo province, the son of shopkeepers Khun Kim Chheng and Chi Eng. In 1953, the year my father died, I began my studies at the pagoda school near the temple of Neang Khmao. From the beginning, I cherished my education.

We are in 1973—73, 7+3, which adds up to 10, the sum of the numbers of my employment number, 118.

Could this be the year that brings good fortune?

And yet I have never succeeded in believing such things...

I fear guns, knives, and batons, and do everything in my power to escape conflict. What little I possess comes from my salary and the exertion of my labors.

I have never brought harm to my mother, teachers, brothers, or friends. And I love my country, the same as any citizen.

I love art and literature, and I believe that everything attained by a nation's art is attained for its spirit, but I haven't the optimism with which Solzhenitsyn writes in his Nobel lecture,

> *So perhaps that ancient trinity of Truth, Goodness, and Beauty is not simply an empty, faded formula as we thought in the days of our self-confident, materialistic youth? If the tops of these three trees converge, as the scholars maintained, but the too blatant, too direct stems of Truth and Goodness are crushed, cut down, not allowed through—then perhaps the fantastic, unpredictable, unexpected stems of Beauty will push through and soar to that very same place, and in so doing will fulfill the work of all three?*

I ask myself, Could art really possess so great a power?

Between politics and me, there are just too many complications. The government and the National Police take me for a political person, and yet I see myself in an entirely different light.

I have never wanted to govern another, and all this scheming for power disturbs me. My curiosities lie in the moral, philosophical, and anthropological. I have neither the taste nor the talent for manipulation; I only wish not to be a victim.

I live like every other human being, profiting from my free time by gazing at the sky, the stars, by letting my spirit drift, by trying to come to an understanding, however small, of others.

I know that the true person of politics does not fear permanent disquiet, separation from family, imprisonment, torture, or even assassination.

Whereas all I want is to live, sheltered from physical harm, surrounded by my loved ones.

When my curiosity and desire to write perish, then, dear reader, you must consider me gone.

I live confined between walls. I have known this since I reached the age of reason. I am obliged to live with them. I am obliged to live like them. I have to adapt myself, there is no other way. I would prefer not to obey, but I am besieged by their laws, their prisons, their police, their shotguns, their profiteers, by all those who live on the backs of others and treat humans like things. They surround me.

I would like to discuss. I would like to oppose. I would like to remove these walls and live as I have heard it is possible, free from the imposition of their rules. But I am nothing more than a grain of dust.

When I think of my eyes, my ears, my heart, my skin, fear paralyzes me. One day, one day to come, all that is mine will be hastened down the road to oblivion.

There are times when I imagine my corpse. Someone takes hold of me, they are going to bury me. What pity I feel for my hands, my skin, my heart, my lungs! Why am I dead? Will I ever again see the others? I feel so much fear! But there is no end.

When I consider the ways in which people quarrel, clash, and kill one another, I think: *Such impressive talent!* But I would like to know: For what good? What purpose will it serve to kill the other? Even such an act will not bring the killer closer to immortality.

Each time I see the face of my mother, my father, my children, the grandparents in my family, the elderly in general, I am terrified. Do they understand that they will soon be sinking into nothingness?

If I die at this time today, what will occur? Eventually my books will disappear from the cupboard. My family will arrange the funeral without considering my wishes... of course this hardly matters, since I will be unaware.

Will I be a soul taking leave of substance, or will I be reborn into another existence?

They will speak of me, and afterwards, perhaps, they will cease to recall me because I will no longer be in daily contact with the living. Little by little, my wife and son will no longer remember me, just as I forgot, little by little, the deaths in my family. That is how it is.

Are they afraid, these men in the twilight of their lives, those who struggle in their beds, who endure hopeless operations, who are condemned and brought to the site of execution?

Are they afraid, and where does the fear go? And the young who don't believe in death, are they fearless because they feel so full of life, because they have experienced so little, because they have nothing to lose?

The young are exploited by every revolution. The young are sent out to wage every war, forced to the front, because they are much more efficient than the old.

And the ones used like pawns? The ones who, under orders, give away their lives? And the Japanese kamikaze? And the ones who commit suicide attacks?

And the unfortunate Jews, the scapegoats, assassinated in the millions?

If a death is horrific, does a person have the right to murder another? I answer: No.

No, he does not have the right.

In Solzhenitsyn's novella [*Matryona's House*], the widow, Matryona, possesses nothing. Why accumulate goods, she wonders, only to live in fear of dispossession, only to hold fast to our belongings rather than our lives? Hers is an uncommon way of seeing, certainly, yet I find myself in kinship with her. I have never wanted to possess villas nor land nor wealth because I imagine that, at the moment of my death, my attachment to them would bring me only sorrow. Far better to lead an untethered existence.

Night. Fifteenth of the seventh lunar month. The moon, a quarter full, visible behind the bars of the prison window, shines more luminously now than on previous nights.

Ah, moon, elixir of the heavens, you are a freedom within the quiet sound of the wind. You bring consolation. You are the smile, the open space of a long moment of forgetfulness. You are so lovely, moon, your pure surface like the gold leaf an artist lays on the ceiling of the sky. Despite the miasma of our world, despite the impurities displayed before you by our greed, you retain the same radiance, beautiful, immaculate, integral.

The distance between us, moon, is the only fault you possess.

I remember myself, a little boy at the pagoda. I remember myself, seated, bowed, both legs folded alongside my body, in the company of classmates the same age who have since disappeared from my life. Nearby, a half-dozen monks, emblems of the tranquility of the soul, of virtue and the renunciation of personal desire, rest; nearby, two or three candles and a few sticks of incense gently diminish, releasing thick curls of smoke. I prostrate myself from time to time, palms pressed together, before the smile and serenity of the Master.

I know it is dangerous to live among men. I have known it for more than twenty years, ever since I reached the age of reason.

But twenty years ago, I never felt terror as I feel it now. Never.

The inspector interrogates me from every conceivable angle before rising, brutally, and moving quickly to the cupboard beside me. A grand cupboard, large, solid, heavy, which had assessed me with a sinister and oblique gaze. What is the inspector reaching for? What will he withdraw from its body? My heart hammers. I think of a train in the night. I am trembling everywhere. My lungs burn. My hands and feet are ice. I try to suppress my bodily responses, but my nerves no longer obey the dictates of my mind. Abruptly, an old expression returns to me: to piss myself from fear.

A kind of hope remains in me. Microscopic. I know that I am innocent and wrongly accused. So I try to change my thoughts, I try to be hopeful: the inspector is Khmer, he has the same dark skin and the same blood as me.

Will someone let my mother know? Of this, they say nothing. She lives far from this place. Still, I've been dreaming of her. So I am no different from the other prisoners. Our nights are identical. We are all people of laughter, tears, and nightmares.

In my dream, my mother no longer wears her familiar smile. Her face is gaunt and her hair is graying; normally her cheeks are round and her hair jet black. Panic stricken, she holds my eldest daughter by the hand. She hurries forward, gripped by a single desire: to secure me in her arms, with all the clumsiness of too long an absence, with all the force of her love... but she is blocked by a guard who forces her to stop and turn around. She begins to weep, looking at me for a long time without moving until at last she says to me in a frail voice, choked by sobs, "My child, what have you done?"

My daughter—she, too, gazes at me. Her small hand beckons, as if she were trying to tell me, "Come home."

Her gesture shattered me, and I woke with a start, my eyes filled with tears.

I wanted to rejoin them, to embrace them, but in this place where I remained, all I could hold was the night.

I was freed on September 6 at 1 p.m. I said goodbye to everyone, even the guards. Too much joy! My feet barely felt the ground. I had the unreal impression of having been summoned to an examination, a trial.

In the hospital, I stayed five nights at the bedside of my mother. Five long nights before she was allowed to leave. On entering these sick rooms, I was overcome by dizziness, the same dizziness that swept over me last year when I came to this very same hospital to help the wounded. Ah, cast your eyes on all the maimed, all those at death's door. Naked life! A great spectacle! Men enacting massacres on other men. I wanted to cry out, *Enough!* But already I heard the comrade revolutionaries mocking me: *Enough of your pathetic humanism.*

In the hospital, my mother's breath was cold.

That night, the moon shone with an unfamiliar light. The sky was clear.

Since then, on many nights, the moon has shone with the same strange light.

Since then, on many nights, questions have twisted inside my mind. The same questions. Forever the same, unanswerable questions.

Sleepless, I remember *Les Misérables*. A storm in the mind. Jean Valjean, pseudonym Monsieur Madeleine, could have passed a life of ease, basking in the esteem of others, if only he had remained in his home. An innocent had been condemned in his place. However, the innocent could be freed if Valjean confessed, but then Valjean would be the one to end his life in prison, the object of derision.

This scorn he is familiar with. When he was nineteen, he stole a loaf of bread and was condemned to a penal colony. He does not want to return there. He is old. He no longer has the same fortitude as in the past.

At last, he chooses to turn himself in to the tribunal.

I must choose between the path of wisdom and the path of desire, between city and countryside, between Cambodia and the world, between the present situation and a future I must make for myself. In short, to stay or to go. I must choose. No one can do it for me. And I will be responsible for my choice.

I think of my aging mother. I think of my little room. I think of my writing desk, the cupboard I would open to take out my books, the chair on which I would sit. I think of my family, friends, loved ones. Their faces smile at me. My lips return their smile. A courgette soup with anchovies brings me pleasure. I think of the surface of the river. I think of the vast sky. I think of the light breeze. I think of my salary of more than ten thousand riels. I think of my electric lamp. I think of asphalt roads, running water, the radio, the television, all the beautiful songs we listen to. I remember everything.

How can it be that my anger is never aroused? When another looks at me with hostility, I react with pain. I do not have material assets, and when I see the conditions in which the majority of people on this earth live, I have no ambition to acquire things. I have never known an enemy.

If I do not move from this place, my life will contract. I must go. I need to explore the chasms and the wide spaces. I must come to know the places of which I've been told. I fear to get my hopes up, yet France, England, America, China, Japan . . . I feel these countries await me. I want to go very far away and turn my back on war. Oh! How I wish men would stop their killing and finally be reconciled. Finally, only compassion can salvage the world.

There are others who work for the common good. There exists a political movement that fights for the benefit of humanity. I find this right and good, but I do not participate. I want neither to exploit nor be exploited, neither to command nor be commanded. All I want is to let go of the comfort of my habits and seek a guiding philosophy for my life.

Translated by Madeleine Thien from the French translation by Christophe Macquet

SOTH POLIN

Command Me to Exist

One day, while working as a low-level supervisor in a private high school in the capital, I got the pink slip. Staff reduction. Due to the disastrous management of the school.

Sacked! Dismissed! Bang! Kicked right in the head!

For years I had lived under the authority of the principal. Every day, except Sundays, he commanded and I executed: "Welcome the visitors, Sam On! Answer their questions! Answer the phone! Collect the students' tuitions! Sign the receipts! Track down the defaulters! Do the weekly books! Find me this go-between! Call this fixer! Do this! Do that! Like this! Like that!"
 It was nonstop.
 Then, from one day to the next, nothing.
 A void.
 I spent entire days on my porch, slouching in an old weather-beaten folding chair, legs hanging, arms crossed, gazing into space.
 I would like to clarify something.
 When I say "nothing," I don't mean "no more work," but rather "no more orders." It might not make a big difference to you, but to me it's paramount.

Let me tell you the whole story.
 For an entire month, I ran around the city, from east to west and west to east, seeking employment. I spent more than a month roaming the streets, like a sickly dog, discombobulated, without any success. And then, one morning, hiding under my blanket, raging and despairing, attempting to fool myself into extending my sleep —"I still sleep; I am still sleeping; I am dreaming that I am still sleeping"—I heard my wife's booming voice.
 "How much longer are you going to hide, Sam On? Have you seen the time? Ain't you ashamed, you big slob? Come on, *My Lordshit*, move that ass of yours. Go empty my chamber pot and fetch me some noodle soup."

My wife's words weren't very kind, were they?
 And unremarkable—to you—I imagine ...

But, to me, you see, they were sweet and cool like white-sugar ice cream.

And they had an immediate effect.

My brain circled around itself a few times, like a plane performing successive loops. "Come on, Sam On, shake your fat ass, you old goat. Empty the chamber pot and bring home something to eat."

These were orders.

Very specific, unequivocal, like those I received at work.

All at once, my body lit up. A tremor ran from my toes to my skull. I straightened my head with lizard-like alertness. I threw the blanket to my side. I put my feet on the ground, wrapped a sarong around my waist, and squatted under the bed to grab the chamber pot.

In short, I obeyed the order that was given to me.

And while I complied, I thought that if I applied myself, I could stretch one single order, as absurd as it may sound, into a series of secondary orders.

"Empty the chamber pot," for example.

I could break down this action into a succession of steps:

1. Carefully lift the chamber pot.
2. Watch the level to avoid spilling urine on the way like an EPILEPTIC PIG.
3. Smell the liquid so you will know if it will have to be soaped once or twice.
4. Put on your flip-flops.
5. Walk down the stairs and empty the chamber pot at the foot of the mango tree across the street, or in the toilet bowl, which is far behind the house, next to the white acacia hedge.
6. Clean the chamber pot.
7. Put it back where it belongs, under the bed.

As you can see, this required that I perform quite a few complicated moves—actions I would have never accomplished had I not received my wife's initial order.

There was a sequence.

A production line of commands.

Order number 1 led to number 2, order number 2 led to order number 3, etc.

After thoroughly and conscientiously cleaning the chamber pot and putting it back under the bed, I noticed some tiny drops of urine on my forearm. The chamber pot had been filled to the brim—the urine, of a rust color, had a thin layer of white scum that resembled sea foam. I must have spilled some on myself by accident.

I needed to scrub away the bad smell to make sure it wouldn't reach my wife's nostrils.

"Such a big deal for two insignificant little orders!" you're thinking.

But let me tell you something, ladies and gentlemen: I was happy, do you hear, happy! My life had meaning again. After days and days of morbid prostration, I was alive again; I was moving again.

Ever since the high school showed me the door, I—a minor employee exploited at will—had drifted along in a state of pitiful unreality like a bird stuck in midair, flapping its wings but not moving.

Thanks to my wife's orders, I got my vitality back, I was back in business. I FUNCTIONED LIKE A NORMAL HUMAN BEING AGAIN.

I was an engine regaining power after a first-rate oil change.

And so, that morning, after emptying the chamber pot, I quickly washed myself, combed my hair, and dressed, then rode my bike to the Olympic Market, near our house.

Fifteen minutes later, I came back with a bowl of noodles, freshly made, piping hot.

I forgot to tell you that my wife worked as a secretary in the private sector. She went to her office every morning without fail.

That notable morning, after gobbling down the bowl of noodles I had just purchased for her, she sent me to hail a pedicab, gave me 50 riels, and compiled a long list of tasks for me to do:

"Look, Sam On, buy us some *rah* [snakehead] fish. Don't spend more than 15 riels, it will be plenty. Simmer the fish in a caramelized stew. You will need 3 riels of sugar, 3 riels of glutamate, 2 riels of pepper, 2 riels of condensed soy sauce. For tonight, you will buy beef, the neck part. Also get a very tender fillet and prepare and prepare a bowl of *samla mchu krasang* [sour *krasang* soup]. Make sure you don't forget to bring me a few spare ribs. You will grill them the way I love them. When you come back from the market, clean the house from top to bottom: polish the floors; wipe the tables, the cupboards, and the chairs. Then you will do the dishes: you will scrub the plates, the pots, the glasses. Everything must shine and look perfect! Then you will fetch some water and fill up two to three jars under the house. Finally, you will cook the rice. By the way, I don't want Aunt Yom to work for us anymore. It doesn't make sense. Going to the office now. That will be all for today."

She climbed into the pedicab and vanished.

Fire Aunt Yom so I become my wife's servant.

She was trying to hurt me, for sure, to punish me because I was jobless. She just had no idea how happy she had made me. WHAT A BEAUTIFUL DAY LAY AHEAD! I grabbed a basket and biked with a smile on my face to the market. When I came back, I put all the groceries in the pantry after making sure that the wire-mesh gate was locked so that no cat could get in and steal our food. Then I cleaned the house from top to bottom; I washed the dishes; I fetched the water; I filled up the jars and I cooked. All exactly as ordered by my wife.

The next day, I started over, with the same enthusiasm.
   I didn't need to accomplish great things. Domestic chores provided all the happiness I needed.
   Really, I could have done anything.
   As long as she gave the order.

Thus, little by little, my wife became my new boss. Her orders became more concise and humiliating.
   If, in the past, she called me "big brother" with the most tender voice, nowadays she hurled "good for nothing" and "parasite" at me every chance she got. "Move your ass, parasite," she'd say. "Stop bumming around; I'm gonna cut your ears into a point one day, you'd better watch out... you puny little man... entitled bum... Come on! Hurry up! Wash the plates, earn your keep, sweep the floor, do the laundry, go to the market, clean the bedroom, and cook the rice... I'M GONNA TEACH YOU SOME MANNERS, YOU'LL SEE!"

Not satisfied with just ordering me around, she had to add insults and threats. But I couldn't have cared less, as long as it fueled my engine. I memorized the orders she shouted, regardless of how many, before she left for work in the morning. And during the day, I executed them, one after the other, to the letter.
   Each order was a turn of the key.
   And each turn of the key wound me up.

When I could find a quiet moment during a hectic work day, I sometimes pondered my situation.
   My life depended upon the presence of my wife and solely on her.
   I saw that she, and she alone, could stir my body, my organs, my hands to action.
   My love for her intensified.
   I was infinitely grateful that she lived by my side.
   I had absolute faith in her.

For almost a year we lived on good terms.
   Until dark clouds appeared on the horizon.
   The engine sputtered.

The structure began to falter.

Did my wife finally understand that her daily orders, far from bothering me, actually motivated me to live?

Did she find someone else to do my job?

One morning she left for the office without giving me a single order.

She seemed worried. She dressed in a hurry, quickly made herself a cup of coffee, then left in a pedicab without saying a word.

I was dumbfounded. My arms crossed, legs hanging, gaze lost in the distance. Like a puppet without a master.

That evening, she came home really late.

And the following days, it was worse. On several occasions, she even stayed out all night.

Since she no longer issued any orders to me, I stopped my daily chores. I didn't do anything anymore. Absolutely nothing. I only ate as a last resort, when my stomach cried from hunger and ordered me to eat. I would then scrape an old rice crust that I dipped in fish sauce. The house was in shambles. Everything was in disarray and so dirty it looked haunted. Everything had fallen into disrepair with unbelievable speed. A stench came from the filthy dishes, which had turned the color of snot. The floor was covered in a layer of garbage at least two inches thick: bird nests, hardened mud, old newspapers. Dust flew everywhere. You could hardly see anything.

My wife seemed oblivious to the wreckage.

But it was impossible that she didn't notice.

I waited. I waited.

I waited for her to order me to clean this awful mess!

But maybe it was already too late.

Maybe she had given up, faced with damage beyond repair.

Then came this infamous Sunday morning.

When I opened my eyes, my wife was packing her belongings in a large suitcase at the foot of the bed. She walked back and forth between the bed and the closet.

I felt a burning sensation. This pain issued an order I didn't want to obey.

I could feel my tongue throbbing in my mouth, and my lips struggled to move.

"But...But what are you doing?"

My words startled her; she turned to look at me. Then she sat on the bed next to me.

"I am leaving, Sam On," she said. "I tried to get you to face this fact in many different ways, but you just didn't want to know. Now I'm going to set the record straight. Here you go. You and me—it's over. I'm seeing someone else. He loves me, and I'm crazy about him. We've been sleeping together for more than two months now. I made up my mind today. It's nonnegotiable. I'm starting a new life with him. He's downstairs, in his car. He's waiting for me. You've been very cooperative until now, Sam On, and I would like you to be useful one more time by helping me carry my suitcase to the car. It's the last thing I will ever ask of you."

Sacked! Dismissed!
  I thought my chest was about to burst open.
  My pain was now yelling its order at me, making it critical that I obey.
  "But I can't live without you, Jasmin," I said to her. It was true, ladies and gentlemen. How could I go on living if my wife no longer commanded me to exist?
  "I can go on without you, Sam On," she replied. "You're a nice boy. You're devoted, like no other. I don't deny it. But it's not enough, you see. You must be irreplaceable. And I can replace you as easily as I can get a new sewing machine, a pen, a pillow."

My pain soared to new, unbearable heights. I stuttered, "But I... What am I going to do without you?"
  "Don't be childish; come on, get dressed, and you will take my suitcase downstairs."

I was torn.
  For the first time, I was receiving two contradictory orders.
  My pain urged me to hold on to my wife by any means necessary, while my wife commanded that I take her suitcase downstairs.
  Who should I obey?
  I got dressed without solving this dilemma.
  My wife paced back and forth in the bedroom.
  When she finally closed her suitcase, she fixed her makeup in front of the mirror.
  As she stood with her back to me, I stared at the nape of her neck. So beautiful. So soft.
  Suddenly I snapped.
  "No, no! It can't be happening; you cannot just leave like that!"
  Like a madman I threw myself on her and grabbed her by the throat.
  She stammered, "Help... Sam On... Help..."
  These words were enough to return me to reality, and I loosened my grip.
  She was shaking all over.
  She rubbed her neck, turned to me, and gave me a strange look mixed with fear and anger.
  "How could you do that? What's got into you?" she said.
  "I can't bear the thought of losing you..."

I had lost my mind. I had almost strangled my wife. Now that I was regaining my senses, I was horrified at what I had done. I kneeled at her feet and begged with joined hands.

"Don't leave, Jasmin, please have mercy on me… Without you, I die… Please… Be kind enough to let me live by your side, by your panties… Please… If you don't want me as your husband anymore, just keep me as your coolie, your servant, your slave… I will do everything you ask… I will never complain… You can hit me over the head. You can kick me over and over again… You can pee all over me… I will always be happy… I will always be willing… I will serve you at any hour of the day or night… Command and I will obey… Send me off somewhere and I will go… Tell me to do something and I will do it… You don't believe me? Go ahead, order… Command me to steal for you… to rob a bank… to jump from a window… One word from you and I kill myself."

This long tirade only made her laugh (and I saw the two most adorable dimples appear on her cheeks).
 I was overwhelmed.
 I shook from head to toe like a motherless chick.

"That's a bunch of nonsense." She laughed. "How can one love to that extent?"

I hugged her knees with passion. I kissed them in a frenzy and buried my nose in her crotch.
 "Jasmin, my love," I said breathlessly, "I swear: one word from you and I jump out of the window."
 "You're really ready to do anything I want?"
 "Yes, yes."
 I had made up my mind. I was ready to die, if that's what she wanted.
 "Alright then: TAKE MY SUITCASE TO THE CAR."
 I almost died on the spot.
 I bit my lips till they bled.
 But this time my wife's order won out.
 I brought down the suitcase and crossed the yard.
 The car was parked in front of the gate. Blinded by the sunlight, I couldn't see the man behind the wheel.
 I walked around the car and loaded the suitcase in the trunk.
 Then I went back, walked up the steps, and collapsed on the old folding chair. My arms crossed; gaze lost in the vast, empty sky; legs as limp as a frog's.
 Waiting for a NEW ORDER.

Translated by Francoise Bénichou from the French translation by Christophe Macquet

SOTH POLIN

from *The Anarchist*

Published in 1980, L'Anarchiste has never earned Soth Polin the status in France that its literary quality merits. The reason may be that the first French journalists who reviewed the edition had taken a strong pro–Khmer Rouge position in the 1970s, and they did not approve of its caricature of a French ethnographer.

The first part of L'Anarchiste *is based on Soth Polin's Khmer novel* Chomtet Ot Asor *(Pitiless Provocation), which was banned in Cambodia upon its publication in 1967—making it wildly popular. Polin translated it into French himself, and it was accepted by his Parisian publisher on the condition that he expand it. The excerpt here is from the second part of* L'Anarchiste, *written in Paris in three months between 1979 and 1980, after the end of the Khmer Rouge regime and the death of Polin's father.* **PE**

My Peugeot 504 crashed into the metal parapet separating us from the Seine, but instead of going through the barrier and plunging into cold water, the car swerved to the left, just like an American Thunderbolt jet banking on its wing in the Pacific war. I surrendered for my own safety, letting go of the clutch and the brakes, trying to get back in control. No use. The car turned multiple somersaults on the recently paved street. What was running through my mind in those seconds? Nothing. Other than clinging to the steering wheel through sheer instinct, I felt neither fear nor any other emotion. Utter emptiness. But from somewhere I heard a faint cry: "I'm affffraid …" Then a second collision, stronger than the first, pulverized the railing. And we ended up below the overpass, close to the water.

My fare, a young English girl, was thrown from the car at the moment of the second impact, snapping her neck and disfiguring her cherubic features. Khmer poets of old compared the beauty of a woman's breasts to the persimmon fruit. Hers were crushed. So young. She couldn't have been more than twenty.

She can't have gotten anything out of life by that age. Not much anyhow. What a terrible loss for mankind. It was like the destruction of a work of art. And who was to blame for this catastrophe? A miserable Cambodian taxi driver in Paris.

As for me, I got out of the car unhurt. As miraculous as it might seem, I escaped without a scratch. I got off with a fright. But what joy, what pain. That moment shook me out of my torpor, my prostration, my mental hibernation. Shock forced me out of my melancholy cocoon. And that was tough enough.

Looking back over the span of my life, it has to be said that I am unbreakable, assisted by incredible luck. I'm the guy who wanted to die but can't stop living.

You suspected as much, didn't you? And now it's you who's the broken blossom.

It's not fair, I'll give you that. But you know, that's how I am, have always been: a cold fatality for others, the bringer of doom and disaster. My rotten luck has harmed everyone I've ever touched, everyone I've ever loved. Along the way, while I've thrived, scores of friends have taken the blame for my own ill fate.

Do you realize that I've been the epitome of absolute evil from birth? I'm sure of it. I'm not my father's son but the child of the devil. As a tiny baby who'd just opened its eyes to the light of the sun, naked and pure, I'd already brought ill fortune down on my family.

The day of my birth, my dad had an accident that nearly killed him. I should tell you that I came into the world under the same star chart as my father's, in the same dragon year; in the same month of April; on the same weekday, a Tuesday—and that had not turned out well for him. In the popular belief of those days, such a child as I would always be crossing his father's path.

I was born in Memay village, in Kampong Cham province, in a little wooden house, newly built, raised up on columns, with an unfinished verandah. It was an equally bad omen to live in an unfinished house. Who knows how many heads of households have died from such an oversight. A hole in a pillar, if not filled in, could harbor a spiteful spirit. A swarm of bees clustering around the end of a beam that someone had forgotten to saw off could bring death and desolation. On the night I was born, under a wavering, smoldering light fueled by fish oil, my dad chased a huge moth out of the house. It had a revolting wing pattern like a coat of gray paint, and had roosted in a gaping hole in our verandah, a part not yet boarded over. My dad took a hard fall, and the right side of his chest struck a bamboo pillar. For weeks he was delirious with fever, hovering between life and death. My grandparents' pitiful inheritance—spent on buying him the best possible care—melted away like wax under a hot sun.

I never recovered from that... Listen up, girlfriend! I can tell you, no kidding, that the man I thought the most of in this world was my father. But the more I loved him and the more I strove to help him out, the more heartbreaks he suffered on my account.

All through my youth, especially after I moved to Phnom Penh and started college, my greatest desire, my overriding obsession, was to get my dad a new car. I'm from humble stock and spent my childhood in poverty. Most days, all that my parents, my brothers, and I had to eat were a few bites of morning glory from our vegetable patch. And when we did luck into a few salted chops for a family meal, it was such a feast that my dad kept telling us, "The meat is better closer to the bone."

Back then we lived in Tuol Tompoung district, smack dab in the middle of a big marshland next to a huge lake called Boeng Slang, whose dark and unblemished waters fascinated me. That's where, after nearly drowning twice, I taught myself to swim. At night, I'd stretch out on my rattan mat, which was all that came between me and the gnarled, warped floor boards, savoring delights by the wavering, wan light of a storm lamp: the Three Musketeers or the woes of Uncle Tom. But I shared a bed with red ants whose bites burned like hell, and Buddha's Brushes—tiny millipedes who could crawl into earholes with ease—scorpions, and even slender snakes. And when the floods came, huge rats swam around me at ear level, their snouts nosing through the drifting debris like miniature submarines.

Oh, those flood days are unforgettable. Water the color of pus rose like a festering wound and covered this godforsaken place. It bewitched me.

Our water jars floated away from their place at the foot of the stairs leading up to our house. Propelled by the wind, they washed up about fifty meters away, nearly always by the outdoor toilet. I had to swim out to bring them back and then strap them tightly to the railing, out of reach of the swell.

At night it rained so much our thatched roof caved in. A gaping hole appeared, with blinding lightning, and rain ... The sky became our ceiling. Our wisp of a cabin shook violently. None of that stopped me from sleeping. But my father would always rouse me from the deepest dreams, at a point of such pleasure that my flea-ridden mat seemed like the softest bed in Nirvana.

Virak, child of mine, come help me.

I had a helluva time pulling myself out of my dreams. If it hadn't been for Papa, I would not have stirred, not even for all of Ali Baba's treasure. But I had to help him collect the rain in our jars, to save it as drinking water, since our well had flooded. Bravely I pulled myself out of my torpor, yawning over and over. I'd sit up with a start, huddle back into a ball for a few minutes, my head between my legs to gather my spirits. Then I would head out somewhere, staggering along in search of pails of water. The jars filled, I would climb back under my mosquito net on all fours. Drenched, soaked to the bone, I would get back into my comfort zone like a mollusk retreating back into its shell. I could never get to sleep right away. I would shiver under my covers, teeth chattering, and bring out the photo of Elizabeth Taylor from under my pillow. I couldn't take my eyes off her, this feisty slip of a woman. She was in a bikini, kneeling before a beach ball, on a beach in the Côte d'Azur. I'd linger over her eyes, her chest, her behind, and the sweetness of sensual dreams would steal over me. I'd wish with all my soul that one day I'd find a wife with such a sweet body. I was only thirteen.

Yes! All this ... harsh living forged an indestructible filial love in me. Little by little my adolescent brain sketched out a plan of revenge against my fate that became an obsession: one day, when I had finished my studies and got rich, I'd gift my father a dazzling car; if I couldn't manage a Mercedes, then a Peugeot maybe.

Naturally this project went nowhere. I was too wound up in my desire to pull off the thing that mattered most to me in life. And when the moment came to "do the right thing," I didn't bother to do it because I was already worn out by my own restlessness. So the important thing got by me. Later, when I became the manager of a chain of newspapers in Phnom Penh and had money and influence at my disposal, not only did I not carry out my promise—my secret childhood vow—but when I finally departed for France, I completely ruined my father. He had climbed up the slope and out of poverty—all alone and without any help from me—yet on my account he was destroyed, defeated, and left groveling in front of the powers that be, completely undone…

I, the loving son who kept aflame the memories of our misery years, nearly brought disgrace on him by leaving. I could not even bring myself to say farewell, yet I reduced him to slime. Now it's too late! I'll never see him again. That season's over. Time cannot return… The door to happiness has shut in my face forever.

Oh, my friend, motionless you lie, spread-eagled in the white snow that your scarlet blood stains in a long trail all the way to my flipped car… You see, that car would have made my father so happy! So listen to my story, told with the brute honesty that the sight of your crushed beauty inspires in me… I am capable of the vilest lies, but not in front of this, not in front of you…

My tragedy… the tragedy of my life, this life full of wounds, erupted in 1974, with the death of my good friend. No, it began earlier than that, in 1963… because the unfolding of a destiny is a complex thing. It's crawling, tortuous. You can't imagine the itinerary of a life like mine. How could I have got here? There's more than one story… It's a series of complications that mobilize, organize themselves, as if they were inserted into a clockwork that nothing can stop: a devilish intelligence shadowed my footsteps, contrived my downfall in minute ways, creating or rather spawning, with each twist in my path, little incidents that seemed like nothing but had disastrous results.

Sure, 1974 was the year my friend Savouth was assassinated, and his murder triggered everything: my political vendetta, my exile, the ruin of my family, my country's descent into hell. But in 1963, the dice were cast. My destiny was already mapped out. These two dates are indissolubly linked, and the second was just the consequence of the first. By 1974, wounds upon wounds had turned into nitroglycerine. And, now, after all this fuss, after the explosion, I realized that the truths I'd always told myself were no more than a pack of lies.

It's tough, my dear, to tell Truth from lies. Truth is no more than an Idea, if I use this term in Plato's sense. And the Idea, in its incarnation, becomes prisoner of a world made up of contingencies and, therefore, of irrationality. Like the beauty that inhabits a woman's body. But while you can know exactly when and how ugliness takes over a body and chases away its rival, you can't pick the moment when a political system begins to topple. What's harder still is that sometimes Truth or the Idea of it becomes embedded in a political system that you thought was fossilized but that you don't or won't listen to because it's not dressed in the latest style. The Truth is there, crying out, imploring, solitary, desperate. It gouges your eyes out, but you don't see it. Because other people are attacking the Truth, you let go of the Idea. All of a sudden, you flex your arm and it does the craziest thing. You knock her out, to finish her off, so you don't have to put up with her sniveling any more. You slit your wife's throat while she is still beautiful because, through your insanity, you take her for a witch. You don't realize any of this until it's too late, of course.

In 1974, I thought I was serving my country—for which I'd risked death a hundred times—with a pure heart, out of patriotism and selflessness. In reality, it was an unbridled thirst for power, a pressing urge for stardom, that drove me. And at the end, this self-absorbed malady, this modern egoist that I'd become, only helped to destroy his country, even more effectively than its enemies. Result: the country sank into the most terrible communism, one whose horrors eclipsed those of Stalin and Mao combined.

But I must start at the beginning, or you'll see nothing but fire and stars. Even though there's a big leap between 1974 and 1963, we must begin in 1963 because it explains what comes later... because in the serene skies of my youth, there was a tiny black dot, distant and almost invisible, which grew suddenly into a monstrous bird of prey that swooped down and devoured my life...

Look, my dear. Look with me through this tiny keyhole. It's a miniscule hole, but you can see everything. Look at this young man of twenty-three, this young Cambodian, sitting in bed, reading *La Dépêche* while listening with a distracted ear to the news filtering through his pocket radio. All of a sudden, he nearly falls over. The ground shakes, the sky rips open. The radio announces the assassination of President Kennedy. This Achilles, struck down in full glory... It can't be true! A god of war, pulverized into smithereens.

A world ends. All values collapse. It's not as if Cambodia enjoys good relations with the U.S. But everyone except for Prince Sihanouk and the Communists admires the American president: young, handsome, intelligent; the most powerful man in the world who, what's more, had a pretty wife. At any rate, for this naïve, dreamy young boy, what's left to live for after an event like that?

That news ruined his whole day, this young Cambodian... because, guess what, it was his wedding day. There was no possible link between the two events, but let's just say the assassination came at the worst time: his idol fell off the pedestal on his day of Bliss.

A bachelor of law from Phnom Penh University, the top graduate in his class from the Department of Diplomacy at the Royal School of Administration, he is destined for great things. That very evening, he will marry the daughter of the governor of Kampong Cham province. She has a cute name, Sao Myra, and is only seventeen. Languorous eyes, sensuous lips, and a splendid pair of legs. One day, while spying on Myra as she played badminton, he had glimpsed those legs through a tamarind hedge. Because he had a mind forged in the West, for that young Cambodian, unlike for his compatriots, the legs and not the face are the symbol of femininity. And what a fine match, marrying the daughter of the governor! It could open up vast horizons for him... perhaps even—who knew?—a diplomatic posting to Paris, the city of his dreams. Of course, it was a marriage arranged by his parents, a marriage of convenience, an almost mercenary trade. What do you expect? In Cambodia a degree can help you snare a pretty wife who's been pampered in the conservatories of the well-to-do. A lamentably popular catch-phrase that was laying waste to our elite—an elite that was particularly speculative and non-creative—went "Money's number one, sex is number two, partying is number three." It's disgusting, vulgar. But this young Cambodian, who was already sliding unawares into his era's collective cynicism, was killing two birds with one stone. He was making his parents happy with such an alliance—and the girl seemed as though she would please him. It was at this juncture that the ground beneath his feet gave way, with the assassination of the world's most powerful president. He was devastated. As foolish as it may sound, he had the impression that if he hadn't been about to get married that day, the president would not have been killed.

And then, over the evening during the lavish ceremony of his wedding banquet, where guests of honor, high-ranking officials, military generals, and even a minister were mingling, the ground beneath his feet again collapses. Overhearing by chance an indiscreet conversation, he learns that the woman he's just married is not her father's daughter, but instead a girl adopted by the governor. He's been duped, and for him it's a phenomenal act of deceit. His is like the seething rage of a fanatical collector who discovers that he's paid a huge sum for a fake Van Gogh or a fake Vermeer. Like the raving madness of a thief who's just pulled off the heist of the century, only to find the banknotes are counterfeit. Or a feeling even more childish. Once, as I was driving back to a suburb in the south of Paris … I can't remember where … oh yes, it was to Verrières-le-Buisson … a fare in my taxi told me about his eleven-year-old son. The boy learned through malicious gossip that his father spoke French with an accent. It was excruciating for the child, as though out of the blue a deluge of fire and sulfur had laid waste to his garden. Yes, it feels something like that to this young Cambodian groom. Fire and flood merging, like Vishnu and Shiva joining their destructive forces. He was not marrying an authentic wife who was beauty incarnate, but instead some bastard. However much he tells himself that he's marrying the daughter and not the father, and that it's she he'll fuck and not him, it's no use. He can't be content with a fake.

A lover of the infinite and the absolute, this boy wants all or nothing. The slightest, most humdrum defect upsets and torments him. In his teenage years, he'd once broken a racing bike (a Bertin) that he loved, because some of the original parts were rusted beyond repair. Foaming at the mouth, boiling with rage, he confronts the governor—straight into his big, fat, lump of a face, bloated with alcoholism—and accuses him of having ripped him off with "spoiled merchandise."

From that moment on, this young Cambodian begins to go off the rails. He consummates his marriage. He spends his honeymoon completely normally, making the trip to Siem Reap–Angkor with his wife, Myra. She's decent in every way. But the spell is broken. He will never be able to love her deeply. He fucks her properly; she gets pregnant the first time. But on their return to the home where he now lives, under the same roof as the governor... the demons are unleashed. He seduces his sisters-in-law, who are their father's real daughters: Sophary, Sothea, and Mona. The first two, eighteen and nineteen respectively, are unmarried. But Mona, the eldest, is twenty-eight, married to a respectable pharmacist. She's also the most beautiful and—perhaps as the forbidden fruit— the most delectable, and it's on her that our hero will wreak the most havoc.

Our young friend is not handsome, but he is well built, with the sad eyes of a tired child. Girls love that. He doesn't only take physical possession of his sisters-in-law; he also breaks their spirit. He leads their souls astray, especially Mona... whom he seduces last of all. He weaves his web meticulously... always arranging things so that it's they who seek him out.

I should make it clear that the devil's also mixed up in all this. This family of the governor, like most of the upper crust, is already "wild," contaminated by the frenzies of the West. These sisters-in-law adore modern dancing. Now, what do these lascivious movements mean, this concupiscent miming? Are they not the prelude to love making? Why dance at all if not to end up in the same bed?

Look hard through this little keyhole, my dear.

It's a Saturday night. Nobody's home except for our friend, Mona, and the servants. But the servants could not care less about the goings-on in their master's upstairs bedrooms. Mona, although a mother of two, loves studying and is preparing for her baccalaureate exam in philosophy. So she asks him, this distinguished mentor, to help her with her essays. He opens her door softly, surreptitiously, but certain of himself, because tonight she's invited him to come to see her.

The previous week they had danced together, the whole family, during Chaul Chhnam, the Khmer New Year. He'd grabbed the opportunity to pull her chest up close to his, caress her backside, and whisper verses from Shakespeare and Ronsard in her ear. Joy is brief. Nothing lasts. Everything drifts. Let's make haste and enjoy those moments that don't deign to wait around for us... On the way home, it was just the two of them in the front seat of the car, and he'd touched her thigh by accident. She had gotten excited by it.

Now, he edges his way into her room. He sees his sister-in-law stretched out on the mattress, flat on her belly, offering up the sight of her behind while drafting an essay entitled "Is Habit an Instrument of Liberty or Slavery for Man?" One look at her and he's out of his mind. He goes wild over petite women because he imagines that he can envelop them completely with his kisses and that their sex is lush, blooming, more fleshy than that of other women. Mona is petite, with a slender waist and plump buttocks. There's nothing better. Her sampot has ridden up a little, and beneath it are the most stunning pair of legs he's ever seen.

He sits down on the bed, next to the buttocks that he wants to sink his teeth into, his hands itching to touch her.

She looks up at him, smiles. He's so mesmerized that he can't tear his eyes from her round arse.

"Has Bang Phon gone to Phnom Penh?" he asks. Phon is her husband's name.

"Yes, he has important business to attend to. I didn't want to go with him, because my baccalaureate is only a month away. But I sent the kids along so that they could get a change of climate."

"If Bang Phon saw me sitting on your bed… He'd be terribly jealous."

She turns to face him again and, troubled by his look, laughs quietly, feverishly.

"Just sitting on my bed's not going to make him jealous."

She raises herself halfway and kisses him on the cheek. It's a quick, burning, clumsy kiss. She takes the plunge, and he hears her heart pounding.

"And even that's nothing to worry about," she says.

The boy stops chewing gum and stares at her, nearly nose to nose, and sees her blush.

"Spit out your gum," she orders, only this time she's using the affectionate *tu*.

He pulls the gum from his mouth in a long thread, presses it into a ball, and tosses it into the far corner of her room. She turns onto her back, waiting for him. He's about to jump her when she says:

"Go bolt the door, Virak."

He obeys her right away. When he comes back, he pounces on her like a brute, and they embrace with abandon, writhing and grimacing as if in pain. He presses his mouth to hers violently, licks her nose, her ears, nuzzles her neck… bites her breasts through the fabric.

"I love you… I love you, my Mona… I'm crazy about you… you are better than all the other women," he says, panting. Mona's weakening, but she still has the strength to gently push him away.

"Undress," she sighs.

He rips off his clothes in a frenzy, scattering them any old way, while she manages to slip out of her sampot by letting it gently drop. Then, expertly, she offers herself to him, propping up her rear on a bolster and tucking her legs up against her chest. Faced with this spectacle, the young man thinks he's dreaming.

What whiteness! How chubby it is! How full! he tells himself, overcome with dizziness. With a graceful move of her head, supporting herself on her outstretched arms, Mona throws her hair back while arching up her breasts. Without gentleness, without tenderness, he is about to sink into her when suddenly she pushes him away.

Translated from French by Penny Edwards

SOTH POLIN

from *The Aroma of Desire in Fresno*

1991. The Persian Gulf War began. Lady Luck dropped me like a kidney stone. My business was in ruins, dissolved like salt in water and wax in the sun. I imported luxury goods: Chanel La Crème Douce, Mahler, and medications such as Calcium Corbière, Becozyme, Bepanthen, Mysteclin. One night in Los Angeles, burglars broke into my van and swiped all my beauty products, a cruel loss of several grand. In quick succession, my heavily cylindered vehicle, which transported rice and groceries to Long Beach via Utah, collapsed on the freeway, an incredible omen that magnified my losses by thousands more in perishable goods.

With me buried to my neck in misfortune, my young wife decided this marginal businessman with a bottomless financial setback was equal to a man condemned to death. She left me. Bye, bye! She abruptly disappeared from my landscape, pursuing her Mexican ex-boyfriend in San Jose. No money, no honey. This is the norm in the adventures of everyday life in the U.S.A. When the evil eye strikes, the rabbit's foot escapes us. We lose the things we have, but we also lose the things we don't have.

After that Great Vehicular Disaster of '91, I thought I could get into mussels and shellfish, which were harvested in Modesto. But the rivers were polluted that season; this deep-water activity was not a good idea. One of my merchant friends suggested garlic, Texas via Fresno. He told me that he made a lot of profit, three to four grand per interstate shuttle from Houston via Fresno in his pickup. This also failed to work out: garlic season had not yet arrived.

My ambition to harvest mussels and mollusks and garlic was further demonstration of my inexperience in this field. I was a Baudelarian albatross fallen from the sky, ill-prepared to walk on Earth, tangled up in its injured wings. Those in my circle, family, friends, riddled me with sarcasm, mockery, and criticism I had little use for at this point in my life. It was rumored that what I did now was not indicative of my past glory, and that this did not result from congenital maladjustment but from insanity... nothing more, nothing less.

My new vehicles were broken down. There was nothing left for me but an Astro cargo van in my last fight against destiny. This van, which I had driven for only 40,000 miles, was already giving me signs of exhaustion, in the form of costly repairs. The cause of these operations had occurred during my trips to Utah; I was used to sleeping innocently and blissfully with my car running, while the air conditioner hummed. I didn't realize the damage I was causing until a mechanic told me.

The sister-in-law of one of my friends, a well-advised Vietnamese woman who once sold duck eggs, whispered in my ear to sell "tough hens" in Fresno (hens with firm flesh). These *moan svet* were very well appreciated by Laotians in Fresno, but the venture required me to stock up from an enormous henhouse fifty miles from Long Beach on the way to Vegas. This transaction would bring me $400 to $500 per ride, just enough to pay for my minor survival needs without having to depend on money from other sources.

The price of these "tough hens" came to eighty cents per hen. I could easily sell them for $2.50 or $3, going door to door. This was a wise thought but quite a poor calculation. Each household, in theory, would be able to take five or ten, and the contents of my cargo van would vanish in no time. But here was the flaw. We were used to plucking these "tough hens" and reselling them in Long Beach, whereas in this case, I had to travel in the opposite direction to ship them from Long Beach all the way to Fresno, 300 miles from my residence. My frantic desire to go elsewhere, this irresistible peregrination towards a faraway landscape, made no sense for a guy who was broke. I was a man living on the brink of dreams, deserting my own garden of self.

In the midst of all this trouble, my left eye started to gyrate. Uncontrollable tremblings of the pupil every five minutes! This was not a good sign.

I am seldom superstitious, disbelieving in angels, demons, or even dreams and omens. During the last several months, I had been pursued by an incredible series of episodes of bad luck. How many more were in store for me? The evil eye had not had enough of my being.

My cargo van only had seats up front, and in the back, chicken coops that a Chinese man from Santa Ana had made out of old wood. Each coop held nine or ten hens, which prevented the chickens from trampling each other during the course of the trip. I cargoed two hundred hens on each of my trips to Fresno (this was my fifth). During the drives, I lowered my windows so that my hens would be calmed by the breeze.

My left pupil continued to twitch, grating my nerves. I was dying to curse my own destiny. Rumor has it that men were given intelligence in order to overcome obstacles. Without problems we wouldn't have solutions, nor intelligence. No! No! And no! I didn't want to be an intelligent person. For what? My predicaments came en masse like waves from the sea. The first one barely shattered at the border of my consciousness, the second was already penetrating. The problems piled on top of each other, merged together, ambushing me to the point where I lost the North Star, my bearings. I was nothing but a cynical character, an agnostic who didn't have faith in good or bad (as much as I always dreaded the bad that came from my personality, I didn't fear the bad that came from others). I had lowered myself to fear the blinking of my eye. I understood nothing!

I was scared of the future, of the passage of time. I was scared of surprises, because they were always bad. I was afraid of the day of reckoning, now impossible to postpone. I was afraid of the pure truth, the subjective, anything that related to me. I was especially afraid of the acts I might commit toward others. If I hadn't committed any sins, how could I explain the irrepressible twitching of my left eye?

While lost in these ludicrous thoughts, a group of *moan svet* laying hens frantically escaped from their cages. They flew in all directions, twirling feathers in an indescribable cacophony of cackling, searching for a place to lay eggs. My van was a cargo of craziness. Some of these hens wandered onto the passenger's seat. A brood hen curled up between my thighs to lay fresh eggs, which rolled onto my knees and boots. In a brief moment, many eggs cracked because the mother hen stepped on them. One hen pecked my shoulder, another my head. One covered my head with liquid shit. I couldn't do anything against an orgy of leaping and chuckling witches other than try to wave them off with my free arm.

I experienced a powerful feeling of self-pity. I was nothing but a loser. I had the desire to cry like a child. Was this a tangible result of the blinking of my left eye? Or because I was going to sell these chaotic hens alive to the Laotian consumers of Fresno, who would sever their throats? What a business. Damn! From the moment we find ourselves, why are we driven to the brink of dishonor and shit?

I was faced with this unsolvable problem when my car finally reached the border of the city of Fresno. I searched for the Walnut exit, having in mind to stay at the place of Mesrok Young, a friend in the city.

Mesrok Young rented a three-room apartment on the first floor, equivalent to a four-room apartment in France, three miles from the Walnut exit. We called him "Me Srok," leader of the district, because he had a lot of influence in the Cambodian community of Walnut Avenue. People feared him. He liked to have eloquent discussions, and he knew many influential people in the city. He even maintained regular relations with American journalists in the region. Through the use of malicious gossip, Mesrok Young had the power to turn recalcitrant individuals to his politics. He had the power to make a show-off disappear, as he used to do in the refugee camps on the Thai border.

We discreetly arrived, my hens and I, in front of the home of Mesrok Young, at the same moment that he was about to celebrate the Khmer New Year, with the participation of the Cambodian community of Fresno. It was already 4 P.M., and a large crowd was forming. Two groups of players of pétanque, a game of boules, confronted each other for money, lifting clouds of dust in the large backyard. Everyone was dressed in new clothes, and each side shouted at the top of their lungs to intimidate the opposite side. Booing, encouragement, shouts of triumph, and the sharp noise of bowls striking one another with a terrifying efficiency all gave me vertigo. Naturally shy, I wanted to pull myself away from this celebration, which made me feel like a complete stranger. I wanted to escape far away from this place, where no one could see me covered in mud and hen feces. But what could I do? I had no choice. In Fresno, my only crash pad was the home of Mesrok Young. I especially needed his son, a likable adolescent, well devoted to my cause, to help me sell my hens to the Laotians of the neighborhood.

The twitching of my pupils ceased for the time being, but it was just taking a break. I didn't get a chance to shower, because there were too many people in the bathroom. I didn't have clothes to change into. My outfit reeked of chicken shit. As for my cowboy boots, they were covered with dried-up mud from my fishing trips the week before. I was a monkey among worldly people.

In Mesrok Young's large living room, an orchestra of traditional musicians played the *tro*, the *takhe*, the *chapei*, the *khim*, and excelled in accompanying the throaty melodies of a group of young girls. This evening of the Choul Chhnam Khmer was genuinely magical and entertaining. Mesrok Young had great instincts for party planning, like all the leaders of Cambodian villages.

There was first the *ayai*, the court of love in which a couple of singers reply to each other with saucy songs. And then there were the charming young girls who sang choruses of ancient verses shuddering of obsessive nostalgia: "Phko Loan Kokrik" (Roaring of Thunder), "Trapeang Peay" (Windswept Pond). There was a young Chinese woman who sang "Chumno Khae Prang" (Summer Breeze) in a pleasing voice, an incredible novelty. My whole life, I had never seen a Chinese woman sing Khmer so wonderfully. Maybe she learned these songs in Khao-I-Dang camp, or during Pol Pot's reign?

As for Mesrok Young, who had insisted I stay for the celebration, he had the greasy face of an obsessive libido. He had a spouse and grown children, but that didn't stop him from resigning himself to women. He wore a beautiful trois-pièce, a tie of flowered silk, and on his wrists, gold bracelets as large as chains, and on his middle finger, a diamond ring as thick as Mike Tyson's big toe. He sprayed himself with half a gallon of Lancôme, which released a "1001 Arabian Nights" fragrance over the entire room, more powerful than the smell of an American plane dropping retaliation bombs on Saddam Hussein.

Presently, Mesrok Young eyed the young Chinese woman without protest from his wife, who was very close to him. Mesrok Young whispered into my ear, "You know, Saroeun, this A Muoy is just twenty-two. She studies in the same E.S.L. class as I do. You notice she's the indisputable star of the festivities. Each of us dreams of having her. But this A Muoy here only wants to have fun with me. She probably won't be able to escape Mesrok Young. She already chased after me several times at school."

Honestly, I could not see any sign that this young woman was pursuing Mesrok Young. If he was so sure of himself, why did Mesrok Young bathe himself in expensive Lancôme? Even President Bush would not prettify himself like that.

I noticed a number of overly dressed guys shamelessly pursuing this Chinese singer, like flies on a morsel of palm sugar, without embarrassment, without any scruples. If they could eat her, they would sink their teeth into her like a sandwich in front of all the guests.

But I wasn't that interested in this joyful mob, in this place of thinly disguised senses, since I was nothing more than a forlorn soul. I was nothing more than a small boat in distress in the middle of an ocean of indifference. It wasn't that I was not attracted to women, or that I was unsociable, but rather that I was overwhelmed by a consuming anxiety over an unhappy love affair.

I didn't want to stay close to anyone or to remain in the middle of this celebration. I didn't want to discuss, or listen to people converse about, politics or passionate love. Given the fact that my cash box was empty, the most important thing for me was to get rid of my hens as quickly as possible.

The beautiful Chinese woman had surreptitiously risen out of her rattan chair to sit beside me. I hadn't even finished laughing at myself when I discreetly noticed her two gorgeous legs and her lavender-blue mini skirt. Our bodies were almost touching, and I could smell her breath and exquisite perfume. I was in the ring with a kick-boxer. Despite my precautions, I did not see the kick from my adversary; in other words, the shin bone of her leg slammed against my thoughts like a bolt of lightning.

How could I allow a blow to reach an area so vulnerable? One kick and there I was, groggy, incapable of striking back, and very close to collapsing. But I realized that it was already too late to defend myself against anyone. This Chinese bewitcher had already succeeded in capturing me in her nets and holding me down at her mercy, like a fish.

What's the use in attempting to avoid these blows dealt by fate? I wore clothes that reeked of hen feces from twenty yards away—that should have kept anyone at bay. Instead, this pretty girl had sidled up to sit beside me. Or did the chicken shit attract her? Had chicken shit become a fragrance, a love potion?

"Can I have a moment with you, Bang?" the young Chinese woman addressed herself to me. Man! The shit hit the fan. Young girls always called me Uncle, not this endearment. Even my wife called me Papa. This saucy Chinawoman had just called me Bang [older brother or darling], using her most enterprising yet smooth tone. I decided to play the same game.

"Of course, Aun Lang," I said. "You can discuss with me whatever you like. I thank God for sending me a woman so ravishing to spice up my conversation."

"I despise you, Bang! It's me who came to sit beside you, yet instead of complimenting me, you have thanked God, who's done nothing for you. Is it possible you've been influenced by a foreign culture?"

"Dear Lang, you have American citizenship, and your name has already changed to Suzy Mei Lang. Please spare me your hypocrisy."

"Between the two of us, I don't know who has reacted the most under the influence of foreign culture."

"Oh! You know my name, and my history?"

Instead of being vexed by my sarcasm, she burst into laughter, and our conversation took off from that argument. My goodness! Why was she so fixated on me? I had pinned myself against this corner of the wall, like dried mango preserves, feeling nothing, no longing, no desire for the consideration of any woman. I had become as asexual as the men of Pol Pot's revolution; in other words, when they saw women holding up their sampots to sow rice, they felt no attraction whatsoever, because they dreamed only of roasted chicken thighs and sandwiches. I wanted to strike a blow to the moral preaching of this professor of tortures. I considered myself to be a man decapitated by the evil eye. A little middle-class man penniless and helpless was not going to tremble with excitement for a woman he perceived as nothing more than a symbol, like a piece of pork or beef. I suddenly realized that I had sat by myself in this corner of Mesrok Young's living room for more than three hours already, and that I had hardly spoken to anyone other than Ms. Lang. I noticed Mesrok Young throwing furtive glances over at us with what seemed a mixture of fear and deception. It had probably been awhile since he had invested energy in courting this Suzy Mei Lang. And now it was me, his guest, who was pulling the rug out from under his feet. He must have resented me. Nonetheless, he reacted like a gentleman, keeping himself from interrupting our conversation.

Other predators, all the same, seemed resigned to lose their prey. They noticed that I was keeping the rest of this meal to myself. I somehow found myself one of the final candidates of opportunity. If I seized the great prize of this evening, it was because I had collected by chance the winning ticket, and no one could reproach me for it. In any event, I had the impression that the tempo of this Khmer New Year celebration was slowing like a dying libido.

"What are you thinking about?" Ms. Lang asked.

"I'm thinking about two epilogist women who gave me kicks in perfect combinations." I meant my wife, who had just exited my life, and this other woman, this Suzy Mei Lang, who had abruptly sunk her teeth into it. Ordinarily, when I was obsessed with a woman, I was inaccessible to any other woman. So how was it that this time, this Suzy Lang had introduced herself so quickly into my life, crushing my defenses with one blow?

"What are you talking about, Bang?" she asked. "What woman gave you the boot?"

"No!" I responded. "No woman has given me the boot. I was awaiting the blow, like an idiot!"

"You are strange, Bang. You have the attitude of someone who came from somewhere other than Fresno. I heard word from afar that you specialize in selling French perfumes, isn't that right? Me, too. I sell perfumes that come from France."

My eyes widened, and I looked at Ms. Lang with disbelief. Never had Ms. Lang seemed so beautiful to me than at this moment. Her charms were intense, but she seemed a hundred times more attractive as a result of my excitement, which was not unlike that of finding a new client for perfumes or chicken, or discovering a buried treasure. A man drowning in a river's current would be happy to see even the floating carcass of a dead dog. But how much greater would his happiness be if an angel descended from the sky to rescue him?

"What, don't you believe me?" she asked. "I sell French perfumes and toothpaste, the same brand as yours, Émail Diamant. What is the wholesale price of a tube of your Émail Diamant?"

"How did you know I sold these toothpastes?" I stammered.

"How did you know I had American citizenship? It's exactly the same thing! When someone doesn't say anything, don't go believing that he knows nothing of your business. Tell me how much a tube of your toothpaste costs wholesale."

"I sell for seven dollars apiece."

"Here in Fresno, I can easily get rid of them for ten dollars apiece. And in certain locations, this can go as high as twelve. Can't you see we should be partners, Bang? Would you like to see my collection of perfumes?"

"Yes, I would. Where are they? Do you have them with you?"

"No. I keep them at my place, several miles from where Mesrok Young lives."

"But I can't leave this place. I must honor this celebration with my presence, until the end," I said without conviction.

"Let's go. Come on, don't say no, this will only take fifteen minutes, we will come back afterwards. Uncle Mesrok can't say anything."

She suddenly got up, took one of my hands, and proceeded to drag me forcefully. I was flabbergasted. I didn't know what to do. Not going with a beautiful woman who asks you to follow her would be stupid and cowardly, especially in front of this audience of adventurers and thrill seekers. But to leave with her at this moment would be extremely convenient. Leaving with a woman when one was on the brink of financial ruin, as in my case... and where were my hens? I didn't even know whether they were sold or not. In the end, I ran across the room, pursuing the Chinese diva of this musical celebration, who must have belonged to the sphere of influence, the private property of Mesrok Young. I asked him for permission, babbling pathetically, "Bang, Ms. Lang wants me to go take a look at her perfumes. It won't be long. I'll come back in a few minutes."

I felt guilty for everybody. I lowered my face, advanced on the tips of my toes like a thief, and exited towards freedom outside, behind the voluptuous Ms. Lang. All things have no value. Nothing is permanent. *Anicca vata sankhara,* as the Buddhist prayer goes.

I no longer feared Mesrok Young's admonitions. I was not embarrassed at the idea of a scandalous relationship, or the dishonor of being a bankrupt man. I no longer thought about the future. I only thought about the present. Whether I was a womanizer or kidnapped by this woman, it would end up the same. I didn't believe that Suzy Lang asked me solely for the sake of her perfumes. And I didn't think that pursuing her was motivated by the same. This had nothing to do with perfumes.

At the bottom of Mesrok Young's stairway, I asked her, "Lang, where is your car?"

"I didn't bring my car, we will take yours."

"But mine is full of chicken shit."

"That's alright, Bang. There's nothing like the smell of chicken shit. It contrasts with the fragrance of the perfumes. Thanks to this smell of chicken shit, I found you so intriguing!"

Translated from Khmer by Bora Soth and Norith Soth

TY CHI HUOT

from *Sky of the Lost Moon*

Editors' Note
Known for his novels and his scripts for traditional theater, Ty Chi Huot is one of the most celebrated authors of the 1980s. His works include Back to the Nest *(1984) and* Sky of the Lost Moon *(1985), which was broadcast on national radio.* Sky of the Lost Moon *tells the story of a young Laotian man, Bophan, sentenced to time on the harsh French prison island of Poulo Condor (Koh Tralach in Khmer) and then imprisoned in Phnom Penh. After being released, he finds refuge with a Cambodian fisherman family and falls in love with their daughter, Mealea. In one of the most moving passages of modern Cambodian literature, their story ends when Bophan returns from fighting in Laos in the 1970s and discovers that Mealea and her father have been killed by the Khmer Rouge.*

CHAPTER 2
FLOATING LIKE DUCKWEED

In Phnom Penh Prison, I was separated from Chan, my Cambodian friend, as they placed the inmates from Koh Tralach into cells with existing prisoners. The mosquitoes and intense cold kept me from sleeping. Families of the Cambodian prisoners had brought them mosquito nets, but my hometown was so far away, and no one in my family even knew I was imprisoned here. I didn't own another set of clothes—let alone a mosquito net or a blanket.

One evening, when it was almost dark, as I was lying on the prison's floor feeling sorry for myself, a bundle dropped in front of me. I turned to see where it came from and saw a female prison guard smiling outside of my cell. She waved to me and spoke softly in Khmer, "Don't tell anyone..."

Then she left. Her words were short, but from her gesture I understood that the bundle was for me. Not wasting any time, I opened it up, and my heart filled with happiness. I never expected a prison guard to be so charitable. The guard, who was in her thirties, was the same one who supervised the inmates and brought them from the cells to the work site. Without me noticing, she had seen and understood what I needed most right now, and provided it.

In the bundle was a change of clothes. They were not new, but for me at that moment, they were worth more than an emperor's robes.

I embraced the clothes and thought about the actions of the prison guard. Despite being a woman in uniform, she behaved like other Khmer women I had observed: sweet and gentle. She must have realized that I spoke only a little Khmer, as she often used sign language to direct me in my work tasks. She never cursed or used foul words with me. However, I never expected her to be so kind as to secretly give me clothes.

I wore my new shirt over my ragged one and covered myself with the *krama*, which had been used to make the bundle. I leaned my back against the wall and bitterly recalled my past.

I am a Phuthai from Khammouane, which lies along the Lao-Vietnamese border. I was born to a poor farming family with many children. When I graduated from high school, I was supposed to study at a college in Vientiane. However, since the trip to the capital took about two weeks and staying in Vientiane would be expensive, my father decided to send me to Hue, in Vietnam, instead.

At my university in Hue, I was studying with Lao, Vietnamese, and Cambodian students. At the time, the revolutionary movement had exploded in Vietnam, but I did not yet know what a revolution was. In 1945, as the revolutionary movement was spreading all over the three countries of Indochina, I returned to Laos. Then the French colonial administration lost the war and withdrew, but Indochina was soon occupied by Japanese Fascists.

The war raged as Cambodians, Laotians, and Vietnamese rose up and fought against the foreign powers. Outraged by the invasions and caring about the fate of my country, I began to realize my obligations as a citizen. I became immersed in the revolution and Marxist-Leninism and eventually joined the Lao People's Liberation Movement.

Six months later, I was assigned to work in the propaganda group to recruit more people to our cause. When the Japanese lost World War II and sent their army home, the French resumed their occupation of Indochina. However, under the guidance of the Indochinese Communist Party, the nationalist movements in the three countries still fought for independence.

Unfortunately, one rainy season, I was arrested in a village and deported to Phnom Penh. I was sentenced to imprisonment in Koh Tralach, where I remained for two years. But now I had good reason to hope that I would soon be freed. The French had brought prisoners like me from Koh Tralach for a retrial in Phnom Penh because the island was overcrowded with political prisoners. The French had decided to release some who had been given light sentences.

As I was lost in thought, someone shoved me to ground so that I could be shackled. That night, I was able to sleep soundly for the first time since being imprisoned because I had a blanket—the *krama*—thanks to the kindness of a prison guard whom I would never forget.

I was the only foreign inmate there; the rest were Cambodians. I stayed in Phnom Penh Prison for three more months before my retrial took place in a military court. The judges were all French, but my two attorneys were Cambodians. Probably thanks to the large number of political prisoners and the lack of space for more, the attorneys kept demanding my release, which was eventually granted.

A few hours later, I was brought before the Prison Chief. After giving me many warnings, he issued me a letter of release and let me go. My only possessions were a change of clothes and the *krama*, both gifted to me by the kind guard. I had no money, nothing else at all.

For someone new in town like me, Phnom Penh seemed huge. The markets were crowded with people while the roads formed a giant chessboard. I saw shops selling expensive goods and people smiling. I felt I was the only one who was sad and lonely. I walked and walked without any specific direction until nearly dawn. Finally, I reached a small hill with a massive stupa and temple at the top. It was a clean place, so I decided to rest there for the night.

I used a broken tree branch to sweep a small open space for me to sleep, south of the temple, and then lay down, my stomach growling. When night came, I trembled in the sharp cold, but my spirit felt as free as a bird that had just been released from its cage. For the first time in two years, I was able to sleep without being shackled or watched by guards.

I don't know how long I slept, but when the noises of birds in the trees woke me, the sun was already high. When I sat up, I saw an old monk holding a broom and staring cautiously at me. I knelt and bowed to him and asked for the broom to sweep the place for him. He smiled gently, and after learning I was Lao, he spoke to me in Thai. "I'm sure you understand Thai, don't you?"

"Yes, sir, I can understand some. Thai and Lao languages are similar."

"Don't you have a home? Why were you sleeping here?"

"I was arrested by the French in Laos, and they detained me in Koh Tralach for two years. They just released me yesterday."

He slowly nodded. "My dwelling is in the north of the temple. You can go there later to have some porridge."

That day, I wandered around the city, thinking about what I could do for a living and how I could save money to return to Laos. I did not speak enough Khmer or know about the daily life of Cambodian people.

Southeast of the hill was a large market crowded with people and big shops owned by Chinese. Vietnamese people sold their goods in the market, while Cambodian vendors peddled their stuff from baskets on the street. South of the market lay a port, where ships and small boats entered and exited every day. There I saw many coolies who made their living carrying heavy loads. Seeing them, I realized there was a job for me.

That evening, I went back to my place near the temple. By now I knew that the hill was called Phnom Daun Penh while the temple on it was known as Wat Phnom. Everyone here knew Wat Phnom because it was the symbol of Phnom Penh, as Pha That Luang was to Vientiane.

Not long after I lay down, the monk who spoke Thai appeared again. He gave me a mat, a blanket, and a piece of cloth to cover myself while bathing. I knelt and bowed before him for his kindness. After giving me a few words of advice, he left. His kindness reminded me of the charitable prison guard who had given me clothes.

That night I slept soundly and more comfortably than ever, like a rich man sleeping in his mansion.

CHAPTER 3
COINCIDENCE OR FATE

The next morning, I went to the port to ask for work as a coolie. The job wasn't hard; besides, I had served two years of hard labor in prison.

One day, I was carrying a hundred-kilogram sack of beans on my back from the pier to the shoreline. As I balanced on a wooden bridge, a Khmer coolie shouted to me, "Wow! Lao, you can carry really heavy weight!"

None of the Khmer coolies at the pier knew my name, but since they knew that I was Lao, they called me "Lao."

"After just a few days, our Lao friend can carry such a heavy load!" another Khmer coolie shouted.

Dropping the bean sack in its place, I wiped the sweat from my forehead and began walking back toward the pier where several coolies were taking a rest. On seeing me they called out, "Hey, our Lao friend! Come for a smoke break."

All the workers here liked me because they saw that I was softspoken and kind. As I heard my new friends beckoning me, I saw a young lady washing clothes on the bow of a large fishing boat and looking at me timidly. When our eyes met, it gave me a strange feeling of confusion, and she too turned her face away.

Chatting with my friends, I felt some sort of mystic force compel me to look at the young lady again and again.

After a while, she turned her face up to look back at me, but at the moment she met my eyes, she looked down again—this time revealing a shy smile.

I rested, then returned to the ship to carry more bean sacks. As I dropped a sack onto the pile at the shoreline, an old lady carrying a large basket filled with her shopping approached me and asked, "Excuse me, can you help me carry that bag to my boat?"

As she spoke, she pointed to a sack containing about two *tau* [about four pecks] of rice.

I replied as I wiped dirt off my shoulder. "Yes, which one's your boat?"

"Just follow me."

I lifted the rice sack onto my shoulder and followed her to the pier. At the top of the ramp, she walked to the boat where the young lady was washing clothes.

Seeing the older woman approaching, the young one got up and took the heavy basket from her, then said happily, "Mother, you are back from the market? I haven't cooked the rice yet."

"It's okay. The sun is not high yet."

I understood then that the older lady was the owner of the boat and the young one was her daughter.

After telling me where to place the rice sack, the old lady put her hand into her pocket and said, "How much do I owe you?"

"It's okay, auntie. I want nothing for it," I replied, shaking my head.

"Ah, why don't you want to be paid?" the old lady asked, opening her eyes wide.

"Your sack of rice isn't heavy at all. Please think of it as me just helping you out."

Despite my answer, the old lady hesitated. Her daughter discreetly watched me and said, "He is a Lao national, Mother."

Hearing this, the old lady gave me a friendly smile and said in Lao, "Please tell me your name."

"Yes! … My name is Bophan Suvanthon," I replied.

As there were still many bean sacks in the ship I had been working on, I hurriedly said goodbye to the old lady and left to get back. I did not want to lose any of my wages for the day.

At noon, I and the other coolies had our lunch break. I walked to wash myself at the pier and get ready to buy my lunch at the nearby market. Just then, I saw the young lady appear at the bow of her boat and call out to me. "My parents want to invite you to join us for lunch."

I was shocked; I hadn't expected her to speak to me in Lao. I started to wonder whether her parents were Lao or Khmer. Even more surprising, I had just met her mother and had only carried a small sack of rice for her. Why was she kind enough to invite me for lunch?

Seeing that I was hesitant, the girl spoke again. "Please come on up! My father and mother are waiting to meet you."

When she said this, it would have been impolite for me to refuse. Also, I wanted to keep my manly bearing. So I smiled back and headed toward her boat.

The boat was bigger than the others around it and had a large, strong roof. A wall of wood divided the interior into two spacious rooms with clean wooden floors.

Inside, a man in his forties and the old lady were waiting for me. I guessed he was the young lady's father.

I greeted him politely and sat facing him. His wife brought a teapot and poured hot tea into three cups, handing one to me.

"Have some tea first, my dear," she said.

"Thank you," I replied, reaching for the cup with both hands.

Her husband stared at me, eyeing me from head to toe, and finally asked, "I heard you are Lao, is that right?"

"Yes, I am."

"Which ethnic group are you from?"

"I'm of Phuthai heritage."

"From what province?"

"I'm from Khammouane."

"What's your name? And how old are you?"

"My name is Bophan Suvanthon. I'm twenty this year."

He sipped his tea, and then continued. "I heard from my daughter, Mealea, that there was a port coolie from Laos. So I wanted to learn more about you. How did you end up here? In Phnom Penh, we rarely run into Lao people."

Since his Lao was so much better than his wife's and daughter's, I decided to ask, "Excuse me, but are you Lao too?"

"No, I'm Khmer. But my hometown's in Stung Treng; that's why I can speak Lao. My wife's hometown is Kratie, and that is where my daughter, Mealea, grew up, so they can also speak Lao."

I understood then why all the members of this family could speak my country's language. The father's hometown, Stung Treng, bordered Champasak, in Laos. Many Lao people resided in Stung Treng!

I took another sip of tea and said, "I don't know anyone in Phnom Penh and have never encountered any Lao nationals either. Meeting you and your family really makes me happy."

The boat master chuckled and asked me sympathetically, "If you don't have any relatives or know anyone here, why did you come to Phnom Penh?"

I suddenly felt hesitant and ashamed to tell them the truth: that I had been in prison at Koh Tralach. Maybe they would stop being friendly. Yet lying to them would mean betraying my conscience. Eventually, I told them all about myself.

Afterwards, the husband and wife looked at one another without speaking. Then the mother called out to Mealea in Khmer to bring our lunch. The daughter responded in a lovely soft voice, then brought out a tray with hot dishes.

As Mealea disappeared back inside, the couple asked me to enjoy the meal. In the awkward silence, I wondered what they were thinking about me. I felt as if I were riding a tiger's back: I could neither stay on nor get off. I tried my best to bear my shame and continue sharing the meal with them.

After the meal, Mealea came to take away the dishes. Her father was smiling again and handed me a small package of tobacco, while rolling a cigarette for himself. "My name is Reus, and my wife is Hem," he said. "I have two children. You already met my daughter. Her little brother is at our home."

I tried to change the subject by asking him, "Where is your home?"

Hem, who had been quiet, answered for her husband. "Our house is in Chroy Chongvar, but I come to sell our fish at this pier every day. I am very sorry for your being so far away from your hometown. Please come to visit us whenever you see our boat. You can have all the fish you want."

Not until then had I understood my hosts' minds. Their earlier quietness was caused not by their disapproval of me but rather their pity.

So I sincerely thanked them. "I really appreciate your kindness for a homeless person like me…"

The father exhaled cigarette smoke and said, "The Khmer character is to sympathize with the poor and underprivileged. Don't be ashamed of your job. No work is lowly as long as you don't steal from anyone. In my younger days, I used to struggle like you. I used to pull a rickshaw, and worked as a coolie and a servant. It was not until I reached this age that I managed to build a proper life for my family."

The consoling words of my host warmed my heart and melted away my shame.

As I chatted with her father, Mealea kept looking at me demurely. She was petite and had long hair that fell below her shoulders, dark eyes, a small nose and lips, and clear brown skin. Whenever our eyes met, I felt my heart thumping and my body warming all over.

As my mind was distracted by her, I worried that I might say something wrong, so I hurriedly said goodbye to the couple and their daughter.

From that day on, whenever her boat was at the pier, Mealea always offered me fish from her mother. Her parents asked me to join them at lunch. As time went by, our friendship grew. Mealea and I gradually became bold enough to tease each other. Whenever I didn't see her boat at the pier, I felt a perplexing sense of ... loneliness.

Translated from Khmer by Rinith Taing

SOK CHANPHAL

The Kerosene Lamp Ghost Stories

Editors' Note
Sok Chanphal is well known for his short stories, novellas, and song lyrics. He was awarded the Southeast Asian Writers Award for Cambodia in 2013. His collected short stories, Dream, *published in Khmer in 2019, includes many of his best known stories, including this one. While ghost stories are very popular in Cambodia—and sharing them is a form of entertainment—one terrible consequence of the Khmer Rouge period was that countless people died without receiving funeral rites and, many survivors believe, became wandering spirits.*

One evening, a ghost-story contest was held at the Tuol Sleng Genocide Museum. A prize of one hundred thousand riels was offered to the person who could tell the best scary story. The event was organized by Mr. Chak, who also made himself one of the judges. The master of ceremonies began the evening by asking Mr. Chak to give a speech. Looking very serious, Mr. Chak spoke slowly.

"First of all, I would like to thank the MC for giving me this chance to open the contest," he said. "I'd also like to thank all of you who have come to this event—especially the ladies and children—and also the contestants. We are all together now. I would like to acknowledge Mr. Buth, the head janitor at Tuol Sleng, who has made the venue so welcoming. And I'd like to give a nod to Mr. Sarak, the electricity manager in Tuol Sleng, who has been most cooperative. He's turned off all the lights to ensure that Tuol Sleng is dark, to heighten our fright."

Mr. Chak paused to give the audience a chance to look around the darkened room. The inky blackness made everyone feel even more deliciously frightened; the only illumination came from a couple of kerosene lamps at the front. One lamp was on the MC's table; the other was in front of Mr. Chak. Plastic ghosts had been hung from the ceiling, and they flapped in a breeze that passed through the room. Everyone shuddered. The twenty or so people in the audience avidly enjoyed ghost stories and had paid two thousand riels each for a ticket.

Mr. Chak resumed his speech. He greeted Mr. Bunly, the head security guard, who would protect the audience against the evil ghosts and not let them interrupt the event. "Also," Mr Chak said, "I would like to say thanks to the grandmothers and grandfathers, and to the little children here. I'd like especially to greet the contestants who signed up to tell ghost stories. And even more, I'd like to especially thank the audience members sitting in the back who can't hear me well. Finally, I would like to acknowledge the other judges sitting next to me: Mr. Phann and Madam Srey Pou. And out of respect, I would especially like to greet all the souls that died at Tuol Sleng, and—"

Someone in the audience shouted, "Stop with all the greetings! You are wasting so much time. Let's start the program; you keep saying 'especially this, especially that.' When are we going to start hearing the stories? We bought tickets to hear stories—not to hear you thank everybody!"

Mr. Chak fell silent, and the MC took over. "I would like to greet the grandfathers, grandmothers, aunties and uncles, and little children again," he said.

"Let's start the program!" someone else in the audience yelled. "If you keep greeting people like this, you won't be done until tomorrow morning."

The MC blinked. He gazed down at the paper, which he wanted to keep reading from, but couldn't decide whether or not to skip his prepared remarks. Members of the audience were yelling, "Let's start the program!"

This annoyed the MC, but he folded the sheet, put it in his pocket, and resumed talking without reading from it. "Let's begin the contest. And so, currently we have only two contestants. If anyone else wants to participate, you can come up and sign in now to take your turn. However, I don't want to waste more time or make the audience wait any longer. So, please welcome the first contestant, Mr. Samrak. He will tell a story called 'The Trip to Hell.' And I want to inform you that everyone in the audience will be judging the contest because I don't want anyone to criticize how we handled the program or accuse any judge of taking a bribe. So please, everyone, pay attention and decide at the end which story is the scariest. And by the way, we have to excuse all the judges from voting on the first contestant as he is Mr. Chak's son. Okay, now it is time for Mr. Samrak to tell his story. Please give him a round of applause." Faint clapping from the audience greeted Mr. Samrak, a skinny young man with a pointy face and protruding lips. He began his story.

THE TRIP TO HELL

I answer my cellphone and see it displays the numbers 333. A creepy female voice speaks. "Hello," she says. "I'm calling from Hell to invite you to visit. Please, don't be surprised. You don't need to pack anything. In just a moment, my team from the Ministry of Tourism will come by to pick up your soul. Hell will provide for your transportation, hotel, and meals. You don't need to worry about spending any money at all. Now, just go to sleep as you normally would, and be sure not to tell anyone about this. If you do, I will cancel your invitation. Goodbye."

"Wait!"

She talks so fast that she doesn't give me a chance to ask any questions. What should I do with an invitation to Hell? It could be the greatest opportunity of my life!

It's around midnight when two ghost officials arrive for my soul and escort me to a modern-looking subway station. There I see about ten people waiting.

As the train leaves the subway station with all of us aboard, an older man turns to a lady sitting next to him. "Have you ever been to Hell?"

"This is my first time," the lady replies. "I've heard that being given a chance to visit is rare. When I got the invitation, I was so happy I fainted, and my soul left before I could inform my children where I was going."

"Do you know why they invited us?"

"I heard that they give invitations to Hell as a reward to good people, because when good people die, they go to Heaven and don't get a chance to visit."

"How long do you think this will take? I need to get back to care for my sick mother."

"Don't worry. It's just one night. When we wake up, we will be in our own beds at home. I can't spend a long time here either, since I need to attend a Buddhist ceremony and tomorrow I need to donate to an orphanage."

The train continues nonstop across a dark domain, then pulls into a station. An announcement comes over the speaker: "Welcome, ladies and gentlemen. Please step off the train. You have arrived at Hell Station. We welcome you to Hell." Then the speakers boom in English, "LADIES AND GENTLEMEN!"

Outside the station we see a number of well-dressed ghosts standing in a welcome line and smiling at us. A lady ghost, maybe the tour guide, says, "Over there is the mayor of Hell. He's here to welcome everyone." She points at an old man who is dressed in traditional Cambodian clothing and waving at us.

Loud applause greets the mayor as he begins to speak. "On behalf of Hell City," he says, "I warmly welcome all ten of you. For a thousand years, our Ministry of Tourism has been planning this trip for good people. And today you are our first guests to Hell."

Then everyone steps forward happily to receive a copy of the itinerary.

Mr. Samrak fell silent until the audience started yelling at him. "What happens next?!"

Mr. Samrak turned to Mr. Chak, his father, then pointed at him and said to the audience, "If you want to know more, please ask him."

Someone from the audience shouted, "You are the contestant telling the story! Why are you asking your father to tell the rest of it?"

Mr. Samrak smiled. "This story came to me in a dream, but when I reached this point, my father woke me up to tell me to take him to the toilet." Mr. Chak looked embarrassed. "He won't go to the toilet by himself," Mr. Samrak explained, "because he is afraid of ghosts." He sat down, shaking his head. "I guess the story is unfinished." Someone else yelled, "What's going on here?! Since your father woke you up, please allow the other contestant to tell his story. And, what's more, go back to your dreams and get your storytelling prize in Hell."

The MC rose. "Let's show our thanks to the first contestant. Now please, everyone, don't be angry—whether or not his story gets a prize depends on you. Anyway, I guarantee that you'll like the next story because it will scare you very much. Everyone, please give a round of applause to our second contestant, Mr. Srun. He's come to tell a story about Neangneak's ghost. Please, go ahead."

Mr. Srun had short hair that shone with coconut oil and wore his shirt tucked inside his pants. He held a kerosene lamp as he stepped in front of the crowd.

"I wish to greet you and bow respectfully to everyone," he said. "I would like to respectfully greet the MC of this program and the neutral judges. And even more, I'd like to respectfully greet the audience because you are the important judges who will give me the award. Please, everyone, accept my genuine appreciation."

Then Mr. Srun stopped and took a long breath. The audience was thinking that this guy had the same chatty style as Mr. Chak and, moreover, sounded like a phony. But they nevertheless waited to see what would happen, knowing they would not give him a good score unless he told a really scary story.

Mr. Srun continued. "I'm really delighted to be here." He paused. "You all look frightened already. I'm Srun, and I'm going to tell you a story called 'Neangneak's Ghost Baby' to entertain you. Oh, sorry, actually to make you frightened. Please give me your attention."

NEANGNEAK'S GHOST BABY

When Neangneak died, all of the villagers at her death ceremony were frightened because the village's Buddhist priest wasn't there. The sound of the monks chanting was eerily sad and resonated in the mind of Mr. Seth, a guy who was old enough to be someone's husband but was nevertheless still afraid of ghosts.

Mr. Seth pulled the bed covers up to his face, not covering it because he was afraid he would look like a ghost. He was frightened all the way to the tips of his toes. He was afraid that a cold, ghostly hand would grab him and drag him away. He was so afraid that he could not even close his eyes, afraid that a ghost would sit next to him. He was so afraid that he could feel his soul rising into his throat, ready to escape his body. His heart was pounding, and he trembled as the wind blew through the room. When he heard a mouse scamper across the floor, his lips quivered.

He started talking to himself. "Is a mouse an animal that isn't afraid of ghosts? Or is a mouse only afraid of a ghost mouse? The next time I see a mouse witness another mouse die, I'll have to see if it's afraid of that dead mouse's ghost. I won't be afraid of a mouse ghost! I may see a mouse ghost scaring other mice, but it won't bother me. If I met the ghosts of people, though, I'd be horrified. For example, suppose it's a ghost with long, sweeping hair and a white dress and black eyes—speaking slowly without opening its mouth. I would be very frightened of such a lady ghost ... just like Neangneak's ghost. I knew Neangneak when she was alive, and even then her face was scary. She would be even more frightening as a ghost. Yikes. So crazy! Why did I think of her? I need to calm down and think about beautiful women instead of Neangneak's face. I'll pretend not to be afraid, but there is nothing I can do about it. I'm still thinking of Neangneak's face."

Mr. Seth was alone at home. His parents and sister had gone to the provinces and would return the next day. Although Mr. Seth was afraid of ghosts, he'd never actually met one. Ghosts were merely a figment of Mr. Seth's imagination, the result of what he'd seen in the movies.

The next day, on his way to the field, Mr. Seth passed Neangneak's miserable-looking hut; a spirit flag was hanging out front. It was so quiet around there. Seth felt scared and ran away. Because he hadn't attended Neangneak's death ceremony, he wasn't aware that her body was buried in that very field. He started to clear the land with a hoe, intending to plant potatoes. But when he heard the rustling of bamboo interrupt the silence around him, he began trembling. Holding the hoe, he suddenly heard the sound of someone crying in a high voice. He immediately dropped the hoe and ran. Not paying attention to where he was going, he ended up at Neangneak's grave. Sitting in front of it was a figure in a white dress.

"It's a ghost, a ghost haunting me!" He wanted to scream and run, to find his way back home, but he was powerless to move.

"Uncle Seth." It was the voice of a little girl.

"Oh, a ghost is haunting me, calling my name!"

He tried to run, but he stumbled and fell. Behind him, he heard the voice again. "Uncle Seth, it's me!"

"I know who you are. You are Neangneak. Don't hurt me. I have done nothing to make you want to scare me. " He closed his eyes, his body trembling as he could neither get off the ground nor turn around to face the ghost.

"A Seth! A Seth! Little Seth!" said another voice. "Why are you lying here trembling? What happened?"

Mr. Seth looked up to discover that this second voice belonged to Mr. Sau. Reassured, Mr. Seth said, "The Neangneak ghost is haunting me. Can't you see her?"

"Where do you see Neangneak?" Mr. Sau asked.

"You don't see anything? Maybe that's because she isn't haunting you! When she saw you, she disappeared."

Mr. Seth stood up and looked around. He saw Neangnee, the daughter of Neangneak, staring at him.

"You're Neangnee, aren't you? I thought you were your mother haunting me; I got confused because you are wearing a white dress," he said.

Mr. Sau shook his head. "You are too old to be afraid of ghosts; you're just like a kid."

"If you were me, you'd be afraid too. Neangnee's crying sounded just like a ghost's voice." Mr. Seth and Mr. Sau turned to Neangnee. Her eyes were red from crying.

"Do you miss your mother? Don't worry, your mother has gone to heaven—no need to miss her," Mr. Sau said.

"My uncle has told me he will take me to live with him, since I am an orphan, but I don't want to leave my mother here alone. I'm afraid she'll feel lonely," Neangnee said sadly.

"So you'd rather stay here by your mother's grave?" Mr. Seth asked.

"When my mother was alive, she was afraid of ghosts. She used to tell me that when she died, she wanted me to come to visit her. If I go to Phnom Penh to live with my uncle, how will I be able to comfort her?" Neangnee asked.

"Don't think like that, Granddaughter. If you want to visit your mother, come back for the ceremony on each anniversary of her death. Meanwhile, think of your future. If you live with your uncle, will he allow you to study? I'm concerned that instead of treating you like a daughter, his family will look upon you as a servant," Mr. Sau said.

"I heard that he will make me be a doughnut seller for him," Neangnee said.

"Oh, my god!" Mr. Seth replied.

"That would be child abuse," Mr. Sau told her.

"But I am not his daughter. How can I expect to stay in his home for free without being of any benefit to him. How could he afford to feed me?"

"What she says is right, Uncle," Mr. Seth added. "It wouldn't be child abuse to make her work, as long as he feeds her. Besides, if he doesn't support her, who will? On the other hand, with this reasoning he could justify exploiting her."

Mr. Sau slapped Mr. Seth on the head. "How foolish! Nobody but you thinks about it that way," he said.

Then he turned to Neangnee. "Granddaughter, before you go live with your uncle, please ask him whether he will allow you to study. If he will, please return his good deed by helping out his family. Then it would not be child abuse."

"But I will have to sell doughnuts, Grandfather, because he is a doughnut seller."

Mr. Sau nodded. "There is nothing else you can do to support yourself. Let it go. It's okay to live with him and work for your room and board." Then Mr. Sau turned to Mr. Seth and said, "I heard that you are going away to Phnom Penh to study."

"Yes, Uncle. I'm leaving for Phnom Penh next month."

"When you get there, don't forget about this girl! Be sure to find out where Neangnee is living with her uncle and go visit her often."

Later on, Neangnee went to live with her uncle in Phnom Penh, and Mr. Seth studied at a college nearby. Whenever there was an anniversary ceremony for her mother, Mr. Seth brought Neangnee back to their hometown. Time passed, and Mr. Seth graduated and became a medical doctor in the village. Although his parents tried to force him to marry, he wouldn't. He was waiting for Neangnee to receive her high school diploma, and then he planned to marry her.

As for Neangnee, being the daughter of the ghost Neangneak, her life was sorrowful and hard. But when she married Mr. Seth, her fortunes changed. There was only one problem: Mr. Seth was still afraid of ghosts.

"The end," Mr. Srun said. "Thank you for your attention."

Confused, the audience looked around, and someone shouted, "That's it?!"

"I think this story has surprised you, but don't forget to give me your vote for the prize. I would like to say thank you in advance." Mr. Srun bowed.

Smiling, Mr. Srun was about to leave the speaker's platform when someone in the audience yelled at him. "Stop! Why didn't you talk about Neangneak's ghost? You just told us about Neangnee!"

"Sister, thank you for your question," Mr. Srun responded. "As I explained, Neangnee is the daughter of Neangneak's ghost, which is why I talked more about her."

"No one wants to hear about Neangnee; she is a living human!" another person protested.

Mr. Srun smiled. "Yes, I'm so sorry. But you see, this is a true story, not a made-up one. After Neangneak died, she never came to visit the village as a ghost or wrote to tell the villagers about her ghost life. I don't know anything else about her."

Mr. Srun walked off the stage and sat down. He thought that everyone had been very interested in his story, and that his story would win the prize. The people in the audience, however, were shaking their heads over his story.

Then the MC got up to speak. "These two candidates have tried their best, and the audience is considering which story deserves the prize. But we still want to give the award of one hundred thousand riels to the best storyteller. So, please, if there is anyone else who wishes to tell a ghost story, we welcome you to come forward now."

The room was completely silent. There were no volunteers. Then Madam Srey Pou, one of the judges, stood up to speak.

"On behalf of the judges, I would like to say something. Nowadays our society is all about gender equality. Take me, for example. I served as a judge to provide a gender role model for women. And I'm really sad that among the three judges, I'm the only woman. But no matter; some members of the audience are women, which is good."

"Madam!" said someone from the audience, "we're not here to discuss gender."

Madam Srey Pou didn't care if anyone was listening; she just kept giving her opinions. "Yes, now I'd like to urge a woman contestant to come up to challenge the men. How many women are here? I notice there are fewer women than men. I would encourage a brave woman, who dares to come on the stage, to challenge the male contestants and to let them know that women have the same abilities as men. I would like to give you some examples. Women nowadays are very clever. They have official positions in government and in the various ministries. In fact, in some countries, a woman is even the prime minister."

"Sorry, Madam, please finish speechifying," said the MC. "Don't bore the audience; we have to continue on with our program."

Madam Srey Pou ignored him. "Yes, I'm just opening up the subject so we can talk about gender. And I want to leave all you women with this message: we must be aware of our own self-worth and not simply accept the value placed on us by men. Now, I'd like to turn to tonight's contest. We've already seen that these two contestants are unable to tell a good ghost story. One talked about a dream and the other talked about the orphaned daughter of a ghost. And the accomplishments of the orphan girl do not represent the potential of all women; the story just describes a particular young woman who merely graduates from high school and then gets married. We should—"

Mr. Phann nudged her lightly as a signal to stop, but she paused only briefly before continuing. "Yes," she said, "if there is a woman here who can really compete against these men, please come up and tell a genuine ghost story. Remember, we are in Tuol Sleng prison, a place with a history of genocide and torture. That is another reason why I want to embolden a woman contestant to tell a ghost story—to talk about people who died during the Pol Pot regime.

"Having made my point, I still have more to say. Actually, I know a ghost story—a ghost story from Pol Pot times—but I didn't want to beat out the contestants here, so I didn't register. When I was young, I won many contests and accomplished many things—"

She noticed that everyone was yawning. "Well, anyway, I would like to finish my thoughts. Let's please encourage a brave woman to come up here and be a contestant."

The MC was about to say something when a woman wearing a black dress appeared on the platform and walked over to the kerosene lamp. Her arrival made Madam Srey Pou very happy. The people in the audience stared at this woman with a mysterious face and wondered where she had come from. They figured she might be a good contestant who could tell a real ghost story, since just looking at her frightened them.

"Now, I see we have a volunteer to tell us a ghost story," the MC said in a quavering voice. "Can you please tell us your name and the title of your story?"

A keening voice filled the room. "My name is Phin. I want to tell a story called 'My Story.'"

When everyone heard her voice, they suspected they would be the most frightened by her and would want to give her the prize. The MC rushed off the speaker's platform without asking any more questions. Now, even Madam Srey Pou looked frightened, nodding her head as a signal for the contestant to begin.

This is a strong woman, Madam Srey Pou mused, *though the title of the story is a bit strange. I've already decided to give her a higher score than the others.*

MY STORY

During the Pol Pot time, I was forced to evacuate Phnom Penh to a village in Battambang. I was separated from my relatives and, most significantly, from a young man who lived near me and whom I'd loved since childhood. At this time, my entire life consisted only of tears. But I could only cry in secret, because if the villagers heard me crying, they would kill me. The young people in the Khmer Rouge were the cruelest—like beasts. They considered us people from the city to be subhuman. I suspect they were all illiterate peasants. Every day they tried to catch someone doing something wrong, so we were constantly worried about being caught.

One day when I was working in the rice field, I was cursing them in my mind when all at once my stomach began to cramp painfully; it was time for my menses. I couldn't bear the pain, so I sat down. Then a young Khmer Rouge woman came toward me, yelling and cursing. "You are lazy and acting crazy in order to get out of work!" she scolded. She wanted to drag me off to be "re-educated." Luckily, at that moment a young man came by and begged her to stop, telling her, "She's my relative." So the Khmer Rouge girl released me and began flirting with the handsome young man. She stopped threatening me in order to bat her eyes at him. His name was Veasna, and although skinny, he was still handsome. We'd never met before, but because he dared to protect me, I fell in love with him instantly.

Later on, Veasna and I would exchange glances, but only secretly, because we feared being accused of acting immorally and being "disappeared."

Unfortunately, one day when I walked to the outdoor latrine, I happened to see Veasna. Oh, my gosh! I sighed in embarrassment. I turned my back, with my eyes closed, until he was finished; and after I'd finished, we walked together back to the village. He told me that he thought about me all the time—even when going to the latrine. I was so happy. But as we passed by the Khmer Rouge girl's house, she called out to Veasna and ordered him to come inside.

I walked home alone, really angry. There was nothing I could do. I could only wish that she'd "disappear" herself forever. I imagined that she called Veasna to her house so she could seduce him. I felt sorry for him. I tried to calm down and concluded that he should just give in to her and forget about me. The important thing was to stay alive. His body was still his own.

That is not the end of this tragic story. When the Khmer Rouge girl found out about our love, she reported us, and I was taken to Tuol Sleng prison. We never saw each other again.

Having reached this point in her story, Phin began crying pitifully. She wanted to continue, but someone in the audience yelled at her, "Stop speaking! When you started, you made your voice sound very frightening; but as you went along, all we heard was you talking about yourself and nothing about scary ghosts."

Phin responded slowly. "My story isn't finished."

The person in the audience continued. "Everyone here was bored by your story. If you don't know how to tell a ghost story, just stop."

"But I've never seen a ghost," Phin said.

Another listener shouted at her. "So stop speaking now! We want to hear ghost stories."

"But I've already told my story," Phin replied.

"So your story is a ghost story?" Everyone jeered.

"Yes, because I'm a ghost."

At this, everyone jumped to their feet, gaping at her in fright, and started running for the exit. The hall quickly emptied, except for two people too frightened to move. One of them was Madam Srey Pou.

"Madam, you are a well-educated person," Phin said to her. "Your speech made a ghost lady like me very happy. You are the reason why I appeared in front of the audience. The ghost men here were too afraid to reveal themselves. You know, I was cruelly killed by Pol Pot. So why didn't those people want to listen to my sorrowful story? Now I have something more to say. Because you are an intelligent lady, I would like to ask you for help. Would you please help me sue for justice for my soul's sake in the Khmer Rouge Tribunal, the Extraordinary Chambers in the Courts of Cambodia, for war crimes? Madam, please assist me!"

Madam Srey Pou sat trembling as she listened to Phin, and then she fainted. Phin turned to the other person, Mr. Chak. A disembodied voice from elsewhere in the room said, "What's wrong with him? Why didn't he run out with the others when he had a chance?"

"Why didn't you run away?" Phin asked. "What are you doing here? Do you want to continue listening to my story?"

Mr. Chak couldn't speak. His legs shook. He staggered towards her, presented her with the award, and fainted.

Translated from Khmer by Soknea Nhim and Teri Schaffer Yamada

SOK CHANPHAL

Buried Treasure

Do you believe in dreams? Last night, I dreamed that someone told me where to dig for a box of treasure! Maybe it wasn't a heavenly being. Maybe it was a wandering ghost who came to make fun of me.

This morning, the sun is smiling so hard that it's showing its teeth. I am thinking about my dream: a box of gold buried on a hill under the palm trees. I'm not overly excited, but it would be untrue to say I'm not intrigued. I have mixed feelings about the whole idea. I have never thought that fortune would just fall from the sky; but then again, I'm fed up with my unlucky life. Still, why would someone come to me in a dream and tell me where to dig for treasure? Even if I found a real chest full of gold, as dumb as I am, I wouldn't know what to do with it. All I can think of is to buy food, eat, sleep, and turn myself into a pig.

palmyra palm (Borassus flabellifer) is the national tree of Cambodia

In any case, here I am walking toward the spot revealed to me in my dream, my mind full of uncertainty. I notice that the grass along the path toward the hill looks like it has been trampled by oxen and cows, and the earth is torn up, as though horses ridden by soldiers have just run over it. No, I see that it wasn't horses, oxen, and cows that have chewed up the path: it was villagers.

In wonder, I stop and look around. Oh! Under the palm trees on the hill, villagers have gathered in a group, chattering like sparrows who have just returned to their nests in the evening. The crowd looks exactly like the people I saw in my dream, standing beside these very palm trees.

Oh, my goodness! I'm too late. There really must be some buried treasure on the mound under the palms. Who came in their dreams to tell the whole village to dig here?

"Hey, diggers!" a person on the fringes of the crowd yells out. "Have you found any treasure yet?" Like me, he is too late to get a chance to dig.

Crash! Don't be alarmed. It's not the sound of falling palm fruit. It's the sound of two men fighting, and one of them has fallen down. If palm fruit were to fall on these men, they would both be seeing stars.

"Hey, stop fighting! What evil has gotten into you?" an old lady yells. "If you fight like that, you won't get a share of the treasure." The two stop fighting and rejoin the crowd.

Bang! When a loud noise rings out, everyone turns to look. A frightened child begins screaming. A big-shot policeman fires his handgun into the air. Looking around at the villagers, he shouts arrogantly, "Get off this mound now! Back off!"

Bang! Another gunshot. The villagers look at each other, and when they see that an old lady has fallen to the ground, they cry out in panic.

"Don't make any false moves!" the policeman yells. "Carry this old dying lady to her house. Lend a hand." The child is screaming again. "Who is that child's mother? Take him away and feed him," the policeman orders. "This crowd is too disorderly. What do you mean a treasure is buried on this hill? Get! Go home!"

"We are not that stupid, you know!" says a fearless youth. "You plan to take the treasure yourself, don't you?"

Bang! The bold young man turns blue and backs away. Waving his gun, the policeman yells again. "This is an order from the head of the village commune! I'm not going to repeat myself. Go home now! Treasure or no treasure, leave it to the commune leaders. Whatever is here is not yours. If it is a treasure, the head of the commune will inform the government office. It's the property of the nation. The leaders will give the commune a portion of it for development."

The villagers stop talking and watch. The National Working Group—that is, the commune leaders—arrive and start eagerly digging. The faces of the commune head and his wife look like those of feverish gamblers expecting at any moment to hit the jackpot.

The village leader shows up, smiles at the commune head, and says, "If the village leader does not get involved here, the villagers will fight among themselves to get their shares, so it will be difficult to divide the treasure fairly."

"Hey! If it's real treasure, I'll give you a cut. But is it true; is the treasure real?" the head of the commune asks.

"Yes, absolutely. All the villagers had the same dream. I, my wife, and my three children dreamed it, too."

One of the villagers asks aloud, "I wonder why all of us had the same dream."

Oh! None of the villagers is going home. They hover around the diggers. Each villager may be thinking that if they all rush him, the policeman doesn't have enough bullets to kill everyone. If he starts shooting, he may kill somebody else first. So, I'll just stand here and observe until something happens.

Suddenly, I can see that they have found what looks like a metal box. I hear the head of the commune shouting, "Bring it to me! Let me open it myself."

The villagers squeeze in to watch the head of the commune open the box. I think to myself, *Just forget about it.* Treasure or no treasure, there are too many people, and anyway I don't think I deserve to share any part of it. I shrug and turn toward home. About three minutes later, *kreang!* My ears tell me the blast wasn't a gunshot. It sounded like a land mine.

Translated from Khmer by Yin Luoth

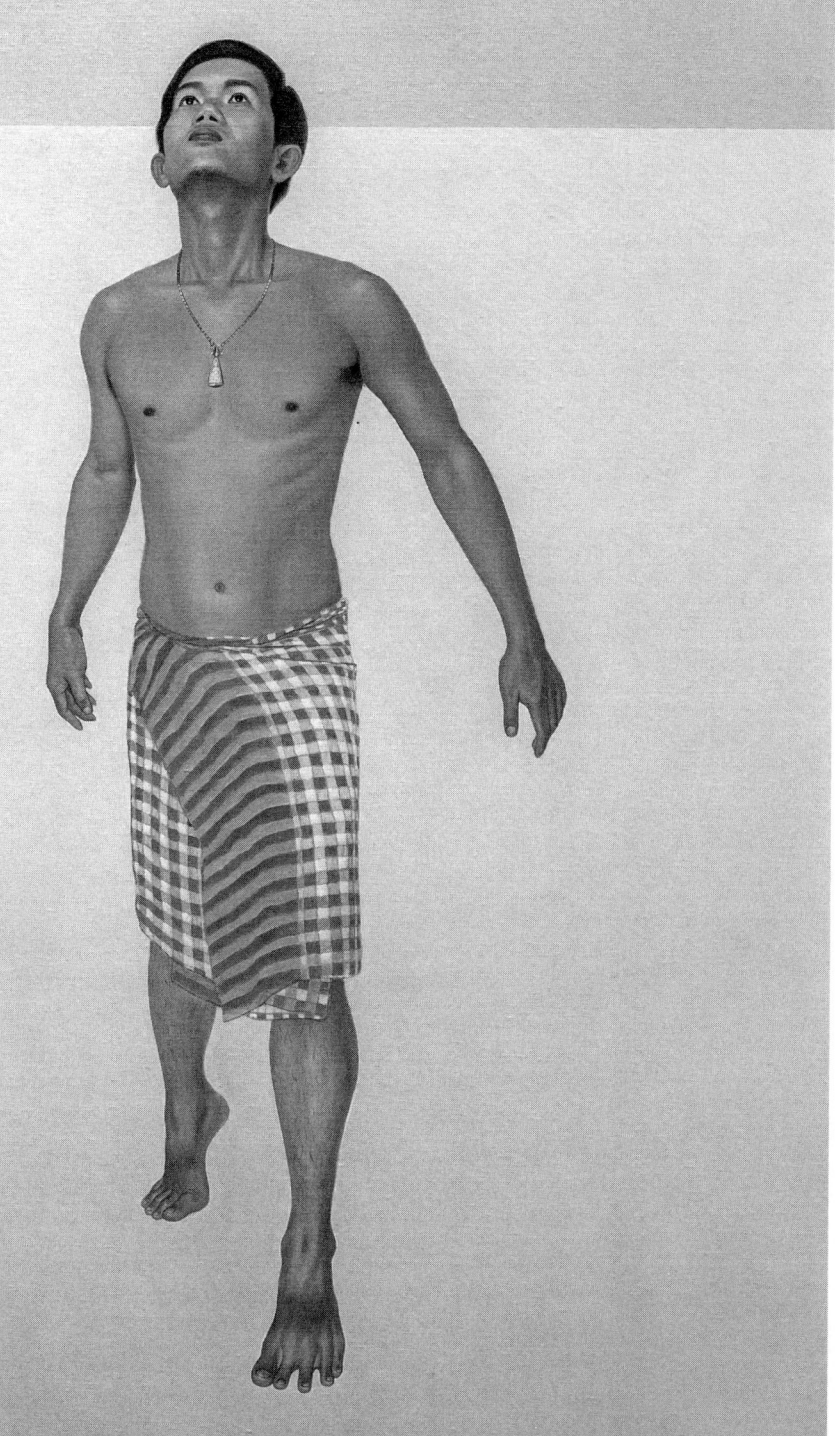

BUNCHAN MOL

from *Political Prison*

Editors' Note
Bunchan Mol was arrested and imprisoned by the French after joining a large demonstration in Phnom Penh calling for the release of Hem Chieu, a highly respected Buddhist monk and activist in Cambodia's Nationalist Movement. In his memoir, Political Prison, Mol describes his experience in prison from 1942 to 1945 on the island of Koh Tralach, recounting the cruelty of the French against those who opposed their rule in what was then called Indochina. Hard labor, torture, lack of medical care, and starvation killed many of the prisoners. After the Japanese briefly drove out the French in 1945, Mol was released and continued his anti-colonialist activity. In 1971, his prison memoir was published in Phnom Penh and became a bestseller. The following translation contains excerpts from chapters 7, 9, and 14. The kickboxing fight described here took place when he was twenty-two years old.

VOYAGE TO KOH TRALACH

At around five in the evening, the ship crew brought us prisoners some food: a big pot of steamed white rice and hot wax gourd and pork soup, with finely chopped salted greens and pepper on the surface. Dear readers! Since being arrested and imprisoned, suffering from miseries in Phnom Penh and Prey Nokor [Saigon] jails for three months and twenty days, I had not tasted white rice. Now, with a lot of rice and proper side dishes, I ate and ate until my stomach swelled to where I could barely breathe. I lay on the floor, and Eum, my friend from Takeo, saved me by slowly rubbing my belly. He scolded me for being such a pig. When what was in my stomach appeared to digest, my pain went away.

At six, the guard came in and shackled us. He ordered us to sleep. Around two hours later, we heard a loud whistle as the ship began its departure from the port. A sailor came and loosened the shackles, telling us that if the ship ran into grave danger, we had to free ourselves and jump into the sea to save ourselves. This puzzled me, so I asked a Khmer Krom man [Cambodian from Kampuchea Krom in what is now southern Vietnam], who was familiar with Koh Tralach island, about the warning. He explained that the ship had just entered the deepest area on the Cà Mau Sea, somewhere around a few kilometers beyond Cap Saint Jacques [Vũng Tàu], and the crew was cautious because there was a chance we could hit a floating mine laid by the Japanese. It would have been a disaster, and all of us prisoners would easily become fish food. We were placed below the bow, and since that part of the ship would be the first to hit the explosive, we would definitely be the first to depart this life. There would be no one to help us get unshackled because every crew member would be too busy saving his own neck. Even if we could free ourselves, there would be no time for us to escape. There was no hope, and all we could do for now was to pray to Buddha, Dharma, and Singha and ask our faraway parents for their blessings. It was every man for himself.

A few hours into our journey, all of us got seasick and threw up; the disgusting smells of our vomit gave us headaches. I tried my best to keep from throwing up, but eventually I had to give in, and the delicious meal I had just consumed came out. Suffering from dizziness, we soon dozed off. By the time we woke up, it was dawn, and the ship had already anchored.

Around an hour later, someone opened the hatch, and I saw people looking down at us. One of them said in Vietnamese, *"Chuyến này thuyền ít người."* I asked my Kampuchea Krom friend what that meant.

"Fewer people this time," he translated.

A few moments later, I heard the cargo on board being transferred to large boats that carried them to Koh Tralach's shore, which was about two kilometers from the ship. When all the offloading was finished, the crew unshackled us and brought us up to the deck. I then got my first look at Koh Tralach, an island with breathtaking scenery.

My dear readers! I couldn't believe Koh Tralach was so big, even bigger than Kampong Speu's municipality, and had rows of houses. The sight of beautiful mountains, beaches, seas, and forests was wonderful, but as prisoners, how could we enjoy it? All our thoughts were on our next destination. The guards ordered us to get into a boat and sit on sacks of rice, next to jars of fish sauce and baskets of dried fish.

When we reached the port, the guards ordered us—the new inmates—to form two lines to be counted while we waited for a prison guard to fetch us. The prison was about two kilometers from the port, and the current inmates arrived to transport the goods from the boats to the detention center. Some of these men asked me to name the price I would take for my sandals, which were quite new. However, a friend of mine, who was more experienced in such deals, suggested I wait and sell them at the prison, where I could get more for them.

As we walked, I kept listening to what the others were saying. Without realizing we had arrived at the prison, I found myself at a small cell designated for new arrivals. We were ordered to form two lines again and to strip naked. Then they called us in, one by one, to be searched. Two Vietnamese guards were being supervised by a Frenchman. First, they ordered us to open our mouths wide and cough loudly so they could see if we had a letter or 100-riel [piastre] note hidden in our mouths or throats. Next, we had to squat, and an inmate was assigned to search our anuses. Then they examined our hair and ears before allowing us to return to the lines. Every one of us had to go through this.

During the search, several friends of mine were tortured—beaten to the brink of death with a rattan rod or a whip—just because they did not cough loud enough or failed to follow orders. Thank heavens I was able to escape such punishment; because I was the fifth to be called, I had been able to observe what happened to those who went before me. When my turn came, I just copied the ones who didn't get beaten. After the search, we were allowed to put our clothes back on and were taken to small cells, where we stayed for the next fifteen days. Because we needed to recover from seasickness, we weren't put to work yet.

At this time, the friends of mine who had been here before told me everything I needed to know, which scared me. The French forced the inmates to do various kinds of labor, both heavy and light. Sometimes the inmates could choose the work they did, but it could also depend on luck. The hard jobs included logging, diving for coral, making lime for construction, making white salt and black salt, and so on. The easier ones included serving the Frenchmen, making bricks, and working on the plantation. The other desirable jobs were hunting tortoise eggs and joining the *recherche* teams assigned to watch out for inmates who wanted to escape to the mainland on a bamboo or cloth raft...

In any case, the inmates were forced to work like slaves from dawn to dusk, without rest. They were treated like machines, like the ones used at rice mills...

The *recherche* team consisted of around 300 to 400 inmates, mostly Cambodians. The French had devised this colonial tool to control the Vietnamese by authorizing the Cambodians to torture them (not much different from the French appointing Cambodians as colonial agents with the power to arrest their countrymen). There were many methods of torture, which frightened everyone...

One of them was to strip the prisoner and make him lie naked on a table. A guard tied the inmate's testicles with a rope hanging from the ceiling. Then he would tighten the rope or squeeze the testicles as the prisoner was crying out in pain. If the prisoner confessed, he would be released immediately. But if he denied wrongdoing, the guard would tighten his grip. Dear readers, can you imagine how painful that was? Could you bear it?...

The prison physicians, either French or Vietnamese, appeared to be doing experiments on the inmates in order to sharpen their surgical skills. They would perform all kinds of procedures, as though the inmates were animals; no one cared whether they were killed or crippled. The physicians performed unnecessary surgeries even when an ailment could be treated with simple medication.

Koh Tralach island was itself a criminal—one that murdered people. Once you were sent here, you could only pray that you would get out alive.

BOXING MATCHES ON KOH TRALACH

One day, having gotten a ten-day break from logging, I visited Mr. Pouk Ny at the brick kiln, where several of my friends were working. While we were talking, a Khmer guard called Sum joined us. He said he knew my family, who lived in Chbar Ampov district in Kandal province. Sum told me that when the time was right, he would request that I come to work at the kiln so that we friends could be together, and I thanked him. Then Mr. Pouk Ny told Sum, "Bunchan Mol is an outstanding boxer." When Sum asked me if this was true, I humbly replied that I knew how to box, but I had never been in a competition.

Then Sum told me that he had been searching for a Khmer national to go up against a Vietnamese inmate known as Ah Be, who worked on the public work team. Ah Be had been undefeated for seven years, and barely anyone had the guts to fight him. Sum asked me directly whether I was brave enough. The New Year competition was coming, he added, and the organizers were looking for a Khmer opponent.

"He's very strong and fast," Sum said. "All of us Cambodians on Koh Tralach are afraid of him."

I did not answer at first since I was wondering about Ah Be's stature.

"Are you brave enough?" Sum asked again.

"I can't say yet," I replied. "May I go and see him with my own eyes first, and then I will give you my answer in a couple of days."

The next morning, I went to observe Ah Be at the beach area, where he was driving a road roller. I looked him over from head to toe and saw that he was a bit shorter than me. He had a slender waist, though, which was a sign of great agility, but having been in Koh Tralach for eight years, he was probably rusty. Also, in boxing, the one with greater height has an advantage.

After half an hour, I went back to the brick kiln. Sum bid me closer and asked, "So how is it? Did you see him?"

"I did, sir."

"And do you have the guts to face him? Please help save the Cambodians' face here! He has beaten every opponent in the past seven years, and every year the Big Boss [prison chief] has a hard time finding an opponent for him."

"I noticed that he is not that strong, but who am I to underestimate him? If you want me to volunteer, sir, I hereby agree, but I cannot guarantee a win. Let's allow fate to decide."

"Hurray! A Khmer man agrees to fight Ah Be," Sum cried happily as he jiggled my shoulder. "Tomorrow, I will go to the Big Boss and ask him to give you a break to train for your match on January 1, 1943."

Back then, my lack of experience made me both excited and nervous. I heard that Ah Be was very strong; his single punch or kick could easily kill a man in the ring. It was indeed frightening, but I knew I had to prepare myself. If I was going to be killed, so be it, since it was fate for my life to end here. Still, I admit I was reluctant; everyone, Khmer and Vietnamese, was intimidated by Ah Be's strength, as if he were a tiger. That's why no one had volunteered to be in the same ring with him.

Three or four days later, the news about my upcoming match spread all over the island. The Vietnamese inmates were joking about the new Khmer inmate who had the guts to face "our Ah Be." They said he wouldn't need more than one punch or kick to kill me. This was the typical attitude of the Vietnamese; they always boast when they feel brave but never take a single step forward when they are afraid. This is the truth I learned while living alongside them. When you live with thieves, you know how a thief acts.

Ah Be also took a break to get in shape to fight me. Meanwhile, Cambodian inmates kept bringing herbs to enhance my strength. Pouk Ny gave me a root, which he asked me to keep sucking. I accepted all their gifts, not wanting to disappoint my friends.

Time flew by, and January 1, 1943, arrived. The boxing event took place in a theater crowded with French, Vietnamese, and Khmer citizens, as well as thousands of inmates. There would be five matches that night, all fought between Khmer and Vietnamese boxers. In the first match, the Khmer boxer was defeated. The second one was a draw. In the third bout, the Khmer lost again. A Khmer athlete eventually scored a win in the fourth match. The last was my match against Ah Be.

Before the fight, I prayed, focusing on all the good karma I had amassed and my parents' merit and hoping for a win to improve Cambodia's reputation on Koh Tralach. My hope increased when Ah Be displayed a posture from an ancient martial art known as *võ sĩ* [Chinese *wǔ shi*, "warrior"]. I thought that if he used that style, I would definitely win.

The referee rang the bell to start the bout. Ah Be and I got up and walked toward one another. He took the offensive and threw the first punch, which I dodged. His next two punches also missed me, and I threw my first jab at his face, followed by an uppercut to his chin and a kick to his gut. I jumped back as he collapsed. The referee counted to seven, waiting for him to get back on his feet. But Ah Be raised his hand to tap out, saying that he was still dizzy from lack of sleep the previous night. It was a KO victory in the first round.

A deafening cheer went up from the crowd, giving me goosebumps. At nearly the same time, a French official known as Toustou climbed into the ring, rubbed my shoulder, and asked for my name and prison number, which he wrote down in a small notebook. He gave me a quick smile before leaving the ring. Some French officials gave me money—some five piastres, and others ten. I received fifty piastres in all. Meanwhile, hundreds of Khmer inmates came to embrace me, barely allowing me to breathe or get out of the ring.

"That's the Cambodian champion for you!" some shouted. "He defeated Ah Be! Long live Cambodia!"

Sum was over the moon; he asked the French chief guard who supervised the logging team to give me one night outside of prison. I went to the brick kiln with him, and Sum asked his serving men to kill chickens to make chicken congee, which we happily ate with his herbal moonshine. Many inmates joined us. I enjoyed the party with them until three in the morning…

The next morning, a prison guard came to me with a summons from Monsieur Toustou. I followed him to the *Recherche* Bureau, which was headed by

Toustou, but he was not there when I arrived. After a short wait, he came in, smiling broadly when he saw me.

"Do you want to work for the *Recherche* Bureau?" he asked me.

"Yes, sir. I am at your mercy. I will accept any work you assign to me."

He smiled again and entered his office. When he returned, he ordered an official to take me to the *recherche* team...

After I was with the *recherche* team for twenty days, Monsieur Toustou summoned me again, this time to be a *caporal* [supervisor] of a remote district known as Guérêt, a place where inmates grew such crops as coconut, sugarcane, spinach, herbs, pineapple, and lemons.

THE LIGHT OF FREEDOM

Dear readers, after the last several chapters, you may feel that I had become a free man or even a government official after I was sent to work in Koh Tralach.

To become a *caporal* who inspected inmates, lived harmoniously, and was recognized by so many people was indeed a rare thing on the prison island. You may think I would have succumbed to my good life and stopped caring about everything but doing my job well in order to gain favor with the Frenchmen.

That was not so! My idealism remained in my heart. The great cause that had compelled me to swim across a sea of miseries, from Phnom Penh Prison to Prey Nokor Prison and then to Koh Tralach, the Death Island, stayed strong because of idealism for the revolution: to liberate my motherland from French colonialism. So how could I have been happy? I had no idea about how the revolution in my country was progressing. Indeed, I was downhearted to be marooned by the French in the middle of the high sea, away from my friends. The French hoped to weaken our patriotism or make us abandon political involvement. But how could we ever give our loyalty to the colonial masters?

Inside, I was eagerly waiting for the outcome of World War II, which by then was spreading like fire through Asia. I understood that if the Japanese triumphed over the French, I would have a chance of repatriation before the end of my sentence, which imposed "five years in prison with hard labor and fifteen years in exile."

Otherwise, I would have to remain a prisoner here for another two years and stay away from my country for the next twelve, which was a very long time. If that was what was destined for me, I had no hope of going back and continuing political activities alongside our national heroes.

Yet, as politicians, we always had hope! I kept my dream that one day I would be free and return to the Land of the Khmer, and with other heroes reclaim our independence from the foreigners. Living in Guérêt, I was always looking forward to the war's outcome.

The change came in late 1944. The Japanese started to drive the French out of Indochina. Koh Tralach came under Japanese occupation, bringing an end to French power on the island. Yet, not soon afterward, in February

1945, the Allies helped the French get back on their feet. On February 8, 1945, Koh Tralach was heavily bombed by the Alliance. A week after that, a squad of Japanese soldiers, with a telegram from Phnom Penh, came to the island to fetch four politicians: Hem Chieu, Nuon Duong, Pach Chhoeun, and me. Hem Chieu had died in prison, so only three of us were able to leave the island.

At about six in the evening, we boarded a battleship off the coast of Koh Tralach. It was a World War II Japanese destroyer. Also on board were a hundred Kampuchea Krom soldiers, along with their wives and children, who were heading for Prey Nokor. They had been assigned by the French administration to work on the island.

Koh Tralach! The Island of Torture! Criminal Island! The Death Island had imparted unforgettable memories! And now I had to leave! I waved goodbye to the island... with sadness. I mourned the death of Hem Chieu. His grave was number 1,113. I was very sorry for not being able to say goodbye to him. O Koh Tralach! Please take care of his remains. One day, when we succeed in our cause, we will come back for them and thank you.

Translated from Khmer by Rinith Taing

BORETH LY

Of Performance and the Persistent Temporality of Trauma: Memory, Art, and Visions

Physical pain has no voice, but when it at last finds a voice, it begins to tell a story.   Elaine Scarry, *The Body in Pain*

OCTOBER 11, 2005, SALT LAKE CITY, UTAH

My own experience of violence suggests that trauma is forever a painful feeling, a bodily and mental pain that resurfaces unexpectedly. This traumatic experience is a form of obdurate history waiting to be articulated and written about, but it refuses to be written about in the past tense without the unpredictable—and persistent—intervention of the present tense. Interestingly, the experience I had during and after the performance of my text at the "War Capital Trauma" conference resonates with what Raymond Williams advocates in his seminal essay, "Structures of Feeling," on thinking and writing about history, culture, and society in the present tense: "In most description and analysis, culture and society are expressed in an habitual past tense. The strongest barrier to the recognition of human cultural activity is this immediate and regular conversion of experience into finished products."[1] Indeed, the experience of trauma resists being categorized into a "finished product." Memories of traumatic events, both great and small, are often ineffably and surprisingly evoked by body language, images, words, sounds, and silence; trauma always continues to haunt us. As I recall, the emotional experience evoked by my reading and performance was most unexpected, both for me and for the audience. I hope to capture some of the violence, the fragmented (or fractured) sensory experience, and the unpredictable and persistent temporality of trauma and memory with this performative text.

A WOUND (ROOM) OF ONE'S OWN

Laurie Sears introduces Boreth Ly. He is dressed all in white, the color of mourning in Southeast Asian tradition, and sits in the back of the room. Miriam Bartha starts playing the third movement of Mahler's Symphony No. 4. A slide with the phrase A WOUND (ROOM) OF ONE'S OWN *is projected onto a white screen. Boreth approaches the podium and signals Bartha to stop the music. He then begins to read his prepared text.*

My journal dated Sunday, April 17, 2005, reads:[2]

It is 7:52 p.m. and I am sitting in my windowless office at the Simpson Center for the Humanities, University of Washington. I have been awarded a fellowship so I can reflect and write about trauma, arts, and history. It was on April 17, 1975, that the Khmer Rouge entered the city of Phnom Penh, the place of my birth. It is exactly thirty years ago. It is hard to imagine that I survive and am now thirty-eight years old. I became a university professor. I have worked hard all these years to overcome the horrors I experienced when I was a child. I spent the next twenty years of my life suppressing the painful memories—it is due to a sense of loss that I narrate my personal trauma to myself and to you today. I needed a sense of perspective. My own reflection reminds me of what Anaïs Nin wrote in her journal dated April 1933; she described the frustration and the anger that her friend, Antonin Artaud, felt after a conference at Sorbonne University, when he tried to show the audience a true "Theater of the Plague." She quotes Artaud as saying: "They always want to hear about; they want to hear an objective conference on the Theater of the Plague, I want to give them the experience itself, the plague itself, so they will be terrified, and awaken ... Because they do not realize they are dead. Their death is total, like deafness and blindness."[3]

PRELUDE

Poetic justice? On April 15, 1998, I saw from the comfort of my Berkeley, California, apartment a photograph of Pol Pot's corpse on television.

Apparently the man responsible for the genocide of 1.7 million Cambodians between 1975 and 1979 had just died a natural death. Although I had experienced Pol Pot's atrocities firsthand, I learned his name only in 1979, after Vietnam had overthrown the Khmer Rouge regime, for until then we Cambodians had been obeying the orders not of a man, but of Angkar: "The Organization." Recently an international tribunal has investigated the crimes committed by Pol Pot and other Khmer Rouge leaders, and trials are currently being conducted in Cambodia. The names of many have come to light, but whether just verdicts will occur is still questionable.[4] For those of us Cambodians who lived through that bloody era, during which entire families disappeared overnight, these acts of public justice leave us still asking ourselves: What happened? Should we remember or try to forget? If we remember, how do we envision the past?

A slide reading UTOPIAN VISION *is projected on the white screen. Bartha starts playing the beginning of the fourth movement of Mahler's Symphony No. 4; it will play for three minutes before it is stopped.*

UTOPIAN VISION

We enjoy heaven's delights,
So we can dispense with earthly things. No worldly turmoil

Is to be heard in heaven:
Everything lives in peace and calm. We lead the life of angels
Yet are gay about it; We jump and dance, We skip and sing…
Gustav Mahler, *Symphony No. 4*, fourth movement, "Sehr behaglich"

When sung by a boy soprano, these lyrics from the fourth movement of Mahler's *Symphony No. 4* capture the utopian vision of my childhood in Cambodia: a young boy's innocent vision of his protective family—paradise on earth. Ironically, the Khmer Rouge regime also had a vision of transforming the capitalist society of Cambodia into an agrarian utopia. Hence the word *utopia* is used throughout this text to embody these highly incompatible ideals and to capture these ironies.

I was born on February 14, 1967, in Phnom Penh, where my family had lived for generations. Because of a civil war fought continuously from 1970 onward, mostly in the countryside, the political situation in the city became increasingly unstable as I grew up. My mother's worries about the future of her children increased accordingly.

In 1975, in the midst of this political turmoil and the occasional drop of a bomb, arrived the annual celebration of the New Year, which that year fell from April 15 to April 17. As we customarily did on the first day of the New Year, my brother and sister and I helped my mother, grandmother, and aunts prepare festive foods. In addition, all the women and children in my family participated in the preparation of *baisei* (ritual offerings made of banana tree trunks, banana leaves, miracle flowers, and incense sticks) to be placed on an altar set up on the balcony to greet the new *devata* (a deity who annually descends from his heavenly realm to look after the well-being of the Cambodian nation).

While we were making *baisei*, I overheard my mother, a fervent believer in the power of visionary monks to predict her future, tell her mother and sisters that in a distant province a few months earlier she had consulted just such a monk, who foretold Cambodia's destiny: "The water of the Mekong River will turn blood red and rise up to the height of the elephant's stomach." The tone of my mother's voice became more somber as she continued to describe her visit. Little did I know that this cryptic prediction would foreshadow the most horrific event of modern Cambodian history.

At about noon on April 17, the last day of the New Year celebration, Khmer Rouge troops arrived in Phnom Penh and jubilantly declared their victory over General Lon Nol's regime. From our balcony we saw a parade of tanks and jeeps proceeding down the boulevard in front of our house. My grandmother immediately rushed into her bedroom and cut up a white cotton bed sheet, which she transformed into a flag that she hung from the balcony to welcome the troops, but even more significantly to signify surrender. The rest of our neighbors did the same. On the front of each house appeared a white flag and, in some cases, a white shirt.

Shortly thereafter, the Khmer Rouge troops started to open fire on the government soldiers. To avoid being struck by bombshells and bullets, my entire family descended to the dark bomb shelter below our house and hid. My mother tightly embraced me, the youngest of her four children (my oldest brother had been sent to Paris for schooling), in her arms. Every time we heard a grenade or bullet explode in the street, she would whisper in my ears, "Don't be afraid; they're only firecrackers." Half an hour later, a loud knock reverberated on our front gate. Two Khmer Rouge soldiers, each holding a gun, told us to evacuate. "Don't worry. You will be back in three days," they assured us.

I was eight years old on April 17, 1975.

This particular date is forever engraved in my memory. Because I had been playing around the house with my brother and sister, I was barefoot. Like our neighbors, we obeyed the soldiers' orders, quickly exited our home, and spilled onto the streets of Phnom Penh, confused and disoriented. Even now, the sights and sounds of that day haunt me. I remember especially the bullets and the shattered glass lying on the ground—debris from the violence that had taken place earlier. Since I was barefoot, I could not walk on the scorching pavement, so my father carried me on his shoulders while my two siblings continued to walk this difficult road, this road of no return.

By 1979 only one member of my family besides myself, my grandmother, was still alive. My mother, brother, and sister had perished of malnutrition, starvation, and illness, and my father had been murdered.

HAUNTED VISION

Between 1975 and 1979 the Khmer Rouge regime killed roughly 1.7 million Cambodians.[5] One of the many sites in which the killing took place was Tuol Sleng Prison, also known by its code name, S-21, situated in the heart of Phnom Penh. Tuol Sleng had been a high school until 1975, when the Khmer Rouge came to power and converted it into a "reeducation camp." Roughly fourteen thousand Cambodians, mostly intellectuals and members of the elite, were interrogated and eventually tortured to death there.

After Vietnam invaded Cambodia in 1979, the Khmer Rouge regime ended. When the Vietnamese entered Tuol Sleng early that year, they found the bodies of recently slain victims chained to their beds, as well as decaying corpses.[6] I first saw Tuol Sleng, which the Vietnamese converted into a museum documenting the Khmer Rouge genocide, at the end of the year en route to the reopening of the Olympic Stadium to see a soccer match between the Vietnamese and the Cambodian teams. I was twelve years old and had just returned home with my grandmother after having spent four years doing forced labor and almost dying of starvation. But our house was an empty shell, looted of all our material possessions. My grandmother and I looked in vain for photographs of our relatives, but they had all vanished. In horrifying contrast, I had recently seen on the walls of Tuol Sleng a multitude of black-and-white photographs of prisoners who had been executed.

The Tuol Sleng compound, literally and metaphorically, was a slaughterhouse. Now it is a repository for the collective memories of those Cambodians victimized by the political violence of the Khmer Rouge. Not surprisingly, this slaughterhouse is haunted by the brutal memories of the violence there. Both the museum's staff and visitors have reported seeing ghosts wandering in the buildings after dark.[7] The haunting became so intense that in 1999, Buddhist monks were invited to the museum to offer foods to propitiate the restless souls of the victims who had been murdered inside the prison cells. A photograph published in the April 13–29, 1999, issue of the *Phnom Penh Post* shows four monks reciting sutras and sprinkling holy water onto the skulls of the victims to calm their angry souls.

DEVASTATED VISION

Only seven prisoners survived Tuol Sleng. Now six of them are dead. One of the survivors, a sculptor named Im Chan, died in 2000. In an e-mail sent on February 14, 2000, my friend Ingrid Muan told me of Im Chan's death:

I have just come back from Vat Langka. Im Chan died yesterday. It seems to be the season for dying. He was a sculptor who was imprisoned in Tuol Sleng and is best friend of Chet Chan.[8] I sat at a Buddhist temple for a long time with Chet Chan who looks suddenly old and grey but was as angry as ever. The cremation is this afternoon. I went to tell Vann Nath because no one had yet. He is sick himself and looked off into the middle distance a lot, saying over and over again, "Now I am the only one left." It made me think of what we wrote in The Legacy of Absence *and the burden of giving testimony. How do people not cry here?*

I responded the next day:

I am sorry to hear of Im Chan's death. I think the "blank" you saw registered in their eyes is a deceptive facade. They cried, but internally, inside their hearts. Do you remember the opening lines from Paul Verlaine's poem? "Il pleure dans mon coeur / Comme il pleut sur la ville."[9] Perhaps veiled behind those blank eyes are outpourings of tears comparable to the torrential rainstorms that we once experienced in the climate and landscape of Cambodia. Im Chan's death represents the loss of another witness to the genocide.

Now Vann Nath is the sole survivor, a painter who was imprisoned at Tuol Sleng from 1976 to 1979.[10] In August 1980, the joint Vietnamese and Khmer governments commissioned him to create a series of paintings titled *Scenes of Life at S-21*, which vividly document the different methods of torture used by the Khmer Rouge during his imprisonment. Hanging on the prison's walls as visual narratives of the violence that took place inside Tuol Sleng, the paintings are social realist in style. Although their purpose is to describe the violence that the artist witnessed, they lack an analytical perspective on the horrific ordeal that he experienced. I would like to suggest that like many other survivors, Vann Nath's ability to see analytically was devastated while he was imprisoned at Tuol Sleng.

Like many oppressive political organizations, the Khmer Rouge was very visually focused. It was a scopic regime that enforced visual surveillance on its victims and deliberately traumatized and destroyed their vision.[11] The terror and power of the Khmer Rouge were disseminated through a modality of surveillance expressed in two memorable metaphors widely used by the regime. One was, "Angkar has the eyes of a pineapple."[12] Just as a pineapple has eyes that face in all directions, Angkar has panoptic vision. The second metaphor was embedded in an often repeated phrase: "If you want to live, grow a *ko* tree in front of your house." The threat is implied by a play on words; the kapok tree (*Ceiba pentrandra*) is also a pun on the Khmer word *ko*, which means "mute." Angkar's advice in both cases was to watch your words, stay mute, and be blind.[13] The Khmer Rouge's scopic regime also employed psychic surveillance, which is made manifest in the "Ten Security Regulations," found outside Building A1 of the Tuol Sleng compound.

The Khmer Rouge watched every move that we made, and they even systematically photographed their victims before executing them.[14] Many of these interrogation photos are reproduced in a coffee-table book, *The Killing Fields* (1997).[15] Dinh Q. Lê, a Vietnamese-born artist, along with many other scholars has contested the claim made in this book regarding the transparency of the victims' state of mind: "If you look in these people's eyes, you could try to see or relive what had happened."[16] I share Lê's opinion that these victims did *not* know what was happening to them, nor did they know what they had done wrong. We know from looking closely at these interrogation photos that the prisoners were blindfolded as they were transported from elsewhere to Tuol Sleng. The blindfolds were then removed, and the prisoners were immediately subjected to the gaze of the camera. Thus the petrified, shocked, and confused expressions on their faces, especially in their eyes, are opaque, suggesting that their vision had already been traumatized and destroyed by the surveillance of the camera.

This trauma would eventually lead to both literal and metaphorical blindness. Two of Vann Nath's paintings further demonstrate this devastation of vision. In one painting we see a group of blindfolded men being led to the Killing Fields of Choeung Ek to be executed. The other image shows a blindfolded prisoner at the moment of his execution. The blindfolds literally ensure that they are kept in the dark about their surroundings and their eventual fate. In addition, many of the skulls found at Choeung Ek were in fact found with blindfolds. Ironically, the victims' ability to see had already been robbed during their imprisonment at Tuol Sleng, during the act of interrogation that was recorded by the blinding flash of the camera.

The devastation of vision among the victims of the Khmer Rouge contributed to the absence of visual representations of the genocide. "The Legacy of Absence," a 2000 exhibition organized by Ingrid Muan and Daravuth Ly for the Reyum Gallery in Phnom Penh, included paintings by Cambodian artists who drew on their knowledge and experience of the genocide.

Other horrifying cases of devastated vision emerged after the genocide among Cambodians who had immigrated to the U.S. In 1982, physicians reported that a group of female survivors living in Long Beach, California, were victims of "hysterical blindness": they had lost their sight after witnessing their loved ones being killed by the Khmer Rouge.[17] Between 1982 and 1986, roughly 150 Cambodian women were interviewed by doctors, who reported that their symptoms ranged from blurred vision to complete blindness.[18] All the women were middle-aged and had witnessed violent acts, such as seeing their daughters beaten to death by Khmer Rouge soldiers or witnessing their husbands and sons executed in front of them.[19]

MEMORIALIZED VISION

This phenomenon of hysterical blindness inspired Dinh Q. Lê in the fall of 2000 to create a series of works titled *The Texture of Memory*, a title he borrowed from James E. Young's book, *The Texture of Memory: Holocaust Memorial and Meaning* (1993).[20] *The Texture of Memory* consists of more than twenty framed white cotton cloths embroidered in white thread with portraits of Khmer Rouge victims, taken from interrogation photographs. For each work, Lê drew a sketch of a photograph onto one of the cloths and then commissioned a group of women in Ho Chi Minh City to embroider the outlines of the sketch.

In January 2001, I met Lê in Phnom Penh, where we visited Tuol Sleng together. As we walked through the haunted chambers, we spoke about *The Texture of Memory* and he told me the significance of this series. White is a color for mourning in Southeast Asian funerary custom, and he wanted the white embroidered outlines to be read like braille; over time the oil from the viewers'/participants' hands would help to articulate the faded images.

Lê's white cotton cloths remind me of the white flag that my grandmother hung on our balcony on April 17, 1975, as a symbol of our surrender to the Khmer Rouge. I am haunted by this connection, and I am astonished by the fact that a white cloth that signified surrender in my childhood is now a symbol of insistent remembrance. One of the works from *The Texture of Memory* series particularly resonates with me. In this work, Lê presents three embroidered portraits of one victim that overlap one another so as to create a disoriented image of three faces with four eyes. The image is baffling, and it invites viewers to seek to clarify it by touching the embroidered white lines—an action comparable to untying knots of interwoven thread—an act of coming to vision.

The reconstruction of vision traumatized and devastated by the Khmer Rouge depends on the will of the living. Remembering equals seeing equals remembering. The reassembling and sharing of a series of fragmented images from the minds of survivors contributes to the collective memory of the massacre and violence that took place under the Khmer Rouge.

There is a memorial pagoda located at the Killing Field of Choeung Ek. Housed inside this transparent glass pagoda is a series of skulls of victims, many of whom were blindfolded before they were decapitated and had their heads and bodies thrown into shallow mass graves. The skulls are arranged so that they face outward, their empty eye sockets looking out into the four cardinal directions. They offer another reference to the metaphor of the eyes of a pineapple. But in this case, the powers of vision are reversed: it is now the dead who do the surveillance. The dead stare hauntingly and obdurately back at both the survivors and the killers, reminding us all of this violent chapter in Cambodian history and memory.[21]

FOUR MOVEMENTS

The four sections of this presentation correspond to the four movements of Mahler's *Symphony No. 4*. I remember my childhood rather well because it represented a utopian world, which many Khmer orphans of my generation choose to hold on to because of our longing for that one brief moment of peace. This longing for totality and wholeness, for a history without brutal fragmentation, explains my desire to structure my narrative according to this symphony by Mahler.

Bartha starts playing the third movement of Mahler's Symphony No. 4. It lasts for five minutes, as Boreth gathers his text and circumambulates slowly three times around the audience in a counterclockwise direction (symbolizing a funerary ritual) and finally returns to the table.

EPILOGUE

My journal dated Friday, May 11, 2005, reads:

> *I am utterly exhausted. The reading performance of the text went rather smoothly but I was unprepared for the painful emotions that resurfaced during the delivery of the text. I thought since it had already been published, I could reread the text objectively, but I was most surprised when I became overwhelmed by the horrific memory. I was so overcome with the emotional pain evoked by my reading of the words and showing of images that I started to cry during the performance and at times, the painful experience almost incapacitated me, preventing me from reading the text out loud. As tears unexpectedly streamed from my eyes in the beginning of the performance, I felt that I had literally regressed back to childhood—an extremely physically and emotionally vulnerable period in my life—and I begged my audience to forgive me for my display of emotion. I don't think I ever want to repeat the performance; the emotional and physical pain was absolutely unbearable.*

APRIL 17, 2006, SALT LAKE
CITY, UTAH—REFLECTIONS

It was thirty-one years ago today that I was forced to exit my home in Phnom Penh, Cambodia. I am now writing from my apartment in Salt Lake City, Utah, where I teach at the University of Utah. The view outside my windows is of the barely visible Wasatch Mountains, and they are covered with snow. Yes, it is snowing again—April snow. Clearly this snowscape is very different from the tropical landscape of Cambodia where I spent my childhood and early adulthood. As I look out into the falling snow, I wonder what many Cambodians of my generation or older are doing today and how they feel about the traumatic events that happened. I know that Soth Polin, a well-known Cambodian novelist in the 1960s and 1970s (now living in Long Beach, California, and driving a taxi for a living), holds this perspective:

> *It is the atrocity of the Khmer Rouge. Even if you are reaching in your imagination for a new destination, you cannot get past their cruelty. When you try to write something without mentioning the Khmer Rouge, you can't. The next generation will forgive that, they will forget, but for us, we cannot forgive it.*[22]

Much has been said about the need to address the issues of conflict and reconciliation, and the following words came to my mind:
Crime Punishment Accountability Tribunal justice
Memory Remembrance Forget Forgive Poetic justice

EMPATHETIC EYES/VISIONS

I remember that my impression and vision of the audience's emotional reactions during and after the performance of my text were wide ranging. I remember seeing:
Teary eyes Stoic eyes Skeptical eyes
Bewildered eyes Empathetic eyes Perplexed eyes Compassionate eyes
Angry eyes Meditative eyes Inquisitive eyes Blindfolded eyes

FEBRUARY 14, 2007, 11:55 P.M.,
HILTON HOTEL, NEW YORK CITY

I have just returned from celebrating my fortieth birthday with a group of close friends: Carol Becker, Ann Hamilton, Moira Roth, Shahzia Sikander, Nora Taylor, Lydia Matthews, Amy Lyford, Janet Kaplan, Kara Olsen Theiding, and Holland Cotter.

It is hard to imagine that I turned forty today and that I even lived until the age of forty.

I have never celebrated my birthday, but I decided to gather a group of close friends to celebrate this astonishing day; it is astonishing because I never thought when I was a starving child having to do forced labor under the Khmer

Rouge era that I would live until the age of forty. Here I am, though, alive and well. I am writing from my room at the Hilton Hotel in New York City. It is snowing outside. We had dinner at a restaurant called Cendrillon, located in Soho. I felt such warmth seeing my old and new friends on my birthday. I asked my friends who came to dinner to share their thoughts on the following questions about trauma and memory:

What is trauma to you? Or, what are your thoughts on memory?
Shahzia Sikander (artist): "War."
Ann Hamilton (artist): "Forgetting... loss of memory... the inability to remember... to make present."
Nora Taylor (art historian): "Psychological pain induced by painful experiences."
Amy Lyford (art historian): "Loss of control, bodily invasion, and the recognition of being a disciplinary subject. I am coerced, coercive; that is another level of trauma."

What is memory to you?
Shahzia Sikander: "Fantasy and nostalgia."
Ann Hamilton: "Remembering... embodied knowledge."
Nora Taylor: "Personal narrative of one's life experiences."
Moira Roth (art historian and writer): "A sense of loss and determination to recall that loss."
Amy Lyford: "Projection out of the past to the present necessarily engages with or recognizes blind spots; misrecognition."

WHY PERFORMANCE AND NARRATIVE?

Clearly, my friends' thoughts on issues of memory and trauma are diverse and complex. Indeed, there are no easy answers to these seemingly simple questions. Moreover, two of the most pressing questions that I have been asking myself concern why I feel the need to perform my profoundly personal pain and why I want to externalize it to a group of strangers (albeit intellectuals). As I mentioned earlier, I narrate this story to make sense of my own traumatic past. My experiences concur with Susan Brison's assessments of the study of trauma and memory:

The study of trauma also supports the view of memory as multiform and often in flux. Memories of traumatic events can be themselves traumatic: uncontrollable, intrusive, not chosen—as flashbacks to the events themselves. In contrast, narrating memories to others (who are strong enough and empathetic enough to be able to listen) empowers survivors to gain more control over the traces left by trauma: Narrative memory is not passively endured; rather, it is an act of the part of the narrator, a speech act that defuses traumatic memory, giving shape and temporal order to the events recalled, establishing more control over their recalling; and helping the survivor to remake a self.[23]

It is this necessary narrative process that explains my desire to narrate for myself and subsequently to perform my traumatic and painful memories to a group of empathetic friends and strangers; in turn, this process contributes to the remaking of a self for me. This is not to say that my traumatic experience disappeared as a result of this externalization; quite to the contrary, this painful experience is forever imprinted in my body and mind. But now I have intellectual control over this initially repressed and painfully chaotic experience, and I achieve this on an ongoing basis by giving structure to these events that now live outside time. Trauma will remain forever unpredictable and haunting.

NOTES

A longer version of this text was published in 2003; see Boreth Ly, "Devastated Vision(s): The Khmer Rouge Scopic Regime in Cambodia," *Art Journal* 62 (2003): 66–81. I conceptualized the essay to be read with Gustav Mahler's *Symphony No. 4* playing in the background. This is a highly condensed version of the original essay that I read as a performance at the conference "War Capital Trauma," organized by Tani Barlow and Brian Hammer at the University of Washington in Seattle, May 10, 2005.

I would like to thank all my friends and those in the audience at my performance, particularly Miriam Bartha, Kathleen Woodward, Romila Thapar, Tani Barlow, and Laurie Sears; without their understanding and empathy, I could never have had the courage to perform the above text. I especially thank Tani Barlow, whose friendship and support are unconditional. Laurie Sears and Tikka Sears were also there for me in very important ways; they helped make my time at the Simpson Humanities Center both enriching and productive. I would also like to express my gratitude to my dearest friends and colleagues, Kara Olsen Theiding, Ming-bao Yue, and Gema Guevara, who have always been there for me. I am indebted to them for their enduring friendship. Dipika Nath has been wonderful to work with, and I thank her for all her help with the editing process. Finally, I would like to thank Ann Hamilton, Shahzia Sikander, Moira Roth, Nora Taylor, Janet Kaplan, Lydia Mathews, Amy Lyford, and Carol Becker for enduring the snowstorm and coming to my birthday dinner on February 14, 2007.

1. Raymond Williams, "Structures of Feeling," in his *Marxism and Literature* (Oxford: Oxford University Press, 1977), 128.
2. The title of my subheading is deliberately chosen to reference Virginia Woolf's seminal essay on feminism, "A Room of One's Own." My essay was written in a tiny room I rented while I was a graduate student at the University of California, Berkeley, and it is from within the interiority of this room and thus my interiority that I wrote the essay "Devastated Vision(s)." See Virginia Woolf, "A Room of One's Own," in *The Virginia Woolf Reader*, ed. Mitchell A. Leask (New York: Harcourt Brace Jovanovich, 1984), 168–88.
3. Gunther Stuhlmann, Ed., *The Diary of Anaïs Nin* (1931–1934) (New York: Swallow, 1974), 1:192.
4. See the full coverage of the trial in the *Phnom Penh Post*, April 14–27, 2000, and less thorough coverage in the *New York Times*, January 5, 1999.
5. David Chandler, *Voices from S-21: Terror and History in Pol Pot's Secret Prison* (Berkeley: University of California Press, 1999), vii.

6. Ibid., 3.
7. Chea Soheacheath, "Keeping the New Year Ghosts Happy," *Phnom Penh Post*, April 13–29, 1999.
8. Chet Chan teaches traditional Khmer painting at the School of Plastic Arts in Phnom Penh.
9. Paul Verlaine, *One Hundred and One Poems,* Trans. Norman R. Shapiro (Chicago: University of Chicago Press, 1999), 78. "Il pleut sur mon coeur /Comme il pleut sur la ville" ("It weeps in my heart/Like it rains in the city") is from "Romances sans paroles" (my translation from the French).
10. Vann Nath, *A Cambodian Prison Portrait: One Year in the Khmer Rouge's S-21* (Bangkok: White Lotus, 1998), 24–26.
11. The term *scopic regime* is borrowed from Martin Jay's essay, "Scopic Regimes of Modernity," in *Vision and Visuality,* ed. Hal Foster (Seattle: Bay, 1988), 3–28.
12. John Marston, "Metaphors of the Khmer Rouge," in *Cambodian Culture Since 1975: Homeland and Exile,* ed. May M. Ehibara, Carol A. Mortland, and Judy Ledgerwood (Ithaca, NY: Cornell University Press, 1994), 107.
13. Ingrid Muan and Daravuth Ly, *The Legacy of Absence: A Cambodian Story* (Phnom Penh: Reyum Gallery Press, 2000), 13.
14. Sara Colma, David Chandler, and Vann Nath, "Arrest," in *The Killing Fields,* ed. Chris Riley and Douglas Niven (Santa Fe, NM: Twin Palms, 1996), 94–101.
15. Allan Desouza, *Dinh Q. Lê: The Headless Buddha* (Los Angeles: Center for Photographic Studies, 1998), 4. Also see Riley and Niven, *The Killing Fields.*
16. Ibid., 5.
17. Alec Wilkinson, "A Changed Vision of God," *New Yorker,* January 24, 1994, 52–68.
18. *Ekleipsis* (Dir. Tran T. Kim-Trang, Video, 1998). See also Irene Small, "Blind Spot: The Video Art of Tran T. Kim-Trang," *Art Asia Pacific,* No. 30 (2001): 52–57.
19. Ibid., 52–54.
20. Dinh Q. Lê was born in 1969 in Ha Tien, on the border between Vietnam and Cambodia. He experienced the Khmer Rouge invasion of his village in 1979. See Moira Roth, "Obdurate History: Dinh Q. Lê, The Vietnam War, Photography, and Memory," *Art Journal* 60, No. 2 (2001): 38–53.
21. The annual day of Remembrance is May 20. See Annette Marcher and Yin Soeum, "Will They Find Peace?" *Phnom Penh Post,* March 17–30, 2000.
22. Sharon May, "Beyond Words: An Interview with Soth Polin," in *In the Shadow of Angkor: Contemporary Writing from Cambodia,* ed. Frank Stewart and Sharon May (Honolulu: University of Hawaii Press, 2004), 16–17.
23. Susan J. Brison, "Trauma Narratives and the Remaking of the Self," in *Act of Memory: Cultural Recall in the Present,* ed. Mieke Bal, Jonathan Crewe, and Leo Spitzer (Dartmouth, NH: Dartmouth College, 2000), 40.

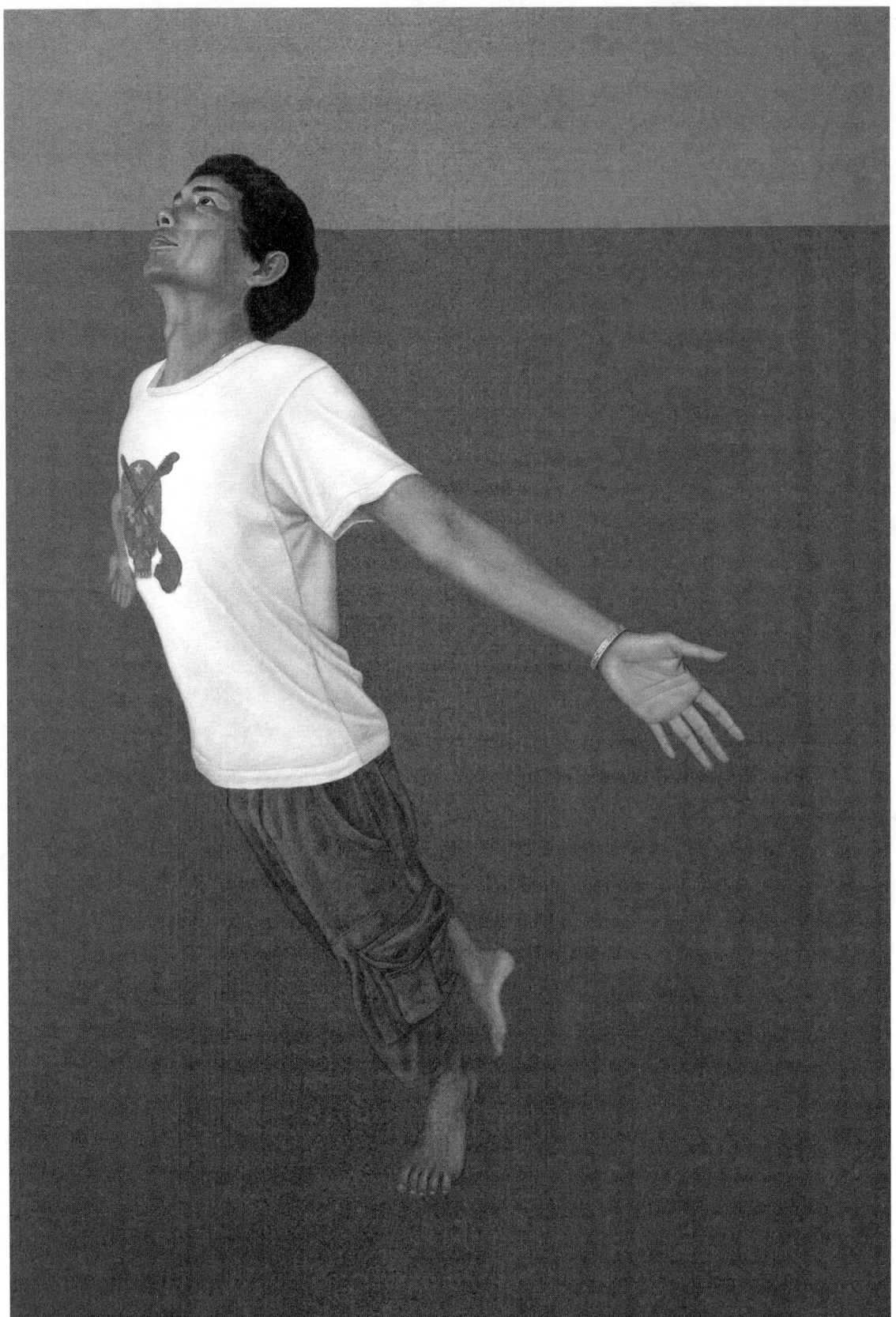

ALICE PUNG

from *Her Father's Daughter*

Editors' Note
Alice Pung's father named her Alice "because he thought Australia was a wonderland." Pung's first memoir, Unpolished Gem, *recounts the life of her Chinese-Cambodian family pursing the Australian Dream in working-class Footscray, a Melbourne suburb, with humor and wit. In her second memoir,* Her Father's Daughter, *her quest to understand her father's story takes her to Cambodia, where he spent four years under the Khmer Rouge regime before escaping with her mother. The book alternates between her father's voice and that of her own, presented here.*

DISMEMORY

DAUGHTER—

There should be a word for a memory that you had deliberately forgotten to remember: a Dismemory. This is what her father had. Dismemory sounded like a foreign country filled with heaps of miscellaneous cast-offs. And people in clusters, picking up the pieces, also called Dismemories. People wearing their Dismemories like armor, or perhaps sewn into a strangely colored suit with small lapels. But maybe a person grew until their Dismemories became too tight and the seams could not help but tear. Had she ever walked around with an enormous hole in the middle of her back that she did not know was there because she could not see it? Or maybe another time her knee had been exposed, right in the area where doctors tested your reflexes with a small hammer, to make sure you still felt the feelings that kept you alive. Her Dismemories were small, but her father's were enormous.

What if it gets worse, she wondered, but never asked him.

What if what gets worse, he would have wanted to know. Your dismembered memories. Your Dismemories. No such thing. But of course there was. There was Dismemory in his trying to cut off the sharp tip of a knife with another knife, and Dismemory in the way he wrapped an unpeeled banana in cling wrap so it would not be contaminated in his children's school bags. Dismemory in the way he surrounded himself with a kaleidoscope of ever-evolving electronics. There was Dismemory when he took walks near the Maribyrnong River and feared drowning, and Dismemory in the way he plotted that she would either move back home or stay inside the college. Dismemory in the secret glee he felt that his daughter could find a job where she sat in one warm safe room for eight hours a day. Dismemory in the way he loved innocence. During her childhood, she found that the most difficult thing was to argue with her father. She could never win, because you could never argue with anyone who wanted so much for you, whose very arguments were motivated by this love. As the years progressed, nothing seemed to have changed.

"Why can't I stay out past eight p.m. in summer?"

"Why do you whine so much? Why don't we just let you wander the streets? See how far that gets you." Even in her second year of university they still imposed that ridiculous curfew on her.

He made her so furious sometimes. But you could never question the paranoias attached to this love, because to him it would mean questioning the love, which was unconditional. And what kind of ungrateful troublemaker would ask questions about a gift many families lacked? So instead she asked him about the people he had loved before. "What was Chicken Daddy like?"

"He was a very hard-working man," her father would reply.

"How did Chicken Sister look?" she'd inquire, and he'd give her a blurry description of what colonized Indochinese considered beautiful.

"She was very pretty, big eyes and pale skin. So perhaps you'd better not write that her brothers called her Spider when she was young or no one will have any sympathy for her."

She understood how he thought people would respond: sympathy for beautiful and perfect characters only. But she couldn't make any of it perfect. Perfection did not bring them back to life. She gave her father her writing to read, and he corrected only the factual errors.

"Thanks, Dad, but do you have any other suggestions?"

"No. I don't know much about writing."

"Come on, Dad, just tell me whatever comes to mind."

"Do you think there's too much suffering in the Cambodian part? Maybe white people don't want to read about too much suffering. It depresses them."

She didn't know what to say about that. She knew exactly what he meant, though. Her first book had been filled with the sort of sardonic wit that came easily to a person whose sole purpose in life was to finish university and find her first graduate position, knowing full well that she was on her way to becoming comfortably middle-class. She had refused, just as her father did, to look beyond the here and now. If you looked at darkness through rose-colored glasses, all you got was a congealed-blood color. A color that should have a specific name, like *blug*, a clotty mixture of mucus and blood. A word that was not in her father's dictionary. It was best not to look at all. But now that she was older, she saw that in his quest for modernity and upward mobility, her father had given his children a completely different history, drilled into them that they were part of a Chinese culture that spanned centuries, which was true;

made sure they were also aware they were bona-fide born-in-Australia kids. But in doing so, he had wiped out the most significant part of their identity.

How could she forget the men and women who came to their house in Braybrook when she was young, who had no idea of privacy? They would poke their heads into any room and *wahhh* when she and her toddler brother were getting changed. Whenever they were expecting visitors, her parents would hide the valuables, but they never failed to offer food, and as much as anyone wanted. "We're having dinner! Join us! Join us!" And before the person could refuse, a bowl heaped with rice would be thrust into their hands and a chair pulled out. Her mother would cook Vietnamese food because that was what she was taught in Saigon: Bánh hói, Bánh canh, fish soup, and rice-paper rolls with hot Thai basil and mint. The family fridge was filled with jars of homemade fish sauce; their bedrooms were guarded by glassy-eyed porcelain Buddhas. The Goddess of Mercy floating on her lotus had watched the children grow up from her place on the mantlepiece, but gradually they ignored her as they dismantled their filthy former habits.

When one of her uncles first arrived in Australia, he kept a wastepaper basket beside his loo. He thought that flushing used toilet paper would block the pipes. Some migrants washed their hair with dishwashing detergent because they couldn't read the labels, but the pictures of lemons gave them a feeling of zesty succor. Others dried meat on flat pieces of newspaper in the living room, or pickled onions in empty Nescafé jars. They were always afraid of scarcity because they were not Mainlander Chinese but Diaspora Chinese, driven from place to place, destined never to feel a sense of belonging; knowing they would never belong unless they kept themselves separate and hid the most important parts of their heritage inside the home. In Cambodia they were the walnut-faced grandmothers selling boiled eggs in the marketplace, or the goldsmiths making jewelry for weddings. In Australia they were the model minority only once they were no longer scrambling in the factories and picking fruit on the farms, and once their kids could speak English.

And when she and her brother came home from school speaking English, her father knew it was time. He wanted to whitewash their history so they could begin anew. No prying ways, no crap on scraps of paper lying around the house. Her father had named her Alice because he believed this new country to be a Wonderland, where anything was possible if only she went along with his unfailing belief. His patriotism rang truer and more annoying than any bogan supremacist's. *Australians all let us rejoice,/for we are young and free.* This to him was the most beautiful national anthem in the world. There was golden soil and wealth for toil. Who wanted to be anywhere else? In other countries, the anthems were all about rinsing the land in the blood of brothers. He would never let her go to Cambodia. "You can travel anywhere in the world except there," he told her generously, but still she would not relent.

When she reached adulthood, she kept at it. "But Alexander went when he was nineteen!"

"That's different. Your brother is a boy." The boys were allowed to return on holidays, and, after the age of thirty, if they were still single they were sent back to find wives for themselves.

"If you want to go back to Cambodia, you must stay with Uncle Kiv," her father had told her. "He'll look after you." Uncle Kiv was her father's hero. Her father would show every visitor to their house brochures of Uncle Kiv's banks in Cambodia—shiny full-color pamphlets designed to entice investors. These brochures clearly were not literature, but inside their pages her father found a story of success that he could not resist sharing whenever any of her friends' parents came to pick her up. "But I want to go with you, Dad," she kept insisting.

"It's too dangerous still," he'd reply. Finally, ten years later, he relented. He and her younger sister Alison were going with her. She was to travel to Beijing for a week-long writers' festival, then meet them in Hong Kong, and then would fly to Cambodia together.

"I'll bring the best Panasonic camcorder that's on display at the shop," her father told her, "so you can remember the details of the place exactly as it is." These weren't fields of golden wheat or barley they were going to see. Her father was going to show the killing fields to her, the daughter he wouldn't even let out to see movies at Highpoint mall in her early teens.

When she left her parents' house, her father was waiting outside on the porch in his woolly old argyle jumper, black buildings behind him against the quiet sky, still dark but ripening for the day. He watched her taxi drive away, no doubt memorizing the number plate in case the driver didn't take her to the airport.

THE FIELD
DAUGHTER—

Her senses became more stretched, as though they were working their hardest to take in the world. At first there was the field. And then there was the heat, when the sky breathed its fever breath over the field. Then back to the field and its unyielding dust. Nothing grew on it. "When the floods came," her father said, "this was raised ground. This was where I buried people." How could such a hot land be filled with water? "In Cambodia, there are only two seasons," her father explained, "wet and dry." Like he was explaining the latest Philishave razor. Wet and Dry. It had meant nothing to her until she stepped onto this soil.

When she imagined people dying like flies, what she saw in her mind was ice and snow and skin-thin sleet deaths. Too many movies about Stalingrad and the Holocaust and the Long March. Silly, she knew, because death here had hot halitosis that withered away the bodies much faster. Its rotting gums melted organs into miasmic matter. "The best fertilizer in the world," her father told her. "Besides shit, of course."

And that was all her father said about that.

How do you feel about being here? she had wanted to ask him, but she knew what his answer would be.

Nothing much. It's just a place.

Yet it wasn't nothing much. It was nothing at all, and yet suddenly this flat stretch of nothing was everything. All that existed at that moment was this space. And she knew—all her father's life had been about filling this emptiness. All he probably wanted to do after five minutes in the field was to climb back into the air-conditioned car and talk about Kiv's buildings, which spread across the city and rose into the sky, and the seaside resort that sprawled across the beach like a beautiful blinged-up woman, to lose himself in those generous sandy arms. But in the middle of the field, with nothing, you had only your own body. And how treacherous your own body can be, she thought. How strange that most people woke up each morning with the certainty that life would go on for them, when it was entirely dependent on the body, a body over which you had absolutely no control, a body that every once in a while would let loose with an awful surprise. You could vomit on a public bus. You could collapse on a dirt road because of a weak ankle. Exhaustion might blur your vision. Tinnitus could put a brake on your sense of balance. A migraine might make you taste tin in your mouth and bleed from the nose.

The field left her exposed, as no other place in the world had, left her standing there with her loved ones, realizing how little she knew about anything or anyone, even how very little she knew about herself. It stripped her of all certainty.

Dad buried bodies here, she realised, bodies that needed to be held, that once moved and exhaled and blinked just as she and he were doing. Bodies no one would ever talk about again.

She looked around at her family. There were bones beneath their feet, souls between their breaths. The distance between the living and the dead was only the fade of a heartbeat away. She felt a sudden need to grab them, her loved ones; to hold them close, to make sure they were not going to dissolve.

At that moment, her father was seeing something else. He pointed to the trees. There weren't many, and they were skinny coconut or sugar palms, huddled at the edges of the yellow field, as if afraid to step into the soil of a thousand souls.

She waited for him to tell her about the trees. "Look at those bamboo ladders," he said. "They're used for climbing to the very top, to collect the juice of sugar-palm plants or coconuts."

She grabbed the ladder and started climbing. "Only the first few rungs," he said, "or you could fall." She let go.

They were surrounded by ex-soldiers now working as her family's bodyguards. Dressed in a khaki uniform, one of the soldiers carried a hessian bag of bullets across his chest. Another had a hoe and was digging a hole in the ground. This time it was not for burying a body but to make a fire and burn their Heaven Banknotes in memory of Auntie Suhong's mother, who had been buried in this ground. They had brought along two cartons, and each banknote was printed in gold on one side and in silver on the other.

"When I was digging up the ground the year after your auntie's mother died," her father said to her, "I unearthed the marker of her burial spot. Your auntie and uncle had written her name on a small piece of wood."

"Did you stow it away and keep it?" she asked.

"No, of course not." If you picked up a handful of dirt from the ground, you were stealing from the revolution.

"People dug the graves up, over and over again, after the liberation," Uncle Kiv told her. They were looking for rings and gems looped around finger bones and wrists.

"There was nothing," her father confirmed. "When I buried those bodies, they didn't even have proper clothes." Now there were not even bones left. None of those people seemed to have existed, and yet her auntie was kneeling on the dirt in front of an incense urn, with three sticks of incense clutched in her hand. On the ground a rattan mat was laden with food: platters of roast meats, bowls of fruit, and bamboo shells filled with rice and red beans. When Auntie Suhong rose up after her third bow and turned around, her shoulders were shaking with the memory of her mother.

The villagers were watching. They had been steadily growing in number, and some had stood for hours beneath the sugar palms. A mother with a growth on her neck that gave her face the profile of stoic nobility. A cluster of naked children with faces she wanted to kiss. Her auntie and uncle handed out the food to the villagers. More children appeared out of nowhere, running across the field.

There was a man with them. An old man who had once led the children's army in their collective. Murderer of children! she thought when her father told her who he was. She could not believe that her father and Uncle Kiv were talking to him so calmly and casually, as if he were some ordinary neighbor with whom they had shared a street. She could not believe how, after their visit to the field, the man invited them back to his house, which was no more than an empty hut raised on stilts. He showed them a photograph of his daughter's wedding.

"Look," her father said to her, pointing out figures in the photograph. "This is his only daughter. That man standing next to her is his son-in-law." On the wall of his hut, alongside two family photos, was tacked a peeling picture of some movie stars. On the floor was a small used tube of teenage makeup for face blemishes. How strange to see it there. This man also had children in his life, children he loved. He also had the grace of his community and their goldfish memory spans.

She felt that this country was something precious—brutal, split open like a pomegranate, with hot breath and a million red and buried eyes. A country she would never understand, but that had shaped her father and made him who he was. The real miracle in this, she realized as she watched him standing there in the heat holding a straw hat to his head, was not that he had lived. The real miracle was that he could love.

At Sea, and Seeking a Safe Harbor

This past December, after not talking to me for several months, my mother called from her rural Oregon home. I listened from Seattle as she offered updates on cousins in Cambodia, inventoried her latest aches and pains, and noted my father's failing memory.

Her talk was sprinkled with the Khmer word *koun,* meaning "child," an endearment she had stopped using with me months before.

When, at the end of our call, she summoned me home, a knot tightened in my gut. "Come alone," she said.

We had been sparring over broken hope. I'm gay, or a version of it. I came out to my mother in my twenties as gay because there is no word in our Khmer language for bisexual.

And if there is, I don't know it. I was living and working then in the Bay Area. She flew in for the weekend. I wasn't sure she knew what *gay* meant, so I drove her to the Castro.

From my Honda Civic, she pressed a chubby cheek to the window and pointed at two men in leather chaps, holding hands, their bare behinds hanging out.

"That the gay?" she asked.

"Yes, Mom," I said, embarrassment flaring at the back of my neck. "Stop pointing. Yes, that's the gay."

On the drive back to my apartment, she told me she loved me. I thought she understood this essential thing about me: that one day I may walk down the street holding hands with a woman (minus the nudity), and it would be totally normal.

I miscalculated the moment, completely.

Twenty years later, after learning I had left a career in international media to move to Seattle to be with my partner, a woman, my mother let loose a verbal squall: "You're crazy. You're being disrespectful, dishonorable, disloyal. You're not normal."

I spent weeks slumped on the sofa, mentally scanning my insides for injuries.

When she cornered my siblings to sway them to her side, I called her to lob a shot back. "What kind of mother are you?" I hissed, and we each retreated, for the next six months, into our own hurts.

I resolved to keep my distance from her, but when she called last December and asked me to visit, I agreed to make the four-hour drive.

A week later, my parents were in the kitchen eating rice and salted fish when I arrived. My mother wedged two scoops of steaming jasmine rice into a bowl and nudged it toward me.

I brought oranges from their favorite Asian market in Portland and holiday cookies that my partner had made and arranged in a tin tied with red ribbons. My father pinched a piece of fudge from the tin and told me to thank my partner, while my mother just stared deeper into her rice bowl.

Then she started talking, bits and pieces of news. As an hour stretched into two, we moved into the family room, where my mother eased into her rocking chair, waving me over with a flick of her wrist and clamping her arms around my waist. "What do you want for Christmas?" she asked. "Money? Clothes?"

"I want you to be happy for me," I said.

I was the happiest I had ever been. I was finally with a partner who loved me for whom I was, who laughed with me until we were stumbling around the house, drunk on raw joy. Who inspired a better version of me through her grace, generosity, and loyalty.

My mother started sobbing, her head pressed into my belly.

"I'm not happy," she blurted out. "Ma wants you to get married. Be normal, like your brother and sisters, and find a good man to marry before Ma and Pa die."

I froze and flipped the switch in my heart to "closed."

Her sobbing soon escalated into the kind of wild crying I saw her do when someone died. I did not console her.

Instead, I peeled her fingers from my waist and stepped back, angry at her ambush, and then felt ashamed for not being more compassionate. "Maybe she could use a hug," I thought. "Maybe that would save us."

I was too enraged. Not only was my mother genuinely not happy for me, but she insisted she would never be happy as long as I was gay.

I had always been so proud of my mother, using adjectives like courageous and resilient whenever I spoke of her. She raised my siblings and me to be solid citizens, grounded in morals and mission. She taught us how to grow gardens, stack wood, pickle plums, patch anything with holes, and be proud of who we were, refugees who had come to America with almost nothing.

Forty years ago, as genocide gripped Cambodia, my family fled on a Cambodian navy vessel built for a crew of thirty with some three hundred people crammed on board. For three weeks, the ship plied the waters of the Gulf of Thailand, turned away by countries unwilling to grant us asylum.

Halfway into the journey, a baby with a swollen head and shriveled legs went sallow inside my mother's sarong. The baby hadn't cried or moved in days.

The captain of the ship, surely smelling rot, eventually came around.

"Your baby is dead," he said. "Throw it in the water. The corpse will contaminate the others."

"We're Buddhist," my mother pleaded. "Please let me bury my baby in the earth."

The captain relented, allowing my mother to cradle her listless baby for another week or so.

That baby was me.

I had heard this story dozens of times before it occurred to me one day to ask her, "Did you think I was dead?"

She paused and glanced past my shoulder to some other place. "I had hope," she said. "Just a little hope that you were still alive."

I had survived on my mother's hope, on the dreams she breathed into me and on the drops of water she put on my unmoving lips. I had spent my life with this story as my albatross, trying my best to repay her by being a good daughter and not disrupting the bond between us.

Over the years, my mother bragged to her friends about how I had bought my own home, sent her and my father on vacations, and traveled the globe as a journalist, even when she protested certain dangerous destinations like Afghanistan. ("I brought you safely from war," she told me. "Why do you want to go back?") After I went against her wishes that time, she didn't talk to me for nearly a year.

I was a good daughter. But out of my parents' sight, I rebelled, dating people I knew they would find inappropriate. Yet I had plenty of conventional boyfriends, too, and these I brought home. I also brought home an occasional girlfriend, but my mother didn't take any of them seriously.

I hadn't considered, until way too late, that tacking between genders could be confusing to my mother.

Since visiting her last December, I stumbled into a newer understanding of her while watching a documentary film set in Cambodia.

In one scene, as a young Khmer bride gets her face drawn up with mascara before her wedding, the camera pans to the bride's beaming mother, who announces how happy she is that her daughter is fulfilling her duty.

Duty. As I considered that word, I finally understood the depth of my mother's disappointment. It was tied up in an ancient pain left over from when she was corralled into an arranged marriage after being badly beaten by her father with a steel rod for shaming the family when, instead of marrying someone chosen for her, she tried to flee.

To my mother, my being gay was worse than running away. It meant not fulfilling my ultimate duty as a daughter: to marry a man.

It also robbed her of her birthright in blessing me on my wedding day, in symbolically clipping a lock of my hair and tying red string around my wrist for an auspicious new future.

We're left wedged inside too tight a space, Ma and me. If I am to be a good Cambodian daughter, I must sacrifice an essential part of who I am and lose my partner, who loves me with her full nurturing force. If I am true to myself, I cause Ma to lose a fundamental part of who she is as a Cambodian mother.

I see no middle ground, no safe harbor for us to come ashore together. But I know who I am, and how I am like her. I know that same impulse of hope in Ma is alive in me, beating beneath my ribs, something she breathed into my soul on a wayward ship so long ago.

It's a hope that she will one day come to a better understanding of me, a hope that we will survive this journey, too.

There's always hope, even if it's just a little.

ELIZABETH CHEY

Painting History: An Artist's Reframing of Memory and War from Survival to Healing

When I remember the painting Vann Nath shared with me fifteen years ago, I see again the glimmering hope in his deep eyes.

Recalling the painting unravels a flurry of memories, their feathers floating, circling in the mind with a tint of jasmine and blue.

On a cold winter evening in 2002, Vann Nath appeared in my apartment, a bit to my surprise. The Cambodian family I lived with in Brooklyn had offered him and his travel companion some refuge, warm beds, and Cambodian home-cooked meals for a few days. In the U.S. for the first time, Vann Nath was to receive an international recognition called the Hellman/Hammett Award for persecuted writers and artists, administered by Human Rights Watch. But he would never let on how important he was. He wasn't the kind to like attention or recognition, and his nonchalance and humility intrigued me more.

He appeared taller and broader than average for a Cambodian man. His head of silver-white hair so starkly contrasted his dark skin. I wondered what in his life had made his eyebrows and hair so wispy. He looked tired, worn, and disoriented by the pace of New York City, its rhythms nothing like the slowness of Phnom Penh, Cambodia.

Time has washed away much of my memories of this evening, yet I still feel the awe and admiration I had for him when I first met him, and relish hearing his gentle tone and singular sentences.

As he unrolled the painting, he patted his palms over the image, and said: "Here, elements: water, fire, earth and air."

My eyes lingered on the edges of the painting, on his weathered fingers.

"Buddha describes what is in all living things in four elements," he said.

Silently, we appreciated the elegance of Buddha's teaching, and as my eyes scanned the painting, I began to see motion.

The lofty white clouds billowed against a turquoise sky and quivered with silver linings. The subject, a man with the same deep, dark eyes as Vann Nath's, holds his hands up in prayer, humbly surrendering to nature—the elements. He appears as if held up to the sky by the earth like an offering. But there is apprehension in his expression: some fear, some worry, some guilt; possibly a gnawing sense of unworthiness. The expression in the man's face displays a raw tension: some part of him obediently complies with the thing that is larger than himself, and yet there is a desire to be free from the thicket of a meticulously, sadistically, orchestrated history.

During our meandering conversation about paintings and life in Cambodia, I learned that Vann Nath had been a prisoner inside S-21, a high school the Khmer Rouge turned into a torture center. The S-21 guards were prepared to kill him, but by chance discovered he had a talent with paint and brush. The Khmer Rouge kept saying they'd kill him, but meanwhile gave him painting assignments, portraits of their leader Pol Pot, under whose reign nearly two million Cambodians died. When the Vietnamese invaded in 1979 and removed the Khmer Rouge from power, Vann Nath was one of only seven people to survive S-21 prison, where an estimated seventeen thousand prisoners were killed.

Years later, out of what he once described to me as his own sense of wanting to preserve the history of the place for future generations of Khmer people, and to free the ghosts from inside his mind, Vann Nath painted images he could remember which documented life in S-21. In those paintings, which remain in the prison, now Tuol Sleng Museum, a starved Vann Nath stares vacantly at a dirt floor. His collarbone and rib cage poke through his black, ragged clothes. He sits, disheveled and disoriented, chained to horrific memories of the murders he witnessed.

None of those images matched the dignified Vann Nath sitting quietly with me then. Nor did the Vann Nath embodied and emboldened in the painting he had shown me resemble those historic paintings of his life in Tuol Sleng.

In this visceral image, the man on the knoll has his vulnerabilities exposed. I saw Vann Nath's desperate veneration of justice—an immovable quest for truth which was audaciously raw and rare.

I could see Vann Nath's hope that beings in higher, divine planes saw his suffering and the injustices faced by his people. He held an unshakable faith in *kamma* [karma], the Buddhist law of nature, its justice system, where those who performed good deeds would get good fruits, and those who sowed evil seeds would get evil results in undeniably equal measure.

This struck me as Vann Nath's most endearing quality, his faith that justice had its way of playing out. Maybe it was because he was from Battambang, where my mother's family also comes from, where faith and veneration for the Buddha's teaching play a deep role in families and communities. Maybe it was that strong base in the faith of *kamma* that we shared which drew us to talk about this painting. Clearly, the painting was his conversation about redemption and justice which also revealed some of his doubts about whether his own *kamma* was a slimy slosh of good and bad deeds—fruits of past deeds and histories irretrievable and not fully reconciled from its shadows.

Vann Nath's longing to visualize a better version of himself in the painting told me more than he could say in words. Was this self-portrait Vann Nath's rejection of memory? Was he aspiring to be free of his past and the narrative that made him a victim? Could this longing to be free of his history's sordid implications be what Elie Wiesel called in his 1986 Nobel Peace Prize Lecture the "divine curse," that which plagues a reluctant hero, burdened with the bad luck of being a witness to genocide, and a survivor?

In Wiesel's lecture, he said:

> *For us, forgetting was never an option. Remembering is a noble and necessary act. The call of memory, the call to memory, reaches us from the very dawn of history... It is incumbent upon us to remember the good we have received, and the evil we have suffered... Man appeals to God to remember: our salvation depends on it. If God wishes to remember our suffering, all will be well; if He refuses, all will be lost. Thus, the rejection of memory becomes a divine curse, one that would doom us to repeat past disasters, past wars.*

In Wiesel's urgings, he makes it a moral obligation for people across the world, leaders and governments, to remember history and protect humanity from repeating wrongful acts against itself. By speaking up and bearing witness to violations of human rights, Wiesel charges victims of war, violence, and genocide to speak of their experiences as evidence, encouraging the notion that collective memory can shield society from repeated crimes against humanity, war crimes, and genocide; thus becoming the means to stop cycles of suffering. Wiesel's perspective on commemoration takes on a moral and biblical connotation, rooted in Jewish tradition, a culture which calls for remembrance above all else.

But in Vann Nath's world, the Buddhist construct defies calls for remembrance in the form of holding any people above others. Instead, it aims for a more universal sense of humanity. In a practice where all living things can be characterized by four great elements, and the only constant is *anicca*, or change, the Buddha's first tenet is for practitioners to accept as truth that *existence is suffering*. Wiesel's call to action and his trust in memory to save others from repeating mistakes relies to a fault on romanticism within its core.

We see again and again, history being repeated and forgotten, or collective memory being overpowered by dark forces: Armenia, Bangladesh, Bosnia, Burundi, Cambodia, Darfur, Rwanda... Aleppo. Memories of war live on within one or two generations, but in times of peace they begin to falter within three or four.

We do not lack evidence of individuals and their witness of atrocities. What we may be more vulnerable to is mis-remembering or not identifying ourselves as also part of the same humanity. We fail not because of a lack of intelligence, or repeated documentation of war, or efforts to record what happened (as with the Nuremburg Trials or the Khmer Rouge Tribunal), but rather, we fail because memory documented in the form of sterile facts and records have lost their emotional impact, and can be readily shaped for political purposes. The emotional vibration of experience, the trauma itself, cannot be contained in historic records. Painful and stirring lessons from war and violence do not transmit from history books as vibrantly as sensations in the body.

Cognitive scientists like Oliver Sacks suggest humans are constantly rewriting history. At the autobiographical level, the act of recalling contaminates memory, and the constant flow of information to the brain is a cohesion that melds past and present, riddling both with inaccuracies. At the societal level, history is like soft wax, molded and re-worked to fit the needs of each society's yearning for lessons, symbols and occasions, or yearning for evidence to confirm conditioned biases. Sacks writes: "We now know that memories are not fixed or frozen, like Proust's jars of preserves in a larder, but are transformed, disassembled, reassembled, and re-categorized with every act of recollection."

As we continuously take in sensory signals from outside environments, we jumble up new data with old memories. Our genetic impulses to self-protect encourage us to assess and reassess, and tap into a backlog of memories, views, and perspectives that continuously shape the way we live, adapt, and survive. This is nature's process, its bio-chemical mechanism of adapting to ever-changing realities. We are constantly creating new and vaguely familiar memories, views, and perspectives with every blink of an eye.

We don't even need to work at forgetting. The destruction of memory, or rather *the de-constructing and restructuring of memory*, the choices which allow us to reframe situations in our mind, are the very adaptive qualities of the human mind that possibly helped Vann Nath, and generations of survivors, make it through impossible situations.

In interviews I conducted with women who survived the Khmer Rouge, between their sentences, amid words and long silences, floated ghosts of shame and denial. A denial of the reality of those moments was a way to escape. These women subconsciously reframed what they had to live for: a child, a husband, a mother.

They decided what was worth fighting for by secretly saving a ladle of watered-down rice porridge or conjuring a false identity to save a sister. With malnutrition and severe forced labor as added factors, who knows how the mind and body worked to alter beliefs, fragment views, and reconfigure what was necessary to stay alive. Many I interviewed still expressed a sense of guilt, of moral corruption, and brokenness, for having lied to live.

I read the witness testimonies of the Extraordinary Chambers in the Courts of Cambodia (ECCC), and see how perpetrators of crimes against humanity dance around questions with non-answers, I wonder if anyone can remember anything from that time accurately, given the stakes of being put on trial.

When I read heroic stories of Cham leaders organizing small rebellions against the Khmer Rouge, or read of how women and men were forced into marriage, then read countering arguments from expert witnesses chiming in with their own misguided evidence (most of whom were never even there), I feel a kick to my gut. Can institutions seeking "truth" ever reach deep enough into the psyche of the killers to pinpoint their intent? What motivates us to keep drawing out these stories, and how reliably can we distinguish between memories of what *actually happened* and the current perspectives, emotions, and reasons for remembering? Why do we seek to learn from these experiences and who will listen?

Long after the Khmer Rouge, nearly four decades after the genocide, only a few Cambodian schools have been allowed to teach this history in classrooms. Parents, so traumatized by their past, speak little about what they experienced to their children. A younger generation of Cambodians cobbles together stories from Western media and weaves together different impressions, shouldering the burden of their parents' suffering in silence. They carry the weight of this history but have no specific details, pick up fragments of history in disjointed pieces of narrative overheard when elders are talking amongst themselves, from whispers or angry shouts in those moments when their parents or grandparents heave under the pressure of rebuilding a life after Year Zero.

Every weekday I bike past Tuol Sleng Museum on my way to work and home. People living around there go about their daily lives, but superstitions linger. Families clear off the streets by dusk, lock their metal gates at night, because people still believe the place is haunted. Signs, hung on the barbed wires along the wall surrounding the complex, read: "Two hundred dollar fine for urinating." I laugh a little at the signs, and get mildly upset by how surreal it is that a place of torture has become a tourist destination.

I don't go inside Tuol Sleng anymore. I tell my guests that they should go to the Museum, but I won't take them. Riding past the periphery every day is enough, but I'm not frightened; I'm protective of an experience I can no longer regain after Vann Nath's passing.

The last time I went inside, Vann Nath walked in with me, and told me details of his imprisonment. I could see the fear and sense of degradation he experienced in his eyes. The shape of his body warped while retelling those memories; his stance leaned left and inward.

Rarely do I initiate a conversation about the Khmer Rouge these days, but sometimes among older Cambodians, I'll ask what they think of the ECCC trials. They shrug their shoulders in dismay: "It doesn't bring back my dead wife." "It won't bring back my father." A friend of mine said, "I never really knew my parents were forced to marry each other under the Khmer Rouge. My mother freezes up. She won't talk about it when I ask."

For some of the Cambodians I talked to, the ECCC trials represent a crude form of justice in a world where everything has been turned upside down, especially under a current political regime where many former Khmer Rouge still run the country and reap the spoils of war. In Phnom Penh today, privilege and wealth are symbolized by the multitudes of Land Rovers that fill the streets, and the rare Bentleys accompanied by trucks of armed guards. Those signs of prosperity and development contrast wildly with the poor street-cart pusher collecting recyclables from heaps of trash. One person I talked to essentially said the Khmer Rouge's effort to create social equality was a disaster and current conditions make the divide even greater: "They stomp on poor people's heads to get rich; they dig up skulls to build luxury apartments. The whole country is for sale to the highest bidder."

The trials may encourage people to learn about the past, and to break their silence, but I doubt they will feel justice and redemption within the Western structures of courts, testimonies, and limited reparations.

Every day, in front of Tuol Sleng Museum, busloads of foreign tourists walk in wearing tank tops, shorts, and sunhats, as if they were going to a beach. I often wonder what impressions they come out of there with, and imagine they see us, Cambodians, as wild beasts—demented, vile, bloodthirsty over ideology, and crazed with a mandate to kill. I worry they see us as lepers, diseased by an enigmatic darkness which lurks only inside the blood of rare breeds, fashioned out of a convoluted understanding of communism and a mean streak of vengeful populism tainted with extreme nationalism. Such a perception of Cambodian culture is an illusion perpetuated by the media. I can only hope some walk away from Tuol Sleng seeing that hate, ill will, and the capacity to harm is within us all if social, political, and economic conditions are rife with fear, intimidation, and manipulation. But sometimes I give in to doubt that until they experience it themselves, history remains a philosophical abstract.

As a writer who did not experience the horrors of the Khmer Rouge regime, I cannot be an eyewitness, but I am still drawn to tell the story of a genocide I never directly experienced. Unlike Vann Nath, I am not exorcising ghosts, or seeking redemption or justice. Maybe this makes me a culprit, complicit in perpetuating the narrative of humanity's dark side. Maybe the ghosts of millions of victims permeate the Cambodian landscape in ways that talk to the heart of things which every artist strives to touch, but cannot always because she or he lacks the depth of suffering needed to tell the human story. I am prone to sympathize with the painful experiences of my aunts, uncles, and other Cambodian elders who identify themselves as the victims, while wanting to dispossess those uncles and aunts who were Khmer Rouge leaders or agents.

At the heart, I find myself pondering this question: what makes a human mind lean towards corruption? Does it happen slowly, where one small lie supports the space for another lie, then a slightly bigger and dirtier lie, until the mind becomes immune to what is truthful, moral, and just? Do the lies and denials get to a point where the perpetrator can no longer determine what is real and right anymore? Or do hatred and delusion grow out of preconditioned, latent tendencies, lurking in the mind, needing only extreme stress to lure them out?

In a heart-wrenching scene from the documentary *S-21: The Khmer Rouge Killing Machine* by famous Cambodian filmmaker Rithy Panh, the director turns the tables on history. In this scene, Vann Nath, the prisoner, sits at a table with two former prison guards nearly twenty years after his detention, addressing one of them as Khan, his first name. Vann Nath calmly asks them questions about their motives for killing and torturing people.

> *Vann Nath: They created a law that forced people to lie... not to lie to the interrogators... but to lie to ourselves, to lie to ourselves. We denounced people we didn't know, confessed to acts we never did, but we had to answer so they'd let up a little, and not harm us too badly.*
>
> *Khan: The interrogator, too: "No answer? I don't believe it. [whispering:] You had to make up stories. True or False, you had to answer."*
>
> *Vann Nath: And so then, we lost our sense of being human, isn't that right?*

Vann Nath continues to prod his former torturers, but scene after scene, they inch back on excuses and deny their own agency in the act of killing. During their regime, the Khmer Rouge called themselves *Angkar*, which is Khmer for "organization." They described Angkar as having pineapple eyes—with the all-seeing, all-knowing, and omniscient power to invoke terror and reinforce the fear that those who went against the organization would be treated as traitors.

> *Vann Nath: If everyone only thinks Angkar, discipline, obeying orders, "carry out orders or be killed," then that's it, it's over for our world of justice. We don't have a moral center, what we call human conscience—that which separates humans from animals.*

As I watched the scenes clinically draw out the details of how these ordinary men, then Khmer Rouge cadres, killed and dumped bodies into mass graves, my chest felt like caving under the daunting weight of never understanding their intent. The killers kept repeating the lies they were telling themselves. There's a moment when Vann Nath says bluntly: "We are not here to cleanse your bad deeds. I am here to understand, so that what happened was not a waste."

After forty years of research and documenting, can we adequately answer Vann Nath's question, and fulfill his wish to understand? Can we offer solace to those survivors who still suffer daily their very private and personal tragedies in Cambodia today? Though we try, through the Khmer Rouge tribunals, news coverage, films, stories, art performances, talks, and history lessons, we have yet to find a way to address crimes against humanity sufficiently enough to stop them.

Before his death, Vann Nath may have surrendered to never knowing why what happened to him happened. He may have realized the difficulty of achieving an understanding of *kamma*. *Cetanā*, what the Buddha called volition, intention, and directionality of mind, that which generates *kamma*, is hard to trace. Can anyone ever know what intents drove the Khmer Rouge's physical actions, spoken words, and thoughts (expressed or suppressed)?

And yet, I sympathize with Vann Nath's journey to balance a doomed perspective with some audacious hope. He was not merely asking for the whole world to bear witness to the suffering he and so many others faced. He wanted Khmer Rouge leaders, the guards and keepers, killers and perpetrators, to own their agency, to own their own *kamma*. Before he knew if a high court would be set up to put Khmer Rouge cadres on trial, and well before Pol Pot died, Vann Nath offered his captors the chance to be human again.

While writing this essay, I scoured the Internet in hopes of finding the same painting Vann Nath showed me, because I needed evidence, something outside of my head to confirm it was real, that my recounting of its details would not be prone to mis-remembering. I doubted whether I'd find it, and imagined it hung in a back corner of a hallway or in the library room of a private collector. I was determined to find some evidence of what I saw, and finally decided to go to Vann Nath's home in Phnom Penh, where I last saw him.

At Vann Nath's gallery, his widow, Kith Eng, and his daughter shuffled through old photos, prints and papers in search of the image I remembered. While we reminisced, Kith Eng told me about his funeral and the fifth-year commemoration ceremony of his death. After an hour of looking, we couldn't find any trace of this painting. Vann Nath's widow looked at me apologetically, with kind eyes, but I was not disappointed. Without the image, I'm unsure whether my memory is reliable—exactly what I have been questioning from the start. Without material evidence or documentation of the painting, I feared my story could easily misrepresent the artist's intention. Like many testimonies, it lives unverified, untrustworthy, and a fabrication of moments irretrievable.

Instead, I am open to imagine the painting and its meaning to my own liking.

When I imagine Vann Nath in the painting he showed me, I see him as the arc of this story, a story I have fashioned with flawed memories. Offered up by the earth, my Vann Nath, the Vann Nath that I want you to love, levitates in technicolor. He masters the four great elements, overcoming sensory desire, ill will, sloth, worry, and doubt. He finds himself no longer shrouded in self-denial or self-doubt, but confident and open-hearted, beaming with loving-kindness. In the Vann Nath I paint for you, he is freed of his suffering, able to look his torturers compassionately in the eyes and say: *We are all human. I accept both the light and the dark in you, and believe you and I have the agency, the human conscience and ability of mind to act in ways that move us towards enlightenment.*

SOKUNTHARY SVAY

Cambodian Requiem

The large choral room has unflattering fluorescent light. There are two baby grand pianos, red velvet curtains entirely covering one wall, a timpani set, a gamelan gong, storage lockers, and numerous folding chairs placed in a semi-circle and facing a conductor's stand. On any given Wednesday, at least eighty singers are waiting to begin rehearsal. I'm sitting with folks half my age and with others who are twice my age. They are primarily White, with just a few East Asians. I seem to have little in common with these people, yet here we are, gathered together in this room to sing our way through Mozart's *Requiem*. The last time I sang in a choir was nearly a decade ago.

My family's emigration story began far from a rehearsal room. I was born in a refugee camp in Thailand shortly after my parents left Cambodia during the fall of the Khmer Rouge, a genocidal regime that ruled from 1975 to 1979 and took the lives of roughly 1.7 million citizens in a failed attempt at an agrarian utopia. During this time, intellectuals, people of Western influence or religion, even people who wore glasses, were identified as the class enemy. City people were corralled into the countryside, where most died of malnutrition or execution. When the regime fell, the Vietnamese moved in and took power. My parents left for the Thai border. Then, in 1981, my mother got off a plane in New York on a chilly autumn day, wearing sandals and a sarong, completely unprepared for this new world, as were all the other Khmer refugees who made it to the U.S.

Eventually, a makeshift Khmer Buddhist temple was established on Fordham Road in the Bronx. Cambodian New Year events were held there, with Khmer pop music and dancing. At other times, when the children of survivors got married, their weddings were conducted at the temple according to our practices. The Khmer Rouge had replaced our traditional court and folk music with the gongs and mantras of communist ideology; by celebrating our rituals in the Bronx, we were saving a part of our history and identity.

Cambodian prayer ceremonies *(bonn)* were a time for redemption. At one home or another, people would host a *bonn*, inviting monks in orange robes and other Khmer Buddhists to pray for loved ones who had been lost, for those living, and for survival and success. A room would be emptied of everything but the people and offerings, and was soon filled with woodsy incense and the serene monotone of sutras being chanted in the ancient Buddhist language, Pali. We kids would run amok outside, only occasionally joining in. When we did, we sat with our legs tucked respectfully sideways, pretending to know what we were doing. Afterward, once all the monks had accepted their alms from the community, the laypeople would eat together, sharing a potluck.

When it came to Cambodian music, though, sacred had little to do with it. My parents' musical connection to their home country was on cassette tapes with pictures of American women pasted on their sides, cut from clothing catalogs. On the tapes were recordings of Khmer pop stars from their time—Ros Sereysothea and Sinn Sisamouth, among others—and sometimes traditional music. Many of the original recordings were destroyed during the regime; some were only found decades later in hidden archives or private collections. As kids, we taped over my parents' cassettes. In hindsight I cringe at what we did. For my mother, the traditional Khmer wedding songs were reminiscent of her own wedding—traditionally, a nearly week-long ceremony with countless ornate dresses to change into, almost an entire village in attendance, and feasting and dancing into the night. These tapes stirred my parents' feelings of nostalgia, and allowed them to return briefly to their past lives.

Yet all of these reminders of Cambodia, the things that comforted my parents, were absolutely foreign to me. While I became used to the religious and cultural rituals, they didn't connect to the person I wanted to be. My life had a Cambodian soundtrack, but it confused me. I wanted my parents to encourage me to be different, but still be their child.

I had to eke out my own way of being in the world as an inheritor of my parents' experiences. Unlike my older brother, I didn't personally experience the trauma or guilt of surviving what my mother called "the war." But I lived with their fear and isolation from the non-Khmers around us—people my parents called foreigners. Our apartment door had eight locks: two pairs of chains linked by master locks, a floor-mounted police lock, a couple of deadbolts, and a smaller chain lock with an alarm. If we weren't expecting visitors, we didn't open the door. In fact, hearing American voices on the other side, sometimes we stood by the door listening until we heard their footsteps walking away down the hall. Most of the time the voices belonged to Jehovah's Witnesses; only they would be so bold as to knock freely on a stranger's door in the Bronx.

But away from my family, in school, I didn't share their fear of strangers. I joined the glee club and rehearsed with the group every Friday. I picked up the flute and started playing in the school band. Especially in glee club, I didn't feel like just an individual in a classroom striving to get good grades for myself; I became part of something bigger, contributing to my school's community through music. I later auditioned for a special performing arts high school in Manhattan and was accepted as a flutist. In spite of my parents' disapproval of music as a career and of their only daughter traveling to Manhattan on the subway alone, I pleaded my case—a rare thing—and they reluctantly agreed.

For many years, my family lived by rote: my parents going to work and making practical decisions; and my brothers and me going to school, obeying our parents without question. But as a budding musician and teenager, I felt it wasn't enough for me to go through the motions of life. I needed to experience and feel all the many emotions that no one in my refugee household explored.

As a flute major at the LaGuardia High School of Music & Art and Performing Arts, I walked past Juilliard every morning after my train ride to Manhattan from the Bronx. I listened to Mary J. Blige sing "My Life" as I dreamily imagined performing flute solos at Lincoln Center. To me as a fourteen-year-old, nothing seemed odd about that juxtaposition. I wore baggy jeans and gold hoop earrings and called something "dope" if I liked it. Although I eventually became disillusioned with my time at music school, I had a brief, childish desire to be bigger than what I was. I always knew that I wanted to sing, but the school didn't allow for double majors, and my previous music experience was in flute. I felt obligated to continue with the instrument since my father had purchased a student flute for me early on—a rare indulgence, given how careful my parents were with money.

Like a lot of students at that age, I felt lost and alone, more so because learning and practicing an instrument is a solitary vocation. I practiced by myself for hours, and my parents were indifferent to the process. In my twelve years of playing seriously, I had never heard a good or bad word from them. I had no idea if they even liked the sound of my playing. I felt ashamed by what I didn't know, and practiced timidly all those years, as though playing in secret, as though it was my burden alone. Although I do imagine that somewhere in the South Bronx in the 1990s, some Puerto Ricans and Dominicans could hear my flute playing across the housing projects—shrill as the Number 2 that traversed aboveground across my entire neighborhood.

My parents stopped coming to my concerts after elementary school. The year I was in the Bronx Borough-Wide Band's Carnegie Hall concert, my mother came to pick me up after it was over, missing the entire performance. I didn't have a picture from that evening, and I've lost contact with many of my band mates. I was thrown into a dark time due to my family's lack of support and acknowledgement of my abilities—and because of the awkwardness that comes with being a teen. Sometimes I wept myself to sleep out of sadness and frustration. In my household, the moment we felt anything negative, we shut ourselves off emotionally and went to our respective rooms. My family could love through acts of sacrifice, but had no idea how to communicate affection.

In between flings with teenage boys to fill the emotional gaps in my home life, there were school concerts put on each semester by the various music ensembles. In junior high school, I had only played the notes in front of me—a far cry from real artistry. I had four music lessons where I learned a great deal about sight-reading, but had learned nothing about emotion, interpretation, intensity, or musicality. I viewed my instrument from a practical standpoint: how best to make a sound come out and to play technical passages as quickly as possible. I was a typical, untrained, immature student. Then this changed one day, when I sat in on a vocal class of choral music and heard "Lacrimosa" from Mozart's *Requiem*. This was the first time I listened to the *Requiem*, and I was astonished by what I heard. The four young African American singers stood in front of the classroom and sang in a foreign language I'd only read about. It would be thirteen years before I understood the words, but I could feel the sighs, hush of eighth notes, and swelling of emotion in the room. "That day of tears and mourning, / when from the ashes shall arise, / all humanity to be judged. / Spare us by your mercy, Lord, / gentle Lord Jesus, / grant them eternal rest. Amen."

Despite having no job and little money, I managed to scrape together ten dollars for a recording of Mozart's *Requiem* by the Berliner Philharmoniker, conducted by Herbert von Karajan. I began to listen to the recording on my shoddy computer speakers every day, sometimes twice a day. Here I was at sixteen, a Cambodian Buddhist with no context for a Latin Mass written by a classical Western composer. I came to know all of the melodies by heart. All the anguish and loneliness I felt was encapsulated in Mozart's motifs. I exhaled my anger through his *Dies Irae,* and I submitted myself to his *Confutatis*. It didn't matter that outside my window I could hear basketballs being bounced as I tried to sleep, or that it wasn't safe to be out at night in my neighborhood, or that I had been shunned by my social circle because they thought me a "slut," or that I barely heard a tender word from my father. I was safe here with Mozart. When the sopranos sang *"voca me,"* I was being called by something I couldn't comprehend.

I came to understand the beauty and tragedy of classical music. The *Requiem* opened my ears and heart to other major works. That particular year at our annual concerto competition, I heard Mendelssohn's *Violin Concerto in E Minor,* a well-known work capable of evoking tension, desire, and awe in just its first movement. I admired but was jealous of the violinist's virtuosity. I skipped classes to attend midday rehearsals and submit to this beauty again and again. I sat alone in the concert hall's balcony. From that seat, it felt like a private concert. I found a transposed score for flute, which I knew I could never play but bought anyway. Another year, the senior chorus sang Carl Orff's *Carmina Burana*, a joyous collection of musical vignettes. I found an affordable recording of that work as well and spent another few weeks entangled in the piece, all to the puzzled looks of my mother, who couldn't understand my musical obsession with a language so foreign to her. For once I felt truly connected to the music I was hearing.

After a tumultuous few years at LaGuardia, I worked in retail and entered college, enjoying a brief time as a music major. However, I seemed out of place as a classical flutist in a primarily jazz program; I earned an English literature scholarship instead, which covered my tuition and provided a stipend. After my lifelong fight to keep music in my life without support and guidance from the school or my parents, I'd thrown in the towel and taken the path of least resistance and practicality.

Although I had once envisioned myself developing a singing voice, I instead began to develop a literary voice. With writing as a requirement in my major, I took up poetry as an outlet and was surprised at my interest in prosody. My advisor was like a second father to me, a more encouraging, emotionally available figure who looked out for my academic interests. Later, I received a fellowship that introduced me to a community of students interested in my literary projects and thesis. I found my niche; I wasn't alone anymore. I was surrounded by a world of creativity, literature, and supportive scholars. After graduation, I worked at the CUNY Graduate Center, an institution offering a Ph.D., and spent time in a creative writing MFA program before dropping out mid-semester to give birth to my child, Soriya Annabel. Suddenly, I couldn't remember why I was writing.

Issues that I thought I had left behind came to the surface. I had spent most of my life unable to talk about my anger towards my family, my guilt for wanting anything for myself, and my frustration over my inability to speak up. Having a child forced me to reflect on how I was raised and whether that experience was worth passing on. I became bitter and had a dream of being a child again, abandoned by my family. Exasperated by my daughter's refusal to sleep and by reading too many "expert" books, I forced her onto a sleeping schedule. This caused us all to lose sleep, and I became irritable and cried often. I fell into deep postpartum depression, trapped in my body and mind and unable to articulate my pain.

I found a therapist who helped me articulate the repression of my childhood, and helped me understand the trauma of my parents' experience and the damage of their survival mode of parenting. I slowly began to forgive them for how I was raised, while also discovering what my parents had given me that I was grateful for: pragmatism, independence, respect for elders, loyalty, integrity, and unconditional love. I had to find a way to mourn a painful childhood, subjected to their undiagnosed post-traumatic stress disorder, a condition prevalent but untreated in much of the Khmer refugee community.

Once I began to address my childhood memories, I slowly found music again. I discovered the Queens College Choral Society, a student- and community-driven chorus that performs two concerts a year. They were holding auditions for all parts and would be performing Mozart's *Requiem*. Having spent years removed from my musical aspirations, I felt the timing seemed right. I had dreamed of singing this piece, a Mass for the dead that had once brought me to life in a household that had witnessed death, yet never spoken about it.

I found my first private voice teacher, a music director at a church connected to Juilliard, and made friends with moms who were also singers. My long-term goal was to become a better musician—something I hadn't considered since I was a child. I always felt stunted in my musical growth, partly because we couldn't afford private instruction. I viewed my ability to play the flute as a means of being noticed and loved. Since my parents couldn't show affection, I sought that fulfillment at school, and when I couldn't advance beyond my abilities, I felt like a complete failure. The flute represented issues of self-worth. Singing, however, evoked childhood memories of Friday-afternoon glee-club rehearsals and the joy of discovery; it became a way to express things that I couldn't say in words. I found my voice, emotionally and literally.

The sacred choral music experience is different from that of Pali chanting, which I grew up with. Monotonal music sometimes has a negative connotation, but I like to think that in Buddhist or medieval chants, the uniformity of tone evokes a feeling of peace and the monotone doesn't detract from the musicality. Arguably, Western choral music provides something similar using the conventions of Western harmony. Whether singing in harmony or unison, human voices converging create a rare place in the world where groups ranging in size from ten to over a hundred—individuals with seemingly little in common—can work together in peaceful unity.

Requiem helped me heal from my own struggles, but it also represented to me the healing of the Cambodian diaspora. The Cambodian rites for the dead play an integral part in leading souls to their rebirth. Many of the casualties of that regime were denied their Buddhist rituals because religion was outlawed by the Khmer Rouge. At the temple in the Bronx, we continued—through *bonn* on various occasions, such as Pchum Ben (Ancestors' Day) or Cambodian New Year in April—to honor those we lost. Although Cambodia doesn't have the tradition of the Requiem Mass, I think Mozart's "Lacrimosa" would be a fitting tribute to those who died and to the pain experienced by the country.

Back in the Queens College choral room, I'm anxious to sing, but do I still remember how? The pianist begins to play the opening chords to the first movement of the *Requiem*. Our conductor, wearing a black turtleneck, sets the mournful tempo with his baton. Everyone is looking intently at the score, but I don't need to because the opening passage is burned into my memory. I know it from all those days in my teenage bedroom. It's the piece that saved me. I feel tears welling up as I open my mouth to finally become part of this work as a performer rather than merely as a listener. Then we finally get to my beloved "Lacrimosa," with its musical landscape, composed mostly in minor keys. As it ends on "Amen," the final cadence shifts to major, and we mourners experience a brief feeling of hope and its possibilities.

RINITH TAING

The Bookrenter of Battambang and the Master of Uselessness

THE BOOKRENTER OF BATTAMBANG

On a blustery evening in October 2017, my fellow journalist Alessandro Marazzi-Sassoon and I were on our way to Battambang province, which borders on Thailand in the northwest. We were two young and enthusiastic reporters from the *Phnom Penh Post* hoping to write a feature about why the province has produced so many of the country's most famous artists. The golden-age singer Ros Sereysothea, writer and poet Kong Bunchhoeun, master mason Tan Veut, painter and writer Vann Nath, and more recently the acclaimed sculptor Sopheap Pich were all from Battambang. Even the legendary Sinn Sisamouth, known as the Elvis of Cambodia, made Battambang his home, composing countless songs that mentioned the province and its artists. His famous love song "Champa of Battambang" personifies the city as a beautiful woman to whom he longs to return, and has come to be regarded as expressing nostalgia for all of Cambodia.

While we were searching, we were also hoping to find any material from which we could develop an additional feature; we couldn't justify having asked our editor for three days in Battambang if we returned with only one story.

This was my first trip to the province, and even though I grew up in Cambodia, I did not know much about it; Alessandro knew even less. So we decided to leave everything to chance, rented two motorcycles, and set off in search of an interesting story.

As we were drove along the southern side of Battambang's Phsa Nat Market, I spotted among the many cafés, pubs, and shops, which were mostly selling souvenirs, an odd hole-in-the-wall storefront. Above the door was an iron statue depicting an aspsara, a Hindu female spirit of the clouds and waters, like those carved in bas-relief at Angkor Wat. Below it was a sign: GRANDPA APSARA—BOOK RENTAL SERVICE. We went inside and saw a shop that was dusty with age, but the shelves of old books, some yellow with age, were well organized and clean.

The owner of the shop, Tran Sab, is seventy-nine years old, small in stature, and has a hairless head and hands covered with paper cuts. While we were waiting to talk to him, we overheard him lecturing a young woman who had come into his shop searching for a translation of a Korean novel. "When you read Korean novels, you are supporting Korean writers," he admonished her. "When you read Khmer novels, you are supporting writers with your same Khmer blood." After greeting us, he told me that his eyes were now too bad for reading, but he still took pleasure in helping other people enjoy books—especially people who could not afford to buy them. In any case, compared to what happened to him about forty years ago, the loss of his ability to read is not the worst calamity in his life.

Sab was born in Kampuchea Krom, an area that was long part of Cambodia before falling under Vietnamese control, a change formalized by the French in 1949. He has always been proud and protective of his Khmer identity and culture, especially Khmer literature. In 1958, soon after coming to Cambodia, he enrolled in Phnom Penh Municipal Pedagogy School, hoping to become a primary-school teacher. There, he met Khieu Samphan, who at that time was on the law faculty of the University of Phnom Penh. Samphan would later become one of the most powerful officials in the Khmer Rouge. After the regime fell, Samphan was convicted of crimes against humanity and sentenced to life in prison—all the time denying that he knew anything about the atrocities committed during the genocide. At present, Samphan is still appealing his sentence. Nevertheless, looking back, Sab said, "I found Khieu Samphan to be a good, articulate person; he helped me become a communist."

While in school in Phnom Penh, Sab participated in demonstrations and protests. He even claims he was one of the leaders in the famous attack on the U.S. embassy by a mob of 20,000 students on April 26, 1965. The demonstration was prompted by U.S. cross-border air attacks that had killed many Cambodian citizens, and by a malicious article about Prince Sihanouk and his wife, Monineath, published in the April 5, 1965, issue of *Newsweek* magazine.

As a result of his political activism, Sab was prevented from finding a job after graduation in 1963. The only capital he had then were the dozens of books that he had bought with the money he saved by living frugally and skimping on meals. Therefore, he decided to start the first book-rental business in Phnom Penh, in a stall located in front of Chao Ponhea Yat High School, later known as Tuol Svay Prey High School, and finally as S-21.

"Book prices at that time were exorbitant," Sab said. "So my business was popular with students, especially those from poor families or from the provinces. I was also happy because I could read books and make money at the same time." From textbooks and technical manuals to novels and folktales, Sab's books provided knowledge and entertainment to the students, who paid about five riels to rent a book for a week. He loved it when he saw his customers reading his books, he told me, and when they kept coming back to rent more.

When the Khmer Rouge came to power in 1975, Sab was among many educated and intellectual people who at first were delighted by the black-shirts' victory. On the afternoon of April 17, while Khmer Rouge soldiers were entering Phnom Penh, Sab put on his best clothes, grabbed a white flag, and rushed out of his house to welcome them. But what happened next was not what he and other educated people expected.

"They suddenly forced me to evacuate Phnom Penh," he said. "I was carrying nothing. They made me leave thousands of my books behind. It was the worst moment of my life."

Although Sab had been a supporter of the regime, the Khmer Rouge labeled him one of the "New People," mostly urban, educated Cambodians who were driven into the countryside, where they were forced to do menial labor, often beaten, starved, and moved from place to place. During this period, Sab secretly searched for books in old houses and brought them with him when he found any. One day, a Khmer Rouge cadre discovered the books in his bundle and accused him of being an enemy of the revolution.

"They tied me up and were going to kill me with a hoe," Sab said. "To save myself, I pretended to be insane and did a comedic act to make them laugh. That was the way I escaped death."

During the Khmer Rouge regime, the only written materials allowed were filled with propaganda. After the fall of the regime in 1979, Sab learned that all his books in Phnom Penh had been either burned or made into toilet paper or cigarette wrappers.

"They destroyed my entire collection and turned the school where the students had been my customers into a prison," Sab said, almost breaking into tears. "I was wrong to support them."

In 2002, after many years of struggling to collect books, Sab reopened his book-rental business in Battambang. But compared to four decades earlier, business has not been good. His shop used to be crowded constantly, and now only four or five people enter in a day. Everyone is distracted by new technology, he says, from smartphones and video games to social media and the Internet. As readership has fallen, the incomes of writers, as well booksellers, have been declining. Many writers—including the best of those who remain and who were lucky enough to have escaped slaughter by the Khmer Rouge—have given up writing and looked for other ways to make a living.

Sab, however, is committed to keeping his business going as long as possible, until he simply can't sustain it anymore. He is ashamed, he said, that sometimes he has even had to ask his customers for donations so that he can make ends meet.

"Young people today miss out on the kind of information and moral values that books provide," Sab said. "I wish they would realize that not so long ago, if you even picked up a book, you would be executed."

After about two hours, I said goodbye to Sab and hit the road to go back to the office. The only way I could compensate Sab for his story was to give him my appreciation, but I was sure he deserved much more than that. After meeting him, I stopped calling myself a book lover. He may be the person in Cambodia who deserves that title more than anyone else.

THE MASTER OF USELESSNESS

In high school, I too collected old and rare books as a hobby. When my friends found out, they began calling me the Master of Uselessness. They were more interested in video games and computer software, and wanted to talk about the latest movies rather than about authors whose works they had never read. It hurt me because I thought of literature as embodying the spirit of the nation.

I have treasured books more than almost anything else in my life. I have read them to keep my imagination alive and to remind myself that there is a larger world out there. I have found books wherever I can—in out-of-the-way bookshops like Grandpa Apsara's, in old markets, on the Internet, and in libraries. About fifteen years ago, I was in a public library in Phnom Penh, reading some newer literature, when on a shelf in a far corner, a book caught my eye by being the oldest there. Its cover displayed a painting of the Tonle Sap, a beautiful woman carrying a basket of fish, and a man in traditional Lao clothing. I grabbed it, found a quiet place, and started reading—immediately intrigued by this story of an outsider, a Laotian revolutionary, who is befriended by a Cambodian fishing family. The title was *Sky of the Lost Moon* by a Ty Chi Huot. As I would learn later, the author, born in 1952 in Takeo province, had worked many jobs before becoming a writer, including baking bread, waiting tables, and cutting hair at a small stall near the Orussey Market. His first novel, *The Sea Coast Gangsters,* was published in 1970 and sold in the fish market. As it turns out, the novel in the library was the last book he wrote before he died in 1987 at thirty-five. I wished he would have lived longer. I wished I could have met him.

From the age of seven, I wanted to be a writer. But I sometimes felt I was born in the wrong place at the wrong time. I never wanted to become the next J. K Rowling, Stephen King, or John Grisham. I simply wanted to write books of fiction that would be read. My mind was filled with characters living in imaginary worlds. I dreamed about a Cambodian time traveler who goes back to the past to try to prevent the fall of the Angkor Empire. I imagined a daring Cambodian spy traveling the world for his country. I began to write these stories down, and to passionately read fiction by well-known authors. I started with *Sophat,* widely considered the first Cambodian novel, written in 1938 by Rim Kin. After that, I read Nou Hach, Chuth Khay, and others. When I learned English, I began reading Western literature—a simplified version of Daniel DeFoe's *Robinson Crusoe,* then Charles Dickens's *Oliver Twist* and *A Christmas Carol,* and much more.

I asked myself, Why do people around the world know DeFoe and Dickens, but not Ty Chi Huot or Chuth Khay? I realized the answer was that millions of people could read English while only a handful could read Khmer, my mother tongue. Furthermore, almost no Cambodian authors had been translated into English. And so I made it my life's mission to become a writer and to help bring world attention to Cambodian literature.

When I told my parents—both of whom were successful professionals in the fields of education and medicine—they were shocked. They could not believe such ideas came from their only son, whom they expected to rise even higher in a professional career than they had. They told me that my dream was unrealistic and being a writer was a terrible way to make a living. From that day on, they did all they could to discourage me from becoming a writer.

They threw away my manuscripts, punished me when they found me writing or reading novels, and even asked my teachers to report me if they caught me writing stories at school. Friends and relatives also discouraged me. I couldn't blame them, though; I would have done the same if I had been in their place. After all, unlike in the golden age of Cambodia's modern literature, during the 1960s and 1970s, it is nearly impossible nowadays for writers to earn a living in this country.

I did my best to overcome all the opposition, but in vain. Soon, my imaginary characters faded away along with their worlds, new stories stopped coming into my head, and I stopped writing. I struggled to put all my effort into my schoolwork, though on the side I still secretly read as much literature as I could.

Then, after high school, I entered the "stubborn stage" of my life. I rejected the path my parents had planned for me. I refused to go to medical school and instead accepted a scholarship in English and international studies at college. I was re-committed to achieving my childhood dream.

Unfortunately, I would fail again. Completing a dual major in the university was not as easy as I had hoped. I spent most of my time reading textbooks, doing research, and writing essays for class. There was barely time left for reading novels and even less for my own writing. By the time I graduated, I considered myself a passable wordsmith, but my instincts as a creative writer had left me. Also, it became obvious to me that I needed to have a regular income in order to have a future. I accepted that in the real world, making a living as an author was nearly impossible. So I ended up becoming a journalist.

In the years that followed, I published hundreds of articles in English and received several journalism awards. But, unfortunately, I wasn't able to return to my own writing. Disappointing as this was, journalism gave me the chance to meet and interview many iconic Cambodian authors and to write about their lives. I interviewed Chuth Khay, known for his revolutionary use of everyday vocabulary and conversational style, and his iconic ghost stories of the 1970s, which have influenced writers today like Sok Chanphal. "I write books to be enjoyed by everyone, no matter whether the reader is an intellectual scholar or an ordinary person with only a few years of schooling," Khay told me in 2019. Now in his eighties, he is, apart from his friend Soth Polin, one of the only veteran fiction writers alive today. After surviving the Khmer Rouge by pretending to be deaf, dumb, and mute, then working for many years as a taxi driver in France, he at last resumed his literary career in 2000, writing several books based on his childhood and his brief return to Cambodia.

I also wrote investigative stories about Bunchan Mol, one of the founders of the Khmer Issarak and the author of *Political Prison* (Kuk Noyobay), a memoir describing his incarceration in the 1940s in Côn Sơn prison in southern Vietnam during French colonial rule. Today, the prison is a museum dedicated to the Vietnamese who fought for independence from the French; it has been almost forgotten that Cambodian nationalists were also locked up in that brutal space. I could find no record of what happened to Mol after the Khmer Rouge entered the city in 1975. It is presumed he died in Phnom Penh.

Finally, more recently, I've started translating Cambodian fiction and memoir. I have even begun translating the last novel of Ty Chi Huot, *Sky of the Lost Moon,* that so captivated me fifteen years ago when I discovered it on a dusty library shelf. In these ways, I am keeping alive my promise to make Cambodian literature and information about Cambodian authors more accessible to the world. Perhaps I'll even get back to writing fiction of my own.

chapter 8

Let us abolish the monarchy and establish Angkar*!
Let us abolish taxes and establish voluntary contributions!
Let us abolish the white and glorify the black!
Let us dignify the ignorant and eradicate the learned!

*Angkar: organization

from Year of the Rabbit

It is the mark of a talented artist to be able to give the illusion of simplicity to an account of the unthinkable. This story is so painful that for years, survivors were unable to tell it to their children. The experience of chaos eats away at our insides and leaves us helpless, torn between wanting to live again and the fear of not having the strength. It's like standing in front of a bridge that lies in ruins and looking at the other riverbank, where our souls might find peace and ease.

Conceived by radical ideologues and implemented by zealous leaders, the murderous utopia of the Khmer Rouge regime could only be achieved through the unleashing of a reign of terror, one that isolated individuals and destroyed every vestige of traditional society. Family ties, solidarity, respect, faith, compassion … All moral foundations were annihilated, just as the people who believed in them were exterminated. It was not only a matter of killing, but of erasing us and denying our dignity. How can one understand what those blackclad men inflicted on others?

But humans are not easily eradicated, and that is their strength. In Tian Veasna's description of his family's desperate escape, disaster is repeatedly averted through minor miracles. Like the Khmer Rouge chief who lets the young doctor get away, the old peasant who intervenes to save the family from execution, and the villager who offers his hut so the young woman can give birth. As long as humans resist, it seems as if nothing truly irreparable could happen, even when everything is collapsing and fear is destroying society. But how long can a person hold out against the spread of a totalitarian terror that only gradually reveals its true face? Where can a person find refuge when every door is locked? Who can be trusted when every movement is watched? When divulging a name can result in death?

Rithy Panh

After their arrest by Khmer Rouge militia, Khim and Vithya's families were sent to a village to be reeducated according to the principles of Angkar. There they again met Song, the young man on the bicycle. As one of the "old people" from the countryside, Song was assigned to help relocate the "new people" from the cities. He suggested that the two families come to his village of Roneam.

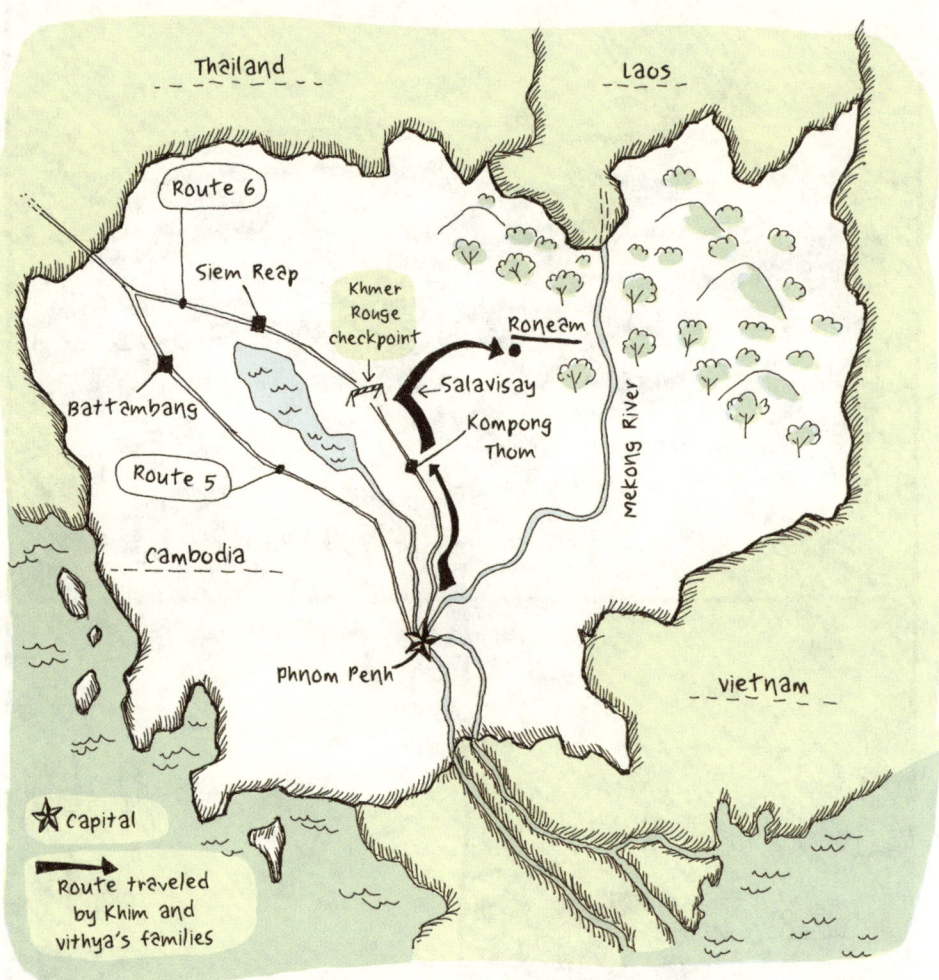

PHINA SO

Contemporary Writing and Publishing in Cambodia

In the mid-eighties, five to six years after the genocide ended, Cambodia slowly came back to life. When I enrolled in school, my mother was involved in the book business, and I remember stacks of books kept in piles in the corners of our house. She rented those books to the villagers. I often saw her noting down the villagers' names, book titles, the dates the book needed to be returned, and the rental fees. She told me she made a living renting out books, and it was evidence of the thirst for reading that arose after the genocide. In time, books became available in printed versions, unlike the handwritten copies that my mother rented, one notebook at a time.

The notebooks were the same type used in classrooms. Most were very nicely produced, copied out for a fee by people with good handwriting. Because they were created by hand in pencil, a novel might exist in several versions. My mother bought them from Battambang province; some of the most popular were written by Tonsay (Rabbit), a pen name of Mao Samnang. My mother told me that while she bought the books and rented them out herself, she also rented the books to a secondary dealer in her home district. According to her, a novel could have seven to ten chapters—one chapter per notebook. Each was rented for around 20 to 30 KHR—about US$.05 to US$.07 today. Then, in the early 1990s, when my mother became seriously ill, she gave up her book-rental business. For a long time, I used to search for those kinds of books, but could not find any that still existed.

A lot of the most popular books for rent were romance novels. I remember that Mum was not keen for me to read them. Like many traditional parents, she was raised to believe that reading brought more bad than good to girls. I could not understand why, so when she was not around, I secretly read the novels anyway. Later, during a cultural leadership workshop organized by Cambodian Living Arts, a colleague asked me, "Was this when your feminism started?" I think it was.

Having witnessed the popularity of my mother's book-rental business, I came to believe that Cambodians—including my own parents—are eager to read when books and stories are available to them and are affordable. One night, when my mother had spent almost the entire evening reading her favorite novel, she was so engrossed that her hair caught fire from the lamp beside her. My father was a reader too. In the early 1990s, whenever he came home from a business trip, he always brought back a dozen books and magazines. I remember being so happy to hold those wonderful books.

After high school, I left our home in Pursat to study psychology at the Royal University of Phnom Penh. At the time, I never thought much about being a writer. I didn't have a clue that writing could be a profession, and I had never heard of the Khmer Writers Association or writing classes. Nothing. So I continued studying for my degree, graduated, found a job, and got a scholarship to study for a master's degree in social work in Melbourne, Australia. I wrote a blog, but being a novelist or a poet still didn't occur to me.

When I came back to Cambodia in December 2012, I'd become a more outspoken person. With my close friend Huot Socheata, I started to think about writing short stories for fun. About that time, I saw a frightening incident: live on Facebook, a beautiful young woman tried to cut her wrists. I thought about all the stories I'd heard of young girls who reacted tragically when their boyfriends ended their relationships. In those days, ten or twenty years ago, if a girl had lost her viginity, it was a serious situation. In those cases, a young woman was made to believe that she was worthless from then on. Many women would do whatever they could to hold on to relationships, including trying to force their boyfriends to marry them. And when this didn't work, some chose to harm themselves or commit suicide. They believed their lives had no value anymore because they had been told that no man would marry a woman who was not a virgin.

As a feminist and an advocate for gender equality, I felt it was important to address this situation. My friend and I decided to encourage the creation of stories depicting strong young women in professional careers, daring to express themselves and able to move on with life in spite of the disapproval of men. We solicited submissions and put together our first anthology: *Crush Collections: Heartbroken? Not a Problem!*

When we started looking for a publisher for the anthology, we discovered that in Cambodia there were no genuine publishers, only printers. Moreover, the printers had no respect for an author's rights and paid no royalties. In addition, they gave us no guidance on editing, revising, or other aspects of publishing. Writers might be offered a low, one-time payment for their manuscripts and that was it. That was not the kind of arrangement we were looking for. So my friends and I decided to establish our own publishing business. At the time, we didn't really know what it meant to say we had a publishing house. There was no formal way to register the business or become official. We just named ourselves Kampu Mera Editions, created a Facebook page, and have been going ever since.

The first anthology we published, *Crush Collections,* was relatively successful and received recognition from the literary community. As a result, we decided we shouldn't publish just one book and quit. We developed a theme for a second anthology and again invited submissions. Then we made a third, fourth, and started publishing other kinds of books, including translations.

Having started Kampu Mera Editions, I was invited to attend various international literary festivals. The writers would ask me if Cambodia, too, had a literature festival. I didn't know, but I soon found out about the Kampot Writers and Readers Festival. However, I realized that they didn't have as much local content as I wished to see. So in 2017 I established the Khmer Literature Festival, which is now in its fifth year. Last October, the theme was "The Art of Literary Translation."

Along with the immense joy I get from doing this work, there have been many challenges. One of them involves intellectual rights. The Ministry of Culture and Fine Arts has a Department of Copyrights and Related Rights. However, because of the surge of the Internet—and a lack of knowledge about copyrights—there are many instances of people sharing, copying, and reproducing writers' works without compensation or permission. They falsely believe that since they bought a copy of a book, they can do whatever they want with the contents. Many others believe that they are promoting a writer's works when they read the book aloud on YouTube. In the worst cases, books are photographed, then resold online for US$.25 to US$1 per copy without the permission or knowledge of the authors. This unethical behavior by people is essentially theft, and the lack of laws and penalties to stop the practice discourages many authors from writing and publishing at all. At the same time, ethical, independent publishers such as Kampu Mera Editions get few of the grants that are available to promote literary work.

The same lack of regulations means that many of the unethical publishers also illegally translate and sell foreign-language books without any consequences. Besides stealing from authors and legitimate translators, their behavior creates unfair competition for those businesses—again, such as Kampu Mera Editions—which are committed to obtaining permission from translators and authors before publishing their work and to paying royalties and other costs.

Clearly, legitimate publishers need the support of government and relevant ministries to regulate, encourage, and sustain a cultural ecosystem for literary artists and publishers. But at the present time, Cambodia does not ensure protection of freedom of expression. Lack of access to creative writing courses, workshops, and publication further limits literary freedom.

Despite these barriers, Cambodian writers are resilient and we are learning fast. Through our commitment, love, and passion, we writers and publishers are jumping in and doing the work. Cambodians have many stories to tell that have not emerged, and there is still a long way to go.

PHINA SO

Freshwater Crayfish and the Trouble with Names

By the time I wake up, Mum is already home from the market. Having been away from the family in Siem Reap for five days, I want to be more helpful to her than I usually am. "Is there anything at the market you forgot and want me to pick up and buy?" I ask. Over the fish porridge she's cooking, she replies, "Maybe some crayfish? I'm making a Vietnamese sour soup today, and crayfish would be perfect for it."

I know what she is implying: she hadn't forgotten the crayfish. Instead, she had decided not to buy them because she was worried about money, fearing that such a purchase would quickly deplete the amount I had given her for the monthly household expenses.

In fact, there are three things Mum asks me to get. First, of course, the crayfish. Second, pineapples, which are an ingredient in Vietnamese soup; however, she says, pineapples are up to me because she herself doesn't like them. Third, *phka snao,* the name of a yellow flower *(Sesbania javanica),* to be eaten as a raw vegetable with our dinner.

My nine-year-old-daughter comes along with me, and as we walk I am thinking about the Vietnamese sour soup. Its name includes a word that's recently caused debate because of its connotation. In the Khmer language, the soup is called *samla mchu yuon. Yuon* refers to people from Vietnam. I have heard that some people—mostly in the West—are saying that the word has derogatory and racist origins and shouldn't be used. As a result, many Cambodians, including me, are now calling the soup *samla mchu Vietnam.*

This makes me think of other names you hear in the marketplace. Some are being debated, with people saying they should be changed or used more carefully. Other names are regarded as acceptable and not given a second thought.

For example, in Khmer, the term for onion literally means "French bulb." In general, when an introduced vegetable is large, we refer to it as *French.* I am not sure if this is related to the comparatively larger size of French people, or to the introduction of the onion during French colonial times.

The pineapple that my mom didn't quite ask for is another example. It has a tough outer layer that, when sliced away, leaves behind little round recesses or "eyes." The phrase "pineapple eyes" was used by the Khmer Rouge to intimidate people from keeping secrets—that is, it suggested that the regime had eyes everywhere and could see in all directions.

Considering these names and their political references, it occurs to me that even the name of the marketplace I'm going to is questionable. The market is called Phsa Chhouk Meas, which means "Golden Lotus Market," because the land on which it was built originally had thousands of lotus ponds. Lotus plants filter pollution, so the ponds were established there to manage sewage from Phnom Penh as the city expanded. I imagine that because the ponds also provided good habitats for fish, city people could harvest food from them. But as the urban population increased, the land containing the lotus ponds was sold to developers for the construction of houses, and the ponds were filled in.

Three years ago, developers abandoned a small pond in front of my house. It was overflowing with debris, but after I worked on it for a few months, the water became clearer and a few lotus plants appeared. The neighbors seemed to love it. But then the developers came back, and the little pond ended up being filled in like all the other "Golden Lotus" ponds in the area.

At the marketplace, my daughter and I walk through a narrow lane between two rows of stalls. As we pass, someone shouts, "One kilogram 6,000 KHR, mother!" I cannot see the young woman's face because she is bent over her display of cauliflower. "Will you take 5,000 for it?" I reply. She hesitates so long that I am already past her stall before she straightens up. But our brief exchange lingers with me. I ponder the custom of a young person calling an older woman "mother," and the way the Khmer language marks the hierarchies in families.

We keep walking until we find fresh crayfish piled up in a wooden stall. "How much for a kilogram?" I ask. "60,000 KHR," the vendor replies. Seeing my reluctance, she says, "Big ones! Look at them, sister! Other stalls sell them cheaper but theirs are so small. Not like mine!" I agree that her crayfish are big. But I am not convinced that the price is good, so my daughter and I continue on to a stall where they're sold for 45,000 KHR per kilogram. The vendor here tells me that her freshwater crayfish come from Takeo province, in southwest Cambodia, which is renowned for its freshwater prawns and crayfish.

After our purchase, we go in search of the *snao* flower. We hear a vendor call out, *"Chanthou, chanthou, chanthou!"* My daughter asks me what the word means. I think it's a type of flower, but I check with the man at the stall to make sure. Yes, he tells me, *chanthou* is the name of the flower he is selling. He is holding four bunches of them wrapped in lotus and banana leaves. I remember a story about the flower that I don't tell my daughter. Another name for it is *phka kbat pdey*—"husband-cheating flower," referring to an adulterous woman. Girls who love *chanthou* flowers are often teased because of its name. Yet for some reason, *chanthou* is also the flower people most often buy as an offering when praying to the Buddha. I don't want to confuse my daughter by telling her about the contradictory meanings of the flower's name. And I also decide not to tell her about the irony concerning Phsa Chhouk Meas, or Golden Lotus. Once so plentiful in this area, the Golden Lotus is usually made of plastic these days.

If *phka chanthou* refers to unfaithful women, why do people pray to the Buddha with it? If the Golden Lotus is as valuable as its name suggests, why have developers filled in all the ponds? My daughter and I return home, and before I can enjoy my lunch of *samla mchu Vietnam,* I wonder if the Khmer dictionary has ever been updated with all the nuances of the word *yuon.*

Translated from Khmer by the author

MARIA HACH

An Archive of Haunting

The photo album feels rough, like sandpaper. I pick at the faded yellow cover with my index finger. It's dry and flaky. Tiny crumbs fall off and I gently brush them away. I think that it could be the oldest thing in the house. I am sitting on my parents' bedroom floor, hungry with curiosity. I bring the photo album up to my face and close my eyes. It smells musty and familiar.

I am eight and these are the things that I know:

My mum used to have long hair.

My dad used to wear flares.

This place is hot, because the children didn't wear many clothes.

But I am eight, and there are lots of things that I don't know:

What my parents looked like when they were kids.

Why we burn incense.

Where Khao-I-Dang is.

What happened before.

"How did you and dad get to the refugee camp, Mum? You know, the one we were born in."

"Well, there was a bus parked in front of the gates. We saw people getting on, so your dad and I ran over and got on at the last minute. We didn't have anything with us and we didn't know where it was going. We only knew that it had to be better than this place," she says, chuckling.

The smallest amount of hope can sustain you.

When I was eight, nothing existed before the refugee camp. As far as I was concerned, my parents were born there! I'd never seen photographs of their childhood in Cambodia: no New Year's water fights, no temple visits, no family barbeques, no primary-school portraits. The only photos I'd seen of our lives before this one were taken in the refugee camp. And it was a version of life that I didn't recognize. Red dirt, bamboo huts, crying toddlers. It was a place that I liked to visit sometimes, because even though I saw myself in the photographs, it wasn't real. "The camp" was an abstract concept in my imagination—an in-between place that served only one purpose: to get us to a better place. A place full of promise and new beginnings.

In 1987, my family moved from one haunted place to another. We thought we'd found peace on the lands of the Kulin Nation, in Southeastern Australia.

New migrants like us thought we could rebuild our lives without ever having to confront the ghosts of Australia's colonial past.

I read a story and I'm struck by a sentence—"the dead move on ... but the living we just stay here"—and I wonder if the dead ever mourn the living.

As I got older, I started to feel what happened before. I had vivid dreams. I noticed strange occurrences and sensed rumblings in the background. I heard whispers to ancestors and observed, in every Cambodian house I entered, an altar with offerings of persimmons and sweet biscuits. I watched my parents hoard rice and water. Every Sunday morning, the smell of burning incense filled my nostrils. Forgotten names and forgotten places. Things spoken and unspoken. Every time I turned a corner, there were traces of the past: the everyday reminders that my parents had lived a life—many lifetimes—they would rather not remember, but could not allow themselves to forget, before this one.

The sociologist Avery Gordon says that the past is not over and done with, but rather, it's living and breathing, and it remains a part of our worlds. Haunting, according to Gordon, is unresolved pain, social wounds, and "hidden" histories of abusive systems of power coming up for air. What we do with what remains is up to us. I didn't live through the Cambodian genocide and yet my life has been indelibly affected by it. What started as a whisper slowly morphed into something much bigger than me and my experiences. It began with just one thing: a feeling of being haunted. Sometimes by actual ghosts, sometimes by fragments of stories I'd heard, sometimes by silence so palpable it consumed me for days. This haunting feeling led me to write a Ph.D. thesis exploring how the traumas of the past continue to shape the lives of the Cambodian diaspora.

I don't need to read history books to learn about the brutality of the Khmer Rouge. I was exposed to their violence through my mother's grief and broken memories.

My parents carry lots of stories—stories carried, but rarely told. I grew up learning about what happened in Cambodia by reading history books and by watching the Hollywood movie *The Killing Fields*. These stories about Cambodians were told through the eyes of Western historians and filmmakers, in a language that took me further and further away from my mother tongue. For a long time, I recognized my history only through violence. In my thesis, I wanted to tell a different story. No skulls. No landmines. No body count. As Vietnamese American writer Ocean Vuong explains, when you are most recognizable in your research as a corpse, it does something to you. He says that for the cover of his first book, *Night Sky with Exit Wounds,* he wanted to have Vietnamese bodies that were living.

"How can narrative embody life in words and, at the same time, respect what we cannot know?" For me, this question by writer and historian Saidiya Hartman perfectly captures the opacity, complexity, and beauty of haunting as a topic of exploration. While the past demands our attention, it's also deeply fragile. How could I write about the legacies of violence, dislocation, and loss that have affected Cambodians everywhere, with caution? How could I capture something that felt unnameable? How could I write about genocide without perpetuating its brutality? I wanted to show what I knew to be true about intergenerational haunting: that while tied to histories of pain, haunting encompasses longings, loss, movement, ambivalence, love, and hope. Haunting can be generative and open up new ways of thinking and writing about trauma. But just as there are limits to what we can "know" about our parents' lives in Cambodia, there were limits to what I was prepared to write about. While language helps us to make sense of our worlds, I think some things can never be put into words.

Sometimes, I dream of my mum working in the fields, dressed in black. I want to call out to her, but my tongue feels stiff, or missing, or as if it has been cut out of my mouth. My body, tied up like knots.

I wanted to reimagine how the past, and its place in the present, could be told. I looked to queer and feminist writers whose work exploring the textures of emotional life resists the notion that history is linear; that lives are linear. Scholar Ann Cvetkovich writes that trauma challenges understandings of what constitutes an archive. She uses ethnography, cultural texts, and oral history interviews to "archive feelings" and to create new narratives about the experience of suffering. My "archive of haunting" was an experiment in capturing fragments and affects; states of being that move, and that move us. I collected everything and nothing, because haunting exists in bodies and in stories. Haunting exists in daydreams, silence, and ritual; in grainy photographs, songs, and in memories that are not our own. They can never be ours, and yet, somehow, they're always there.

I met other second-generation Cambodian women whose stories of intergenerational haunting seemed to be intertwined with mine. Generously and warmly, they shared their stories about growing up Asian in Australia. They talked to me about their process towards understanding; their careful navigation of their parents' trauma; the anxiety and joy of moving in and out of different worlds. Thick skins, heavy hearts. Their words expanded the possibilities of what it means to be haunted.

What happens if we allow ourselves to feel the tremors?

It took me five years to write my thesis. During this time, the ghosts, which were once on the periphery, came into full view. I read Grace Cho, a Korean American scholar who writes about haunting and the Korean diaspora. Her ghosts are animated through her writing practice, which uses nonlinear temporalities, repetition, fantasy, and fiction. And Saidiya Hartman, who uses the colonial, Western archive of trans-Atlantic slavery to interrogate and redefine the archive. She calls her work a "history of the present." I read Maria Tumarkin, a cultural historian who writes about how physical places can be "wounded" by tragedy. Whether buried or laid bare for all to see, these places shape mourning and remembering. Humans, we want to make meaning of traumatic events because it helps us make sense of the present, says Tumarkin. Then writers like Alice Pung, Ocean Vuong, and Monica Sok, whose tender memory work, infused with love and respect, showed me how I could write about painful things with care. Through their counter-narratives, these writers challenge what counts as "evidence" and speak back to histories of trauma produced by mechanisms of power.

When I lost my tongue, I did not try to reclaim it. Because I realized that my silence is fraught with fear and respect for family. Because how can you talk about violent histories without hurting the ones you love?

It had been almost eight years since my last trip to Cambodia when my research pulled me back there. I didn't have a plan. I only knew that I wanted my archive of haunting to float, like trauma, across time and space. I'd travelled to Cambodia for the very first time when I was twenty. I went without my parents, who always had a reason to say no. After that first trip, I went back several times because split, hybrid, in-between, and torn is not always, as writer Trinh T. Minh Ha reasons, a tenable place to be. Yet there was something more at play in that in-between place, something deeper than the pain of not quite fitting in. I felt the pull of a distant "home" and an aching in my bones.

In Cambodia, I came to expect the unexpected and I never knew what I would hear—a funny joke one minute and a heart-shattering anecdote the next. I met Cambodians my age, and we talked about politics and history. They asked me about my research, and they told me what they learnt at school. *Not much.* When I heard this, I thought about how at school, I hadn't been taught about the genocide that happened in Australia either, nor its continuing effects. In Cambodia, I visited breezy, old Cambodian houses and felt so calm within their walls. But the houses whispered stories of pain and loss. "These floors were destroyed by the Khmer Rouge; can you see the marks?" one guide asked, pointing to the stains on the wooden floor.

I wonder if objects hold memories.

In Cambodia, I visited unmarked graves and local genocide memorials. *The schoolkids are too scared to ride their bikes past them.* I stood in places where people had suffered cruel deaths and where people had survived the unimaginable. At each one of these sites, I felt memories of the past crawl up through the earth and seep into my body.

Most mornings I woke up to the sound of monks chanting, both beautiful and melodic. A familiar melancholic feeling hovered, but sometimes my heart felt so full, I thought it would burst. I visited temples and libraries. I watched, and wrote and stored things away. I prepared for Pchum Ben, a religious ritual in which Cambodians pay respect to their departed kin. It felt strange to be thousands of kilometers away from my family in Melbourne. I spent the day with my friend Sopheak, whom I met over ten years ago while I was working there. She is like a protective, older sister. We visited Angkor Wat and then a local pagoda to light incense and pray. We had lunch by the river and ate rice with fried fish and mustard greens. When I asked Sopheak what she thought about Pchum Ben, she told me that "the ghosts are always around," but during Pchum Ben, she "feels them more strongly."

Being in Cambodia was like being in a strange place where past, present, and sometimes future collided. I was constantly confronted with Cambodia's past, and my relationship with that past. I saw the person I could've been and the life I could've lived. Sometimes, I had moments of clarity, where I caught glimpses of the kind of person I wanted to be. Stronger, maybe. Braver, definitely. Strangers called me sister and then asked me where I was from. They told me I was lucky because "Australia is a good country and not poor like Cambodia." Sometimes the questions exhausted me, and I thought, *I'll just pretend to be a tourist today.* But the guilt of being one of the "lucky ones" meant that I never went through with it. *What makes you think you deserve a day off?* Even though I had the face, I'd never felt more visible in my life.

In Cambodia, different things comforted, energized, and broke me. At the same time I felt a gentle familiarity and stillness, I also felt a simmering anxiety. There were moments when I felt like I was in a crowded room with hundreds of other people, pulling at me, yearning for their stories to be told. Sometimes, I felt like I was experiencing Cambodia not as myself, but as someone else—my mum perhaps, whom I thought about every day while I was there. I imagined her as a teenager, walking to school on the same dusty roads that were beneath my feet. After my parents escaped in 1979, they didn't return to Cambodia for over thirty years. My mum told me that when they finally went back and their plane hit the runway in Phnom Penh, she unexpectedly wept. She said that when she heard the announcement over the speakers welcoming them to Cambodia, it felt like her soul was returning home.

She is more beautiful than the dusty pink skies after the rain, more beautiful than champa *flowers in full bloom, more beautiful than bright-green rice paddies after monsoon season.*

Gordon writes that haunting alerts us to what's in our blind spot or what's been sidelined by dominant narratives. She says that while haunting can be disorienting and unsettling, devastating even, it can compel us to do something different from before. It can compel us to act, create, resist, envision, and transform. Haunting connects us to real people and real struggles that can't be ignored, no matter how hard we try to push things aside. To archive haunting is not simply about remembering the past, or even about restoring what was lost. We trace the past because we want to understand the present.

When I was younger, I was told that the reason we didn't have photos of the time before the refugee camp was because the Khmer Rouge forced my relatives to destroy them; I felt like I had lost one of the only tangible things that connected me to my history. But then I learnt the story of my name. My name was given to me by my uncle, who was already in Australia when I was born. My mum, dreaming of a better and easier life for her daughter, wanted me to have a name so common that I would go unnoticed in Australia. Now, when I look at the photos of my family in the refugee camp, it doesn't so much feel like an abstract place but a piece of the past that I carry with me everywhere I go. I've realized that my history lives and breathes in me.

MA LAUPI

Two Love Songs

Called the "Golden Parrot," Ma Laupi was Cambodia's most famous lyricist, composing for Sinn Sisamouth and other singers. He is renowned for his finely crafted verses, strong evocation of nature, and his mastery of the Khmer style of expressing emotions in a light, allusive, but deep way. "A Pair of Turtledoves," first recorded in 1962 and sung by Meas Hokseng, is regarded as one of the most beautiful Cambodian songs of its time. "The Fishing Eagle of Scarf Lake" was sung by Sinn Sisamouth; its melody was composed by Pov Sipho, who also set Suy Hieng's poem "The Orphans" to music. In Khmer poetry, traoey *(the shore) represents the object of desire, love, salvation, or a metaphysical destination; "reaching the shore" can also refer to marriage. The Khmer verb* yum *means to weep or mourn but it is also used for creatures such as cicadas, monkeys, and birds, meaning to make a strident sound, to cry out in pain, or to call seeking an answer.* **CM/SM**

A PAIR OF TURTLEDOVES

Two turtledoves, we'd call to each other
as twilight turned to darkness,
returning to our shared bower,
unafraid of ever being parted.

We didn't foresee cruel karma at daybreak,
the pitiless hunter that stalked and shot you down,
severing the pledge that bound us,
our promise to stay joined forever.

O Buddha! See this predator who deceived
with a thousand strategies, killing my love,
and leaving me alone in a narrow world of sorrow.
It would have been better to shoot us both.

I remember the rice fields in the sweet breeze
of the harvest season, when I would call
then listen for your answering song.
Unceasing, I cry out in my widowed solitude.

THE FISHING EAGLE OF BOENG KANSAENG (SCARF LAKE)

In a deep valley, in a forest of deeper silence,
lies the still waters of Boeng Kansaeng.
Along its shores of pleasure in the morning,
lake weeds and water lilies happily play, entwined.

At noon, the cry of cicadas resounds in my heart.
Water lilies wilt in the sun, stems bend in the heat.
A fishing eagle cries, complaining of some need,
desire's hunger, the ache of loss.

I see my reflection in the diamond-clear water,
and blink against the light, trying to forget my Chenda.
The breeze off the lake breathes in my ear,
whispering of the rock jetty now underwater.

All that remains: a scarf lost on the wind, teasing the lake.
The eagle cries, calling its soul to answer.
I beat my chest in desolation,
unable to reach the shore of vanished love.

Translated from Khmer by Christophe Macquet and Sharon May

SINN SISAMOUTH

Champa of Battambang

Sinn Sisamouth, considered the king of Khmer music, belonged to the pop music scene that thrived in Phnom Penh from the 1950s to the 1970s. Released in 1962, "Champa of Battambang" was a ballad sung in the bolero-twist style and one of his biggest hits. Still a beloved song, it has come to represent feelings of love and longing for the whole of Cambodia. Sinn Sisamouth was killed by the Khmer Rouge. The champa *is in the magnolia family, an evergreen whose fragrant white flowers are a recurring symbol of women in Khmer poetry.* TW

Oh Battambang, my heart of hearts,
I said farewell, but still you bind me.
So far from you, I live in regret,
caught in grief that won't let me go.

Oh Battambang, my fated companion,
I've yearned for you—an endless ache.
As we are joined in life's long storm,
tell me about the time we first met.

It's been many years, do you remember?
You are as close as my skin, as my breath.
I've hitched my dreams to your sweet face,
hoping that you are my destined one.

Oh Battambang, I've longed for you always.
When will I see your face again?
My heart's on fire, I am all undone,
longing for you, Champa of Battambang.

Translated from Khmer by Trent Walker

KONG BUNCHHOEUN

The Shade of the Tenth Coconut Tree

"The Shade of the Tenth Coconut Tree" is one of several songs that Kong Bunchhoeun wrote for the singer Sinn Sisamouth. According to Kong Bunchhoeun's memoirs, this particular lyric was written during a low point in his life: his mother had died, he had abandoned writing, and he was unemployed. He often sat on a stone bench watching the Sangkae River flow through his native Battambang. He secretly fell in love with a neighbor's daughter, who promised to meet him in the shade of a coconut tree beside the river. She never showed. He recorded the incident in his journal and later turned it into this song. TW

I gaze at the rising flow
of the Sangkae River.
Po Pagoda's gong merges with the howling wind,
moaning a message to the floodwaters
as the sun shrinks and steals away behind your house.

The tenth coconut tree
spreads its shade by the riverside.
Silent and still, I
wait for you into deep darkness.
You've forgotten what you promised me—
that you'd meet me tonight at dusk.

Now I'm lost like a raft adrift,
flotsam in a swirling vortex.
The flower festival at Po Pagoda isn't even over—
how could you forsake me?

Wedding songs from Tuol Ta Ek
become mournful dirges
as a cobra closes her eyes to wed a man.
I stand by the river's edge,
trying to make my tears into a song—
farewell to you: a brute on the outside; a beast within.

Translated from Khmer by Trent Walker

SIM CHANYA

Farewell, Wild Guava Flower

Written by Sim Chanya during the civil war, "Farewell, Wild Guava Flower" was first broadcast on national radio in 1971. Phka trabaek prei *(wild guava flower) is the Khmer name for crepe myrtle. Despite the adjective* prei *(which means "wild"), it is known as the flower of Phnom Penh. A poetic address to the city in wartime, "Farewell, Wild Guava Flower" was originally sung by Dy Sakhorn, who also composed the music, and later interpreted by female singers Sim Touch, Hem Sivon, and Touch Sunnix.* CM/SM

Wild guava flower,
violet like carelessness,
purple as regret,
an evening regret
when a light rain falls
and you feel an impossible love
shudder inside you.

Paper flower,
let us now shed
your melancholy crepe,
it must give way to anger
as our lovely seaside
no longer brings joy
and blood stains our temples.

(refrain)
Farewell, purple flower,
flower of our city,
flower of our frail, despondent sorrow,
of weak, tender blossoms.
Farewell, sadness. Farewell, softness.
This heart can no longer be stilled.
It is time for action—the enemy is here.

Wild flower of the city,
flower of my soul,
the thunder of guns
shakes you on your stem
as hearts tremble on the line.
A young woman picks you
and pins you in her hair,
taking you into the battlefield.

Translated from Khmer by Christophe Macquet and Sharon May

BASSAC FOLK OPERA

When Ream Faked His Death to Win Back Seda

Editors' Note
Bassac folk opera (lakhaon bassac) *originated in Kampuchea Krom in what is now southern Vietnam. From there it followed the meandering path of the Bassac River into Phnom Penh in the 1920s and 1930s, where it was first performed on the decks of barges. It was so popular that actors would jump ship and form troupes in the capital and throughout the country. This form of folk theater is influenced by Chinese and Vietnamese opera (male costumes and makeup, percussion, battle scenes), while remaining deeply rooted in Khmer culture (dance and lyrical art, recitation and arias, elements of farce, and a repertoire of Buddhist, mythical, and historical stories). The Kampong Cham Theater Company, directed by Kang Chanthirith, was created on February 17, 1979, barely a month after the end of the Khmer Rouge regime. It became the best-known* bassac *troupe in the 1980s and 1990s. When the group performed in Phnom Penh, Pich Tum Kravel—the great actor and poet who helped revive* lakhaon bassac *in Cambodia—gave translator Christophe Macquet a copy of the director's handwritten script in Khmer. An excerpt from this rare document has been translated here into English. This folk rendering presents a unique take on the traditional* Reamker, *the Khmer* Ramayana, *telling the story from the perspective of Seda (Sita), not Ream (Rama). The Reamker's plot is well known to the Cambodian audience, and variations are common. In this retelling, after surviving her imprisonment by the evil giant Krong Reap (Ravana), Seda is rescued by Ream, who ascends the throne. However, Ream soon falsely accuses Seda of infidelity with the giant during her captivity. Even though Seda is now pregnant with Ream's child, he condemns her to death and orders his brother Leak (Lakshmana) to execute her in the deep forest. The following excerpt from the play begins there. The entire script was published in Khmer and French in the French daily* Cambodge Soir *in 1999.*

Characters (in order of appearance): Neang Seda (Seda), Preah Leak (Ream's brother, Leak), Tomato (comic character), Venerable Valmiki (hermit), Reamleak (birth son of Ream), Chupleak (magical son of Ream), Preah Ream (Ream), Hanuman, generals, mandarins, ladies-in-waiting, the diviner. A curtain separates the front and back areas of the stage.

SCENE III

On the front stage, Leak is taking Seda away to put her to death, as ordered by Ream.

SEDA   I swear to you that I did not betray my husband.

LEAK   I believe you, but what can I do? No one can oppose the king's justice.

[sings in Sampong style]

> Cruel karma that pursues us
> on his murderous wings.
> What a terrible misfortune
> is yours, dear sister!
> I feel for your immense suffering,
> while the heart of Preah Ream,
> your husband, my brother,
> remains hard as a rock.

LEAK   I can't.

SEDA   You have no choice; it is an order from the king.

LEAK   It is impossible.

SEDA   Kill me.

LEAK   No, I won't.

SEDA   Kill me, I tell you.

LEAK   No.

SEDA   Weak Preah Leak! Is it really you who waged war on our enemies without fear of sword or spear? Is it with cowards like you that we defend our kingdom?

Stung to the core, Leak brandishes the royal sword and brings it down on Seda, but the blade can't penetrate the queen's body. After a second failure, he collapses and loses consciousness.

SEDA   Preah Leak, what's happening to you? It was to give you courage that I said all this, so that you would feel less guilty.

[sings in White Turtledove style]

> It would have been better
> had I died. How many more years
> will I have to live bearing
> this weight on my heart?
> O my king, my lord, you have remained
> deaf to my prayers.
> You have without wavering
> condemned me to death.

SEDA   *[overtaken by pains in her belly, she calls out for help]* Is there anyone here? Help me. Please help me! I am in so much pain. *[loses consciousness]*

LEAK *[regaining consciousness]* Forgive me, Neang Seda, but I must leave you. Stay here and take care of yourself. *[exits]*

Curtain opens, revealing the back area of the stage. Singing can be heard in the distance. Tomato, the hermit's servant, enters.

TOMATO *[sings in comic style]*

> *I am the handyman of the venerable hermit.*
> *Exhausted, I leave the plains to enter the jungle,*
> *I leave the jungle to enter the plains.*
> *I do nothing but drudgery, all the holy day.*

Well, now let's clean up the hermitage. *[While sweeping, he stumbles over the body of Seda. He jumps up in fright and runs for cover. Then he carefully retraces his steps to check on her.]* It's a dead body. Oh, the belly is all swollen. It must have been here for a long time. Hurry up! I have to go tell the venerable hermit. Venerable! Venerable! A corpse, Venerable!

HERMIT *[entering]* A corpse, Tomato?

TOMATO Over there, Venerable, in the place where you usually pray. Look, the belly is all swollen!

HERMIT Where? I don't see any dead bodies here.

TOMATO Over there, go and see.

HERMIT Come and show me.

TOMATO No, thank you. I'll leave that honor to you, Venerable. *[speaks aside to the audience while hermit goes alone to examine the body]* You'll see, in a second the holy man will scurry away with his robes between his teeth.

HERMIT It's not a corpse, Tomato, it's someone who fainted.

TOMATO Nay! Nay! It is a corpse, I tell you! Look, Venerable, how it is all swollen! Well...let's check it out. Oh! But it is true! The corpse is still breathing...

HERMIT She's a woman, Tomato, and a pregnant one at that. I'll sprinkle her with magic water to bring her to her senses.

SEDA Where am I? Preah Leak? Is there anyone here? Help me! Help! *[sees the hermit and rises to meet him]* Holy man, I offer you my most humble respects. *[turns to Tomato]* My respects to you too.

TOMATO Thank you, may the Buddha protect you! But what brings you here? How come you passed out?

SEDA It's a long story.

HERMIT Don't worry. My magic will raise a palace here for you to stay in.

Curtain falls.

SCENE IV

On the front stage, Seda, a jug on her hip, goes to draw water.

SEDA   I am living with the venerable hermit and my heart is full of happiness! Today I draw water and pick flowers for him.

[sings in Lom Smaoe style]

> *Here I am condemned*
> *to live in the forest,*
> *with only wild animals*
> *for companions.*
> *What tenderness I feel*
> *for my poor child, alone,*
> *without any friends,*
> *deep in the jungle.*

Look at those monkeys! How adorable they are! They leap happily from one branch to another, with their little ones hanging on! It must not be easy to carry them! But these creatures do not hesitate! Oh, my son—I left him with the servant of the venerable! Let's go to see how things are going.

Curtain opens.

TOMATO   *[playing with the little prince]* Tweet! Tweet-tweet! Come on, catch! Catch the sparrow! Tweet-tweet! Tweet! Ah! The more I look at you, the more I think you look like me! Maybe you are a little like me after all. *[child cries]* What! What did I say? I was only joking. Don't get angry, my little darling! Don't get angry! *[child cries more]* Oh, but he's shouting louder and louder, the rascal! Venerable! Venerable! Come and help me, Venerable! I cannot console him.

HERMIT   *[entering]* What's the trouble now? It's not so complicated to look after a baby. Is it too much to ask, Tomato?

TOMATO   Oh, and now I'm being reproached too! No, it's not possible anymore, Venerable! I don't know where to turn! I've hardly finished boiling water for tea when I have to take care of the toddler.

HERMIT   Who's blaming you, Tomato? Let me see. Oh, he's just thirsty, this little one. Wait, baby, I'll give you a drink...

TOMATO   He did it, Venerable! He did it! He's done it!

HERMIT   He did what, Tomato?

TOMATO   That's it! That's it! It's happened!

HERMIT   What's happened? What's happened?

TOMATO   Of course! What he ate yesterday... That's why he was crying so much...

HERMIT   Go change his diapers, I beg you, and put him in his hammock. I am going to my place of prayer. *[exits]*

TOMATO   *[changing the baby]* Yuck! This is not pretty! It looks like scrambled eggs with fermented turnips. *[lays the child down in the hammock and rocks him]* Sleep, sleep, dear child, sleep now. *[both fall asleep]*

SEDA   *[entering]* Poor Tomato, he doesn't have a second to himself. No sooner has he finished serving the venerable than he must look after my child. He's asleep now. Let's not wake him up. *[to the baby]* Well, my little one, we will wash you now. *[leaves, taking her child with her]*

TOMATO   *[mechanically reaches out to cradle the child. Feeling that the hammock is empty, he wakes]* Thunder! He's disappeared! He hasn't been snatched by a wild animal by any chance? Ah, let me think about it. The venerable hermit must have taken him with him. Well, let's go and see. *[goes out, then comes back.]* Damn! It's not the venerable! Who could it be then? Poor me! How can I give the child back to his mother? Venerable! Venerable! Help me! Help, Venerable!

HERMIT   *[entering]* Where have you been wandering that the little prince could disappear like that?

TOMATO   Nowhere, Venerable! I rocked him, then we fell asleep.

HERMIT   Very well, but what shall we do now, eh, Tomato? How are we going to return the child to its mother?

TOMATO   Help me, Venerable! I beg you!

HERMIT   Don't worry, I'll get you out of this mess. Go get me a slate. I'll draw a picture and with my magic will make a replica of the child. *[a duplicate child appears]*

TOMATO   *[rushing to pick up the child]* Oh, the resemblance is striking, Venerable. Right down to his little chili! It's amazing! I'll put him in the hammock right away.

SEDA   *[entering, her child in her arms]* Venerable, I offer you my most respectful greetings.

TOMATO   But? You have the child!

SEDA   I took him while you were sleeping. I saw how tired you were, working every day, so I didn't dare wake you up.

TOMATO   Well, you can say that you scared the hell out of me! I thought all my nineteen souls had fled my body to go eat *num banhchok* [rice noodles]! In the meantime, I asked the holy man to make a new child appear. You have only to make it disappear, Venerable.

HERMIT   That shouldn't take long. A simple magic spell and he will be returned to nothingness.

SEDA   No, Venerable! Since this child has been born, let us keep him. He will be an excellent companion for my son. I will take care of him as if I were his real mother.

TOMATO   Ah... One child was already difficult... But two... I will die at the task, help me...

HERMIT   Don't worry, Tomato. I'll recite a magic spell to make them grow up quickly. Put them in the hammock now.

TOMATO   Good, Venerable. *[to Seda]* Let me take your child, madam.

Tomato places the two babies in the hammock. The hermit recites a magic spell and the two children begin to grow. Drums play and they dance. The children bow down before the hermit.

REAMLEAK CHUPLEAK Our most respectful greetings, Venerable.

HERMIT Very well, my little ones. Here is your august mother.

REAMLEAK CHUPLEAK Our most respectful greetings, Mother.

SEDA Very well, my children.

TOMATO That's right, bow down to your mother and to the venerable…While I, who does all the dirty work every day, am not entitled to such respect…

HERMIT My little ones, this is Uncle Tomato.

REAMLEAK CHUPLEAK *[joining hands]* Our respectful greetings, Uncle Tomato.

TOMATO Very well, very well, young highnesses.

SEDA As my two children are grown up now, Venerable, we should give them names.

HERMIT Of course. I will name them in turn.

TOMATO I have an idea, Venerable. The one who was born from a womb, let's call him Womby. And the other one you created, let's call him Sorcery…

REAMLEAK I disagree, Venerable.

CHUPLEAK I disagree too, Venerable.

HERMIT Don't worry, my little ones, I'll find suitable names for you. Neang Seda, your birth son will be called Reamleak [Leak, son of Ream]. And the other one I created will be called Chupleak [Leak created by magic].

CHUPLEAK So I am nothing more than a copy, Venerable?

SEDA *[runs to the child and embraces him by the shoulders]* Don't worry, my little one! You need not have come from my womb for me to love you like a son!

HERMIT Tomato! Go to my place of prayer to get my magic lasso and my fabulous bows. I want to give them to the children.

TOMATO Right away, Venerable. *[goes to get the lasso and the bows; returns and gives them to the hermit]* Here they are, Venerable.

HERMIT Here, my children. This lasso and these two bows have extraordinary power. Beware! If you shoot towards the earth, the arrow will pass through the seven floors of the underworld to the kingdom of the *naga*s. If you shoot straight ahead, it will burn down all the forests of the kingdom. If you shoot in the air, the vault of the heavens will tremble, the heavenly worlds will be shaken. These weapons are not toys, my little ones, you must use them only for good.

REAMLEAK Your word is holy, Venerable, we will always respect it.

SEDA Practice, my sons, and always love one another.

REAMLEAK CHUPLEAK Yes, Mother.

SEDA Venerable, allow me to withdraw.

HERMIT Please go ahead.

REAMLEAK CHUPLEAK Venerable, allow us to withdraw.

HERMIT Go ahead.

Curtain falls.

SCENE V

On the front stage, the brothers Reamleak and Chupleak talk to each other.

REAMLEAK Our noble mother has allowed us to walk in the forest and pick fruit to offer to the venerable.

CHUPLEAK Yes, Big Brother. Oh, look at how these forests are full of fruit. Look at all the colors. What a beautiful sight, Big Brother!

[*sings in Lom Thu style*]

> *I am thrilled, amazed,*
> *to take our leave of the venerable*
> *and of our mother, too,*
> *to explore the jungle.*
>
> *Look, Big Brother, how delightful*
> *are these birds that fill the forest*
> *with their cries and beating wings.*
> *How immense their joy!*

CHUPLEAK Do you see that bird with black-and-white plumage? Look, it has a huge yellow beak. What's its name, Big Brother?

REAMLEAK It's a hornbill, Little Brother.

CHUPLEAK And that black bird with the metallic sheen, with the double tail and a crest on top of its head. What's its name, Big Brother?

REAMLEAK That's a greater racket-tailed drongo, Little Brother.

CHUPLEAK And that proud bird doing the cartwheel? How beautiful! How shimmering his colors are! How he exudes majesty!

REAMLEAK That's a peacock, Little Brother.

CHUPLEAK Look, it flies away, Big Brother. Oh, do you see that tree over there? It's so huge it hides half the sky.

REAMLEAK From what Uncle Tomato told me, they call it the *reangkal*.

CHUPLEAK   It's immense. It shades all the other trees. We should uproot it, Big Brother.

REAMLEAK   Uproot it? Do you see how large it is?

CHUPLEAK   It will be easy with the magic bows and arrows the venerable gave us.

REAMLEAK   Do you really think we can? He has forbidden us to use them indiscriminately.

CHUPLEAK   Just a single arrow, Big Brother.

REAMLEAK   Well, okay, just this once.

They shoot at the reangkal.

CHUPLEAK   Did you see that, Big Brother! We blew it out of the sky!

REAMLEAK   Yes, it's completely destroyed! But it's getting late, Little Brother. The day is nearly gone. It's time to pick some fruit for the venerable and our august mother.

CHUPLEAK   You're right, Big Brother, let's go.

Curtains opens. In the royal city, Ream, Leak, Hanuman, generals, mandarins, the diviner, and ladies-in-waiting gather in the audience hall.

REAM   Go, Diviner, make your art speak and tell us what is the reason for the terrible earthquake that has destroyed our forests and made my whole kingdom tremble on its foundation.

DIVINER   At your command, my King, I am your humble servant. *[bows]* Master of lives, whose divine feet are above our heads! May your majesty allow me the honor of explaining: it is two children, gifted with exceptional strength, who are the cause of this earthquake. With fabulous bows, they have shot at the *reangkal* tree, and the fire has reduced all our forests to ash.

REAM   I want these children brought to me. How can we do that, Diviner?

DIVINER   You must, my Lord, send your royal steed to where the two children are. Around its neck hang a sign with the following words: WHOEVER DARES TO MAKE THIS HORSE HIS MOUNT SHALL BE CONDEMNED TO DEATH.

REAM   Hanuman! Bring my horse to them. Then hide and watch. As soon as you see the children, capture them!

HANUMAN   As you wish, your Majesty. Allow me to withdraw.

REAM   Go. Preah Leak, dispatch a courier to the kingdom of Kaikes. We must warn our brothers Preah Phirut and Preah Sotrut. Let them set their armies in motion now. We are going to make war again!

LEAK   As you wish, Majesty.

Curtain falls.

Translated from Khmer by Christophe Macquet and Sharon May

AYAI FOLK THEATER

A Flirtatious Battle of Words and Wits

Editors' Note
Ayai chhlaoey chhlang is a traditional Cambodian form of improvised musical folk theatre, typically performed by a man and a woman. The two singers stand near the front of the stage, while the musicians play in the back. Ayai combines the art of poetic storytelling with jokes, legends, politics, and history—all done in very clever, rhyming wordplay, often improvised and layered in meanings. As the content is often bawdy and politically charged, the two performers may also play the role of jesters speaking truth to society under a veil of hilarious and sharp-tongued flirtation. Similar to contemporary rap battles, the two singers alternate in a duet—or duel—of words and wit. The name of the male character, smien *(translated here as "clerk") is the title of a low-ranked civil servant who, because he knows how to write, puts on great airs. His character is boastful, flirtatious, and pompous. His role is to make the audience laugh and sometimes to deliver a more profound message. The comic Khmer actors in* ayai *and* bassac *plays and movies are often called* smien *(clerk) or* neay *(chief), followed by their nickname. Except for interludes of spoken dialog, the improvised, poetic verses are sung.*

Most ayai *performances, especially those of the more risqué variety, like this one, are never written down. This excerpt, transcribed by Christophe Macquet, comes from the National Festival of Ayai, Chapei, and Sadiev, performed in Phnom Penh on the esplanade of Veal Men, next to the Royal Palace, in 2003. To our knowledge, this is the first time the ephemeral art form has been translated and published in a Western language.*

PREAMBLE

Ayai music plays.

MAN [alone onstage, hands together in supplication]
Praise be our King Father,
our Queen Mother,
and their royal family.
Praise be the three eminent Samdechs:
Samdech Chea Sim,
our President of the Senate;
Samdech Krom Preah
Norodom Ranariddh
our President of the National Assembly
and Samdech Hun Sen,
our Prime Minister.
Praise be all the Excellencies present here;
praised be your zeal to revive the Khmer Arts
after the genocide;
praise be your efforts to help
the poor singers of *ayai*.

THE BATTLE BEGINS

The man invites his female partner to join him onstage.

MAN Alright, that's enough praise for now.
Who will be my lovely partner?
A madam or a miss?
Or a young virgin? I have my doubts...
If she's not, that's just fine.
It's the cold season, and you have to keep warm somehow.
Any woman is perfect for me!

So a woman, yes, but which kind?
A lady with a child?
I'll take her. She's still good for planting.
A lady with two children?
I'll take her too. She's just as nice as a young virgin.
But a widow?
I don't know... is that a good idea?

WOMAN I'm coming, I'm coming, don't be so impatient.
Here I am! I'm ready. Ready for anything.
Exactly what little game would you like to play?
Go ahead, my dear, tell us what you have in mind...

Come on, or can't you decide?
I asked you a question, and I'm waiting for your answer.

Ayai Folk Theater . *Flirtatious Battle*

| | Come on, handsome, tell us what game you want to play.
An elephant shows off its tusks; a tree, its fruits.
In this Khmer country, when we want to sing, we do it.
So what do you say, my friend, are you ready?
What kind of game do you want to play?
I am open to all proposals. |

MAN   Open, my dear?
          How open?
          Open wide? Half open?
          Open to what exactly?
          Open where?

WOMAN   Yi! Watch your words, little clerk!
          Don't talk nonsense!

MAN   Open, you say?
          As in an open-door invitation?

WOMAN   Yi! Watch your language!
          I'm open, but only to discussion.

MAN   I just hope you're wide open
          because I don't want to hit my head on the way in.

WOMAN   Yi! Careful with your words, little clerk.
          Stop the nonsense!

MAN   I'm afraid I'll knock myself out.
          My head might not take it!

Ayai music plays. They dance the Saiyeut together. The music stops.

MAN   [spoken]
          Well, tell me, you look very sporty to me …

WOMAN   [spoken]
          Well, yes, I train every day at the Olympic stadium …

The woman attempts to hit the man with a karate chop. The man parries the blow. The woman rushes at him and knees him between the legs. The music plays. The pair resumes singing.

MAN   *Yyyyyeow!* Now that's *sportyyyyy, sportyyyyyy!*
          Your shoulders have slimmed down,
          but your belly's well rounded …
          What's your sport? Do you practice it in town?
          Frenzied footwork under the mosquito net?
          Bam! You hit the headboard, the bedside lamp!
          Wham! You hit the wardrobe and it falls!
          You practice so much your belly bulges.

WOMAN	So much empty talk, little clerk, like water off a duck's back, *oeuy!*
MAN	Whoa, so sporty! So coy, so frisky! You practice so much you're all out of breath.
WOMAN	Talk talk talk, little clerk, like playing music for a cow's ears, *oeuy!*
MAN	So athletic! So sporty! You look like a fat tadpole swimming in an old well.
WOMAN	Hey, you, have you looked at yourself lately? Have you seen your own mug?
MAN	And you, have you seen that mess you call hair? Like a ghoul perched on a branch of a tamarind tree.
WOMAN	And you, when I see that mop on your head, I think, now there's one ugly thug I wouldn't like to meet alone at night on the Mekong.
MAN	Well, yeah, I'm a thug, I'm a thief, of the robber species. But I only steal from family, it saves me trouble. I only scam ladies who dare to sing with me. I take them from the top, I take them from the bottom. I grab their *prahok*, I snatch their *pha'ak*. I steal their snacks, I swipe their snooks. And I lick and I lick—and it's so good!
WOMAN	Yi! Little clerk! You're way out of line!
MAN	I'm so crooked I cross the line. I rifle their soy curd, I ruffle their joy curves, I pinch their sweet cakes, I poach their tofu.

prahok: fish paste
pha'ak: chopped fish

The music stops.

WOMAN	[spoken] Well, now, you talk like a scoundrel, but I've dealt with worse! I wonder how well you can handle a riddle?
MAN	[spoken] Pfff, that doesn't scare me. Go ahead, my dear. Ask whatever you want.

Ayai music resumes. The pair continues singing.

WOMAN	All right, fun's over. Now let's get down to business

Ayai Folk Theater . *Flirtatious Battle*

and compete with our wits.
First, I'll ask you to answer a riddle:
Standing erect, he's empty;
Bending down, he's full. So, my dear, what is it?
Do you have even the slightest idea?

MAN Done! I've already guessed it.
Here you go:
"Standing erect, he's empty…"
It's a stalk of rice.
It only stands upright
when the husk is hollow.
Like a man in society:
The emptier he is, the more vain he is,
trying to make himself seem taller.

And the emptier he is, the less he respects his elders.
The less he respects his parents, his ancestors,
the less he respects his masters,
and the less, in the end, he is respected.

The sages say: To stand upright is to show one's emptiness.

Now if this hollow man is a ruler,
he looks down on others,
he despises everyone
and in turn will be despised.

He's an empty shell.
He does whatever he wants,
but karma will catch up with him.

"Bending down, he's full"
means, on the contrary,
that the humble carry a weight within,
like a mature stalk of rice
that bends under its fullness.
They are modest and kind,
following the five precepts
and the Buddhist path.

The sages say: Fruits are born from respect.

He who carries ripened grain bows
before the people, before his brothers.
His heart, words, and gestures are full of regard.
To possess such knowledge
is to own the wealth of the world.

Goods, gold, and silver are one thing.
Rank and titles are another.
But to be loved by the people,
there is no greater wealth.

So, my dear, what do you think?
Has my wit stimulated you?
What do you make of my answer?
How do you like my interpretation?

Now it's my turn to ask you a riddle...

In turn, the woman will brilliantly solve the riddle proposed by the man, and the battle continues...

Translated from Khmer by Christophe Macquet and Sharon May

SONGSAENG RUNGRUEANGCHAI

The Big Tusker

"The Big Tusker" is one of many traditional songs in the genre of kantreum, vocal music developed by the Northern Khmer of Surin, Buriram, and Sisaket provinces in Thailand. The songs are commonly performed at weddings and other ceremonies as well as at modern dance performances. The version here is from a 2010 recording by Songsaeng Rungrueangchai, one of the most popular contemporary kantreum performers.

The first five stanzas comprise a series of old lyrics passed down to Songsaeng by his father. The sixth and final verse is a new addition in which he invokes two of the most respected living masters of kantreum: Yotrak Khoknasam and Samanchai Tongam (Siangrathom). Words appearing in italics are nonsense syllables that are inserted in many kantreum to help set the tone and style, divide phrases and sections, and maintain an upbeat, danceable rhythm. "The Overflowing River" is a reference to a stream in Surin whose name derives from Sanskrit paripurna, "completely full." The phrase "calls the souls" is a reference to a key Khmer wedding ritual in which errant spirits or souls of the bride and groom are invited back into their bodies. Chey hang ("victory" or "success") is a common refrain at Khmer weddings. DH/TW

Nhe, *a-eung-euy eu-eu-euy!*
Alas, *oy euy, chhak-o*, the big tusker,
    chhak-o, alas, *oy euy*, the big tusker!
Chhak-o! He stands at the base of the hill,
    resting his trunk in the fork of a tree.
Chhak-o! His feet pound the earth,
    chhak-o, wriggling and writhing.
His feet pound the earth,
    chhak-o, wriggling and writhing.
Resting his trunk in the fork of a tree,
    tears stream down his cheeks, *yeu eu-eu-eu-euy!*

Nhe, a-eung-euy eu-eu-euy!
The Overflowing River, *chhak-o,*
    the Overflowing River, *chhak-o,*
    the Overflowing River.
The Overflowing River, *chhak-o,*
    I see it flowing clear
    down to the deep.
Chhak-o, I dip my hands in
    and shower my head.
Chhak-o, I dip my hands in
    and shower my head.
Chhak-o, the water's clear, down to the deep,
    where my girl plays, *yeu eu-eu-eu-euy!*

Nhe, a-eung-euy eu-eu-euy!
My soul of gold!
    Chhak-o, my soul of gold!
    Chhak-o, my soul of gold!
My soul of gold!
Chhak-o, walk by the stream.
    Don't chase the sun, *chhak-o,*
    but follow my lead.
Take my hand, love,
    and follow my lead.
    Take my hand, love.
Chhak-o, if you chase the sun,
    it'll leave you behind, *yeu eu-eu-eu-euy!*

Nhe, a-eung-euy eu-eu-euy!
A dove cries "kok,"
    chhak-o, a dove cries "kok,"
    chhak-o, a dove cries "kok,"
A dove cries "kok," *chhak-o,*
    cooing near the village.
My decoy sent out its call.
Chhak-o, I set an old trap,
    but the strap might break.
Chhak-o, I set an old trap,
    but the strap might break.
Chhak-o, I'll set a new one,
    and the bird will lie there,
    flightless, all mine, *eu-eu-eu-euy!*

Nhe, a-eung-euy eu-eu-euy!
A pangolin's scales, *oy euy,*
    chhak-o, are like those of a fish.
Chhak-o, a pangolin's scales,
    are like those of a fish.
Chhak-o, I downed a cup of whiskey;
    now I crave a rabbit's flesh.
If I get a widow for a wife,
    then I'll have wasted my youth.
But if I get a maiden,
    we'd be better matched.
Chhak-o, if I get a maiden,
    we'd be better matched.
Chhak-o, I'll have wasted my youth
    if I plough a field
    that's already furrowed.

Nhe, a-eung-euy eu-eu-euy!
Yotrak sings *kantreum,*
    chhak-o, going "O la nai!"
Chhak-o, Yotrak sings *kantreum,*
    chhak, "O la nai!"
Chhak-o, I listen to the wall of sound
    as Samanchai calls the souls.
Chhak-o, my soul of gold!
    My flawless love.
Chhak-o, my soul of gold!
    My flawless love.
Chhak-o, Samanchai calls the souls:
    "Chey hang," success!
    The bride and groom embrace, *eu-eu-eu-euy!*

Translated from Northern Khmer by Direk Hongthong and Trent Walker

KONG NAY

Lullaby: An Elephant Rocks Its Trunk

Kong Nay is Cambodia's most famous living bard, known for his quick-witted poetry, husky voice, and spirited strumming on the chapei dang veng *(long-necked lute). This transformation of a traditional lullaby exemplifies his gift for reworking old poems with his trademark humor and daring wordplay. The Khmer word* yol, *repeated on nearly every line, literally means "to rock," as in rocking a baby to sleep, but takes on a variety of meanings in this song, including "to swing" and "to depend on."* **TW**

Mmm hmm, an elephant rocks its tail.
My baby, *mmm hmm*, an elephant rocks its tail.
Mmm hmm, love, a bullhorn rocks its battery,
and oh, oh my baby, flies rock the fish-paste barrel.

Mmm hmm, baby, an elephant rocks its ribs.
Little one, *mmm hmm*, curry sauce rocks fresh noodles.
Mmm hmm, my sweet, roast fish rocks a pickled salad,
and oh, oh my baby, fish paste rocks a side of greens.

Mmm hmm, an elephant rocks its unmatched legs.
My darling, *mmm hmm*, cold rice rocks fish sauce.
Mmm hmm, baby, lemongrass rocks minced fish paste,
and oh, oh my baby, fish sauce rocks raw chunks of tamarind.

Mmm hmm, an elephant rocks its trunk.
Dear one, *mmm hmm*, fleas rock a head of hair.
Mmm hmm, dear, the plow rocks the plowshare,
and oh, oh my baby, heads rock full-face helmets.

Mmm hmm, an elephant rocks its shoulders.
My love, *mmm hmm*, gods of the soil rock their shrine.
Mmm hmm, baby, a Vietnamese girl rocks her triangular coconut cakes,
and oh, oh my baby, triangular cakes rock long-shafted Khmer pork buns.

Mmm hmm, an elephant swings its body.
My sweet, *mmm hmm,* a Vietnamese girl rocks silk pants.
Hmm hmm, my dearest, her pants rock me and others too,
and oh, oh my baby, the young miss rocks out as I rock in.

Mmm hmm, an elephant rocks its feet.
Little one, *mmm hmm,* a maiden rocks her cucumber.
Mmm hmm, baby, a widow rocks her sugar jar,
and oh, oh my baby, she sugars her rice at dawn.

Mmm hmm, a widow weeps at night.
My dear, *mmm hmm,* a widow weeps and wails.
Mmm hmm, love, she cries from dusk until first light,
and oh, oh my baby, she weeps to win her own young man.

Mmm hmm, an elephant rocks its mouth.
My treasure, *mmm hmm,* an elephant rocks its mouth.
Mmm hmm, my little love, a crocodile rocks a catfish,
and oh, oh my baby, gaff-prone lay priests secretly rock old nuns.
But not our local priests, of course—only those down in Australia!

Translated from Khmer by Trent Walker

SHARON MAY

A Musician's Life: An Interview with Kong Nay

Master Kong Nay is one of the few surviving masters of the *chapei dang veng*, a traditional Cambodian long-necked lute, registered on UNESCO's List of Intangible Cultural Heritage in Need of Urgent Safeguarding. This interview is excerpted from a longer conversation that took place over two days in January 2010 at Kong Nay's home, at the time on the outskirts of Phnom Penh. Present at different times were his wife, Tatt Chhen (TC); his son Kong Boran; and his *chapei* student Ouch Savy. Since this interview, Kong Nay's friend and fellow *chapei* master Prach Chhuon has passed away, and Kong Nay has returned to his family home in the countryside of Kampot. As we spoke, he was quick to joke and often picked up his *chapei* to play or sing. Despite the sorrow of some of the stories he shared, the room was filled with music and laughter, punctuated by Kong Nay's wit—and often that of his wife of over fifty years.

SM Do you remember anything before you became blind?

KN When I was growing up, I thought other people were just like me. But I was curious why they could walk on their own, while I needed someone to take my hand. I could hear that they could go wherever they wanted without asking for help. When I was seven, I asked my mother, "Mom! Why do I need someone to take my hand?" She said, "They can see, but you're blind, my son." I became blind because I had smallpox when I was four years old.

SM Do you remember anything about that time?

KN My mother told me that when I was sick, I had to sleep on a bed of banana leaves soaked in traditional herbs. If I slept on a mat or cloth, it would stick to my skin, because my body was covered with sores. I was wounded all over my body. I couldn't sleep unless she placed those leaves underneath me.

SM What are your earliest memories?

KN When I was growing up, I remember my mother taking my hand to visit Svay Tong temple and asking me to sit under the shade of a mango tree. I remember it vividly. I was nine years old at the time. That's the first memory. The second one is when I was ten, and I could walk from my home to Svay Tong temple on my own. I could sense the path beneath my feet. By crossing a rice field, I could reach a small road that led from my house. There's a third memory. At the age of eleven, I was walking on the road to the Svay Tong temple. It was in April [hot season], when kids were often sent to fetch water from the temple. A group of teenagers, girls and boys, were also walking on the road. One boy told me to turn left, and another told me to turn right. I suspected that if two people were telling me different things, one of them had to be lying. I turned left and crashed into a tree. The teenagers burst out laughing. I immediately got angry, but at the same time, I also thought that I must have lied to a blind person just for fun in my previous life— and that was why they lied to me and played jokes on me in this life.

SM Can you tell me about how you first came to hear and love music?

KN When I was seven years old, I heard a *chapei* player was coming to play in my village, Daung village, for a festival. I asked my mother to bring me to that performance. Once I heard the *chapei*, I felt intrigued. In that moment I knew, as a blind human being, I'd be able to earn my own living if I learned to sing *chapei*.

SM So you realized that you lost sight and loved the *chapei* in the same year?

KN Yes, when I was seven. I started to learn when I was thirteen. I had to wait because my arms were too short to play the long-necked *chapei*.

SM Did you check the length of your arms each year?

KN Yes, I did! And while I was waiting to be able to play *chapei*, when I was eight or nine, I starting making *chapei* music with my mouth.

SM Was it unusual for a kid to sing like a *chapei*?

KN I was the only kid who could sing and make music with my mouth like that. When I sang, people would give me a little money, a riel or a few coins.

TC In the harvest season, they'd invite him to sing on the paddy dikes to entertain them.

SM Was any member of your family a musician?

KN No, but my big uncle, Kong Tith, taught me to play the *chapei*. He played music for weddings and funerals. He couldn't sing, but he knew how to play the *khsae diev*, *chapei*, and *skor thom*. I kept hoping my arms would get long enough so that I could learn to play. You can ask my wife. When I was young, I was small and skinny. My arms were also short.

TC He was so skinny and small then.

KN My arms got longer and longer each year. After waiting for five years, I realized that I could finally play *chapei*.

SM Did you ever ask your mother if you could learn to play before then?

KN No, I didn't. I told her when I was thirteen. I told her: "Mom! My arms are long enough. Please buy a *chapei* for me because I can play it now." Once my father heard that, he went to buy one for me. It cost 100 riels.

SM Was that a lot of money?

KN It was very difficult for them. One whole cage of pigs could be sold for only 20 riels. We sold four or five cages of pigs back then just to buy the *chapei*. We sold pigs, chickens and hand-woven mats. My father was a fisherman so he also sold some fish to get the money.

SM Do you remember your first day learning *chapei* with your big uncle?

KN When I first asked him, he said it would be too difficult to teach me because I was blind. Without sight, how could I learn? Normally, he could just show me the [fourteen fret] positions for each string that he marked on the neck. But I couldn't see the marks. I begged him, "Uncle! Please just play for me! I'll memorize your Phat Cheay song." I sang the notes after him. When I got home, I practiced on my own. I tried to find the notes to match the sound and tone I had heard. It was sort of difficult for me. To learn to sing a song, it took me two days, then to practice with my *chapei*, it took me ten more days. It took me twelve days altogether to learn a song.

SM How many years did you study with your uncle?

KN I studied with him for two years. After that, as my uncle couldn't sing, I learned by listening to the radio. They played *chapei* singing on Tuesdays, *lakhaon bassac* on Wednesdays, *chapei* duets on Thursdays, and *ayai* singing on Fridays. I learned to improvise lyrics by listening to the singing on the radio. I also bought books of poems and asked people to read them for me.

TC He memorized those verses so he could sing them with his *chapei*.

KN The first stories I learned were *Sovannavong* and *Phka Roam Teuk Roam* [Dancing Flower, Dancing Water]. They were verse novels, so beautiful when they are sung. I memorized them until I could sing them by heart. I'd ask someone to read aloud for me—no one in particular, just people here and there. "If you are free, could you please read this piece for me?" After they read a page or two, I'd go ask someone else to read more.

TC When people read to him just once he could remember it.

KN It took me at least sixty days to memorize a book. They were long poems. *Sovannavong* was written in three books, each book had forty pages, so one hundred twenty pages in all. Each page had six stanzas.

SM Was it difficult for you to remember all that?

KN Yes. It was hard to remember. And it was difficult to seek help from others. People got tired of reading. When I forgot a part, I'd have to ask someone: "I forget at this verse. *Neang moel rukkha* ... what's the next line?" They'd complain, "Hey! I've told you three times already. Why can't you remember?" At first, I sang exactly those seven-syllable verses. They were beautiful poems about giants, stars, different kinds of trees, fish, and scenes like when the giant Sovannavong asked Vantha to be his wife. After that, I was able to make up my own verses. I just needed the name of the king, his kingdom, his parents' names, and so on, and I could make it rhyme.

SM   What age were you when you learned to improvise?

KN   I started to perform when I was fifteen. When I turned seventeen, I fell in love with my wife; and after I got married, when I was eighteen, I no longer had to follow only the verses in books. I could make rhymes on my own, in my own style. Now, as long as I know a theme, I can sing.

SM   How did you meet your wife? Did you know each other when you were children?

KN   I knew my wife when I lived in Daung village, and she lived in Svay Tong village nearby. If I sang on a quiet night, my wife could hear me. I first knew her when I was fifteen.

TC   I knew him before, but I didn't say anything to him.

KN   She knew me, but I didn't know her at the time. It's fate that we met each other. Her older sister lived nearby. When she came to visit her sister, she had to walk past my house. Whenever I heard her voice, I'd ask, "Where are you going, *bang* [older sister]?" She's older than me, so at that time, I didn't call her *oun*, but *bang* instead.

TC   There were many single men and single women in the village. He was very good at recognizing who was who. He would always say something to me when I was walking by.

KN   She would use [the familiar prefix] *a* to address me since she is three years older. When she became my wife, I started to call her *oun* [little sister, sweetheart].

SM   Did you immediately fall for her when you heard her voice?

KN   No! Not yet! I knew her when I was fifteen years old. At the age of seventeen, I started to love her. When I turned eighteen, during the Khmer New Year, I asked my father to propose to her for me. Before I asked my father to propose to her—because I am blind—I talked to her directly. "Bong! I love you and I want you to be my wife. What do you think? If you agree, it's good. If not, let's end it here so we don't get embarrassed."

TC   Many men loved me, but I don't know why I didn't love them—only him.

SM   Did she accept?

KN   Yes, she did. She said yes immediately. I then asked my father to propose to her.

SM   [to Chhen] Did many men come to ask you to marry them before him?

TC   Yes, but I rejected them all.

KN   Many men loved my wife, but she didn't agree to marry them. When she didn't reject me, I had a little hope. However, I was still worried that her father would not give her permission to marry a blind man. She had lost her mother and I had also lost my mother, so we both had only fathers back then. My mother passed away when I was sixteen years old.

TC My mother had died three years before his mother. My mother died when I was sixteen. And you?

KN Same! Both our mothers died when we were sixteen.

SM How did you decide to ask her to marry you?

KN Perhaps we talked three times. I was already in love with her, but she didn't know that. On my fourth time, I decided to ask her. I waited for a time when she walked by, when no one else was at home. [to Chhen] It was like I heard your voice and I fell for you, so I just decided to ask you directly.

TC I asked him, why didn't he love other girls? He said there were many people who wanted him to marry their daughters, but he was not interested in them.

KN It was like, if I love you, I want to tell you. I apologized to her before I asked her. I thought that if I apologized and spoke to her politely, she would not mind if I asked her. I thought if she refused me, no one would know if we kept it in secret.

I was cheated once. I loved a woman before. I never dared tell her myself, but I asked my cousin to ask her for me. In fact, he didn't ask her for me, but for himself! I asked my cousin, "Can you help me to talk to that woman to ask whether she would agree to marry me or not?" He told me to bring my *chapei* and sing at his house. If she came to see the performance, he said he would ask her on my behalf. But he didn't ask her for me. He asked her for himself.

SM Did you sing?

KN Yes, I did. I sang without getting paid because I wanted him to help me out. That woman also came to see the show, but I didn't dare speak to her. Afterward, I asked my cousin, "What did she say?" He responded, "I was about to ask her, but people kept coming to interrupt us. So please bring your *chapei* to perform here again in the next few days!"

SM And did you go again?

KN I went to sing there three times. He kept cheating me.

TC He cheated him because he wanted to hear his *chapei* singing.

KN When I recall that memory about my cousin, I still feel pain. If I weren't blind, I'd stab him to death. He should not have lied to me. When I played for them, I sung the scene when Sovannavong asked Vantha to be his lover. I sang that because I thought he was going to ask her to marry me. I learned my lesson then that if I wanted to marry someone, I didn't need anyone else to ask her for me!

SM How old were you then?

KN I was sixteen. It was just after my mother had passed away. My mother had been sick for five years. It was very difficult then. People were always inviting me to sing. I didn't really want to go to perform because I was afraid that I couldn't be with her at her last breath. Before she died, she told me, "Son, I can no longer take care of you because I am sick these days. As you are blind, no one will marry you. If I die, you can live with your father if he does not take another wife. If your father marries another woman, please go to live in a temple. The monks will look after you. I'm worried that your stepmother would hurt you since you're blind."

SM Did your father remarry after she passed away?

KN No, he didn't. I lived with him until I got married. If my mother knew that I have this woman as my wife, she would be so happy.

SM When did you start to work as a full-time singer?

KN I started to sing since I was fifteen. I would sing for seven nights consecutively, then I'd need to take a break for two nights, then I'd sing again for seven straight nights. That's how it was when I was young. We wouldn't sing for only a couple of hours like now, but for seven or eight hours, after the monk blessings finished at 9 or 10 P.M., singing all through the night until 5 A.M.

SM Were there many ceremonies?

KN Many! In the rural areas, we had rice festivals, gratitude events [for honoring ancestors], village festivals, flower festivals, funerals, and wedding ceremonies. Except for weddings, I would sing at least seven hours for each event. I felt exhausted. But since I was young back then, I could sing for many hours. There was nothing else I could do to support my family. I didn't mind because I could earn money from my performances every night. Though we couldn't get rich, we had enough food to eat just like other families.

TC We also worked rice farming. We only had to buy meat.

SM How did you have enough energy?

KN I was energetic back then. Sometimes I'd start to feel hot in my chest, but I'd continue. Now I can't do that because I get shaky.

TC Before he could sing very loud.

KN Yes, I can't do that now as I'm seventy years old.

SM [to Chhen] Did you go with your husband?

KN No! I didn't allow my wife to come with me because I was worried that another man would fall in love with her!

TC I had to take care of our children.

KN Yes! She needed to take care our children. We had ten children. Are you curious how we had so many children since I was very busy singing *chapei*? If you ask me, I'm going to tell you. If not, I won't.

SM Perhaps you were very energetic …

KN Yes! I tried to sing *chapei* and produce babies. Now, whenever there's a family gathering, there are many people. We have ten children, thirty-three grandchildren, and three great-grandchildren.

SM Do you remember your happiest moment during a performance?

KN The happiest moment was when I sang for a temple inauguration because there were lots of people. In the Khmer context, a lot means over 1,000. Those inaugurations didn't happen every year, and when we had one, people came from all over. An inauguration happened just once for a temple. They were very special.

SM Were you already famous before the war?

KN Before the war period, I sang only in the provinces, not in the city. There were only two *chapei* players in my province back then. The first player's name was Phy Romchea and the second one was me. One time five *chapei* players came together to sing *chapei chhlaoey chhlang* [call and response] for a ceremony.

SM How many years did you sing before the war?

KN I started singing from about age fifteen, so it was twenty years.

SM What work did you do in the Khmer Rouge time?

KN I worked beating the fibers from the inner layer of the stem of palm leaves, then braiding them into rope to tie up cows and water buffalo. I also made brooms from palm fiber.

SM Did you have any problems keeping your *chapei*? I wonder if the Khmer Rouge soldiers would get angry if they saw your *chapei*?

KN They did not feel angry. You know why? Because they also asked me to sing in 1975 and 1976. It was when I was still allowed to live in my own house, before we started having collective meals [around 1977]. They'd invite the people of a particular village to have a meeting and they'd call me to sing for the people. They allowed me to sing only three songs because they needed time for their meeting.

TC They composed the lyrics for him to talk about their regime.

KN They liked my performance, but I needed to sing propaganda for their political regime. I was not allowed to sing poems or folktales. They asked me to sing and criticize the old regime, by saying it was a feudalist society led by the king, whereas now under the Khmer Rouge regime, people were all equal. "Dear people! Please be a part of our democratic society! If we are rich, we're rich together. If we're poor, we're poor together. If I eat chicken and beef, you will also eat chicken and beef." In fact, the farmers ate thin rice porridge with water lilies and those people ate pork and chicken.

SM How did you feel when you sang like that?

KN I was not happy. If I didn't follow exactly what they said, they would kill me.

They listened to every word. If I made a mistake, they'd accuse me of being the enemy and take me away.

SM   Were there many musicians who played for Khmer Rouge?

KN   There were other musicians who played the *tro*, *chapei*, and *takhe* who sang for the Khmer Rouge. However, we all needed to sing to praise their regime and criticize other regimes. In 1977, they stopped all of us from performing. Only musicians in Phnom Penh city could continue to sing.

SM   What else do you remember during the war period?

KN   My life was very miserable during the Khmer Rouge period. As I am blind, I couldn't work as hard as other people, so I received a smaller ration. People who weren't disabled could get three ladles of rice, but I only got one ladle of rice, the same portion as a sick person. That was the first misery. The second misery was they killed my younger brother. He had fled to Thailand during the civil war. When the Khmer Rouge took over, he returned home because he thought we would have peace again, but the Khmer Rouge accused him of being a member of the CIA and killed him. The third misery was that they took me and my family away to be killed. It was right before the fall of the regime in early 1979. They took us to the mountain, Phnom Thkov, in Kampot province, along with other people with disabilities, women who had just given birth, and elderly people. They took away only the people who were no longer useful, so we knew they were planning to kill us.

SM   How many children did you have at that time?

KN   We had seven children at the time. Five were sent with me and my wife, but two were away in a children's unit. They all survived the Khmer Rouge.

SM   Did they want to kill all of you?

KN   Yes! They waited for the other children to be brought there so they could kill all of us at once. They worried if they killed only the parents, the children would take revenge. The Khmer Rouge said they would bring the rest of our children in two to three days. There were around ten families in all. They were mostly elderly or disabled people and women who had newborn babies. We had no hope of escape.

SM   What happened?

KN   We waited there for two days. The only reason that they did not kill us was Vietnamese and KPNLF soldiers arrived the next day. Otherwise, I would be dead already. The soldiers told us to return to where we came from. The Khmer Rouge ran away or surrendered. Some of them changed their clothes to join the other civilians.

SM   How did you feel seeing Khmer Rouge joining the civilians?

KN   I didn't feel anything, because they were the same people and relatives from our village and community.

SM Do you know what happened to other *chapei* players?

KN They killed many *chapei* singers I knew. They were afraid they would sing to tell people about the bad leadership of Khmer Rouge. The first musician who got killed was Ta Changkom Prambey. He was the most famous *chapei* singer. People told me he was killed in Kampong Speu province. Achar Try and Achar Teang were killed in Chhuok district, Kampot province. I felt very upset and sorry for them. Only a few *chapei* singers survived. There was only me and Prach Chhuon. And we are both blind!

SM How did he survive?

KN The Khmer Rouge called him in and said, "We have a question for you. If you answer it correctly, you can stay alive. If you answer it incorrectly, you'll be killed." They asked him to choose between "eat less, work a lot" or "eat lots, but work little." He answered, "I would choose to eat less and work more." If he had chosen the other option, he would have been killed. He ate very little and worked hard so that he could remain alive.

SM After the war, when did you start to sing again?

KN Right away. People started to invite me to sing from the beginning of 1979. The Vietnamese arrived in January, and there were many village festivals and gratitude ceremonies in February and March. People didn't have money at that time. They gave me rice when I sang for them. I started to sing again, but I no longer sang for Khmer Rouge regime. I sang for the People's Republic of Kampuchea.

SM Were you happy when you had to sing like that?

KN I was happy and worried at the same time because Khmer Rouge soldiers were hiding in the jungle. I worried they could still come and harm us.

TC We were happy that we could eat a meal at home again.

SM Did they have other musicians? Or did you perform alone?

KN Most of the time I performed *chapei* alone. However, some families would also invite *tro* and *takhe* musicians when they hosted wedding ceremonies.

SM How long did you live in the village before you moved to Phnom Penh?

KN I lived in my village from 1979 to 1991, for twelve years. In 1992 I came to live in Phnom Penh. They asked *chapei* players all around Cambodia to join a competition. Twenty *chapei* players came. There were two *chapei* players who won the first place, myself and Nen Pe.

SM When you first came to Phnom Penh, did they give you salary?

KN I didn't receive any salary for the first four months. My two daughters and son came to live in Phnom Penh with me. One of my daughters sold boiled corn and the other sold rice porridge to earn some income. My son needed to be with me to take me where I needed to perform. My wife joined me five years later.

SM [to Chhen] Was that difficult for you? Did you miss your husband?

TC It was very tough.

SM You have ten children. How many of them are musicians?

KN Two of my daughters are pop singers and two of my sons are learning *chapei*. Boran can sing now and another son is still learning. Another son plays wedding music on the *tro* and *takhe*. Of the other four, two are fishermen and two are farmers.

SM How many times do you normally perform per month?

KN On average, I perform three times a month, for about one to three hours. In my village after the war, I performed about ten times per month. When I started to be famous in Phnom Penh, I was invited to sing in ten countries, starting in 1997.

SM Do you remember any artists from other countries?

KN I don't remember. I remember an artist from England. His name was [Peter] Gabriel.

SM What do you think about the situation of Khmer arts nowadays?

KN After the war, many *chapei* players had died. Only a few players remained alive. However, Cambodian Living Arts has been giving me a salary to teach *chapei* to young people. Prime Minister Hun Sen has also supported me to teach young people. If the government and other organizations don't help support these masters, they cannot transfer their knowledge to young people.

SM How many students do you have here?

KN I have three students in my village and seven students in Phnom Penh. Three girls and four boys here. We didn't used to have female *chapei* singers, but now we do and they sing well.

SM Are there any masters in this new generation?

KN Not yet! They're very young.

SM Do you want to share anything I haven't asked?

KN There's one thing that I'd like to share with you. Some people believe that they will become blind if they study *chapei*. I'd like to ask you to spread the word that people will not become blind if they study *chapei*. For Kong Nay and Prach Chhuon, we both became blind before we learned how to play *chapei*. He had measles when he was seven, while I had chicken pox when I was four.

SM Do you think that you would still have wanted to be an artist if you hadn't been blind?

KN If I weren't blind, I don't know if I would have learned *chapei* or not. I think I might have studied law.

SM   You are lucky because you chose music.

KN   That's right!

SM   [to Chhen] I'd like to ask you what made you love him.

TC   I felt *anet* [compassion] for him. I thought that if I married him, I could help him after his siblings got married.

SM   Did you also love him?

TC   I felt *anet* for him more than loving him. [*Anet* can be stronger than love.]

SM   Did you know he has a good heart?

TC   Yes! In fact, I was thinking that if I married a man who had sight, he might not be good to me.

KN   Let me tell you so it's easier to understand! She thought that because I'm blind, if she marries me, I won't be able to find other women!

SM   How many years have you been together now?

KN   In two years, it will be our fiftieth wedding anniversary.

SM   I wonder what has made you happy together for all these years?

KN   Let me tell you! The first thing is my wife always listens to me and I always listen to her. In the beginning, I told her, "Now you're married with me, a blind man. No matter whether I can earn income or not, we need to be together and take care of each other until our last breath. Please let's never be apart!"

TC   I love him regardless of whether we have money or not. We share happiness and sadness with each other.

KN   And that's why we have lived together for almost fifty years! To say it briefly, we understand each other.

SM   Do you also feel happy with music?

KN   Let me tell you! After this life, I still wish to become a *chapei* player in my next life. Only I want to have sight so that I can sing *ayai, yike, lakhaon bassac*, all the other forms of art.

TC   He wants to know all the forms. In fact, he knows them, but he can't dance *kbach*. In his next life, he wants to dance!

Translated from Khmer by Tola Say

SACRED DRAMA DANCE

Moni Mekhala and Ream Eyso
as Retold by Prumsodun Ok

Editors' Note
Moni Mekhala and Ream Eyso *is one of the most sacred dance dramas in Cambodia, drawn from Hindu and Buddhist narratives. Closely associated with royal Khmer New Year rites to ensure Cambodia's prosperity, it explains the origins of lightning, thunder, and rain. Here it is retold by Prumsodun Ok. He explains his reasons for creating the retelling, written in 2012, in the essay "Here and Now, into the Future" included in this issue.*

Once, a long time ago, there lived an old hermit named Lok Ta Moni Eysei. Sought across the land for his powerful magic and knowledge, he practiced his craft in the depths of a hidden forest. He had under his tutelage three very promising students.

There was Moni Mekhala, the brilliant goddess of the seas. There was Vorachhun, princely manifestation of the earth. There was Ream Eyso, the fearsome storm demon.

As they neared the end of their studies, Lok Ta sought to bestow a precious gift upon his most deserving student. But seeing they were all very capable, he couldn't decide whom to give it to. Therefore, Lok Ta conceived a contest. He said to his three pupils sitting respectfully below him, his three pupils whom he loved like his own children, "The first person to bring me a glass full of morning dew will be master of this gift."

Before the sun rose the next morning, Vorachhun and Ream Eyso ventured into the darkness of the forest. They left not one leaf or blade of grass untouched, impatiently shaking the clinging liquid into their glasses. It was well past dawn before they collected enough dew, and they each flew speedily to the hermit's hut in hopes of winning.

Arriving at the same time, they were surprised to see Moni Mekhala sitting patiently by Lok Ta's side. Unlike the men, she had laid her scarf out in the open overnight. The goddess had only to wring out the precious fluid, filling her glass in a matter of seconds. With this clever strategy, she won Lok Ta Moni Eysei's contest.

Proud of his students' efforts, Lok Ta decided to give them all gifts. He turned the dew Ream Eyso collected into a diamond axe, Vorachhun's into a magic dagger, and Moni Mekhala's into a crystal ball.

Ream Eyso, the proud demon, nearly laughed at Moni Mekhala's gift. He thought to himself, "How is that harmless ball any better than my powerful axe?" Then, all of a sudden, when Mekhala took hold of it, the crystal began to glow in her hands. Then it began to radiate brilliantly, emitting a powerful, piercing light. Lok Ta Moni Eysei laughed as he saw the wonder on his students' faces. And Ream Eyso decided that he must have the crystal ball!

Several days later, on a day of joyous celebration, Ream Eyso was pacing back and forth in his palace. Both he and Vorachhun had tried to flatter Moni Mekhala into giving up the precious ball. They showered her with flirtatious compliments. They brought her rare gifts. Ream Eyso coveted the ball more strongly with each rejection, jealousy poisoning his blood and consuming his bones. He thought angrily to himself, "How could Lok Ta give her such a gift? I have served him no less! And Mekhala, she's just a silly woman!"

The demon decided he must have the crystal ball immediately. He flew up into the sky in a greedy fury, knowing she'd be dancing amongst the gods and goddesses in the palaces of heaven. On his way, he crossed paths with Vorachhun.

And knowing that Vorachhun would never allow him to steal the crystal, he attacked the righteous prince. Ream Eyso caught him by the leg in the heat of battle and threw him against the side of a mountain, killing him.

Sure of the prince's demise, Ream Eyso flew farther into the sky. He searched desperately for Moni Mekhala until he saw her dancing amongst her friends. The demon descended upon them slowly, his bad energy causing everyone to cease their festivities. Concerned about her colleague's mysterious rage, the goddess asked, "Ream Eyso, what has happened to you? Will you not join us in dance and song?"

"There will be no dance and song!" Ream Eyso said with fiery anger. "Give me your crystal ball. I am the most brilliant of Lok Ta's students! I am the rightful master of Lok Ta's gift!"

The gods and goddesses of heaven looked nervously back and forth between the two of them. Here were two students of Lok Ta Moni Eysei—once even friends—turned into warring rivals. The goddess, unfazed and unafraid, challenged the demon, "Then why have you not won it? This is my gift from Lok Ta. I am its master, the one who shall take care of it."

"If you don't give me that crystal ball, I'll kill you as I've killed Vorachhun!"

Everyone's heart sank at Ream Eyso's admission. Fear began to grow in their bodies, and the vibrant silks and golds they wore seemed to pale and lose their color. They all knew the demon could not be stopped. Yes, they were the gods and goddesses, masters of the universe, but not even they could match the powerful magic practiced by Lok Ta Moni Eysei—the powerful magic now wielded by his protégés.

With new strength, Mekhala responded, "If you want this crystal ball, Ream

Eyso, you'll have to come and get it!" And with that, she flew into the clouds and disappeared. Ream Eyso swiftly followed her, ripping through cloud after cloud to find the goddess. He seemed to lose her when, all of a sudden, he felt the radiant glow of the crystal behind him, and the goddess who held it with calm.

Ream Eyso quickly turned around and yelled, "This is your last chance, Mekhala! Give me that crystal ball or I'll kill you with this axe!"

With her piercing eyes, the goddess looked firmly at the demon saying, "I am not afraid of you."

Enraged, Ream Eyso began to swing his diamond axe at the goddess. But before he could hurl the weapon, Mekhala threw her crystal up into the air. It spun speedily as it climbed the height of the sky, emitting powerful flashes of lightning that blinded the demon and sent him falling backwards. Losing control of his body and sight of his target, Ream Eyso flung the axe in crazed desperation. It flew wildly through the air until it hit the clouds, creating the deep rolling of thunder.

"What have you done to me?!" Ream Eyso screamed in pain and fury. Blinded and defeated, he clawed desperately for his axe and the goddess who had brought him to his knees. "I'll kill you! I swear I'll kill you!"

Moni Mekhala stared as the demon struggled in his violent rage. She held her powerful crystal, the object releasing a light that was gentle yet strong. Around her, the newly unleashed forces of lightning and thunder started to mix. Their union created wondrous seeds of water that fell from heaven: rain.

Floating midair as the rain grew heavier, the goddess contemplated her next move. Should she kill him? Should she avenge Vorachhun? She approached the demon—harnessing all her power, ready to execute justice—when an image of Lok Ta's smiling face suddenly came to her.

Compassion.

The goddess decided to disappear into the clouds instead, and Ream Eyso, recovering from his spell of blindness, found his diamond axe and went searching for Moni Mekhala once more.

Meanwhile, lightning and thunder raged in the sky and continued to produce rainwater that showered the earth. The drops fell like brilliant crystals, feeding rivers and giving life to forests, gracing the bodies of young and old alike.

Some of these precious drops fell upon Vorachhun, reviving the prince and giving him new life.

As he rose from the mud of the earth, his radiant skin golden like a ripened rice field, Vorachhun grabbed his magic dagger and flew into the stormy sky in search of Ream Eyso and Moni Mekhala.

PRUMSODUN OK

Here and Now, into the Future

Editors' Note
In 2012, Prumsodun Ok was named the first associate artistic director of the Khmer Arts Academy in Long Beach, California. The Long Beach Museum of Art Presented his version of Moni Mekhala and Ream Eyso *during that season. From the age of sixteen, Ok had studied with master Cambodian classical dancer and choreographer Sophiline Cheam Shapiro, co-founder of Khmer Arts, a transnational dance organization based in Phnom Penh and Long Beach. In 2015, Ok founded his own troupe, Prumsodun Ok & NATYARASA, Cambodia's first gay dance company and a leader in LGBTQ performing arts in Southeast Asia. This essay was written in 2012.*

Although I've been watching videos of *Moni Mekhala and Ream Eyso* since as far back as I can remember, the story was only told to me in my teenage years. Sitting around Neak Kru Sophiline in her home in Long Beach, the only male student in a living room full of girls, I listened intently to each detail imparted by my teacher. It was a captivating story, a story that would disappear and reappear at different moments of my life, and one in which I continue to find new inspiration.

It was not until my first trip to Cambodia, though, that the story began to reveal its full meaning. It was then, in 2008, that I first witnessed the dance drama in its entirety. And although it is one of the most sacred and oldest works of the Khmer classical dance canon, I found it to be so fresh and alive.

I remember the dancers' presence being so palpable in the open-air pavilion. The transitions between scenes were tight and precise. The dramatic rise and fall of the narrative, expressed through rich and dynamic choreography, defied perceptions of ritual as boring, repetitive, and never-ending. I remember asking Neak Kru Sophiline in surprise, "Is this the original choreography or is this a new version? Was this dance drama re-choreographed in recent history?"

She had no answer for me then. But as I look at the situation with more understanding, it becomes an example of how ephemeral art forms such as dance, traditional or contemporary, are in a constant state of redefinition.

Mirroring the transmission of dance, oral stories are in a constant state of change as well. Different details, plots, and versions surface with each retelling, by different people, in different places, at different times. They also disappear with the fading of memory, and the fading of the bodies that carry those memories.

My retelling of *Moni Mekhala and Ream Eyso* weaves together details from versions passed on to me by my dance teacher, through plot checking with Toni Shapiro-Phim, and through observations of performances I witnessed, both in person and on the internet. My retelling also reflects my understanding of the world I live in. And, even more, it is told to manifest the world I want to see.

As an educator, I've had the privilege of sharing this story many times with my students. Each time, as I look into the faces of my young female students—by the light of a flame beneath the stars in Kings Canyon, at the Khmer Arts Academy studio—I am reminded of how important it is to keep this story alive.

Girls are deprived of empowering images of women. Early on, they watch Disney films that tell them their ultimate purpose in life is to get married. The reality television, music videos, and advertisements they watch instill empty values of materialism and consumerism, telling them they're worthless if they don't fit commodified images of female beauty.

Life gets even more complicated when considering inner-city communities like central Long Beach, where the intersecting problems of poverty, violence, and racial and cultural conflict further suppress young people's growth. In the case of Cambodian American teenagers, a 2011 report by Khmer Girls in Action says they are growing up in an environment of "alarming" rates of depression and high rates of perceived discrimination in education.

Right after concluding my interview with Neak Kru Sophiline for an article called "The Teacher's Gift," I continued our conversation by raising an urgent issue. While teaching at the Khmer Arts Academy studio just the day before, molding and sculpting one of my students as my teacher had done for me, I noticed clean incisions on the girl's forearm on top of older scars. The student demonstrated so much potential as a dancer, and had bravely come forward two weeks before, telling me she had been battling clinical depression.

Explaining that I couldn't understand how someone so young could destroy herself in such a manner, hopeful yet realizing that my love as a teacher might not be enough, expressing my fear that someone might die while under my direction, I began crying. And through my tears, I attempted to explain how I made my student promise to call me if she needed help, how I wanted her to see that she had a home in me and in Khmer Arts. Neak Kru Sophiline, joined quickly by her husband John, calmly, and with great care, began identifying the appropriate steps we needed to take to make sure the student got proper help.

Walking through the streets of Long Beach on my way home that night, my heart heavy and tears falling, I thought about my student, and my other dear students, whom I love so much. Their faces ran through my mind, one by one, sometimes in groups, and I thought about my responsibilities to them, my hopes for them, and my hopes for the art form that brought us all together. These images surfaced a haunting memory that I am only now fully understanding.

When I was four years old, I wrapped my arms around my mother's legs as we watched paramedics roll a stretcher past us towards an ambulance. On it, covered by a white cloth, was the body of my eldest sister, Leang Heang. Exhausted by her physically abusive husband, her spirit broken by his extramarital affairs and being trapped in the prison of an unhappy marriage, my sister chose to leave her two sons and the world by overdosing on prescription drugs. Her only means of triumph, or the only one she could allow herself to imagine, was to end her own life.

Moni Mekhala is a brilliant, shining alternative to all of this. She has been kept alive—through dance and song, from teacher to student—for all the young girls and women, for all the people in our world today. She is a clever woman, a strong woman, an educated woman, a graceful woman, an independent woman who triumphs in a story and universe that appears to favor males.

In my retelling, I have chosen to bring out the latent gender conflicts within the story. I do not want my students to become victims of abusive husbands. I do not want them to enforce violent, meaningless social codes upon each other. Instead, I want to nurture a generation of women armed with and inspired by the story of Moni Mekhala. I want my students to grow to be fearless women guided by love and knowledge. I want them to be innovative women committed to solving the challenges of our world. I want my students—and girls everywhere—to aspire to be visionary women who initiate bold, much-needed change.

My retelling also differs in another way. The Moni Mekhala of prior versions, unaware of the murder of Vorachhun, teased and taunted Ream Eyso almost playfully. In my retelling, she has a serious focus as she contemplates the destructive nature of the killer before her. And, when he has fallen, she is charged with the power and dilemma of executing justice.

As a dancer, I have been subject to the aggression of certain jealous persons. They used my demanding nature as a teacher to tell my youngest and most malleable students that I hated them. They spread rumors about my family. They sought every chance to belittle my work and destroy me. There is a part of me that wants to put a quick end to this unrelenting violence (Moni Mekhala delivers justice, kills Ream Eyso), but it is the voice of my teacher constantly asking for patience and calm that keeps me from delivering the sharp, precise words meant to defend my integrity.

Fortunately, I learned early on to find my own stage to shine on. And, even more, I have learned to make my own stage when one does not already exist. By passing on ideas such as this, through word and example, I intend to curb behavior driven by greed and jealousy. Furthermore, I am committed to molding my students into dancers who perform beautifully, nurturing their capacities as responsible, compassionate leaders and training them to offer themselves in the highest devotion to the tradition.

On a larger scale, this plot difference is a moment of reflection for me as a gay man in a violent society, and as a child, student, sibling, and friend of people who survived a most hellish genocide.

During the trial of Dharun Ravi, the college student who spied on his gay roommate's affair and therefore contributed to the latter's suicide, I didn't know if destroying Ravi's life through years of incarceration was the right thing to do. We had already prematurely lost one person. And after watching *Enemies of the People,* the groundbreaking documentary following former Khmer Rouge cadres through their perpetration of genocide, through our darkest capacities as human beings, I couldn't help but feel the weight of years of guilt and shame that haunted them. It was a guilt and shame that ate at their spirits and bodies, a guilt and shame they felt knowing that they would forever be killers.

What are we to do to those who inflict harm upon us when we know that they inherently suffer in their acts? Why does justice most often come hand-in-hand with a cycle of violence? How do we create an efficacious system of justice driven by love and healing?

The story of *Moni Mekhala and Ream Eyso* gains further meaning as I assume my role as associate artistic director of Khmer Arts. Like the crystal given to Moni Mekhala by her teacher, I have been given precious gifts by my teacher: the art of Khmer classical dance, and now, a space in which to pass it on.

With this appointment, I am further crystallized as an undeniable carrier of this heritage, as someone who will nurture the next generation of leaders who will carry it further. And, fully aware that I belong to a venerable, once nearly destroyed lineage that is over a thousand years old, I am committed to its wholesome preservation, growth, and expansion. I am dancer, am teacher, am choreographer, am writer, am organizer, am fundraiser—I am a caretaker of Khmer classical dance.

Keeping a once-endangered art form alive is no easy task, of course. And I, in light of this, often imagine an alternate narrative progression to the story of *Moni Mekhala and Ream Eyso* when I need motivation.

In the sky, Moni Mekhala has been struck by Ream Eyso's axe. The demon approaches the goddess who, in a calm that defies her pain, surrenders the crystal to her attacker. Ream Eyso laughs viciously as he towers over Moni Mekhala. He proceeds to kill her using her own crystal. Instead of brilliant flashes of lightning, though, there is nothing. The ball begins to lose its radiant glory. It is powerless and crumbles to dirt in the demon's hands.

In my years of practice, I have seen what this crumbling to dirt can look like. Sometimes it is a Cambodian American girl who is overcome by pride and conceit, her dance and costuming nothing but a sad and hollow shell that misleads, misguides, and miseducates audiences and practitioners. Sometimes it is performances that disregard the art form's integrity and spirit altogether, opting instead for modern spectacle that capitalizes on uneducated, indifferent audiences.

I refuse to let this precious gift crumble in my hands. Regardless of being a practitioner in the diaspora, or the resistance of some people to my leadership due to my sexuality—I refuse to let this art form crumble to dirt. I will hold my crystal fearlessly, creatively, and lovingly, imbuing it with the spirit, knowledge, and vision that only I can.

Perhaps then, *Moni Mekhala and Ream Eyso* is more than a story pulled from a large and distant landscape of motherland or collective culture. It is a story passed on to me from my teacher, passed on to her from her own. It is my story. And I offer it to our world.

May Lok Ta Moni Eysei, Moni Mekhala, Ream Eyso, and Vorachhun live in the hearts, minds, and bodies of young people for countless generations. May they be brought to vivid life through dance and song, painting and film, and other forms that only future generations will know. And Lok Ta Moni Eysei, our Grandfather the Great Ascetic, from whom all knowledge of the arts emanates, may you be witness to the colors, intensities, and movements of the light radiating from the crystal that is now in my hands. May you, the spirits of teachers now gone, and my teachers now living, bless me on my journey to sustain and grow the art of Khmer classical dance. Through the dance, and all the arts, may you reveal to us the path of light.

KALEAN UNG

from *Letters from Home: A Multimedia Solo Play*

Editors' Note

In 2016, writer/performer Kalean Ung learned of a drawer in her father's study. It was filled with letters from family and friends living in desperate circumstances in refugee camps, and detailing their lives during the Khmer Rouge regime. A multimedia solo play, Letters from Home *weaves together the stories her father told her of arriving in America in the 1960s as a young music student, her Cambodian family's refugee story, her own story as a biracial, first-generation American, and her experience playing Shakespeare's iconic female characters. These stories are embodied and interwoven with projections, her father Chinary Ung's original compositions, and artifacts that enshrine the people and places of this collective history. The following is excerpted from chapters 2, 5, and 6.*

SETTING

An office filled with objects, artifacts, family pictures, various altars with vibrant colors and textures, a desk and a stool, a red console, a Balinese room divider, stacks of books, music scores, a colorful trunk, a music stand, plants, and other things. Practical lights are hidden throughout the space—behind books, behind furniture, and on the desk. She has collected facsimiles of artifacts, essential props, and drawing material that she has prepared for her storytelling. This is not to say that she knows how the story will unfold, but these are the tools she has decided she needs to tell her story to her confidantes who are listening and watching. She uses a document camera to write, draw, and show us these artifacts as she encounters them. The play takes place in this room only, but we are often transported across time and space. Surfaces will become projection areas. It is important that the space is the space—meaning that a notepad, or a picture frame, or the wallpaper becomes animated as if it were coming to life. Magic is conjured through the embodiment of her storytelling. Sometimes the storyteller conjures a magical transformation, and sometimes the space, as a character, manifests as a presence. The lines of this disintegrate over the time and space of the play. The play is divided into thirteen chapters, and at each intersection we should not pause; rather we should feel like we are stepping into a deeper portal of the storytelling or are peeling a new layer back.

CHAPTER 2. KAW-LEE-YANN

Kalean sits back at her desk. Under a document camera, she awkwardly writes her name in Khmer on a beautiful piece of paper. She transforms into eight-year-old Kalean as her family sits at the kitchen table eating dinner.

KALEAN Dad, how come you never taught us Khmer?

She becomes Dad, as he grunt-shrugs the issue. Her eight-year-old self turns to Mother incredulously. Then she becomes her mother.

MOM Well, Kalean, your father was really upset about what happened, and he didn't really want you to be Cambodian kids. It was just too Goddamn painful.

KALEAN Well, it is painful for us too! *[She transforms back into present-day Kalean and speaks to her confidantes.]* My sister, Sonika, and I are angry with our father because when we play with our cousins and stay with our family, we feel like we don't quite belong.

But where do we belong? As an adult, every time I meet somebody new and introduce myself, they say, "Wow, 'Kalean'? It's such a beautiful name, where is it from? Oh, Cambodia? That's so unique, that's so exotic! I've never heard of that before!"

Of course I know that all of this is out of curiosity and even admiration, but can I tell you that when you say things like that, I feel like some bizarre dog breed that you just discovered.

She finds her Khmer book among a stack. She puts it next to her name in Khmer, which is underneath the doc camera.

Six months before my wedding, I decide I want to learn Khmer. *[She is surprised as she reflects back on this.]* Luckily, I'm in LA, and Long Beach is home to the largest Cambodian population in the U.S. and outside of Cambodia. But there is no one to teach me Khmer. All of the Cambodian people I reach out to point me to a white man named Frank.

Frank or "Lok Kru Frank" speaks Khmer, Thai, Vietnamese, and many other Southeast Asian languages and dialects. He lives in Berkeley and tells me we can have private lessons twice a week over Skype. During our first lesson, he explains to me that my name, Kaw-lee-Yann, means "morally good, charming." No one's ever told me that, and I have to ask him to repeat how to pronounce my name.

An animated box appears around her name on the sketchpad.

He tells me: that in the Khmer culture, I must always speak in a formal way to older people, and that the teacher-student relationship is also formal, so I must always call him Lok Kru Frank. He tells me: that when I greet him with the prayer gesture, I must always greet him at the same level as I would my parents and grandparents. And he tells me: that I must always *initiate* the greeting, as I am of lower status.

She enacts the mini-scene.

KALEAN Chumreap suor, Lok Kru Frank.

FRANK Chumreap suor, Kaw-lee-yann.

KALEAN Sok sabay?

FRANK Sok sabay. Sok sabay?

KALEAN Cha, khnhom sok sabay.

I leave our first Skype lesson so happy and so heartbroken at the same time. How do I not know any of these things?

Learning Khmer is so hard. Lok Kru Frank is a tough teacher, I am a little scared of him, and I feel so, so dumb.

I call my dad.

Hi! Can you help me with my Khmer homework, please?

We start to Skype and speak Khmer to each other every week in preparation for my lessons! It's beautiful because he's a very different teacher than Lok Kru Frank. He happily answers all the questions that I am too afraid to ask Lok Kru Frank, and our lessons turn into stories about his childhood in Cambodia. Like the village where he grew up and his teacher who punished him by forcing him to hold bricks outside in the scalding hot sun and then my grandma who screamed at the teacher for picking on him and the long monsoon season and the rice fields and the French military songs he learned as a child and the more I study, the more he lights up, and the more he lights up, the more I light up, and the more I light up, the more I feel maybe I'll never be fluent in Khmer but at least I have this.

CHAPTER 5. PHONEMES

Kalean is typing. A lightbulb moment. She suddenly stops and goes to find her father's "Inner Voices" score. When she opens it, we hear passages of the music being played. She closes the score and the music stops.

KALEAN My dad took off eleven years from composing music. But not just because he was helping his family escape. He understood that his role in preserving Cambodian arts and culture was essential for refugees. Especially for many of the Cambodian child soldiers who were now orphans. He spent years listening to surviving recordings of traditional music and teaching himself how to play traditional instruments in order to ensure that they knew just how beautiful their country was.

He said he began to wonder if he would ever return to composing at all, and if so, how would he incorporate the traditional sounds of Khmer music within Western music? How would it translate to a concert hall?

Kalean hears her mom practicing the viola through muted walls. It's a complicated passage. Damn, she didn't get it. She repeats. The bow angrily hits the bridge and then... Kalean transforms into her mom with a prop viola.

MOM Chinary! What the hell is this shit?

KALEAN [aside to the audience] My mom storms down the stairs with her score in one hand and her viola in the other.

MOM How am I supposed to play this? You want me to sing this while I play this?!

KALEAN *[aside to the audience]* She runs back upstairs. My dad turns to me—

DAD *[with a grin on his face]* We've got to keep Mommy busy, or else she watches too much news.

KALEAN *[speaks to her confidantes as if at a dinner party]* My dad's music is hard to play. He requires classical musicians to *play* and *sing* at the same time. I mean my mom has to sing, whistle, shout, even bang on a drum while she plays some crazy viola music. Let's just say it's a very specific niche, and my mom may be the only one in the world who has mastered it. My dad always offers to simplify it but she refuses and never fails to rise to the occasion. Then my dad will say, "*Pretty good.*"

One time, my father had to conduct his own music at this Cambodian Festival in New York and he was legit freaking out. We could all tell he was nervous at breakfast on the day of the concert, and as he was flipping through the score he said, *"Oh, why didn't I write this piece in 4/4?"* My mom smiled over her coffee, "karma."

So I ask my dad for a simple lullaby that's a cappella that I can weave through my show, right? And then he sends me a score. *[She grabs the score and it's gigantic and stretches the length of her wingspan.]* But it's not simple.

[She examines the score closely, as if for the first time.] The words are not words but made-up phonemes mixed with some Khmer and even the word "corazon" and it's way too intense to be a lullaby. And then, about a week later… *[The sound of a doorbell interrupts her; she runs to open her door and picks up a box.]* … A big box arrives on my doorstep *[She opens the box.]* and it contains … crotales? A fancy traveling bag? Mallets? This bar thing where you screw the crotales into?

We hear a FaceTime ringtone.

KALEAN Hey, Dad, thanks so much for the piece you wrote for me, it's really beautiful and … hard.

DAD *[Giggles.]*

KALEAN *[She reacts—the audacity!]* Also, Dad, c r o t a l e s *[drawing out the word]* came to my house. Dad, I don't play the CROTALES!

DAD You will learn. It will help you to stay in tune.

KALEAN *[offended]* Well, now I know how mom feels!

[She again speaks as if to friends at a dinner party.] He starts coaching me on the song over FaceTime, telling me the pronunciation of his made-up words. And when we finish this coaching, he says, *"Not bad."* He sends me a text message that day: GOOD JOB ON THE SONG OF COMPASSION. FOLLOW YOUR BLISS. Three rainbow emojis.

Three rainbow emojis are projected.

CHAPTER 6. WHITESKIN

A Cambodian pop song interrupts. In the doc camera, we see a picture of Kalean as a sixteen-year-old in Cambodia. Another flutter from the taxidermy moth. The sound transports her back to…

KALEAN 2002. I'm sixteen and going to Cambodia for the first time. When we get off a small plane in Phnom Penh, there are news cameras everywhere. Apparently my dad is kind of famous here. It's his first time coming back since before the genocide, and he is terrified that my sister and I will get kidnapped, so when we travel through the jungle, my dad hires bodyguards with guns.

VHS footage from her actual trip to Angkor Wat in 2002 is projected. We see Mom, Dad, Aunt Helen, cousin Richard (Bou Bou), and her little sister, Sonika. Kalean is such an American teenager. This shit is golden. We watch for a bit.

On a trip to Siem Reap to visit Angkor Wat, Aunt Helen warns us to stay in the back of the van, and when we drive up to the gate, not say anything, and then—we could pass as locals. If you're Khmer, you don't have to pay anything to visit the temples. But if you are a foreigner, or a "whiteskin" as she refers to my mom *[sixteen-year-old Kalean and her sister giggle]*, you have to pay $30!

[She grabs a krama, a Cambodian scarf, from the trunk.] Walking through the temples, before every checkpoint with the guards, my aunt makes me tie a scarf around my head *[she takes the scarf to do so]* to hide my curly hair and gives me a bamboo flute to play *[yes, this comes out too]* and says that if anyone asks me anything, to just say "Khmer," as in "I am Khmer." *[She looks ridiculous holding the flute.]*

[as sixteen-year-old Kalean] Uhhh, this is so stupid. Seriously, I have to play a freakin flute?!"

[she explains to her confidantes] It's hot and I keep taking off the scarf *[she pulls it down]* as we walk through the temples. But then a guard catches my aunt fussing with my scarf, notices my "difference," and asks me what my name is— *[She pulls the scarf back up.]*

GUARD Chhmuoh ey?

KALEAN *[hesitantly]* Khmer?

[speaks as if to her confidants] There's a huge uproar between two guards, and my aunt starts screaming. My father shows them my passport and eventually they let me go. I am embarrassed and want to die, but he makes me feel better by saying, "Your name is a Cambodian name, you are Khmer," but I think to myself... *[She stares at her pale hands. A beat.]* Am I a "whiteskin?" *[Shame. Where does she belong?]*

A short fragment of her father's composition "Inner Voices" becomes the moth motif, creating a soundscape dream. The framed taxidermy moths on the wall begin to flutter, and one flies across her face. She follows it.

[she confesses to her confidantes as she recalls] When I started learning Khmer, I had a nightmare. I'm in a bedroom, the ceiling is high and the walls a crisp white. My bed is nestled in the corner of the room, and there is a lot of sunlight. But as I look up there are thousands of cocoons. They begin to hatch, and all of these moths start to come out—these brown creatures. They are terrifying. Their wings begin to flap, their eyeballs bulge. But within these moths, there are butterflies too. They are so beautiful. Their wings are colorful, and they are scattered across the ceiling.

What does this mean?

She takes the krama and adds it to the altar.

SINGING KITE INTERLUDE

DAD   *[suddenly]* Kalean. I have these recordings of the Cambodian singing kite that we can put into your play. The sound is very beautiful. Very interesting!

KALEAN   Cool, Dad, but what does that have to do with the music that you're composing *for* the play? Wait, what's the Cambodian singing kite?

DAD   Look it up on the internet.

KALEAN   *[touché, Dad—she looks it up and reads]* "The Cambodian Singing Kite has a bamboo reed that is attached to the kite, and it can sound up to seven tones as it flies." *[Singing kite sound; she has never heard anything like this before.]* Wow. It sounds like a beehive. *[continues reading]* "During the Harvest season when it is windy, Cambodians tie the singing kite at the edge of the rice field. They fly it to pray for rain for their crops and to give thanks for the bountiful harvests. Because it is so windy, the kite is singing constantly."

[We are bombarded with videos and photos of the singing kite. It's as if texts and photos of the singing kite are being sent to her from her dad and are taking over the space. The images are gigantic. Kalean stares at the videos in disbelief. She is so small.]

But—Dad, what is it with the singing kite?

DAD   Well, when I was a little guy, and when the village was quiet, in the middle of the night, I would wake to the sounds of the singing kite that was many miles away.

KALEAN   *[to her confidantes]* He says the sound was haunting. But it soothed him.

DAD   It was a spirit of some sort, an entity. It reminded me of my existence.

KALEAN   *[to her confidants]* Five decades later, he travels back to Cambodia and goes to the rice fields. He attaches a microphone to the kite and flies it through the sky. *[she realizes]* He is trying to find the sounds he heard as a child.

The space is taken over by a giant kite. It flutters.

NOTES ON PRODUCTION

Written and performed by Kalean Ung

Music by Chinary Ung

Developed with and directed by Marina McClure

Letters from Home was developed through residencies, workshops, and performances at Independent Shakespeare Company, UC San Diego, Cambodia Town Film Festival, CalArts, Willamette University, LA Mission College, Madrid Theatre, UC Irvine, Boston Court Pasadena, and The New Wild. It has received support from the Department of Cultural Affairs, City of Los Angeles, and MAP Fund.

About the Contributors

Note: Family names and single personal names appear in bold capital letters.

FRANCOISE **BENICHOU** was a professional freelance writer in French and English. Her translation of Soth Polin's "Command Me to Exist" was her final work.

BUNCHAN MOL ប៊ុណ្ណចន្ទ ម៉ុល (1916–1975) came from a high-ranking family. He served as a monk for ten years, became a boxer, and joined the nationalist movement seeking independence from France. He was arrested in Phnom Penh in 1942 after joining five hundred monks in an anti-French demonstration and was sentenced to five years in Poulo Condor prison on Koh Tralach island (now Côn Sơn island) and fifteen years in exile. After the French colonial government fell to the Japanese in 1945, Mol was released. He later worked under Lon Nol as an undersecretary of propaganda and religion. In the early 1970s, he published *Kuk Noyobay* (Political Prison), describing his life in Poulo Condor, and *Charet Khmae* (The Khmer Mentality). He was executed by the Khmer Rouge in 1975.

CHEY CHAP ជឹយ ចាប was born in 1949 in Kratie and became one of Cambodia's most famous poets of the 1980s and 1990s. He taught at the Royal University of Phnom Penh for many years. In 2004, he received the S.E.A. Write Award for his book *Pi Nih...Pi Nuh* (From Here...From There). His other books of poetry include *Ao Phtei Srok Khmae* (O Khmer Land, 1994).

ELIZABETH **CHEY** works with international, community-based, and small nonprofits on communications, advocacy, strategic planning, and capacity building. She served as assistant regional director of Asia Programs for the American Friends Service Committee and program development officer for Cambodian Living Arts. She earned her MFA from New York University and a journalism degree from Northwestern.

THEANLY **CHOV** ធ្យូរ ធានលី was born in Battambang province in 1985. He graduated in graphic design at the Vocational Training Center Battambang in 2007, then moved to Phnom Penh in 2011, graduating from Chamroeun University of Poly-Technology. His paintings have been shown in numerous exhibitions in Cambodia and abroad, including *Phnom Penh,* at the Musée de l'Hospice Comtesse de Lille, France (2015–2016), and *Cambodia: Looking Back to the Future,* at the Flinn Gallery in Greenwich, Connecticut (2017).

ERIK W. DAVIS studies and teaches Buddhism, ritual, and the theory of religion at Macalester College. In 2016, he published *Deathpower: Buddhism's Ritual Imagination in Cambodia* (Columbia UP). He was an advisor for research projects at the Buddhist Institute in Phnom Penh, and is coeditor of *Sīmas: Foundations of Buddhist Religion* (University of Hawai'i Press, 2022).

KING ANG DUONG ព្រះបាទអង្គដួង (1796–1860) was the last pre-colonial king of Cambodia, reigning from the 1840s until his death. Celebrated today for his efforts to revive Khmer ritual, artistic, legal, and literary traditions, he was a prolific poet, translator, and Buddhist scholar. Trained in Siamese literature, he translated a number of works to and from Thai. He also composed traditional *lakhaon* plays in Khmer and a version of "Code for Girls" *(cpāp' srī)*.

PENNY EDWARDS teaches Southeast Asian Studies at the University of California, Berkeley. She is the author of *Cambodge: The Cultivation of a Nation* (2008) and over twenty articles on the political and cultural history of Cambodia and Burma; she is the coeditor of six volumes, including *Mediating Chineseness in Cambodia* (2013). Her translations from Chinese and Khmer include *A Short History of the Buddhist Institute* (2005). She is collecting writing from Burma that will appear in *Mānoa* in winter 2022.

DIREK HONGTHONG ดิเรก หงษ์ทอง is a lecturer at the Department of Thai Language, Faculty of Humanities at Kasetsart University, Thailand. A specialist in Northern Khmer language and music, he received his Ph.D. in Thai literature from Chulalongkorn University in 2016.

QUEEN INDRADEVĪ ឥន្ទ្រទេវី (late twelfth–early thirteenth century) was the chief queen of Jayavarman VII, the most powerful monarch of the Angkorian period. A renowned teacher of Mahayana Buddhism, she is one of the earliest known female poets in Southeast Asia.

MARIA HACH is a writer, researcher, and community worker living on the lands of the Boonwurrung People of the Kulin Nation. She holds a Ph.D. in cultural and gender studies from the University of Melbourne. Since 2011, she has worked at the Multicultural Centre for Women's Health, a national, community-based organization dedicated to improving the health and well-being of immigrant and refugee women in Australia.

UKÑĀ SUTTANTAPRĪJĀ IND ឧកញ៉ា សុត្តន្តប្រីជា ឥន្ទ (1857–1924) was among the most influential literati of his day. He spent his youth as a monk, and with his background in Pali and Thai, he became a leading poet and intellectual. He was instrumental in reforming Khmer orthography in the early twentieth century and developing the first monolingual Khmer dictionary. Some of his works were widely circulated on palm-leaf and bark-paper manuscripts; others were discovered after his death. His work includes a version of "Code for Girls" *(cpāp' srī)*, a theatrical version of the Buddha's life, *A Journey to Angkor Wat,* and the *Gatilok* (Ways of the World), which combines Buddhist stories, folk tales, and European fables.

HUOT IV អ៊ឹវ ហួត was born in 1940 in Kampong Cham. At thirteen, after visiting the temples of Angkor, he began to write poems. He moved to France in the early 1960s and studied at the Sorbonne. After his retirement, he returned regularly to Cambodia and in 2005 settled permanently in Siem Reap. In 2012, he published *Lbaeng Peak* (Word Play), exploring the secret labyrinths of Khmer sensibility.

KHAU NY KIM ខូនី គឹម was born in Cambodia, studied in France, and returned to Phnom Penh to teach. He has been living in France since 1975. Much of his work speaks to the condition of exile. His poems have been published in the online literary journal of the Association of Khmer Writers Abroad (AEKE) and broadcast on Radio France Internationale (RFI) in the 1970s to 1990s. His novels have been serialized in Khmer newspapers in the U.S. He is one of the few Khmer poets to write in free verse. His recent work is included in *Aksarsel Santepheap* (Literature for Peace), a Khmer literature anthology published in Paris in 2021.

KOSAL KHIEV was born in Khao-I-Dang refugee camp in Thailand in 1980. He grew up in Santa Ana, California, joined a gang at thirteen, and at sixteen was involved in a shoot-out that left two people injured. Tried as an adult, he served fifteen years in prison. While incarcerated, he began experimenting with poetry. Upon his release in 2011, he was deported to Cambodia, a country he had never known. That year, he gave a TEDx Talk in Phnom Penh. He represented Cambodia in the London Poetry Parnassus event at the 2012 Olympic Games and continues to write, teach, and perform spoken-word poetry.

KHUN SRUN យុន ស្រ៊ុន (1945–1978) was born into a poor family in Takeo. When he was eight, his father, a Chinese man who had fled Communism, died, and Srun was raised by his mother. In the 1960s, he worked as a professor of mathematics and a journalist while writing fiction and poetry. For protesting against Lon Nol's government, he was imprisoned in 1971. After a second imprisonment in 1973, he joined the Khmer Rouge. He was killed in Tuol Sleng in 1978. In his short, meteoric life, Srun published three collections of poems, short stories, philosophical reflections, and two autobiographical fiction books. *Chun Choap Chaot* (The Accused) was published in Cambodia in 1971 and in Paris as *L'Accusé* in 2018.

KONG BUNCHHOEUN គង្គ ប៊ុនឈឿន (1939–2016) was born in Battambang. His childhood was marked by the war for independence. A writer in several genres, he is perhaps best known for over two hundred lyrics written during the 1960s and 1970s, many of them for singer Sinn Sisamouth. In 1963 he was imprisoned for writing a novel criticizing an official in the royal government. During the Pol Pot regime, he escaped execution thanks to a Khmer Rouge cadre who had read his novels and testified that he was a writer with a "profound sense of social justice." In 2000, as a result of publishing *Veasna Neang Marina* (The Destiny of Marina), a novel based on an acid attack on his niece by the wife of a government official, he was forced to flee to Thailand and, later, Norway, where he died of cancer in 2016.

KONG NAY គង់ ណៃ was born in 1944 in Kampot. He is Cambodia's most recognizable traditional musician, regularly appearing on Cambodian television and at cultural events. Blinded by smallpox at age four, he began to study the *chapei dang veng*, a long-necked lute, at age thirteen. Within two years, he began to perform professionally. With his trademark dark glasses, he soon earned the nickname Kong Sangha, "Handsome Kong." Having survived the Pol Pot era, he resumed performing. In 2001, he was designated Master of Chapei by the Ministry of Culture and began training future *chapei* players through Cambodian Living Arts. He has collaborated with younger musicians, including rap artists praCh Ly and Vann Da, and was awarded the Fukuoka Prize in Arts and Culture in 2017.

MYLO LAM was born in Vietnam and raised in Los Angeles. He and his family are refugees of Cambodia. His work has been published in *Barrelhouse*, *The Coachella Review*, AAWW's *The Margins*, and elsewhere. His multimedia work won *Palette Poetry*'s Brush & Lyre Prize, and he was a 2019 Sesame Writers' Room fellow.

BORETH LY is associate professor of history of art and visual culture at the University of California, Santa Cruz. She is a specialist in the visual cultures of Southeast Asia and the Southeast Asian diaspora. Her latest book, *Traces of Trauma: Cambodian Visual Culture and National Identity in the Aftermath of Genocide,* was published by University of Hawai'i Press in 2020.

MA LAUPI ម៉ា ឡៅពី was born in 1932, the same year as Sinn Sisamouth, in Kampong Chhnang. During the 1960s and 1970s, he was a well-known lyricist, radio presenter, and speaker, occasionally dubbing and acting in films. It was said that words flowed from his mouth "like fresh water flowing down a mountain." He frequently presented Khmer music concerts and song contests on the Veal Men, next to the royal palace, and he often accompanied Prince Sihanouk on trips to the countryside, entertaining the crowds with his storytelling. In April 1975, while traveling in Pailin, he crossed the Thai border and later found refuge in the U.S., becoming one of the few entertainers who survived the Khmer Rouge. For many years, he lived in Northern California, where he wrote songs for the Cambodian community and helped found Wat Dhammararam, the Stockton Cambodian Buddhist Temple. He passed away in April 1997 in Phnom Penh.

CHRISTOPHE MACQUET is a writer, translator, and photographer. From 1994 to 2004, he was a professor and coordinator of a literary translation program at the Department of French Language of the Royal University of Phnom Penh. Among his many translations from Khmer to French are *Génial et Génital,* short stories by Soth Polin (2017); and *L'Accusé* by Khun Srun (2018). His translations from French to Khmer include *Le Petit Prince* by Antoine de Saint-Exupéry (2002) and *Un barrage contre le Pacifique* by Marguerite Duras (2021). His photographic work includes *L'Oiseau: récit physique* (The Bird: A Physical Narrative, 2014). His latest book of poetry, *DÂH: Dans la nuit khmère* (DÂH: In the Khmer Night), is forthcoming from Éditions Lurlure in 2022.

MAI (M"iṇ M"ai) ម៉ុន ម៉ៃ was a Khmer poet and aristocrat who lived during the late eighteenth or early nineteenth century. He is best known for his version of "Code for Girls" *(cpāp' srī)* and "Code for Boys" *(cpāp' prus).*

About the Contributors

SHARON **MAY** researched the Khmer Rouge regime for Columbia University's Center for the Study of Human Rights, and guest-edited *In the Shadow of Angkor: Contemporary Writing from Cambodia* (*Mānoa*, 2004). Her photography has appeared in *Dancing in Site II: Life and Art in Cambodian Refugee Camps after the War* (2018) and is on permanent exhibit at the Peace Gallery in Battambang. Her fiction has appeared in *Best New American Voices, Chicago Tribune, Mānoa,* and elsewhere. She is the recipient of a Stegner Fellowship in Fiction from Stanford University.

PRINCESS **MOON** is a second-generation Cambodian American poet, teacher, and visual storyteller based in Boston. She was the first woman SlamMaster at the Mill City Slam and served as programs director of the youth organization FreeVerse! In 2018, she founded Let Me Write You a Poem, an online platform focusing on community healing through storytelling. Her book *The Genocide's Love Baby Learns to Sing* was published in 2016.

ROGER **NELSON** is an art historian specializing in Southeast Asian modern and contemporary art, and a curator at National Gallery Singapore. He is the cofounding coeditor of *Southeast of Now: Directions in Contemporary and Modern Art in Asia,* a journal published by the National University of Singapore Press, and has curated exhibitions internationally, including *And in the Chapel and in the Temples* (Singapore, 2018–2019). He is author of *Modern Art of Southeast Asia: Introductions from A to Z* (2019).

KROM **NGOY** ក្រមង៉ុយ was the popular name of the poet born Uk U អុក អ៊ូ, formally titled Anak Braḥ Bhiramy Bhāsā Ū អ្នកព្រះភិរម្យភាសា អ៊ូ (1865–1936). He was one of the most famous traveling bards of the late nineteenth and early twentieth centuries. Cambodia's "poet of the people," he composed poetry and sang while he played a one-string *khsae diev*. Educated as a Buddhist monk, he joined the royal court of King Sisowath (r. 1904–1927). After performing for the Siamese king, he was presented with the title of "Exceptionally Mellifluous" *(phairo luea koen)*.

SOKNEA **NHIM** ញ៉ឹម សុខនា is assistant project nanager for the nonprofit publishing organization Our Books in Cambodia. She served as editor, cotranslator, and assistant project manager for the Nou Hach Literary Association from 2012 to 2017.

NOU HACH នូ ហាច (1916-1975) was born to a farming family in Sangkae District, Battambang. After graduation, he worked as a judge in Siem Reap, and in 1947 for the *Kampuchea Newspaper*. That year he published his first and best-known work, *Phka Srapon* (Wilted Flower). His 1952 novel, *Mealea Duong Chet* (Garland of the Heart), was not published until 1972. In 1952, he served as director of political affairs at the Ministry of Foreign Affairs. Later, he was the Cambodian representative to Vietnam and Indonesia, and a special representative at the United Nations. He was killed by the Khmer Rouge.

PRUMSODUN **OK** ឱក ព្រហ្មសុដន្ត has been associate artistic director of Khmer Arts, a member of the Alliance for California Traditional Arts Board of Directors, and an artist-in-residence at the Baryshnikov Arts Center in New York. He is the founding artistic director of Prumsodun Ok & NATYARASA, Cambodia's first gay dance company, and was named an LGBT+ Creative Leader of Tomorrow by the Championing Diversity project of WeTransfer and The Dots. His 2019 TED Talk was viewed more than 2.5 million times. In 2021, he founded Sereiyos Productions in Phnom Penh to nurture a new generation of actors, musicians, and dancers.

RITHY **PANH** បាន់ រិទ្ធី is one of the most prolific and visionary filmmakers in the world today. A Khmer Rouge survivor who later graduated from the Institut des hautes études cinématographiques in Paris, he has a large body of films, both documentary and creative, that offer an astounding range of historical and artistic responses to the long shadow of Cambodia's darkest years. His 2013 film, *The Missing Picture,* won the Prix Un Certain Regard at the Cannes Film Festival and an Oscar nomination for best international film. He also co-founded Bophana Center in Phnom Penh, dedicated to preserving Cambodia's audiovisual history. The center's namesake is the subject of one of his early docudramas, *Bophana: A Cambodian Tragedy,* the script for which appeared in translation in *In the Shadows of Angkor* (*Mānoa,* 2004).

PICH TUM KRAVEL ពេជ្រ ទុំក្រវិល (born Chhorn Tort ឈន ទត) (1943–2015) was an actor, writer, and director of the dance department at the Royal University of Fine Arts. He published more than twenty books and essays on Cambodian culture and art. In the 1960s, he became famous after appearing in popular movies, such as *Tum Teav.* After surviving the Khmer Rouge, he helped revive the performing arts in the 1980s with the support of the Ministry of Culture. In 2002, he was named National Hero for Cambodian Arts. His collected poems of three decades, *Songs of the Fighting Crickets,* was published in 2011.

PEN SAMITTHY ប៉ែន សមិទ្ធិ (1961–2015) was a journalist and poet. During the 1980s, he studied political science in Vietnam and journalism in the USSR. Returning to Cambodia in 1988, he became editor of the newspaper *Phnom Penh.* In 1993, he founded *Rasmei Kampuchea,* serving as editor-in-chief until his death. He was also president of the Club of Cambodian Journalists.

CHATH **PIERSATH** was born in Cambodia in 1970. His father was killed fighting the Vietcong, and pierSath was put into a work camp by the Khmer Rouge. After the regime's defeat, he returned with his family to his home village. In 1981, he emigrated to the U.S. and graduated from World College West. He volunteered for Human Rights Vigilance of Cambodia and other NGOs from 1994 to 1996. His collections of poetry are *On Earth Beneath Sky* (2020), *This Body Mystery: Paintings and Poems* (2012) and *After* (2009).

ALICE **PUNG** was born in Victoria, Australia, to parents who escaped the Khmer Rouge regime. Her first book, *Unpolished Gem,* won the Australian Book Industry Newcomer of the Year Award. Her second book, *Her Father's Daughter,* won the Western Australia Premier's Award for Non-Fiction. Her third book, *Laurinda,* was shortlisted as Sydney Morning Herald's Young Novelist of the Year. She edited the anthology *Growing Up Asian in Australia* and is the artist-in-residence at the University of Melbourne.

BRAH **RĀJASAMBHĀR** ព្រះរាជសម្ភារ (c. 1602–1631), also known as King Dhammarājā II, reigned for a brief period in the early seventeenth century—some chronicles suggest from 1628 until his death. Described in historical records as a former monk and learned scholar of Buddhism, he was also the author of a number of romantic and didactic poems.

VADDEY **RATNER**, a Khmer Rouge survivor, is the critically acclaimed, *New York Times* bestselling author of *In the Shadow of the Banyan* and *Music of the Ghosts*. Her works have been translated into twenty languages.

PUTSATA **REANG** was born in Cambodia and raised in Oregon. As an author and journalist she has lived and worked in more than a dozen countries, including Cambodia, Afghanistan, and Thailand. In 2005, she received an Alicia Patterson Journalism Fellowship, enabling her to report on landless farmers in Cambodia. She received a 2018 GAP Award to support the writing of her memoir, *Ma and Me* (2022), about growing up gay in a refugee family in rural Oregon. Her work has appeared in the *New York Times, The Guardian,* and elsewhere. She teaches writing at the University of Washington's School of Professional & Continuing Education.

SONGSAENG **RUNGRUEANGCHAI** ส่องแสง รุ่งเรืองชัย is a Northern Khmer Kantreum singer, songwriter, and actor. He was born in 1968 in Surin, Thailand, into a family of traditional musicians. After leaving the military at twenty-three, he joined Ta Yuay's Kantreum Band and was known by his fans as Saengchai. After the band's leader died, he formed his own band and changed his name to Songsaeng Rungrueangchai, a name given to him by the revered monk Luangpu Hong. He has recorded more than twelve studio albums.

GREG **SANTOS** published his latest book of poetry, *Ghost Face,* in 2020. His previous books include *Blackbirds* (2018), *Rabbit Punch!* (2014), and *The Emperor's Sofa* (2010). He is editor-in-chief of the Quebec Writers' Federation's online literary magazine, *carte blanche,* works with at-risk communities, and teaches at the Thomas More Institute. He is an adoptee of Cambodian, Portuguese, and Spanish heritage, and lives in Tiohtià:ke/Montréal.

TOLA **SAY** សាយ តុលា wrote about the Cambodian arts scene for the *Khmer Times* (2017–2019) and for many years has helped organize the Khmer Literature Festival. She was a translator and researcher for the Bophana Audiovisual Resource Center. She has worked on several projects documenting Cambodia's artistic heritage, including *Sonic Cambodia* (2018–2020), *Her Sounds* (2019), *Cambodian Jew's Harp Documentation* (2020), and *Dey Krahom* (Red Earth, 2021). She is currently a research coordinator at Cambodian Living Arts.

SIM **CHANYA** ស៊ឹម ចាន់ញ៉ា was born in 1944 in Battambang. She studied in Phnom Penh, then worked as literature teacher and radio announcer. She was a member of the literary circle that included Khun Srun. Under Pol Pot she was deported to Takeo. After 1979, she worked as the director of the Adult Education Department for the Ministry of Education (1979–1992), taught French (1992–2001), and worked for the Khmer Women's Voice Center of Cambodia (1992–2010). She has published several books of poems, short stories, and novellas.

SINN SISAMOUTH ស៊ិន ស៊ីសាមុត (1933–1976) was born in Stung Treng to a family of Khmer, Lao, and Chinese heritage. At a young age, he moved to Battambang, where he learned traditional Khmer music on instruments like the *tro khmae* (a three-string fiddle) and the *chapei* (a lute). In Phnom Penh, he acquired a large audience for his music when he began performing live on National Radio. From the 1950s to the 1970s, he was part of a thriving pop music scene in Phnom Penh, blending traditional music with blues, rock 'n' roll, jazz, French *yé-yé*, and Latin American rhythms. Appearing in dapper suits, he became an idol, often referred to as the "King of Khmer music." He is believed to have been killed by the Khmer Rouge.

PRINCE AMRINDO SISOWATH (1956–1999) was the son of Prince Methavi Sisowath and Princess Anne-Marie Izzi. A precocious child, he studied mostly in France. Between 1975 and 1981, he was part of the Denis-Martin group of Parisian writers and artists that met regularly in the café Le Denis-Martin. In 1978, he learned that his parents had been murdered by the Khmer Rouge. He wrote poetry in French but destroyed all his work. Only a few poems survived in the typewritten journals produced at Sainte-Anne's Hospital, in Paris—one of the first hospitals in France to offer art therapy to its psychiatric patients—where he was a resident for part of his life. He was editor-in-chief of the asylum's journal, *Trait d'Union*.

PHINA SO ស៊ូ កិណា co-founded Kampu Mera Editions in 2015, an independent press that publishes contemporary short stories, anthologies, novels, and translations. In 2016, she cofounded Slap Paka Khmer, an informal writers' collective in Phnom Penh, and in 2017 she founded the Khmer Literature Festival. Her writing has been published locally and internationally in translation. She is the knowledge, network, and policy program manager at Cambodian Living Arts.

SOK CHANPHAL សុខ ចាន់ផល was born in Kampong Cham in 1984. He is a fiction writer, filmmaker, and lyricist. In 2013, he won the S.E.A. Write Award, the region's most prestigious literary prize. As a lyricist, he has written over one hundred songs, many of them for the best-known pop singers. He is also a director at Antriy Film.

BRAḤ PADUMATTHER SOM ព្រះបទុមត្ថេរ សោម (1852–1932) was born in Kandal. He was ordained as a Buddhist monk *(bhikkhu)* at age twenty-one and remained in robes throughout his life. He composed new or revised versions of several classic works of Khmer literature, including *Tum Teav* (Duṃ Dāv) and *Sabbasiddhi*.

BORA SOTH is a Cambodian American actor who has starred in such films as *The Wife Master* (2012), *The Strange* (2010), and *Bora S.: Private Eye Candy* (2008).

NORITH SOTH was born in Cambodia and raised in Paris and Orange County, California. He is a screenwriter, producer, and editor whose works include *Nicodemus* (2012), *Face* (2012), and *Husky* (2012).

SOTH POLIN សុទ្ធ ប៉ូលីន was born in 1943 in Kampong Cham to an intellectual middle-class family that spoke French and Khmer. He is the great-grandson of the poet Nou Kan. In his youth, he read Cambodian classical literature as well as Western literature and philosophy. His first novel, *Chivit Et Nei* (A Meaningless Life), was strongly influenced by Nietzsche, Freud, and Sartre, as well as by Buddhism. His subsequent novels, short stories, and philosophical tales include *Borah Apsok* (A Bored Man), *Ksai Tae Mdang Te* (We Die Only Once), and *Moranak Knong Duong Chet* (Dead Heart). In the late 1960s, he founded the newspaper and publishing house Nokor Thom (The Great Kingdom), publishing many authors and translators who perished during the Khmer Rouge regime. In 1974, he left Cambodia and took refuge in Paris. He worked as a taxi driver, published a French-Khmer dictionary, and published, in French, his dark novel *L'Anarchiste* (The Anarchist). He later moved to the U.S. with his two sons.

BRAḤ SUGANDH ព្រះសុគន្ធ was the title of a high-ranking Khmer monk of the sixteenth or seventeenth century. Some manuscripts, including "Code of Old Sayings," are attributed to him. A number of Cambodian authors throughout history were known by the same title.

SUON SORIN សួន សុរិន្ទ was born in 1930 in Sangkae district, Battambang. He published *Preah Atoet Thmey Reah Loe Phaen Dey Chah* (A New Sun Rises Over the Old Land) in 1961. It is his only known work of fiction. He is believed to have died during the Khmer Rouge period.

SUY HIENG ស៊ុយ ហៀង (1929–2009) (full name: Ung Tri Suy Hieng អ៊ីងទ្រី ស៊ុយ ហៀង) studied at the Catholic school in Phnom Penh and graduated from the French Lycée, which was rare for women then. In her twenties she owned one of the first and largest Cambodian bookstores and publishing houses, Khemara Pannakea. In 1952, she published the first of three novellas, *Veasna Nei Neang Nakry* (Destiny of Miss Nakry); they were followed by *Stung Kraham* (The Red River) and *Strey Bang P'on Phluoh Pi Neak* (Two Twin Sisters). In 1956, she was the only woman among the ten founding members of the Khmer Writers Association. In 1964, she wrote the novel *Chantrea: Khmer Territory* and in 1971 *Beh Doung Sitha* (Sitha's Heart).

SOKUNTHARY SVAY was born in a refugee camp in Thailand after her parents fled Cambodia, and grew up in the Bronx, where her family resettled. She is a founding member of the Cambodian American Literary Arts Association (CALAA), and has received fellowships from the American Opera Project and other organizations, as well as commissions from the Washington National Opera. Her first book, *Apsara in New York*, was published in 2017. Her first opera, *Woman of Letters*, had its world premiere at the Kennedy Center in January 2020. Her second opera, *Chhlong Tonle* (Crossing the River, or Giving Birth), premieres in March 2022.

RINITH TAING តាំង រីនិត្យ is an award-winning Cambodian journalist and translator. He began his journalism career at the *Phnom Penh Post*, reporting on various topics in Cambodia and other Southeast Asian countries. He has received the Ulrich Wickert International Journalism Award for Children's Rights and multiple nominations for SOPA / WAN-IFRA Excellence in Feature Writing. He is a deputy editor at the *Khmer Times*.

KHUN THEPKRAWI ขุนเทพกระวี (Khmer ឃុនទេពពករី) was the title of a court poet from the northern Siamese kingdom of Sukhothai. Like many other Siamese elites of the thirteenth to fifteenth centuries, he was highly skilled in Khmer.

MADELEINE THIEN was born in Vancouver. She is the author of the story collection *Simple Recipes* (2001) and three novels, *Certainty* (2006); *Dogs at the Perimeter* (2011), winner of the Frankfurt Book Fair's 2015 Literaturpreis; and *Do Not Say We Have Nothing* (2016). Her books and stories have been published internationally and translated into twenty-five languages. Her awards include the Amazon First Novel Award, a Canadian Authors Association Award, and the Ovid Festival Prize. She teaches at the City University of Hong Kong.

TIAN VEASNA ចិន្ត វាសនា was born in Cambodia in 1975, three days after the Khmer Rouge came to power. He moved to France with his parents in 1980 and graduated from Strasbourg's École des Arts Décoratifs in 2001. He then returned to Cambodia, teaching drawing as part of a United Nations humanitarian project. His desire to recount what his family lived through led him to produce a three-volume graphic novel about the Khmer Rouge period, published in France as *L'Année du Lièvre* (2011–2016) and translated into Khmer and published in Cambodia by Sipar. The English translation was published in Canada in one volume as *Year of the Rabbit* (Drawn & Quarterly Books, 2020). He lives in France.

BUNKONG TUON was born in Cambodia. As a child, he spent several years with his extended family in refugee camps on the Thai–Cambodian border before immigrating to the U.S. in 1982. He received his Ph.D. from the University of Massachusetts in 2008. His books include *Gruel* (2015), *And So I Was Blessed* (2017), *The Doctor Will Fix It* (2019), and *Dead Tongue* (2020). He is the director of Asian studies at Union College, in Schenectady, New York.

TY CHI HUOT ទី ជីហួត (1952–1987) was born in Takeo. The eldest son of a poor family, he worked from a very young age as a hairdresser, waiter, and bread-and-dumpling seller to continue his schooling. Under the Khmer Rouge, he was deported to Battambang to make fertilizer. After 1979, he worked at the National Radio of Cambodia. Known for his novels and his scripts for traditional theater, he is one of the most celebrated authors of the 1980s. His works include *Veul Rok Tronum* (Back to the Nest, 1984) and *Mekh Bat Duong Chan* (Sky of the Lost Moon, 1985). He passed away at the age of thirty-five.

KALEAN UNG is a Cambodian American actress, singer, and interdisciplinary artist in Los Angeles. She received her MFA in acting from California Institute of the Arts and is now on the faculty of CalArts. Her solo play, *Letters From Home,* was developed through residencies at UC San Diego, Independent Shakespeare Company, CalArts, and elsewhere. As a companion event to the play, she co-curated an exhibit at the Southeast Asian Archival Library.

TRENT WALKER is a postdoctoral fellow of the Ho Center for Buddhist Studies at Stanford University and a specialist in the manuscripts and chanting practices of mainland Southeast Asia. He has published numerous articles, book chapters, and translations on the religious, musical, and literary histories of Cambodia, Laos, Thailand, and Vietnam. His book *Until Nirvana's Time: Buddhist Songs from Cambodia* is forthcoming from Shambhala Publications in 2022.

TERI SHAFFER **YAMADA** is professor emerita at California State University, Long Beach, where she taught Asian and Asian American Studies. She cofounded the Nou Hach Literary Association in Phnom Penh in 2002 and edited several books on Southeast Asian literature, including *Virtual Lotus: Modern Fiction of Southeast Asia* (2002) and *Modern Short Fiction of Southeast Asia: A Literary History* (2009).

YIN LUOTH យិន លួត was born in Oddar Meanchey (then in Siem Reap province) in 1951. He left Cambodia in 1975 and worked in Seattle for the Asian Counseling and Referral Service. He later cofounded the Nou Hach Literary Association in Phnom Penh. His books include volumes of poetry and three novellas, *Popok Rosat* (As the Clouds Drift), *Phlieng Roleum* (Light Rain), and *Moradak Duong Chet* (The Heart's Legacy). He teaches Khmer at the University of Washington, Seattle.

PRINCE ARENO **YUKANTHOR** (H.R.H. Prince Norodom Yukanthor Vachiravong ព្រះអង្គម្ចាស់ នរោត្តម យុគន្ធរ វជិរាវង្ស [1896–1975]) was the son of the rebel Prince Yukanthor, famous for having denounced the French colonial administration in Cambodia. At twenty-three, he joined the École des Arts Décoratifs of Paris and began a career as a painter and writer. In 1923, he published a collection of poems, *Angkorean Cantata* (under the name of Areno Iukanthor). He produced strange, hallucinatory texts and paintings before returning to Cambodia in 1938 and sinking into madness. He was executed by the Khmer Rouge in 1975.

Acknowledgements

It took a literal world of help to bring this volume of Cambodian literature into being. So many people have assisted in the creation of this book that it is impossible to list them all. We have tried to acknowledge as many as we can here, and we apologize for any inadvertent omissions. To each of you, named and unnamed, our deepest thanks.

Many of the writers and translators published in these pages have contributed to this book in ways far beyond their excellent literary pieces—our thanks to every one of you. For all of those we wished we could have published and could not—for reasons of permissions, time, space, or otherwise—we apologize and regret your absence from these pages. We very much appreciate your work and look forward to your publications to come, as well as more translations of those who are living and those who have passed on.

We also thank an army of booksellers, librarians, tuk-tuk and moto-dup drivers, café staff, students and book lovers, as well as friends, colleagues, and family who supported us through this monumental project. For all those whom we have failed to mention here—who have helped through the decades of creating this book—our enduring gratitude.

On behalf of *Mānoa*, its editors, and all of our guest editors, we thank the following organizations and individuals (surnames in bold):

Association des Ecrivains Khmers a l'Etranger (AEKE)
Bophana Center
Bright Lotus
Cambodian American Literary Arts Association
Cambodian Living Arts
Center for Khmer Studies
Consequence Magazine
Cornell University
Documentation Center of Cambodia (DC-CAM)
Éditions du Sonneur
Éditions Le Grand Os
Revue Europe
Revue Jentayu
Khmer Writers Association
Kampong Cham Theater Company
Kampu Mera Editions
The National Library of Cambodia
The National Museum of Cambodia and its Café and Museum Stage
Nou Hach Literary Association
PEN Cambodia
Stanford University and the Ho Center for Buddhist Studies
The Stilt House Zine
Words without Borders

Ang Choulean
Michel Antelme
Aurélia Aurita
Mohan Bandam
Pichchenda Bao
Be Puch
Eric Becker
Jérôme Bouchaud
Henry Hayden Brooks
Thibodi Buakamsri
David Chandler
Chea Chheng
Youk Chhang
Chheat Sopheak
Kunthea Chhom
Chhorn Samarth
George Chigas
Chin Meas
Chuth Khay
Bernard Cohen
Olivier de Bernon
Theresa de Langis
Aurélio Diaz-Ronda
Randal Douc
Aisha Down
Éric Galmard
Pierre Gillette
Colin Grafton
Dominic Goodall
Chenxing Han
Sobotra (Hang Khmao)
Hang Soth
Susan Harris
Paul Harrison
Melissa Hem
Hem Sivon
Heng Oudom
Vivien Heng
Linda Hess
Hiep Chanvicheth
Huot Ketmony
Huot Socheata
Im Lim
Im Rachna
Phouséra Ing (Séra)

Helen Jarvis
Anna Wolcott Johnson
Kang Chanthirith
Khav Thorn Nhot
Siti Keo
Khieu Sunran
Khing Hoc Dy
Tararith Kho
Khun Khem
Khun Ngeth
Kim Pechpinon
Klairung Amratisha
Koet Ran
Kong Boran
Kroeun Yuen
Ky Soklim
D. Christian Lammerts
Lang Piseth
Lek Chumnor
Leng Kok-An
Kevin Li
Irene Lin
Lon Jadina
praCh Ly
Ly Vonry
Tiffany Lytle
Ken McCullough
Pascal Médeville
Grégory Mikaelian
Valérie Millet
Nikko Odiseos
Laura Jean Mckay
Mak Suong
John Marston
Mao Samnang
Mau Vinna
Mey Son Sotheary
Bruno Montpied
May Ngo
Danny Thanh Nguyen
Nguyễn-Hoàng Quyên
Amira Noeuv
Nol Dara
Ny Monineath
Tomoko Okada

Ouch Savy
Oum Suphany
Santi **Pakdeekham**
Pal Vannariraks
Jean-Baptiste **Para**
Kevin **Park**
Pech Sangwawan
Meas **Pech-Métral**
Penn Setharin
Bopha **Phorn**
Jean-Baptiste **Phou**
Proeung Chhieng
Bertrand **Porte**
Prum Manh
Mengly J. **Quach**
Matthew **Reeder**
Roeun Sarum
Indradévi **Roman**
Santel Phin
Seng Sophea
Seng Sovanndara
Sin Setsochhata
Nalin **Sindhuprama**
Prince Thomico **Sisowath**
Peter **Skilling**
Tossaphon **Sripum**
Angela **So**
Monica **Sok**
Sok Limsrorn
Soleak **Sok**
Sopheak Mara
Sor Sokny
Sou Khemarin
Channbunmorl **Sou**
Khull **Sovanrith**
Soy Sina
Christine **Su**
Sun Sokunmealea
Muyhorth **Taing**
Tat Kimlorn
Tatt Chhen
Ashley **Thompson**
Trans Sab
Peuo **Tuy**
U Sam Oeur

Ung Bun Heang
Kaliane **Ung**
Vandy Kaonn
Vandy Rattana
Voan Savay
Alexander **von Rospatt**
Vong Mayoura
Vong Socheata
Voy Ho
Gail **Walker**
Robert **Walker**
Yan Borin
Yeng Chheangly
Yim Guechsè
Cheryl **Yin**

In thanks and loving memory
༶࿐

Alain **Daniel**
Em Satya (Nono)
Heng Achariya
Keng Vannsak
Nicolas **Ker**
Kun Sopheap
Kimarlee **Nguyen**
Phou Chakriya
Prach Chhuon
Saveros **Pou**
Prum Ut
Anthony Veasna **So**
Michael **Vickery**
You Bo

យថា វារិវហា បូរា បរិបូរន្តិ សាគរំ
ឯវមេវ ឥតោ ទិន្នំ បេតានំ ឧបកប្បតិ

Just as mighty rivers swell the ocean full,
may these pages lift up all those
who've crossed beyond.

សូមអរព្រះគុណ និង អរគុណជាអនេក

With limitless thanks and gratitude

Sources

Warning to Thieves (K. 426)
George Cœdès. *Inscriptions du Cambodge*. 8 vols. Paris: École française d'Extrême-Orient, 1937–1966, vol. II, pp. 121–122.
Ang Choulean អាំង ជូលាន. *Mūlaṭṭhān rien khmaer purāṇ* មូលដ្ឋានរៀនខ្មែរបុរាណ. Phnom Penh: Yosothor យសោធរ, 2013, pp. 241–247.

In Praise of Sister Queens (K. 485)
Cœdès, George. *Inscriptions du Cambodge*. 8 vols. Paris: École française d'Extrême-Orient, 1937–1966, vol. II, pp. 161–181.
Parts of the translation appeared in slightly different form in *Words without Borders* (November 2015) https://www.wordswithoutborders.org/article/from-the-great-stele-of-phimeanakas

Hymn to the Tree of Awakening (K. 484)
George Cœdès. "Une nouvelle inscription du Phimanakas." *Bulletin de l'École française d'Extrême-Orient* 18 (1918): pp. 9–12.
Saveros Lewitz. "III. L'inscription de Phimeanakas (K. 484). Étude linguistique." *Bulletin de l'École française d'Extrême-Orient* 58 (1971): pp. 91–103.
Kunthea Chhom. "Le rôle du sanskrit dans le développement de la langue khmère: Une étude épigraphique du VIe au XIVe siècle." Ph.D. diss., École Pratique des Hautes Études, 2016, pp. 332–340.

Hymn for the Elephants' Feast (Thai: *Dutsadi sangwoei* ดุษฎีสังเวย; Khmer: *Slutī saṅvoy* ស្តុតីសង្វោយ)
Bark-paper manuscript at National Library of Cambodia, FEMC d.934, pp. 5–11.
Buntuean Siworaphot บุญเตือน ศรีวรพจน์. *Kham chan dutsadi sangwoei kham chan klom chang khrang krung kao lae kham chan khotchakam prayun* คำฉันท์ดุษฎีสังเวย คำฉันท์ที่กล่อมช้าง ครั้งกรุงเก่า และ คำฉันท์คชกรรมประยูร. Bangkok: Fine Arts Department กรมศิลปากร, 2545 [2002], pp. 55–57.
Santi Pakdeekham ศานติ ภักดีคำ. "'Dutsadi sangwoei klom chang' khong Khun Thepkrawi: mum mong phasa lae wannakhadi khmen 'ดุษฎีสังเวยกล่อมช้าง' ของขุนเทพกวี: มุมมองภาษาและวรรณคดีเขมร." *Damrong: Journal of the Faculty of Archaeology* ดำรงวิชาการ 3.5 (2547 [2004]): pp. 111–127.

Reamker (*Rāmakerti I* រាមកេរ្តិ៍ ១, i.e. រាមកេរ្តិ៍ ខ្សែ ១ - ៩០)
Buddhist Institute ពុទ្ធសាសនបណ្ឌិត្យ. *Rīöṅ rāmakerti* រឿងរាមកេរ្តិ៍. 10 vols. Phnom Penh: Buddhist Institute ពុទ្ធសាសនបណ្ឌិត្យ, 1959, vol. 1, pp. 1–17.

Saveros Pou. *Rāmakerti (XVIe–XVIIe siècles)*. Paris: École française d'Extrême-Orient, 1979, pp. 1–11.

Code of Old Sayings (*Cpāp' bāky cās'* ច្បាប់ពាក្យចាស់)
Buddhist Institute ពុទ្ធសាសនបណ្ឌិត្យ. *Cpāp' phseṅ phseṅ* ច្បាប់ផ្សេងៗ. Phnom Penh: Buddhist Institute ពុទ្ធសាសនបណ្ឌិត្យ, 1974, pp. 63–66.
Saveros Pou. *Guirlande de cpāp'*. 2 vols. Paris: Cedoreck, 1988, vol. I, pp. 25–27.

My Soul of Gold (*Braliṅ mās öy*) ព្រលឹងមាសអើយ
Bark-paper manuscript, British Library, Or 5865, pp. 2–8 (complete).
Lāṅ Hāp'-Ān លាង ហាប់អាន. *Braḥ Rājasambhār kavirāj satavats* dī 17 ព្រះរាជសម្ភារ កវីរាជសតវត្សទី១៧. Phnom Penh: Srī Puṇṭan ស្រី ប៊ុនដន, 2005 [originally published 1964], pp. 51–59 (incomplete).

Victory in the Eight Directions (*Jăy dis* ជ័យទិស)
Nuon Samān នួន សំអាន. *Gihippatipatti gharāvāsadharm* គិហិប្បដិបត្តិ យរាវាសធម៌. Phnom Penh: Roṅ bumb bhnaṃ beñ រោងពុម្ពភ្នំពេញ, 2547 [2004], pp. 82–83.
Trent Walker. "Unfolding Buddhism: Communal Scripts, Localized Translations, and the Work of the Dying in Cambodian Chanted Leporellos," Ph.D. diss., University of California, Berkeley, 2018, pp. 1336–1338.

Goddesses of the Land (*Praṇidhān* ប្រណិធាន, i.e. *Satrā prāṃmadhdhān sābhauv 1* សត្រាប្រាំមធ្ធាន សាភៅវ ១)
Grégory Mikaelian. "Recherches sur l'histoire du fonctionnement politique des royautés post-angkoriennes (c. 1600–c. 1720), appuyées sur l'analyse d'un corpus de décrets royaux khmers du XVIIe siècle." Ph.D. diss., Université de Paris-IV - Sorbonne, 2006, vol. II, pp. 152–158.

A Selection of Wedding Songs

—Ancestral Offerings (*Nimun banhchoh kraya* និមន្តបញ្ចុះក្រយា)
Cambodian Living Arts. *Offerings to the Ancestors: Traditional Khmer Songs for Weddings* ដង្វាយថ្វាយមេបា ៖ កម្រងធម៌បទភ្លេងការបុរាណ. Audio CD and liner notes. Phnom Penh: Cambodian Living Arts, 2013: Track 10, performed by the Yun Khean Theara Ensemble.

—In Bloom (*Sampong* សំពោង)
Saveros Lewitz et al. "Kpuon Ābāh-bibāh ou Le livre de mariage des khmers." *Bulletin de l'École française d'Extrême-Orient* 60 (1973), p. 306.

—Windswept Pond (*Trapeang peay* ត្រពាំងពាយ)
Hun Sarin ហ៊ុន សារិន. *Vaṅ' bhleṅ khmaer* វង់ភ្លេងខ្មែរ. Phnom Penh: Ministry of Culture and Fine Arts ក្រសួងវប្បធម៌ និង វិចិត្រសិល្បៈ, 2004, p. 102.

—Rowing the Boat (*Om tuk* អំទូក)
Cambodian Living Arts. *Offerings to the Ancestors: Traditional Khmer Songs for Weddings* ដង្វាយថ្វាយមេបា ៖ កម្រងធម៌បទភ្លេងការបុរាណ. Audio CD and liner notes. Phnom Penh: Cambodian Living Arts, 2013: Track 11, performed by the Yun Khean Theara Ensemble.

The Point of the Cape (*Phot chong chroy* ផុតចុងជ្រោយ)
Albert Tricon and Charles Bellan. *Chansons cambodgiennes*. Saigon: Société des études indochinoises / Imprimerie nouvelle Albert Portail, 1921, pp. 83–84.

Yun Khian et al. *Cambodian Forgotten Songs* កំណប់គន្ធីដូនតា. Audio CD and liner notes. Phnom Penh: Bophana Audiovisual Resource Center, 2009, Track 2.

from *Until Nirvana's Time*
Translations: Trent Walker. *Until Nirvana's Time: Buddhist Songs from Cambodia.* Boulder: Shambhala Publications, 2022.
Originals: Trent Walker. "Unfolding Buddhism: Communal Scripts, Localized Translations, and the Work of the Dying in Cambodian Chanted Leporellos," Ph.D. diss., University of California, Berkeley, 2018.

—**The Thirty-Three Consonants** (*Akkhara: 33* អក្ខរៈ ៣៣), pp. 1295–1302.
—**This Life Is Short** (*Braḥ trai lakkhaṇ* ព្រះត្រៃលក្ខណ៍), pp. 1409–1411.
—**Hymn to the Buddha's Feet** (*Sarasör braḥ pād* សរសើរព្រះបាទ), pp. 1245–1254.

Thunder and the Crabs (*Lpök ktām phgar* ល្បើកក្តាមផ្ងរ, i.e. *Satrā ktām* សត្រាក្តាម)
Saveros Pou. *Guirlande de cpāp'*. 2 vols. Paris: Cedoreck, 1988, vol. I, pp. 55–62.

Code for Girls (*Cpāp' srī* ច្បាប់ស្រី)
Buddhist Institute ពុទ្ធសាសនបណ្ឌិត្យ. *Cpāp' phseń pheń* ច្បាប់ផ្សេងៗ. Phnom Penh: Buddhist Institute ពុទ្ធសាសនបណ្ឌិត្យ, 1974, pp. 20–32.
Saveros Pou. *Guirlande de cpāp'*. 2 vols. Paris: Cedoreck, 1988, vol. I, pp. 99–116.

from *Kaki* (*Kākī* កាកី)
Buddhist Institute ពុទ្ធសាសនបណ្ឌិត្យ. *Rīöṅ kākī* រឿងកាកី. Phnom Penh: Buddhist Institute ពុទ្ធសាសនបណ្ឌិត្យ, 1969, pp. 3–18.

A Garland of New Advice (*Cpāp' lpök thmī* ច្បាប់ល្បើកថ្មី)
Anak Braḥ Bhiram Bhāsā Ū hau N"uy អ្នកព្រះភិរម្យភាសា អ៊ូ ហៅ ង៉ុយ. *Paṇtāṃ kram n"uy* បណ្តាំក្រមង៉ុយ. Phnom Penh: Buddhist Institute ពុទ្ធសាសនបណ្ឌិត្យ, 1998, pp. 1–2, 5–6.

A Cycle of Alev Stories
Erik W. Davis, Sor Sokny, Tan Bunly, Chor Chanthyda, Hel Rithy, Sok Ra, Phat Chantamonyratha, Hun Chantasocheata, and Som Vanna, eds. "Roeung Alev រឿងអាឡេវ (The Story of Alev)." In *Tossanavaddey Roeung Preng Khmae Thmey* ទស្សនាវដ្តីរឿងព្រេងខ្មែរថ្មី (The Magazine of New Khmer Folktales: Tricksters). Phnom Penh: Buddhist Institute ពុទ្ធសាសនបណ្ឌិត្យ, 2006, vol. 3, pp. 85–92.

from *Journey to Angkor Wat* (*Nirās nagar vatt* និរាសនគរវត្ត)
Ukñ"ā Suttantaprījā Ind ឧកញ៉ាសុត្តន្តប្រីជា ឥន្ទ. *Nirās nagar vatt* និរាសនគរវត្ត. Phnom Penh: Buddhist Institute ពុទ្ធសាសនបណ្ឌិត្យ, 1969, pp. 1–15, 61–66.
Parts of the translation appeared in slightly different form in *Words without Borders* (November 2015) https://www.wordswithoutborders.org/article/journey-to-angkor-wat

from *Tum Teav* (*Duṃ dāv* ទុំទាវ)
Braḥ Padumatther Som ព្រះបទុមត្ថេរ សោម. *Rīöṅ duṃ dāv* រឿងទុំទាវ. Phnom Penh: Buddhist Institute ពុទ្ធសាសនបណ្ឌិត្យ, 1971, pp. 5–8.

from *On the Threshold of the Khmer Narthex: Nonsense about the Conflict between East and West*
Areno Iukanthor. *Au seuil du Narthex Khmèr: Boniments sur les conflits de 2 points cardinaux*. Paris: Aux Éditions d'Asie, 1931, pp. 332–340.
Grégory Mikaelian. "La bohème parisienne d'Areno Iukanthor (1919–1938). Du Prince de l'imitation à l'initiation du Prince." Bulletin de l'AEFEK 24 (December 2021), pp. 1–36.

The Orphans (*Kmeng kmeng kamprea* ក្មេងៗ កំព្រា, 1964)
Ung Tri Suy Heang អឹងទ្រី ស៊ុយ ហៀង. *Chantrea dey khmae* ចន្ទ្រា ដីខ្មែ. Phnom Penh ស្រី ប៊ុនដន: Srey Bundon, 2003), p. *cha* ឆ.

A Small Request (*Koun bandam muoy* កូនបណ្តាំមួយ, 1969)
Khun Srun ឃុន ស្រ៊ុន. *Kumhoenh ti muoy* គំហើញ ទី 1. Phnom Penh: 1970, p. 34.
Khun Srun ឃុន ស្រ៊ុន. *Samrah chivit* សំរស់ជីវិត. Phnom Penh: 1971, pp. 63–64.

A Hundred Scents, A Hundred Seasons (*Muoy roy klen muoy roy rodouv* មួយរយក្លិន មួយរយរដូវ, Paris, 1980)
Originally published in the online literary journal of the Association des écrivains khmers à l'étranger, edited by Pech Sangwawan, January 2015.

Chey Chap, Two Poems
Chey Chap ជ័យ ចាប. *Ao phtei srok khmae!* ឱផ្ទៃស្រុកខ្មែរ!. Phnom Penh: 1994.
—**Don't Fight the Wind** (*Kom chul neung khyal* កុំជល់នឹងខ្យល់, 1986), p. 7.
—**A Bunch of Coconuts** (*Thleay doung* ផ្លាយដូង, 1985), p. 6.

A Cry (*Un cri*)
Éditions Jentayu, revue littéraire d'Asie (N° COVID-19: En ces temps incertains), pp. 103–104.
Trait d'Union 40, 1987, pp. 53–54.
http://editions-jentayu.fr/numero-covid-19/amrindo-sisowath-un-cri/

Bound to His Father (*Smang euv chang koun* ស្មងឪចងកូន)
Originally published in the *Rasmei Kampuchea* រស្មីកម្ពុជា newspaper, early 1990s.

What Would You Like to Eat? (*Oun chang nham ey?* អូនចង់ញ៉ាំអី?, 1993)
Originally published online at https://pechsangwawann.wordpress.com/

The Race of the Quick (*Puch neak chhap* ពូជអ្នកឆាប់)
Kong Bunchhoeun គង្គ ប៊ុនឈឿន. *Bandam kavey* បណ្តាំកវី. Phnom Penh: 1994, pp. 47–49.

The Fate of Bloodsuckers (*Veasna neak chunhchuok chheam* វាសនាអ្នកជញ្ជក់ឈាម)
Yin Luoth យិន លួត. *Chivit lokey* ជីវិតលោកិយ. Phnom Penh: The Sower's Association, 2008, pp. 16–17.

from *Songs of the Fighting Crickets*
Pich Tum Kravel ពេជ្រ ទុំក្រវិល. *Chamrieng changret daek* ចម្រៀងចង្រិតដែក. Phnom Penh: 2011.

—The Ox with the Broken Hoof (*Ko bak krachak* គោបាក់ក្រចក), p. 48.

—Man and Krasang (*Borah phlae krasang* បុរសផ្លែក្រសាំង), pp. 65–66.

—The Sun Turns Leprous (*Soriya kaoet khlung* សូរិយាកើតឃ្លង់), p. 27.

Chath pierSath, Two Poems
Chath pierSath. *This Body Mystery*. New York: Abingdon Square Publishing, 2012.

—**Exiting Interview**, p. 61.

—**My Brother Thay**, p. 41.

Bunkong Tuon, Four Poems

—**Moon in Khmer**
carte blanche 35 (Spring 2019), https://carte-blanche.org/articles/moon-in-khmer/

Bunkong Tuon. *Gruel*. New York: NYQ Books, 2015.

—**An Elegy for a Fellow Cambodian**, p. 38.

—**Living in the Hyphen**, p. 90.

—**Fishing for *Trey Platoo***, pp. 23–24.

Princess Moon, Two Poems
Princess Moon. *The Genocide's Love Baby Learns to Sing*. Lowell, MA: Bootstrap Press / FreeVerse! 2016.

—**blessing dance**, pp. 12–15.

—**dance, dance, dance**, pp. 26–27.

Kosal Khiev, Three Poems
Original to *Mānoa*.

Reincarnation
Sokunthary Svay. *Apsara in New York*. Detroit: Willow Books, 2017, p. 38.

Ma's Canh Chua Recipe: April–December 1975
https://www.palettepoetry.com/2021/02/18/mas-canh-chua-recipe-april-december-1975/
Originally appeared in *The Coachella Review* (Summer 2019).

Greg Santos, Three Poems
Greg Santos. *Ghost Face*. Montreal: DC Books, 2020.

—**Our Name**, p. 19.

—**Shall We Dance?**, pp. 58–59.

—**Dear Ghosts**, pp. 31–32.

from *Wilted Flower*
Nou Hach នូ ហាច. *Phka Srapon* ផ្កាស្រពោន. Phnom Penh: Rong Pum Reasmey រោងពុម្ពរស្មី, 1947, pp. 1–26.

from *A New Sun Rises Over the Old Land* (*Preah atoet thmey reah loe phaen dey chah* ព្រះអាទិត្យថ្មីរះលើផែនដីចាស់)

English translation: Suon Sorin, translated by Roger Nelson. *A New Sun Rises Over the Old Land: A Novel of Sihanouk's Cambodia*. Singapore: National University of Singapore Press, 2020, pp. 14–27.

An Introduction to *The Accused*
Christophe Macquet, "Préface," in Khun Srun, translated by Christophe Macquet, *L'Accusé*. Paris: Les Éditions du Sonneur, 2018, pp. 7–20.

from *The Accused*
French-English translation by Madeleine Thien. Brick: A Literary Journal 97 (Summer 2016): https://brickmag.com/fragments-from-the-accused/
Khmer-French translation by Christophe Macquet. *L'Accusé*. Paris: Les Éditions du Sonneur, 2018.
Khmer original: Khun Srun ឃុន ស្រ៊ុន. *Chun choap chaot* ជនជាប់ចោទ. Phnom Penh: Pannakear Saravong បណ្ណាគារសារវង្ស, 1973.

Command Me to Exist
French translation: "Ordonne-moi d'exister" in Soth Polin, translated by Christophe Macquet, *Génial et génital*. Toulouse: Éditions Le Grand Os, 2017, pp. 53–66.
Khmer original: Soth Polin សុទ្ធ ប៉ូលីន, "Bangkoap mok bang choh oun!… បង្គាប់មកបងចុះអូន!…" in *Aoy bang thvoe avey.. bang thvoe dae!* ឱ្យបងធ្វើអ្វី…. បងធ្វើដែរ!. Phnom Penh: Nokor Thom នគរធំ, 1969, pp. 35–39.

from *The Anarchist*
Soth Polin. *L'Anarchiste*. Éditions de La Table Ronde, 1980, pp. 128–150.
Parts of the translation appeared in slightly different form in *Words without Borders* (November 2015) https://www.wordswithoutborders.org/article/the-anarchist

from *The Aroma of Desire in Fresno* (*Klen tanha nov Fresno* ក្លិនតណ្ហានៅប្រេស្នូ)
French-to-English translation by Bora Soth and Norith Soth, typed manuscript, 1995.
Author's translation of Khmer original in French, handwritten manuscript, now lost.
Khmer original: Soth Polin សុទ្ធ ប៉ូលីន. "*Klen tanha nov Fresno* ក្លិនតណ្ហានៅប្រេស្នូ," in *Sdech chang* ស្តេចចង់. Long Beach: 1992, pp. 52–105.
Originally serialized in *Serey Pheap* (Long Beach, CA), early 1990s.

from *Sky of the Lost Moon*
Ty Chi Huot ទី ជីហួត. *Mekh bat duong chan* មេឃបាត់ដួងចន្ទ. Phnom Penh: Vappathoa វប្បធម៌, 1988 [second printing; first printing unknown], pp. 10–30.

The Kerosene Lamp Ghost Stories
English translation: Consequence Magazine 9 (Spring 2017), pp. 89–102.
Khmer original: Sok Chanphal សុខ ចាន់ផល, "Changkien nitean roeung khmaoch ចង្កៀននិទានរឿងខ្មោច," in *Yul sap* យល់សប្តិ. Phnom Penh: 2019, pp. 88–116.

Buried Treasure
English translation: Sok Chanphal, translated by Yin Luoth, edited by Teri Shaffer Yamada. *Just a Human Being and Other Tales from Contemporary Cambodia*. Phnom Penh: Nou Hach Literary Association, 2013, "Buried Treasure."

Khmer original: Sok Chanphal សុខ ចាន់ផល, "Kamnap កំណប់," in *Yul sap* យល់សប្តិ. Phnom Penh: 2019, pp. 145–151.

from *Political Prison*
Bunchan Mol ប៊ុនឆន្ទ ម៉ុល. *Kuk noyobay* គុកនយោបាយ. Phnom Penh: 1971, pp. 47–56, 75–80, 115–118.

Of Performance and the Persistent Temporality of Trauma: Memory, Art, and Visions
positions: east asia cultures critique 16.1 (Spring 2008), pp. 109–130.

from *Her Father's Daughter*
Alice Pung. *Her Father's Daughter*. Collingwood, Victoria: Black Inc., 2013, from Part IV, Cambodia ("Dismemory" and "The Field [II]").

At Sea, and Seeking a Safe Harbor
The New York Times: https://www.nytimes.com/2016/07/17/fashion/modern-love-bisexuality-cambodia.html

Painting History: An Artist's Reframing of Memory and War from Survival to Healing
Consequence Magazine 9 (Spring 2017), pp. 108–118.

Cambodian Requiem
Consequence Magazine 9 (Spring 2017), pp. 129–137.

Contemporary Writing and Publishing in Cambodia
Original to *Mānoa*.

Freshwater Crayfish and the Trouble with Names
First appeared in a slightly different form in *The Margins,* the digital magazine of the Asian American Writers' Workshop, at https://aaww.org/freshwater-lobster/

An Archive of Haunting
Original to *Mānoa*.

The Bookrenter of Battambang and the Master of Uselessness
Parts of this essay appeared in a different form at https://www.phnompenhpost.com/lifestyle/life-bound-books-battambang

A Pair of Turtledoves (*Lolok nhi chhmol* លលកញីឈ្មោល)
https://www.youtube.com/watch?v=wOlZNYT4UBo

The Fishing Eagle of Scarf Lake (*Ak boeng kansaeng* អកបឹងកន្សែង)
https://www.youtube.com/watch?v=jls3PvRKOKw

Champa of Battambang (*Champa Battambang* ចំប៉ាបាត់ដំបង)
https://www.youtube.com/watch?v=A86ofe6mhIw

The Shade of the Tenth Coconut Tree (*Mlup doung ti dap* ម្លប់ដូងទីដប់)
https://www.youtube.com/watch?v=m0-mHeAh-Ac

Appeared in a slightly different form in *Words without Borders* (November 2015) https://www.wordswithoutborders.org/article/the-shade-of-the-tenth-coconut-tree

Farewell, Wild Guava Flower (*Lea phka trabaek prei* លាផ្កាត្របែកព្រៃ)
https://www.youtube.com/watch?v=WvBsb0NK-FY

from When Ream Faked His Death to Win Back Seda
Khmer and French bilingual publication, with French translation by Christophe Macquet: "Opéra Bassac: Quand Ream feignit la mort pour reconquérir Seda," Cambodge Soir, May 14–June 22, 1999, from scenes III-V.
Original Khmer source: Handwritten manuscript by director Kang Chanthirith of the Kampong Cham Theater Company.

A Flirtatious Battle of Words and Wits
Transcribed by Christophe Macquet from a performance at the National Festival of Ayai, Chapei, and Sadiev, Phnom Penh, 2003.

The Big Tusker (Northern Khmer: *Tamrey phlu thom* ตำแรียพลุทม; Central Khmer: *Damrey phluk thom* ដំរីភ្លុកធំ)
PR Sound Khmer Surin, 2010. https://www.youtube.com/watch?v=JKsM1Xd5o8I

Lullaby: An Elephant Rocks Its Trunk (*Sranah damrey yol dai* ស្រណោះដំរីយោលដៃ)
https://www.youtube.com/watch?v=BKpOkDanqoY

A Musician's Life: An Interview with Kong Nay
Original to *Mānoa*.

Moni Mekhala and Ream Eyso
Prumsodun Ok, ed. *Moni Mekhala and Ream Eyso*. 2013, pp. 1–6.

Here and Now, into the Future
Prumsodun Ok, ed. *Moni Mekhala and Ream Eyso*. 2013, pp. 73–79.

Letters from Home: A Multimedia Solo Play
Original to *Mānoa*.

Year of the Rabbit
French original, in three volumes: Tian, *L'Année du lièvre: Au revoir Phnom Penh*. Paris: Gallimard, 2011; Tian, *L'Année du lièvre: Ne vous inquiétez pas*. Paris: Gallimard, 2013; Tian, *L'Année du lièvre: Un nouveau départ*. Paris: Gallimard, 2016.
English translation: Tian Veasna, translated by Helge Dascher. Preface by Rithy Panh. *Year of the Rabbit*. Montreal: Drawn & Quarterly, 2020, pp. 137–145.

Permissions

Grateful acknowledgment is made to all the authors, translators, and copyright holders for permission to publish their work. Reprints are not permitted without their written consent. The editors thank the following for permission to reprint previously published works.

Bunchan Mol, *Political Prison*, translated by Rinith Taing. Printed by permission of the translator.

Chey Chap, "Don't Fight the Wind" and "A Bunch of Coconuts," translated by Christophe Macquet and Sharon May. Printed by permission of the author and the translators.

Elizabeth Chey, "Painting History: An Artist's Reframing of Memory and War from Survival to Healing," from *Consequence* 9 (2017). Reprinted by permission of the publisher.

"A Cycle of Alev Stories," translated by Erik W. Davis. Printed by permission of the translator.

Huot Iv, "What Would You Like to Eat," translated by Christophe Macquet and Sharon May. Printed by permission of the author and the translators.

Kang Chanthirith and the Kampong Cham Theater Company, "When Ream Faked His Death to Win Back Seda," translated by Christophe Macquet and Sharon May. Printed by permission of the translators.

Khau Ny Kim, "A Hundred Scents, A Hundred Seasons," translated by Christophe Macquet and Sharon May. Printed by permission of the author and the translators.

Khun Srun, *The Accused*, translated by Madeleine Thien from the French translation by Christophe Macquet, from *Brick: A Literary Journal* 97. Reprinted by permission of the translators. English translation copyright © 2022 Madeleine Thien, used by permission of The Wylie Agency LLC.

Khun Srun, "A Small Request," translated by Christophe Macquet and Sharon May. Printed by permission of Khun Khem and the translators.

Kong Bunchhoeun, "The Race of the Quick" and "The Shade of the Tenth Coconut Tree," translated by Trent Walker. Printed by permission of Tat Kimlorn and the translator.

Kong Nay, "Lullaby: An Elephant Rocks Its Trunk," translated by Trent Walker. Printed by permission of the author and the translator.

Mylo Lam, "Ma's Canh Chua Recipe: April–December 1975," from *The Coachella Review* (summer 2019). Reprinted by permission of the author.

Boreth Ly, "Of Performance and the Persistent Temporality of Trauma," from *positions* 16:1 (spring 2008). Reprinted by permission of Duke University Press.

Ma Laupi, "A Pair of Turtledoves" and "The Fishing Eagle of Boeng Kansaeng (Scarf Lake)," translated by Christophe Macquet and Sharon May. Printed by permission of Pongsavada Ma and the translators.

Christophe Macquet, "An Introduction to *The Accused*," translated by Madeleine Thien. Printed by permission of Éditions du Sonneur, the author and the translator. English translation copyright © 2020 Madeleine Thien, used by permission of The Wylie Agency LLC.

Princess Moon, "blessing dance" and "dance, dance, dance," from *The Genocide's Love Baby Learns to Sing*, Lowell, MA: Bootstrap Press, 2016. Reprinted by permission of the author.

Nou Hach, *Wilted Flower*, translated by Vaddey Ratner. Printed by permission of the Cambodian Ministry of Culture and Fine Arts and the translator. English translation copyright © 2022 Vaddey Ratner.

Prumsodun Ok, "Moni Mekhala and Ream Eyso" and "Here and Now, into the Future," from *Moni Mekhala and Ream Eyso*, ed. by Prumsodun Ok. CreateSpace Independent Publishing Platform, 2013. Reprinted by permission of the author.

Pen Samitthy, "Bound to His Father," translated by Christophe Macquet and Sharon May. Printed by permission of Vong Mayoura and the translators.

Pich Tum Kravel, "The Ox with the Broken Hoof," "Man and Krasang," and "The Sun Turns Leprous," translated by Christophe Macquet and Sharon May. Printed by permission of Chhorn Samarth and the translators.

Chath pierSath, "Exiting Interview" and "My Brother Thay," from *This Body Mystery*, NY: Abingdon Square Publishing, 2012. Reprinted by permission of the author.

Alice Pung, *Her Father's Daughter*, from *Her Father's Daughter*, Melbourne: Black Inc. Books, 2014. Reprinted by permission of the publisher.

Putsata Reang, "At Sea, and Seeking a Safe Harbor," from *The New York Times* © 2016 The New York Times Company. All rights reserved. Used under license. Reprinted by permission of PARS International Corporation.

Songsaeng Rungrueangchai, "The Big Tusker," translated by Direk Honthong and Trent Walker. Printed by permission of the author and the translators.

Greg Santos, "Our Name," "Shall We Dance?" and "Dear Ghosts," from *Ghost Face*, Montreal: DC Books, 2020. Reprinted by permission of the publisher.

Sim Chanya, "Farewell, Wild Guava Flower," translated by Christophe Macquet and Sharon May. Printed by permission of the author and the translators.

Sinn Sisamouth, "Champa of Battambang," translated by Trent Walker. Printed by permission of Mrs. Khav Thorn Nhot and the translator.

Prince Amrindo Sisowath, "A Cry," translated by Christophe Macquet and Sharon May. Printed by permission of Éditions Jentayu and the translators.

Phina So, "Freshwater Crayfish and the Trouble with Names," from *The Margins,* Asian American Writers' Workshop (25 April 2019). Reprinted by permission of the author.

Sok Chanphal, "The Kerosene Lamp Ghost Stories," translated by Soknea Nhim and Teri Shaffer Yamada, from *Consequence* 9 (2017). Reprinted by permission of the publisher.

Sok Chanphal, "Buried Treasure," translated by Yin Luoth, from *Just a Human Being and Other Tales from Contemporary Cambodia,* ed. by Teri Shaffer Yamada. Phnom Penh: Nou Hach Literary Association, 2013. Reprinted by permission of the author.

Soth Polin, "Command Me to Exist," translated by Francoise Bénichou from the French translation by Christophe Macquet. Printed by permission of the author, Éditions Le Grand Os, Christophe Macquet, and Norith Soth.

Soth Polin, *The Anarchist,* translated by Penny Edwards, from *Words without Borders* (November 2015). Reprinted by permission of Éditions de La Table Ronde and the translator.

Soth Polin, *The Aroma of Desire in Fresno,* translated by Bora Soth and Norith Soth. Printed by permission of the author and translators.

Suon Sorin, *A New Sun Rises Over an Old Land,* translated by Roger Nelson, from *A New Sun Rises Over an Old Land*, Singapore: National University of Singapore Press, 2020. Reprinted by permission of the publisher.

Suy Hieng, "The Orphans," translated by Christophe Macquet and Sharon May. Printed by permission of Ly Vonry and the translators.

Sokunthary Svay, "Reincarnation," from *Aspara in New York*, Detroit: Aquarius Press / Willow Books, 2017. Reprinted by permission of the publisher.

Sokunthary Svay, "Cambodian Requiem," from *Consequence* 9 (2017). Reprinted by permission of the publisher.

Tian Veasna, *Year of the Rabbit,* from *Year of the Rabbit*, translated by Helge Dascher, preface by Rithy Panh. Montreal: Drawn & Quarterly Books. Reprinted by permission of the publisher.

Bunkong Tuon, "Fishing for *Trey Platoo,*" "Elegy for a Fellow Cambodian," and "Living in the Hyphen," from *Gruel*, Beacon: NY Quarterly Press, 2015. Reprinted by permission of the author.

Bunkong Tuon, "Moon in Khmer," from *carte blanche* 35 (Spring 2019). Reprinted by permission of the author.

Ty Chi Huot, *Sky of the Lost Moon,* translated by Rinith Taing. Printed by permission of Ty Kesey and the translator.

Trent Walker (translator), "The Thirty-Three Consonants," "This Life Is Short," and "Hymn to the Buddha's Feet," from *Until Nirvana's Time: Buddhist Songs from Cambodia*, Boulder, CO: Shambhala Publications, 2022. Reprinted by permission of the publisher.

Yin Luoth, "The Fate of Bloodsuckers," translated by Christophe Macquet and Sharon May. Printed by permission of the author and the translators.

Prince Areno Yukanthor, *On the Threshold of the Khmer Narthex: Nonsense about the Conflict between East and West,* translated by Christophe Macquet. Printed by permission of Indradévi Roman and the translator.